FOOTPRINTS OF
POLONIA

Polish Historical Sites
Across North America

FOOTPRINTS OF POLONIA

Polish Historical Sites Across North America

edited by
Ewa E. Barczyk

prologues by
Stanislaus A. Blejwas and
Anna D. Jaroszyńska-Kirchmann

HIPPOCRENE BOOKS, INC.
New York

HIPPOCRENE BOOKS, INC.
171 Madison Avenue
New York, NY 10016
www.hippocrenebooks.com

Interior design and layout: K & P Publishing

ISBN: 978-0-7818-1435-5

Preparation of this book was supported, in part, with funds provided by the Polish American Historical Association, a non-profit, tax-exempt, interdisciplinary organization devoted to the study of Polish American history and culture. Founded in 1942 as part of the Polish Institute of Arts and Sciences in America, PAHA became an autonomous scholarly society in 1948. As an affiliate of the American Historical Association, PAHA promotes research and publication of scholarly materials focused on Polish American history and culture as part of the greater Polish diaspora. **polishamericanstudies.org**

TO MY HUSBAND NEAL, FELLOW TRAVELER AND ADVENTURER,
AND TO OUR CHILDREN ANDRZEJ, KRYSTYNA, AND ALEXANDER,
AND THEIR FAMILIES,
AND IN MEMORY OF MY PARENTS WIKTOR AND ZOFIA BARCZYK
WHO INSTILLED IN ME A LOVE OF POLISH CULTURE,
AND TO ALL WHO EXPLORE OUR RICH POLISH HERITAGE

CONTENTS

UNITED STATES

CANADA

CENTRAL AMERICA & CARRIBEAN

MEXICO

_____

EDITOR'S PREFACE

"You can find the entire cosmos lurking in the least remarkable objects."
—Wisława Szymborska

Thirty years have passed since the 1992 publication of the *Polish Heritage Travel Guide to U.S.A. and Canada,* edited by Jacek Galazka and Albert Juszczak, and those intervening years have witnessed major shifts in Polonia neighborhoods. As we well know, Polish immigrants and their descendants made innumerable contributions in their communities and left their visible marks on monuments, bridges, churches, cultural centers, fraternal organizational homes, and cemeteries. The continuing integration of Polish Americans has resulted in newer Polish communities in some larger cities whereas the older historic neighborhoods have become more diverse. As historically Polish places are transformed, rebuilt, closed, or even demolished, it became evident to the Polish American Historical Association (PAHA) that the time had come to create a new guide to interesting and informative sites that highlight Polish American contributions for Polonia, as well as introduce Americans of differing heritage to the important contributions of Polish immigrants. This edition expands on the earlier one but includes the majority of those entries if the places they refer to still exist. The current edition went from twenty-six to forty-seven U.S. states plus the District of Columbia, and five Canadian provinces were expanded to eight. Mexico and the Caribbean are also represented in this book. Most of the remaining states and provinces have Polish societies and organizations but with no physical location, so they were not included.

This book is not meant to be comprehensive from a practical perspective—if every monument, church, or plaque were included, the book would be the size of an encyclopedia volume and not a travel companion. Which sites, markers, churches to include was one of the challenges faced in compiling this volume. First, it was decided they had to be physical sites and not organizations and societies that did not have a permanent residence. Although the most historic and significant sites in the region were chosen based on local residents' recommendations, in regions where there is a much smaller presence of Poles, I was able to be more inclusive compared to major Polonia cities such as Chicago, which alone has over fifty Polish churches. Cuts had to be made but the bibliography provides sources with further resources and research. Commercial sites such as restaurants were omitted with a few exceptions because of the historical significance of their building. Secondly, the original volume generally excluded churches although a few were included. Yet in reading the stories of the early immigrants, one thread was common in that once they arrived, they immediately worked to create a Polish church where they could worship as they had in Polish lands where community life centered around the parish. The church in each community became the core of Polonia and its most formidable institution. Often the priest, who was educated and literate, was recognized as the community leader and the parish was more than a religious entity—it was a powerful social force. It was where weddings, funerals, dances, picnics, sporting events, lectures, immigration self-help societies, and liturgical processions took place, and where the immigrants obtained their information. They sent their children to the parish schools to foster religious and cultural values and maintain their Polish language. They were primarily interested in building magnificent houses of prayer that reflected their Polish identity and ambitions which resulted in the development of what is known as the "Polish cathedral-style" built in Polonia communities, a grand style with tall towers reminiscent of the churches of the royalty and elite of Poland. Thus, the guidebook would not be truly reflective of Polonia without including the churches that were deep expressions of their ethnic and religious identity.

Although historically Poland has been a heterogeneous country, it was decided to limit the scope of the book to focus on the narrower understanding of "Polishness" or *polskość* to a strictly monoethnic sense reflecting traditional Polonia neighborhoods and how Poles in America identified their Polish national identity. Therefore, the preponderance of Roman Catholic Churches with some Polish National Catholic Churches in this book. Groups such as Ukrainian, Lemko, Jewish, Lithuanian, and Tatar who may have immigrated from historically Polish lands are not represented here as generally they had their own organizations and societies in their own ethnic neighborhoods.

As this book shows, Polish sites are found throughout North America. It would not have been possible for the author to travel to all these locations, nor would it even have been advisable to do so due to the Covid pandemic restrictions in place for much of the time of research for this book. Therefore, this project is based on the input of over two hundred volunteers scattered throughout the United States, Canada, and Mexico. Many volunteers from Polish organizations gave of their time and talents to identify the most important sites in their region and provide summaries and pictures. I relied on the input from all of them since they live in these communities and know their region the best. Because of this at times the entries may have different "voices," but I felt it important for them to tell the stories of their Polonia. As the editor I did have to limit entries to approximately two hundred words to make the book a reasonable size. As you can imagine, the volunteers were very enthusiastic to share all their stories. They are named in the list of contributors in the back of the book.

Future plans include the development of an interactive online site with maps, photos, and pinned locations that could be used on a phone when traveling. Many more sites were identified during the research for this book that could not be included so there is already an extensive database for a larger, more comprehensive project. I welcome suggestions from our readers for future sites to include. I apologize beforehand for any errors and would like to hear about them so the future edition can be made more accurate.

I would like to thank my friends and colleagues who agreed to read the entries, provide corrections, make suggestions, and pose challenging questions that hopefully improved the results. I am deeply grateful to Neal Pease, who carefully read the entries for every state and country (thus he will not need a copy of the book) and provided invaluable counsel and support throughout, Martin Kozon, Larry & Martha Romans, Dominic Pacyga, Nadya Fouad, Christine Powell, Mary Wacker, Pien Versteegh, Barbara Rylko-Bauer, Susan Mikos, and Mark Dillon. Special thanks go to Jim Pula, who edited several long sections and whose insightful questions made me rethink other entries, and to Anna Jaroszyńska-Kirchmann, who was like a godmother to the book, always willing to talk through the details of dealing with the organization of the chapters, getting volunteer writers, and reviewing entries. Also, a word of gratitude to my Milwaukee friends who offered technical help when things were not working as expected, Dawn Lee Vue, Ling Meng, and Tamara Johnston. Special words of appreciation to the Book Advisory Committee, listed in the back of the book, for lending their historical expertise, advice, and support in a multitude of ways. A special mention of appreciation to the team at Hippocrene Books especially Priti Gress and Barbara Keane-Pigeon for their insights, editing, and support in making this book a reality. Last but not least, I am very grateful to Gavin Moulton, a Ph.D. student at Notre Dame, who heard about the book and volunteered as an editorial assistant for the last year of the project, tracking down elusive entries, verifying facts, resolving conflicting information, writing entries, and suggesting edits.

We hope that local Polish organizations will be inspired to preserve the historic sites that are found in their midst. Our communities need to have a conversation and then take action on how they will promote and preserve our history for future generations. In collecting the footprints of Polonia across North America before these identifiers of Polonia rich history disappear, this book can be a travel companion for anyone interested in learning more about the rich heritage of and contributions of Polonia. Visitors from Poland can use this volume to discover the extensive contributions Poles have made on this continent. In addition to its primary purpose as an aid to travel, the book can serve as a resource guide for Polish language schools as well as Polish American organizations to learn more about their heritage and instill pride in it. The printed book can be the springboard for further inquiry through websites provided throughout the book. Intended for the general reader and not an academic work, it should serve as a useful overview and guide for anyone exploring Polish heritage in North America.

—Ewa Barczyk, editor
Polish American Historical Association

Style Notes

• The organization of this book is straightforward: Listed under each country are state/province > city/town > sites, with each level in alphabetical order.

• Throughout this book diacritics were used when appropriate—reflecting what a monument is called or how the church spells its name. Many churches are named after Our Lady of Częstochowa but use variant spellings that are then used in the entries for the churches, but I used the Polish spelling for any general references to the icon of Our Lady.

• Thaddeus Kosciuszko and Casimir Pulaski have entered the English lexicon without diacritics so I used that approach, although their first names may be in Polish if that is how they are inscribed on a particular monument or statue.

• Words in Polish are usually italicized except when a proper name, and the recurring ones are not defined throughout the book. In describing parish activities of Polish customs, you may find mention of the following: Boże Ciało (Corpus Christi celebrations), opłatek (Christmas wafer), kolędy (Christmas carols), Wigilia (Christmas Eve) Gorzkie Żale (sung Polish Catholic Lenten devotion), Święconka (Easter basket blessings), or Dożynki (Fall Harvest Festival). Often when Masses are no longer celebrated in Polish, these liturgical traditions continue to be observed in the parishes.

PREFACE FROM PAHA PRESIDENT

The handsome book you are reading, though entirely the accomplishment of the editor in chief, her advisory board, and numerous contributors, began as an initiative of the Polish American Historical Association. Founded in 1943, at first as a committee within the Polish Institute of Arts and Sciences of America devoted to the study of Polish immigration to the United States, and later as an independent scholarly society, PAHA defines its mission in this way:

· To promote the study of Polish American history and culture as part of the greater Polish diaspora.

· To encourage and disseminate scholarly research and publication on the Polish American experience in the fields of history, the social sciences, the humanities and the arts, and advance scholarly collaboration across disciplines.

· To support collection and preservation of historical sources regarding the Polish past in America.

A few years ago, the Board of Directors of PAHA decided the time had come to commission the revision and updating of the predecessor volume, *Polish Heritage Travel Guide to U.S.A. and Canada*, edited by Jacek Galazka and Albert Juszczak, published in 1992, which it also had sponsored. Such is the wealth and variety of the Polish imprint on the New World that the preparation of this renewed and expanded version took several years, but we are confident that readers will find it to have been worth the effort in its informative and encyclopedic coverage of Polish cultural and historical sites in North America and the Caribbean region.

The Polish American Historical Association has broadened in scope over the decades. Its membership has extended widely over the globe, and increasingly its scholarly attention takes in the history of Polish and east-central European diasporas wherever in the world they can be found. But the traditional focus of PAHA has been, and no doubt will remain, the history of Polish immigrants and their descendants in the United States and neighboring lands, and their impact on their adopted countries, so the *Guide to Polish Historical Sites in North America* represents an important and fitting step in fulfilling its core scholarly purpose.

—Neal Pease
President, Polish American Historical Association

PROLOGUE TO FIRST EDITION
—Stanislaus A. Blejwas*

Since its birth, the United States had been constantly present in Polish minds. Kosciuszko and Pulaski distinguished themselves in the American Revolution, Poles followed the debates over the Constitution, and the names of Washington, Franklin, Jefferson and Hamilton were invoked in Polish debates, political polemics, and literature. Early Polish images of America were both simple and varied. There was the exotic, primeval America of the Indian and early settlers. The nobleman and poet Tomasz Kajetan Wegierski was drawn to the colonies in 1783, no doubt influenced by J. Hector St. John de Crevecoeur's *Letters from an Indian Farmer*, which according to Wegierski, presented an "enchanting picture of the happy life of the inhabitants of English America." After the revolution, America became the Republic where freedom and equality mingled with simplicity of manner and industriousness, giving birth to a democratic society without class distinctions. For Poland, which lost its freedom at the end of the Eighteenth Century, America was a needed Utopia, a proof of what man could achieve when free and his own lawmaker upon a virgin land. At the same time, early Polish travelers did not fail to note the double standard of American democracy when they encountered the plight of the Blacks.

The historian, Jerzy Jedlicki suggests that the fiction of the American presence in the Polish mind has been to compensate for all those things missing at home. While Poland lay portioned, America symbolized freedom and the Rights of Man. In the early nineteenth century, nobles, freedom fighters, and political exiles discussed America, but few visited. As he embarked on his two-year journey in 1876, the Polish writer Henryk Sienkiewicz remarked: "The man departing for America is still a rarity among us." But while in America Sienkiewicz observed the early foundations of a permanent Polish presence in the young republic, coming across Radom, Illinois; Krakow, Missouri; Polonia, Wisconsin; New Posen, Nebraska; Panna Maria, Texas; and visiting Chicago. As peasant immigrants arrived in ever growing numbers, America became a new homeland. Sienkiewicz observed that Polish emigres in France might criticize France, but "it would be dangerous to speak disparagingly of the United States to any Pole residing here. He does not cease to love his former fatherland, but after Poland he loves most the United States."

The Polish presence and heritage in America begins with a handful of Poles who landed in the Jamestown Colony of October 1, 1608, on the good ship *Margaret and Mary*. While the Jamestown settlement did not survive, the "Polonians" are remembered as hard workers. Furthermore, they successfully argued for the franchise in the newly formed House of Burgesses. These early settlers were followed by a handful of other scattered about in the early colonies and rapidly absorbed by the surrounding society prior to the American Revolution. The arrival of Pulaski and Kosciuszko begins a Polish political emigration to America. They left Poland because of unfavorable political conditions after the first Partition in 1772, and they participated in the colonists' revolution for freedom. Pulaski organized a cavalry and made the champion's ultimate sacrifice. Kosciuszko marshalled his engineering skills to fortify Bemis Heights and assure the American victory at the Battle of Saratoga, the Revolution's turning point. Other political exiles and emigres followed Pulaski and Kosciuszko in the years preceding the American Civil War and the January 1863 Insurrection, but their numbers were small. The Polish presence in the American consciousness was a faintly imprinted memory of a few heroic individual participants in a common struggle again despotism in the battle for the right of every nation to freedom and independence. These memories, however, were to be less important to American society than to a new generation of Polish emigrants that began to reach America in the 1850s.

It was the Great Peasant Immigration, comparable in importance to the Great Emigration after the November 1830 Insurrection, that imprinted a Polish presence upon the New World. Beginning with the arrival on Christmas Eve, 1854, in Panna Maria, Texas, Polish peasants swelled the immigrant flood from southern and eastern Europe in the years after the Civil War up until Congress adopted exclusionary immigration legislation in 1924. America became the subject of that most popular form of national literature, emigrant letters.

In the rush to America, the peasant immigrants created their own urban villages in the great industrial states of the Midwest, and, subsequently, in the Atlantic states of Massachusetts, Connecticut, New York, New Jersey, Pennsylvania, Delaware, and Maryland. While Poles settled in every state of the Union, they were most numerous where there were jobs, for this was, as Sienkiewicz found, an immigration "in search of bread and freedom." America offered what was unavailable at home. The peasant immigrants worked in steel mills, factories, and mines; only a tenth ever made their way to the farms. As they settled, they organized themselves, developing a remarkably complete series of community institutions; over 950 Roman Catholic and Polish National Catholic churches, numerous parochial schools, insurance fraternals, a Polish language press, and host of sports, cultural, social, and political organizations. By 1930, the U.S. Census counted over 3,000,000 first- and second-generation Polish Americans.

The buildings the immigrants erected to house their community life incarnate their contribution to America's Polish heritage. The churches are often on a grand scale, their size challenging a bishop's cathedral church and other elegant Christian structures. They are a testimony to faith, for God must be worshipped in a great house. They are also an assertion of the Polish presence. God's Polish house had to rival American churches. The immigrant, despite enormous difficulties and often exploitative working conditions, manifested pride in his accomplishments in "Ameryka," pointedly reminding his American neighbors by the size and beauty of his Polish church that he was just as good as any other citizen, and here to stay. Every Polish church, schools, national home, and sports hall is physical testimony to the Polish presence in the New World.

Community organizations and institutions preserved and stimulated the immigrant's Polishness, and at the same time eased him onto the road to Americanization. During World War 1, Polish immigrants demonstrated faithfulness to their homeland and Poland's independence. They donated generously to charitable relief and over 20,000 returned across the ocean to fight in General Józef Haller's Blue Army. At the same time, they confirmed their loyalty to their new homeland, purchasing American war bonds and serving in even greater numbers in the American Expeditionary Forces.

When Poland's independence was regained on November 11, 1918, Polish immigrants rejoiced. At the same time most understood that they had become Americans. Too much was invested in America to return to Poland. In the 1920s and 1930s immigrants and their children, now that Poland was sovereign, focused on their domestic affairs. Democratic and Republican political and citizenship clubs sprang up, and the emerging Polish Americans sought recognition through politics. To confirm their status as equal and valuable citizens, Polish Americans invoked their past, raising local monuments to Pulaski and Kosciuszko, and adding to a growing list of public monuments to the Polish and American heroes dating back to the Kosciuszko statue erected in 1904 in Chicago and the Kosciuszko and Pulaski monuments dedicated in 1910 during the Polish

National Congress in Washington, D.C. Bridges and skyways, avenues, streets, and even American postal stamps, were also symbols of the politics of recognition.

The community was reaching middle age, looking forward to a prosperous future, and new cultural organizations reflected the changes. The Kosciuszko Foundation was founded in 1925, and Polish Americans opened their own national attic in 1935 when the Polish Museum in America was organized. In 1926, the Polish Arts Club of Chicago was established, later becoming a charter member of the national American Council of Polish Cultural Clubs founded in 1948. The cultural interests of Polish Americans were reaching beyond their parents' popular folk culture to Poland's artistic, musical, and literary heritage, which the second and third generation wished to know more about. Modrzejewska, Kochanska-Sembrich, the de Reszke Brothers, Paderewski, and Rubinstein were, after all, well known to American audiences.

An unintended consequence of World War II was the broadening of America's Polish Heritage. A new generation of political emigres and soldier exiles arrived. Included in their ranks were many of Poland's most distinguished scholars, musicians, and artists. Determined to preserve Polish learning and her modern history, this intellectual immigration gifted America with individuals who found new careers in American academia or in the professions; with the Polish Institute of Arts and Sciences in America, founded in 1942 and which counts three Nobel laureates among its members; with the Józef Pilsudski Institute in America, organized in 1943; and with new veteran and scouting organizations.

After 1956 a consumer immigration arrived; and after the imposition of martial law in December 1981, the Solidarity immigration appeared that, in addition to political exiles and emigres, included many talented cultural figures.

America since 1939 remains, as it was in the nineteenth century, a haven and a promised land for Poles. By 1980, there were more than 8,000,000 Polish Americans of all generations living in the United States.

The Canadian-Polish community numbering 254,485 according to the 1981 federal census, shares common bonds with the American-Polish community, but also possesses its own distinctive history. Prior to 1915, a handful of political exiles, including the distinguished Sir Casimir Gzowski, made their way to Canada. The majority of the immigrants, however, were like their American counterparts, farmers and unskilled laborers, most of whom settled on the prairies. Among the best-known Polish Canadians were the Kashubs, who settled in Renfrew Country, Ontario beginning in the 1850s. During the interwar years, Polish laborers came to farms in Western Canada, to the forests of northern Ontario, and to the mines of Alberta, Ontario and Quebec. After World War II, there was, as in the United States, a new immigration of political emigres and soldier exiles. Seeing themselves as the Polish nation in exile, they also altered the nature and increased the size and organizational complexity of the Polish-Canadian community. A consumer immigration from Communist Poland followed them after 1956. These new arrivals were opposed to the Polish political system and dissatisfied with living conditions there. Finally, since 1980, Canada possesses its own Solidarity immigration, including many well-educated individuals and professionals.

The rural Poles who settled in Canada before 1915 carried with them an image of Poland as an oppressed country, their own Polish identity, and, like their fellow Poles in the United States, a sense of themselves as the "fourth" and the only free "province" of the Polish nation. The historian Robert Harney observed that in the years from 1880 to the 1930's, the North American Poles has only a limited sense of the significance of the Canadian-United States border. Canadian Poles received some of their religious leadership from the American side of the border, read the Polish papers of Chicago or Buffalo as well as their own, and shared some common fraternal links and a Polish patriotic consciousness. After World War II, the difficulties of adjustment for the émigré-soldier generation were eased not only by the existence of the pre-war Polish-Canadian organizations, but also by the efforts of the national organizations in Montreal and Toronto, which drew them into the North American Polish community with its comforting sense of shared experiences, common religious faith, and political patriotism. And Canadian Polonia, like its American counterpart, has contributed its share of artists, writers, academicians and educated professionals to a pluralistic New World country.

Each immigrant generation and every individual immigrant leaves a mark in North America, thus enriching the Continent's Polish heritage. The physical signposts are the bronze monuments, steel bridges, concrete streets, stone churches, brick schools, national homes, museums, fraternal lodges, culture centers, and Falcon nests. These structures incarnate and house the human spirit of a nation and its immigrant children and exiles.

North America's Polish heritage is not monolithic, nor can it be discovered and enjoyed on one trip, in a single place, or in a single day. This guide will facilitate your discovery of that legacy.

---

*Stanislaus A. Blejwas (1941-2001) was Connecticut State University Professor and Professor of history at Central Connecticut State University in New Britain, CT. An accomplished historian of Polonia, Blejwas was also past president of PAHA.

PROLOGUE TO SECOND EDITION

—**Anna D. Jaroszyńska-Kirchmann**[*]

Since the time Professor Stanislaus A. Blejwas wrote his Prologue to the first edition of the *Polish Heritage Travel Guide* in 1992, some significant changes have taken place on the North American continent as well as in Poland itself. In 1989, the Polish nation shook off the shackles of communism and elected a new government in the first free elections since World War II. Within a few years, other countries in the Soviet sphere of influence followed Poland's example and rejected communist governments, the Berlin Wall fell, and in 1991 the Soviet Union ceased to exist. As Poland embarked on a difficult road of rebuilding its economy and a democratic political system, it also was admitted to NATO, and in 2004 to the European Union. Political changes affected the direction of migration streams and created new opportunities. While some immigrants from the Polish diaspora decided to gradually return to the free homeland, others remained in their countries of resettlement. In the meantime, large groups of Poles left Poland to search for new economic prospects in European Union countries, for example, the United Kingdom, Ireland, France, and Germany. Immigration from Poland to the United States diminished, compounded by problems with the American visa program.

In the 1990s, the booming economy of the United States facilitated transformative technological developments. The Internet forever changed the way we communicate, get our information, and create virtual communities. In the 2000s, the spread of social media further altered the communication landscapes and built complex networks of global connections. Those new virtual communities offered opportunities to remain connected without the need to be in the same geographical space and time. The technological revolution also influenced urban planning and design, and caused population shifts in cities increasingly dominated by the creative classes in the so-called eds, meds, and techs, or educational, medical, and technological institutions and businesses. Outmigration from the cities to the suburbs that was characteristic for the postwar decades has slowed down, and gentrifying urban neighborhoods attracted young professionals and entrepreneurs looking for new livable spaces, an interesting environment, and stimulating artistic life.

In the third decade of the new millennium a casual visitor or tourist in an American city has a hard time finding the vibrant Polonia neighborhoods of the previous decades, complete with churches, parochial schools, Polish Homes, small businesses, taverns, and other public spaces shared by immigrants and ethnics. Even the largest and most famous of them, like Greenpoint in New York, Trójcowo in Chicago, or the Polish Hill in Pittsburgh, have evolved and changed their character. Historians and sociologists studied and described Polonia's ethnic communities in ethnic spaces for decades, whether in Panna Maria, TX, Philadelphia, PA, Cleveland, OH, Milwaukee, WI, or Seattle, WA. During the period of the Great Migration at the turn of the nineteenth and twentieth centuries, Polish immigrants followed established migration networks and created those communities both because of their need for support and familiarity and because of limited options for settling elsewhere. In the post-Civil War decades industrializing American cities were developing rapidly and chaotically, without much planning, oversight, or regulation. Little Italys, Petit Canadas, Chinatowns, and Polonias located within the city cores became "urban villages," re-creating and re-inventing social and cultural traditions transplanted from the Old Country. Religious institutions played a particularly important role in Polonia, so the impressive edifices of churches, parish houses, convents, and parochial schools became central structures in the ethnic neighborhoods. Polish national homes and other Polonia institutions such as headquarters of organizations, publishing houses, and professional associations served the communities as cultural centers and were also often housed in imposing buildings. Additionally, Polonia's urban landscape included a plethora of businesses—from bakeries, butchers, and grocery stores, to tailors, undertakers, and "parcels to Poland" services. Taverns, bars, and restaurants attracted a steady stream of clients. Neighborhood residential areas with well-kept houses often in specific styles of, for example, Milwaukee's Polish flats or Chicago bungalows spread out around those religious, cultural, and business centers.

Following World War II and the increased social mobility opportunities it fostered, younger Polish American families began to move out to the suburbs in search of larger dwellings, better schools, and jobs. Those who stayed faced postindustrial blight, deteriorating housing and infrastructure, parking problems, and reduced economic prospects. The Housing Acts of 1949 and 1954 facilitated government-funded urban renewal projects, which allocated federal dollars for the clearance of the so-called blighted areas and their redevelopment, which created new modern business, shopping, entertainment, and government facilities to attract the public. In 1956, the National Interstate Highway Act provided funds for the extensive program of highway building and transportation improvement. American cities entered a new age of revitalization and modernist experimentation. Areas that fell victim to the redevelopment projects and highway construction were most often those in which African American and Latino communities were located. White working-class ethnic neighborhoods, however, also frequently suffered from either physical destruction or profound spatial alteration. Searching for inexpensive housing and escaping redlining and redevelopment, racial minorities began to gradually move into those neighborhoods, changing their ethnic composition. The urban tensions of the 1960s and the financial crises and deindustrialization of the next decade further affected American cities. Although the movement to the suburbs continued and some areas witnessed natural aging out of its residents, in many places Polonia neighborhoods persisted due to the influx of new immigration waves in the postwar decades.

Nowadays, the church buildings with their stunning architecture and beautiful art are still a testament to the lives and faith of Polish immigrants. Many of the churches continue to function and draw attendance even from far away suburbs, fulfilling not only religious but also cultural roles, and supporting various organizations, Saturday schools, clubs, and sports and scout teams. Other churches, however, are being closed in waves of consolidations or serve now primarily different ethnic groups. The aging buildings of Polonia's institutions and organizations require funds for updates, renovations, and maintenance. When such funds are not available, they often end up in the hands of developers who either demolish them or transform them into upscale apartments, lofts, or offices.

There are, however, also positive signs of the continuing Polonia presence in the cities. Gentrification, a controversial process of displacement of poorer populations by the wealthier classes looking for attractive but less expensive urban living, affected Polonia's neighborhoods in various ways. Although in some places gentrification erased the Polish character of urban areas, in others it helped to revitalize them economically and culturally, saving Polonia's institutions and businesses that adjusted to serving a new broader clientele. Revitalization efforts are often led by more recent immigrant arrivals from Poland: entrepreneurs and workers in business and art, who invest in restaurants, art galleries, music and theater scenes, and various services. Polish Americans are willing to travel long distances to these Polonia centers to attend cultural events and, especially, to shop for traditional food items.

Poland's history and culture-related place names continue to mark streets, parks, bridges, plazas, and other public spaces. Since the beginning of the twentieth century, American Polonia strove to commemorate historical events and figures, taking pride in the history of Poland as well as Polish Americans. Such efforts resulted in the erection of numerous statues of Kosciuszko, Pulaski, and Copernicus, among others. Like other European ethnic groups, Polonia's leaders looked to legitimize their place within the diverse American society and at the same time to compete with other ethnic groups for respect and recognition. Subsequent generations and immigrant waves continued their labor, enriching urban landscapes with monuments and markers commemorating, for instance, the Katyń Massacre, Solidarity, Rev. Popiełuszko, Pope John Paul II, and other important historical events and individuals.

Elsewhere on the North American continent, Polish immigrant communities developed differently. Polonia communities in both Canada and Mexico remain smaller in size and more scattered than those in the United States, and their physical imprint is more modest in comparison. Unlike in earlier decades, the postwar Polish immigrants to Canada settled mostly in urban centers, and especially in the Province of Ontario. They arrived in several waves: Polish displaced persons and soldiers after World War II, then economic immigrants from the 1960s on, political exiles in the post-Solidarity period, and entrepreneurs in the 1990s. Next to the descendants of Kashubs in Renfrew County, Toronto boasts of the largest Polish Canadian population. Physical traces of Polishness include churches and chapels, Polish homes and halls, as well as a variety of commemoration sites such as museums, memorials, and statues.

Mexico has not attracted larger numbers of immigrants from Poland, although Poles were present in Mexico since the mid-nineteenth century. Immigration from Poland to Mexico increased in the interwar period, and in 1943, thanks to the generosity of the Mexican government, a group of close to 1,500 Polish refugees, mostly women and children, found refuge in Santa Rosa in Guadalupe County, where they remained during the duration of the war. Other Polish refugees who arrived in Mexico during the war travelled either through Soviet Russia, Japan and China, or Spain and Portugal. In the post-World War II period, individual immigrants from Poland settled in Mexico City, and included members of Poland's artistic and intellectual elites. Although Mexican Polonia has not developed large communities, their existing physical imprint needs to be recognized and preserved.

The structure and design of cities on the North American continent is ever-changing, and nobody can predict what the future will bring. Any city on any continent can be read as a text that informs us about the lives, experiences, and aspirations of its past and present residents. Physical manifestations of belonging are important symbols and expressions of both continuity and discontinuity and create a sense of place for the Polish diaspora. This book aims to guide us through the process of cataloging, preserving, and understanding the past as well as celebrating and commemorating it.

---

*Anna D. Jaroszyńska-Kirchmann, Ph.D., Distinguished Professor of History and CSU Professor, Eastern Connecticut State University.

POLISH PRONUNCIATION GUIDE

Below is a brief pronunciation table for Polish letters with diacritics and letter combinations found in this book.

A	**ah** as in t**a**r		Ń	like French palatalized **gn**
Ą	French nasal "**on**" as in **own**		Ó	**oo** as in m**oo**t
C	**ts** as in ca**ts**		RZ	**s** as in mea**s**ure
Ć	**ch** as in **ch**eese		Ś	**sh** as in **sh**eep
CH	**h** as in **h**ot		SZ	**sh** as in **sh**ip
CZ	**ch** as in **ch**urch		SZCZ	**sh-ch** as in fre**sh ch**eese
Ę	French nasal "**en**"		U	**oo** as in l**oo**t
G	**g** as in **g**oal		W	**v** as in **v**ictor
I	**ee** as in m**ee**t		Y	**i** as in s**i**t
J	**y** as in **y**olk		Ż	**s** as in vi**s**ion
Ł	**w** as in **w**hy		Ź	**zh** similar to **rz** and **ż** but softer

UNITED STATES

ARIZONA

PHOENIX
Our Lady of Częstochowa Church
This church was dedicated in 1997 and named as a mission of the Polish Apostolate in 2000. By 2006, the parish had significantly outgrown the church, so it acquired a larger building by repurposing an Assembly of God Church building at 2828 West Country Gables Drive. There are two statues on the Church grounds: one of St. Pope John Paul II and the other of St. Faustina, both dedicated in 2008. The parish received a first class relic of St. Pope John Paul II from the Polish Cardinal Dziwisz in 2013. The altar has a large icon of Our Lady with a contemporary frame. The parish sponsors the John Paul II Polish Language School and Polish Scouts, and its annual Polish festival draws huge crowds from miles around. Throughout the year, cultural events occur frequently—folk dance groups from around the country perform, and lectures and meetings with authors are held. **nowa.polskaparafiaphoenix.com**

Pulaski Club of Arizona
This club at 4331 East McDowell Road, in existence since 1939, supports Polish history and culture by providing activities such as various programs, celebrating Dyngus Day, and hosting frequent dances. The restaurant on the premises helps to support these social gatherings and welcomes visitors. **pulaskiclubaz.org**

Our Lady of Częstochowa Church, Phoenix, AZ

Statue of St. Pope John Paul II
A bronze statue cast in Pietrasantre, Italy, to commemorate the Pope's visit to Phoenix on September 14, 1987, stands at the Virginia G. Piper Plaza near downtown Phoenix.

TUCSON

Arizona Polish Club in Tucson

The "APC," founded in 1967 and located at 1122 North Jones Boulevard, organizes social gatherings, traditional celebrations, and cultural events, both literary and musical. The preservation of the Polish language and customs is of great importance to the club, thus bringing awareness of Polish customs, literature, music, folk dancing, arts and crafts, and the culinary tradition to the general public. They publish a newsletter and maintain an extensive lending library and offer Polish language classes. **www.arizonapolishclub.com/media**

Arizona Polish Club in Tucson (APC)

St. Cyril of Alexandria Church

Polonia in Tucson meets at St. Cyril of Alexandria Church, 4725 East Pima Street, every first Sunday of the month at 3 pm for a Polish Mass. After each Polish Mass, the participants gather at the Parish Hall for some camaraderie and Polish pastries. They also maintain traditions such as the Easter basket food blessing and Christmas Eve community gatherings. **stcyrilchurch-tucson.org**

ARKANSAS

LITTLE ROCK
Bust of Casimir Pulaski

This stylized bronze bust of Pulaski sits on a granite pedestal in the Vogel Schwartz Sculpture Garden, located at the west end of Julius Breckling Riverfront Park on President Clinton Avenue. The 33-acre park, dedicated in 2009, features walkways along the Arkansas River with over eighty sculptures in the garden and an additional twenty-four pieces along President Clinton Avenue.

Bust of Casimir Pulaski,
Little Rock, AR
(Donna Singleton)

MARCHE
Immaculate Heart of Mary Church

Twelve miles north of Little Rock, in Pulaski County, Marche is the only Arkansas town with substantial Polish history. In 1878, the first Polish families arrived with hopes to establish an agricultural community. The settlement attracted Poles from Midwestern cities who built the Immaculate Heart of Mary chapel on a hill named Jasna Gora. After a fire destroyed the church, a brick Gothic building was dedicated in 1933. By 1936, an estimated seventy-five Polish families lived in Marche, but nearby towns were luring younger generations. A picric acid plant constructed as part of the national defense program during World War II forced many families to sell their land and move. While Marche is no longer home to a Polish American community, the Immaculate Heart of Mary Parish (7006 Jasna Gora Drive) organizes an annual carnival that celebrates the site's Polish legacy.

Immaculate Heart of Mary Church, Marche, AR (Patrick Fulks, courtesy of Immaculate Heart of Mary Church)

A Count in the Wilderness

Marche, Arkansas, was a project of Count Timothy von Choinski. Originally from the Poznan area in Prussian Poland, the Polish aristocrat migrated to the United States as a political refugee following the 1863 January Uprising. After he settled in Milwaukee and witnessed horrific working and living conditions among Polish immigrants in cities, Choinski decided to establish an agricultural colony where predominantly rural Poles could apply their expertise in farming. In 1877, an Arkansas newspaper published a letter, in which Choinski expressed interest in buying fifty thousand acres of land for five hundred Polish migrants. Arkansas press reported that the immigrants were enticed to relocate from cities with a promise of forty-acre tracts, out of which ten acres had been planted, awaiting their arrival. When the train with the first families arrived and the travelers saw what one local newspaper called "wilderness," some turned around and left straightaway, while others relocated to a nearby town. Choinski died in 1890, but his dream project, although more modest than he originally envisioned, survived him by several decades. This settlement was one of the most successful immigrant settlement projects in Arkansas.

4

CALIFORNIA

Helena Modjeska Monument,
Anaheim, CA (Maja Trochimczyk)

ANAHEIM
Helena Modjeska Monument
Located in Pearson Park at the corner of Sycamore and Lemon, the Helena Modjeska Monument was built in 1935 as the first Public Works of Art Project in Orange County. The concrete painted sculpture by Eugen Maier-Krieg depicts Modjeska on the stage in the role of Maria Stuart. Sculptures of four vineyard workers on the other side of the monument refer to the agricultural nature of Anaheim during her time there, as she settled in the area in 1876. Anaheim is also the site of the Helena Modjeska Park opened in 1963, with ample picnic and sports facilities, but without architectural monuments.

GLENDALE
Forest Lawn Memorial Park
The Hall of the Crucifixion-Resurrection in the Park contains a monumental panorama, the largest religious painting in the world by Polish artist Jan Styka (1858-1925), commissioned by Ignacy Jan Paderewski in 1894. "The Crucifixion" is 195 feet long by 45 feet high and was first shown in Warsaw in 1897. Styka brought it to the U.S. in 1904 for the St. Louis Exposition. It was later bought by Forest Lawn owner, Hubert Eaton, who commissioned its restoration by Styka's son, Adam. It was unveiled in 1951 in a special auditorium-style hall where it is shown, theatrical-style with a recorded narrative, music, and spotlights highlighting different scenes. A painting of "The Resurrection" was completed by Robert Clark in 1965. Forest Lawn is a cemetery, but its museum holds various artifacts, including Paderewski's portrait by Styka and various other sorts of memorabilia.
forestlawn.com/exhibits/the-hall-of-crucifixion-resurrection

Forest Lawn Memorial Park, Glendale, CA (Maja Trochimczyk)

IRVINE
Langson Library Special Collections, University of California at Irvine
The Helena Modjeska Collection, located on the 5th floor of the Langson Library, has extensive materials about Polish actress Helena Modjeska who lived in Orange County from 1876 until her death in 1909. The Collection includes items dated from 1876-1989, such as personal documents, photographs, letters, theater programs, contracts, notes, music scores, books, and other items authored by Modjeska, Karol Chłapowski, Oscar Wilde, and others. There are five boxes and five oversize folders with unique documents, totaling 3.1 linear feet of archival material. Highlights include Modjeska's handwritten and illustrated fairy tale written for her grandson in 1896.

LOS ANGELES
Astronomers Monument at Griffith Observatory

Built in 1935 on the southern slopes of Mount Hollywood, Griffith Observatory contains various educational exhibits about astronomy and cosmology. On its grounds there are markings for planetary orbits, the directions to summer and winter solstices, lunar standstills, and other astronomical events. The tall concrete Astronomers Monument stands in the center of the lawn before the Observatory and includes on its six sides sculptures of six of the greatest astronomers: Hipparchus, Nicolaus Copernicus, Galileo Galilei, Johannes Kepler, Isaac Newton, and John Herschel. The concrete sculpture by Archibald Garner was commissioned by the Public Works of Art Project and completed in 1934.
www.griffithobservatory.org/exhibits/astronomers_monument.html

Asronomers Monument at Griffiths Observatory, Los Angeles, CA (Maja Trochimczyk)

Our Lady of the Bright Mount Church

This church was consecrated in its current location at 3424 West Adams Boulevard in 1956 and was the first to serve Polish Americans in California. Its predecessor, dedicated to Christ the King, was built in 1926, on land donated by actress Pola Negri. The mid-century modern church by Jerzy George Szeptycki, who designed over twenty churches, includes a large fresco with Our Lady of Częstochowa behind the altar and many relics including those of St. Maximilian Kolbe, Fr. Jerzy Popiełuszko, and St. Faustina Kowalska. The Via Crucis artwork on the walls were donated by Negri and her friend, vaudeville performer Margaret West. The church features large stained-glass windows depicting Polish saints donated by the architectural firm of Yates and Szeptycki. In 1966, new stained-glass windows were created by the Polish artist Ludwik Wiechecki that include scenes from Polish history. The Church's interior was remodeled prior to its designation in 2015 as the St. Pope John Paul II Sanctuary; an imposing sculpture of the Pope stands to the left of the church's main door, with a Pola Negri sculpture seated to the side, unveiled in 2018. **parafiala.org**

Stained glass at Our Lady of the Bright Mount Church, Los Angeles, CA (Parish)

Pola Negri in Los Angeles

Polish actress Pola Negri epitomized the *femme fatale* and was undoubtedly one of early Hollywood's most famous stars. She was born Apolonia Chałupiec in Lipno, Poland, in 1897. After moving to Hollywood as an actor for Paramount Pictures, she donated the land for the construction of the first Polish church in Los Angeles in 1926, as well as Via Crucis artwork for the church in 1956. In 1925, Rudolph Valentino built her a mansion at 621 N. Beverly Blvd., Beverly Hills. She has a star on the Hollywood Walk of Fame; her signature and hand/feet prints are in front of Grauman's Chinese Theater in Hollywood. She was buried at the Calvary Cemetery and Mausoleum in Los Angeles (Mausoleum, E19, block 56).

Ignacy Jan Paderewski Statues

Two identical monuments of pianist and statesman Ignacy Jan Paderewski (1860-1941) are in California. One, unveiled in 2007, is near the Thornton School of Music on the campus of University of Southern California in Los Angeles, where Paderewski received an honorary doctorate in 1923. The second, erected in 2012, is at the entrance to the Carnegie Library in the Paso Robles Downtown City Park where some Paderewski memorabilia are held. A third 790-pound bronze statue cast from the same design by Jessie Corsaut was erected in 2011 at the Institute of Musicology, Jagiellonian University, Kraków, Poland, where the Paderewski Archives are located. The identical statues depict Paderewski in a pose from his 1911 patriotic speech at the Grunwald Monument in Kraków. The initiator and main sponsor of the project, Harry E. Blythe, had owned Paderewski's former winery (Rancho San Ignacio) in Paso Robles and created a Paderewski collection which he donated to USC Polish Music Center. The L.A. statue was initially to be in the Polish Embassy in Washington. The Polish government and Polish American organizations contributed to this project.

Pasa Robles statue of Paderewski (Maja Trochimczyk)

Paderewski's star on the Hollywood Star Walk of Fame (Mariusz Pazdiora CC BY 3.0)

Paderewski Star, Hollywood Star Walk of Fame

On the south side of the 6200 block of Hollywood Boulevard, on the Hollywood Star Walk of Fame, there is a star honoring Ignacy Jan Paderewski, the Polish musician and diplomat who had immense popularity on his eleven tours of the United States.

Polish Music Center, University of Southern California

The Polish Music Center is in Stonier Hall, on the campus of the University of Southern California. It was established in 1985 as the Polish Music Reference Center (renamed in 2000) and consists of the largest archive, library, research, and promotional center for Polish music in America. Holdings include rare manuscripts by over fifty composers (Bacewicz, Bruzdowicz, Baird, Lutoslawski, Paderewski, Stojowski, Skrowaczewski, and others), rare prints and artwork (posters, sculpture, portraits), as well as books, scores, recordings, and ephemera. Activities include Paderewski Lecture Recitals series, concerts, conferences, and a Polish Music History Series of books. There are free concerts and events. The Center co-sponsored a bronze statue of Ignacy Jan Paderewski near USC Thornton School of Music, erected in 2007. **polishmusic.usc.edu**

Papers from the collection at the Polish Music Center, University of Southern California, Los Angeles, CA (Maja Trochimczyk)

MARTINEZ
John Muir National Historic Site

Jan (John) Strentzel, M.D., the father-in-law of naturalist John Muir, was a renowned horticulturalist, vintner, and scholar. He was proprietor of the Alhambra vineyard near Martinez, Contra Costa County, where he cultivated forty-five varieties of grapes as well as pomegranates, almonds, and more. His house is open to the public at the John Muir National Historic Site (4202 Alhambra Avenue) where visitors can view the certificate he was awarded in 1880 on the 50th anniversary of the November Uprising, marking his participation in this patriotic struggle to liberate partitioned Poland.

Our Lady Mother of Immigrants Chapel

The East Bay Polish American Association was established in 1987 by predominately Solidarity immigrants. The newly born Polish American organization purchased a chapel along with a cafeteria in Martinez at 909 Mellus Street. The chapel was named "Our Lady Mother of Immigrants" and quickly became an important center for Polish immigrants in the San Francisco-Bay Area region. The carved wood altar depicts the "Gdańsk Monument to the Fallen Shipyard Workers" of 1970. A large painting of Our Lady of Częstochowa hangs behind the altar. This civic organization owns the chapel where weekly Polish Masses are celebrated by priests from Poland. The association sponsors many events including concerts, meetings with guests from Poland, poetry and art exhibits, and an annual Polish Street Festival. **www.ebpaa.com/about-us.html**

MODJESKA CANYON

Arden: Helena Modjeska Historic House and Gardens

Located in a beautiful rural setting in Santiago Canyon at 29042 Modjeska Canyon Road, Arden is a former residence of Polish actress Helena Modjeska (Helena Modrzejewska, 1840-1909) who resided there from 1888 to 1906 with her husband, Karol Bożenta Chłapowski, and various friends and relations. Modjeska's home, designed by famous architect Stanford White, and called *Arden* after Shakespeare's Forest of Arden in "As You Like It," was designated a U.S. National Historic Landmark in 1992. The site's purpose is to provide a "cultural, educational and recreational opportunity in an historic setting which depicts the life and personality of Modjeska." Most of the furnishings have been provided by the non-profit Helena Modjeska Foundation including modern replicas of her own furniture and costumes. Open by request. **www.ocparks.com/historic/modjeska**

Arden: Helen Modjeska's Historic House (Maja Trochimczyk)

MONTECITO
Ganna Walska Lotusland
This botanic garden was established in 1941 by Polish-born opera star Ganna Walska (Hanna Puacz). Born in 1887 in Russian-occupied Poland, she eventually retired from the stage to care for her garden in Montecito and died in 1984. Walska served as the head gardener and designer of the 37-acre site, featuring 208 plant families and more than 3,200 different plants from around the world, organized into 21 distinct gardens (the blue garden, orchard, cactus, topiary gardens, etc.). The largest collections are of palms, bromeliads; cactus; cycads, aloes and ferns. Open by special request. **www.lotusland.org**

PASO ROBLES
Paderewski Vineyards
These vineyards, which were once part of the larger holdings of Ignacy Jan Paderewski, are located just west of town. They had become fallow but were replanted in 1974 (the tasting room is in Templeton). Paderewski was introduced to Paso Robles in 1914 and then bought over three thousand acres of land and for twenty-five years grew grapes, fruit trees, and almond trees at Rancho Ignacio (named for his patron saint) and Rancho Santa Helena (named for his wife). "Paddy," as he was fondly called, is credited with popularizing zinfandel grapes in Paso Robles wine country. A statue of him stands in front of the Carnegie Library in town (*See* Los Angeles, CA, sidebar: Jan Paderewski Statues, page 6). **epochwines.com/the-land-2/**

Paso Robles Inn
This historic inn at 1103 Spring Street is the site of the annual Paderewski Festival. The inn holds the famous Weber piano that Ignacy Jan Paderewski used during his concert tours in North America. The hand-carved rosewood Weber grand piano was built in 1881 and purchased in 1905 by Paderewski. The piano was in British Columbia for over fifty years until it was purchased by a Canadian Polish organization and donated to the festival which uses it for concerts. Paderewski first visited the Paso Robles Hotel (now Paso Robles Inn) in 1914 during a visit to Paso Robles's healing mineral springs for his hands.

ROSEVILLE
The Polish American Community Hall (PACH)
The Polish American Club of Sacramento was founded in 1959 and moved to this location at 327 Main Street in 1987. PACH is a gathering place for Poles of the greater Sacramento area presenting Polish classical music concerts, lectures, exhibits, language classes, dances; it maintains a library, genealogical club, and hosts an annual September Polish festival. In 1974, Club members helped establish a credit union for the Polish American community of Northern California. PolAm Federal Credit Union, as it is known today, has offices in Sacramento and other Northern California communities. **sacpolishclub.com**

SACRAMENTO
Polonian Cultural and Pastoral Center of Sacramento
The Center was established in October 1985 and opened in 1991 with the consecration of the Chapel of Our Lady of Częstochowa whose large painting hangs over the altar. The original members were Polish immigrants who had been activists in Poland's Solidarity movement. The Center, at 1601 South Avenue, organizes many events throughout the year such as picnics, entertainment, dancing, dinners, and other social gatherings. The Center supports the local chapter of Polish Scouts and offers Polish language classes for children.

SAN DIEGO
House of Poland, Balboa Park

The House of Poland was established in 1938 as one of twenty-two original International Cottages in Balboa Park, together forming the House of Pacific Relations that "serves to promote peace and good relations between nations." The externally similar, simple "cottages" feature interior decorations, displays, and presentations about different nations and their cultural heritage. Polish American organizations keep an open house on Saturday and Sunday afternoons. The house includes displays of Polish costumes, books, and artwork. Lectures and unique events are often held. **www.houseofpolandsd.org**

House of Poland, Balboa Park, San Diego, CA
(Anna Harley Trochimczyk)

St. Maximilian Kolbe Polish Mission

The Polish Mission was founded in 1971 but it was only in 1995 that the Mission finally acquired its own church building at 1735 Grand Avenue in Pacific Beach. The church holds numerous relics including St. Hedwig, Fr. Popiełuszko, St. Pope John Paul II, St. Faustina Kowalska, and Blessed Michał Sopocko. Recent renovations included the installation of stained-glass windows with images of Fr. Popiełuszko, St. Pope John Paul II, St. Maximilian Kolbe, Queen Jadwiga, and St. Faustina Kowalska. The Mission sponsors an immensely popular annual Polish Festival. Masses are all in Polish and Polish customs are observed by the church congregation. **www.polishmission.org/index.htm**

St. Maximilian Kolbe Polish Mission, San Diego, CA
(Anna Harley Trochimczyk)

SAN FRANCISCO
Bernard Zakheim Murals at University of California San Francisco

A series of murals at UCSF painted by Polish-born artist Bernard Zakheim in the 1930s remains the jewel of the University's art collection. The ten-panel series in Toland Hall (first floor) called "History of Medicine in California" includes a panel that memorializes Feliks Paweł Wierzbicki, M.D., one of the most prominent of the Polish pioneers in northern California. Wierzbicki's headstone in the Presidio is reported to be the oldest preserved Polish tombstone on the west coast of the United States and was restored in 1996. Two other panels

The Bernard Zakheim mural that memorializes Feliks Paweł Wierzbicki at the University of California San Francisco campus   (Maureen Mroczek)

by Zakheim are in the Health Sciences West lecture halls. This undertaking was partially funded by the WPA Federal Art Project. Zakheim is best known for contributing the Library Periodical Room fresco and organizing the New Deal art project at the Coit Tower. He worked with Diego Rivera in Mexico City and the University Archives have a set of materials documenting how these frescoes were created and preserved (Bernard Zakheim collection MSS 2014-15).
blogs.library.ucsf.edu/broughttolight/tag/wpa-federal-art-project

Grace Cathedral
John De Rosen (Jan Henryk de Rosen) created eight murals and seven altar panels along the aisles and in the chapels of Grace Cathedral, an Episcopal church at 1100 California Street, including a faux-tile mural behind the Chapel of Grace reredos (1932), and the Chapel of the Nativity's Adoration mural (1946) showing the Holy Family with magi and shepherds. De Rosen also included a little image of his boyhood home in Warsaw in the mural. On a smaller scale, De Rosen painted delicate panels (1949) for the old High Altar, now in the Chapel of St. Francis columbarium. The most visible works of De Rosen in Grace Cathedral are the historical aisle murals (1949-1950) done in a style blending elements of the early Italian masters Giotto and Mantegna. (*See other locations of his murals*: Immaculate Conception Church, Washington D.C.; Cathedral Basilica of St. Louis, MO.)

Joseph Conrad Square
This park, located in North Beach near Fisherman's Wharf, was dedicated in 1971 and named for the Polish author Joseph Conrad (Józef Korzeniowski). Wanda Tomczykowska, president of the Polish Arts and Culture Foundation at the time, is credited with spearheading this project. The nearby San Francisco Maritime Museum has a copy of Jacob Epstein's 1924 bronze bust of Conrad.

Nativity of Our Lord Church
First dedicated in June of 1904, the Nativity of Our Lord Church at 240 Fell Street has been the gathering place for Slavic Catholics for more than a hundred years. It is a personal parish for the pastoral care of Polish, Croatian, Slovenian, Czech, and Slovak Catholics. The walls highlight paintings of several Polish saints. **www.sfnativity.org**

Polish Club Inc. / "Dom Polski"
Located in San Francisco's Mission District at 3040 22nd Street, this club is jointly owned by The Polish Society of California/Lodge 7 of the Polish National Alliance (one of the oldest Polish societies in the U.S. started in 1863), the St. Stanislaus Benevolent Society, and the Polish Literary and Dramatic Circle. The Club building was acquired in 1926 and is used for Polish cultural events continuing its original mission to serve as a center for the propagation of Polish culture, art, language, and community. The Club retains remnants of The Polish Society's original library, founded by actress Helena Modjeska. Historic books may be viewed at the Polish Club's Library, by appointment. A replica of Aleksander Zakrzewski's San Francisco plat map can also be viewed

at the library. Zakrzewski, a Polish 49er and "master of engineering," was an accomplished lithographer from Sandomierz who worked for the U.S. Surveyor General's Office. He drew one of the initial San Francisco Street maps. He is also known for a beautiful map of the mining region of California. **www.polishclubsf.org**

St. Mary of the Assumption Cathedral
In 2017, *Architecture Digest* named this church one of the ten most beautiful churches in the United States. Located at 1111 Gough Street, and known locally as Saint Mary's Cathedral, its Polish Black Madonna Chapel, where St. Pope John Paul II said Mass during a visit to San Francisco in 1987, has a reproduction of the icon of the Black Madonna of Częstochowa, a gift from Wanda Tomczykowska. **smcsf.org**

SAN JOSE
St. Brother Albert Chmielowski Polish Mission
This mission at 10250 Clayton Road is an outgrowth of St. Adalbert Parish in San Francisco and was established in 1989 by the Society of Christ. The patron of the Mission is St. Brother Albert Chmielowski—a Polish monk, elevated to sainthood in 1989; it is the first Catholic parish community in the U.S. to be named after this saint. On the outside of this modern building, there is a large mural of St. Pope John Paul II in front of an image of Jesus of Divine Mercy. Stained-glass windows include one of St. Albert. In addition to an Annual Festival and Polish Masses, the Mission organizes cultural life events with lectures, bazaars, and a weekly café open to all.

SAN MARINO
Huntington Library, Art Museum, and Botanical Gardens
The Manuscripts Department at Huntington Library (1151 Oxford Road) holds the Modjeska-Opid Family Papers, a collection of over three hundred items from 1869-1982. This collection contains letters, photographs, press clippings, programs, reviews, and other items pertaining to the Polish actress Helena Modjeska and members of the family of Ludwik Opid (1865-1948), her

nephew. The family letters show her personal side; imprinted ribbons from flower wreaths given to her in Poland reveal her patriotism; and press clippings document her American popularity, including documentation of her funeral in 1909, celebrated by thousands of Angelenos. Open by special permission.

San Marino Huntington Library, San Marino, CA (Maja Trochimczyk)

Jerzy Szeptycki (1915-2004)

Catholic modernism in Southern California found expression in the many churches of Jerzy Szeptycki. Born in Poland, Szeptycki studied at Warsaw Polytechnic University and graduated with a degree in architecture from the University of Southern California in 1952. At USC, he wrote a thesis about the history of church architecture and his desire to create a style that blended liturgical needs with contemporary materials and modern ideas. A prolific architect, Szeptycki designed over twenty-five churches in California, primarily concentrated in greater Los Angeles, including: St. Lawrence the Martyr (Redondo Beach), St. Bede (La Canada), St. Mary (Fullerton), St. Cyril of Jerusalem (Encino), and Our Lady of the Bright Mount Church. Notably, he was the leading architect for the Shrine of Our Lady of Czestochowa in Doylestown which was dedicated in 1966 and is considered one of Polonia's most important religious sites (*see* Doylestown, PA).

SANTA ANA
Bowers Museum

The Bowers Museum at 2002 North Main Street includes over three hundred items pertaining to the Shakespearean actress Helena Modjeska, who, after coming to California, first lived in Anaheim and then established her residence in Santiago Canyon. (*See entry for* Modjeska Canyon: Arden, page 7). The collection includes costumes, photographs, books, theatrical programs, letters, and a painting by Józef Chełmoński, *Sielanka*, presented to the actress as a wedding gift. Most of the Modjeska Collection is in storage, while temporary exhibitions bring Modjeska to the attention of the public.
www.bowers.org/index.php/past-exhibition/as-she-liked-it-the-shakespearean-roles-of-madame-modjeska

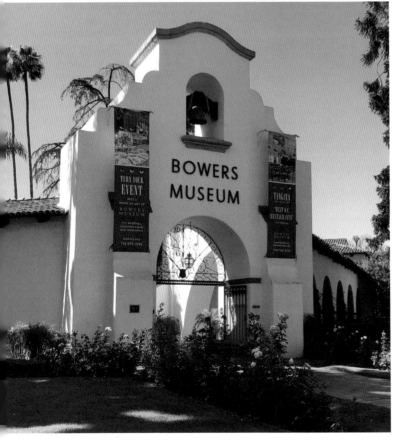

Bowers Museum, Santa Ana, CA   (Maja Trochimczyk)

STANFORD

Stanford University Hoover Institution Library and Archive on War, Revolution, and Peace

Stanford University Library has an outstanding collection of books and documents on Poland, Polish history, language, music, science, and culture but the Polish Collection at the Hoover Institution is particularly extensive. The Institution was founded in 1919 by the future president of the United States, Herbert Hoover, who organized humanitarian relief to newly independent Poland after World War I and remains fondly remembered in that country. The Witold S. Sworakowski Collection on Poland, named after the first curator of the Polish collection, is the largest source of documentation on recent Polish history outside of Poland. The holdings include over two hundred archival and manuscript collections, fifty thousand volumes of books, and three thousand titles of periodicals and newspapers relating to Polish history from the late 19th century until today. Within the collection, there are five hundred boxes of documents from the Polish Foreign Ministry files for the years 1925-1945. There are fifty-four boxes of papers from the Polish Embassy in the Soviet Union during the war years, including many documents reflecting the search for missing officers from the camps in Kozielsk, Ostaszków, and Starobielsk, and over twenty-two thousand prisoners who were massacred on Joseph Stalin's orders in 1940. There are one hundred boxes of documents from the Polish Armed Forced files in World War II, including the papers of General Władysław Anders and the Polish Second Corps. There are 272 boxes of papers given to the Hoover Institution by Leopold Labedz, an eminent Polish journalist. Jan Nowak's papers are deposited there as well. Many of these documents are not catalogued and are not readily available. Prearrangements are advised.

YORBA LINDA

St. John Paul II Polish Center

Established in 1983, this church and community center at 3999 Rose Drive serve as a home for such organizations as Helena Modrzejewska Polish School and Polish Scouting. The Polish Center organizes annual events (Dożynki Harvest Festival on the third weekend of September and Proud

to be Polish Festival with participation of artists and performers from Orange, Los Angeles, and San Diego counties), as well as lectures, exhibitions, performances, and other community events for the entire Polish American community. In 1986, the Center dedicated a plaque in memory of the martyr Fr. Jerzy Popiełuszko. The Bell Tower has three bells cast in Poland.
www.polishcenter.org

Saint John Paul II Polish Center,
Yorba Linda, CA
(Maja Trochimczyk)

14

COLORADO

COLORADO SPRINGS
Colonel Francis Gabreski Bust
Colonel Francis Gabreski (Franciszek Stanisław Gabryszewski), 1919-2002, is honored with a bust at the United States Air Force Academy and a plaque highlighting his military career located in the Honor Court. By July 1944, with twenty-eight kills, Gabreski was already the top U.S. ace in the European theater; in 1952, after downing five MiGs, he became an ace in the Korean War. He is one of the few pilots to become an ace in both propeller and jet aircraft. With thirty-seven and a half kills on his record, Gabreski was, at the time of his death, the top living fighter ace of the United States. Gabreski's numerous awards and honors include the Silver Star, Distinguished Flying Cross, the Bronze Star, and medals from Poland, Britain, France, and Belgium. (*See also* Myrtle Beach, SC, for a marker in his honor; and Pooler, GA.)

Colonel Francis Gabreski bust at Colorado Springs U.S. Air Force Academy (Thomas Napierkowski)

DENVER
Monument to Pulaski and Other Eminent Poles
A 20-ft.-tall granite stele with bas-relief busts of six prominent Polish figures was sculpted by Zbigniew Maleszewski and is in Pulaski Park (3300 East Bayaud Avenue). It memorializes Kazimierz Pulaski, Tadeusz Kościuszko, Mikołaj Kopernik (Nicolaus Copernicus), Marie Skłodowska Curie (Marie Curie), Fryderyk Chopin (Frédéric Chopin), and Ignacy Jan Paderewski. The contributions made by each figure are inscribed below their relief. The top of the monument features thirteen horizontal stripes and a symbolic eagle. Donated by the Polish Community of Denver, it was dedicated in commemoration of the American Bicentennial in 1976.

Polish Club of Denver
The Polish Club of Denver, at 3121 West Alameda Avenue, was started in 1950 by post-World War II émigrés seeking to keep their traditions and language alive. As the Polish population grew, a new building was acquired in 1975. The center supports a lending library, Polish language school, the dance group "Krakowiacy," and scouting. It has hosted many famous literary and political figures, and actors and musicians from Poland, as well as the local honorary Polish consul general. The organization was instrumental in organizing and funding the Pulaski Park monument to six

Monument to eminent Poles, Denver, CO (Alexander Matusiak)

famous Poles. Advocacy of club members also resulted in October being declared as Polish Culture month in Colorado. **www.polishclubofdenver.com**

St. Joseph Polish Church

For more than a century the portal over the church door has read, *Kościół Świętego Józefa (Church of St. Joseph).* In 1902, Denver's small Polish population established a church that would remind its parishioners of their life in Poland and help them feel a bit more at home in the Rocky Mountains. Almost immediately, they instituted a Corpus Christi procession like those held across Poland. Now over a century later, St. Joseph Polish Church (517 East 46th Avenue) is flourishing and continues to preserve and practice the faith with a Polish accent. A few decades ago, the church was added to the National Register of Historic Places, and in the late 1980s Klemens Mituniewicz adorned the ceilings and walls of the church with religious scenes and views of the Colorado Rockies. In the 1990s, the growing Polish population supported the visits of Polish Cardinal Józef Glemp and Pope John Paul II to Denver which brought new energy to the parish. Visitors to Colorado will find Christmas Masses, Lenten services, Easter celebrations, and Corpus Christi liturgies reminiscent of Poland and Polonian Catholicism. **swietyjozef.org**

St. Joseph Polish Church, Denver, CO   (Małgorzata Bielak)

CONNECTICUT

ANSONIA

Kosciuszko Room at the General David Humphreys House Museum

David Humphreys was a general in the Continental Army during the Revolutionary War and had fought alongside Thaddeus Kosciuszko, who had reportedly stayed at his home in Ansonia. The room, established in 1980, is filled with Kosciuszko memorabilia, including correspondence between the two friends. This site at 37 Elm Street is maintained by the Derby Historical Association.

BRIDGEPORT

St. Michael the Archangel Church

St. Michael's was built by the Polish immigrant community of Bridgeport at the beginning of the twentieth century. Located at 310 Pulaski Street, it is a neogothic red brick church that features many accents of contemporary Polish religious art. The parish continues to serve the local Polonia and the church hosts cultural events, a language class, and daily Mass in Polish. **www.stmichaelbridgeport.com**

BRISTOL

St. Stanislaus Kostka Church

The present church building at 510 West Street dates to 1956, when the older structure was replaced with new construction. Its neogothic interior is sparsely decorated although there is a large painting of Our Lady of Częstochowa. Over the years, the influx of new immigrants has helped the parish to maintain a strong Polish identity. Each year the Dożynki festival is hosted by the parish. **www.ststanislausbristolct.org**

DERBY

St. Michael the Archangel Church

This church and parish at 75 Derby Avenue were established by immigrants from Poland at the beginning of the twentieth century. Pressed against a hill, St. Michael's is a neogothic church, designed by architect Joseph A. Jackson. The plain façade contrasts with the richly decorated interior. The church continues to serve the local Polonia community and celebrates traditional Polish events. **saintmichaelsderby.org**

ENFIELD

Polish National Home

Now Old Country Banquets (4 Alden Avenue), the Polish National Home in Enfield was built in 1923 and designed by architect Bruno Wozny. The large and impressive ballroom "Wawel" is used for weddings and major events. Located in the same building is the Pierogi Queen Bakery which specializes in pierogi and nalesniki. The building's exterior also still carries the name "Wawel" along with the date of its construction. **oldcountrybanquets.com**

Polish National Home, Enfield, CT (Tom Kirchmann)

St. Adalbert Church, Enfield, CT
(Romuald Byczkiewicz)

St. Adalbert Church

This Polish parish was formed in Enfield at 90 Alden Avenue in 1915. Most of the immigrants were from Galicia and found work in local carpet mills. The present building was constructed in 1928 in the Romanesque style, supposedly patterned on an unknown church in Poland. Stained-glass windows behind the altar depict several Polish saints. Two grottoes were constructed in 1939 with statues of Mary and St. Adalbert. The church is currently a part of St. Raymond of Penafort parish. **www.straymondenfield.org**

HARTFORD
General Casimir Pulaski Monument

Pulaski Mall at 394 Main Street features a bronze statue of Casimir Pulaski on horseback that was designed by the nationally recognized sculptor Granville W. Carter. The memorial monument was funded by local Polish American citizens and dedicated in 1976 for the Bicentennial celebrations. The overall statue, including the pedestal, rises twenty-two feet and shows the Revolutionary War hero astride his horse, pointing the way to battle and victory with his sword. A plaque includes the

General Casimir Pulaski Monument, Hartford, CT
(Romuald Byczkiewicz)

following quote attributed to Pulaski, "I came here, where freedom is being defended, to serve it, and to live or die for it."

Polish National Home of Hartford

Constructed in 1930 and designed by architect Henry F. Ludorf, the Polish National Home at 60 Charter Oak Avenue is noted for Art Deco style and original features, including bronze grillwork and doors, period light fixtures, and exterior bas-relief decorations. It was listed on the National Register of Historic Places in 1983. The Polish National Home has hosted many noteworthy visitors including the Polish heroes of the Second World War, General Tadeusz Bór Komorowski of the Polish Home Army and General Władysław Anders of the 2nd Polish Corps, renowned Polish pianist and composer Andrzej Anweiler, and Red Sox baseball legend Jim Rice, as well as two American presidents. For many decades, the Home hosted weekly polka radio shows. Now a Polish tavern, restaurant, and banquet venue, it continues to host

live jazz and classical music concerts. Each Christmas season is celebrated with a display of *Szopki* (crèche) and Polish caroling.
polishhomect.org

Sts. Cyril & Methodius Church

Sts. Cyril and Methodius Church at 63 Popieluszko Court was designed by architect Timothy G. O'Connell and constructed between 1914-16. The interior is replete with Polish symbols and images of saints, including a series of medallions over the arches painted by Vincent Mundo in 1937. Notably on the ceiling above the altar is a large painting of Sts. Cyril & Methodius modeled after a late-19th-century canvas by Jan Matejko. The church regularly hosts performances by the Fryderyk Chopin Society of Connecticut.
sscyrilmethodiushartford.org

MERIDEN
Casimir Pulaski Monument

This monument on the green median strip on Broad Street is a six-foot bronze bas-relief portraying General Casimir Pulaski standing with a hand on the hilt of his sword, with an eagle taking flight on the top of the structure. The granite foundation is from Barry, Vermont.

Casimir Pulaski Monument, Meriden, CT
(Romuald Byczkiewicz)

The dedication of the monument took place in 1934, accompanied by a parade and audience of many thousands. The inscription on the monument reads: "Casimir Pulaski Polish-American Patriot Aided the Colonies in Their Fight for Liberty Dying Gloriously in Action. Meriden Polonia."

St. Stanislaus Bishop and Martyr Church

Led by Rev. Antoni Klawiter, Polish immigrants to Meriden organized this parish in 1891, becoming the first Polish parish in Connecticut. Construction on the present church began in 1907. The church at 82 Akron Street was designed by the architectural firm Reiley & Steinback in an Italian Lombard style and can seat nine hundred. In the apse there is a large painting of "St. Stanislaus in Glory," and by the altar a painting of Our Lady of Częstochowa commissioned from an artist in Poland. The church is a part of a sprawling complex that includes a school, rectory, community center, and convent. It is part of St. Faustina Kowalska Parish.

MIDDLETOWN

St. Mary of Czestochowa Church

Middletown's Polish community organized their first parish in 1903, but the church built in 1917 was destroyed by arson fire in 1980. The new church building at 79 South Main Street was built in 1983 and offers a modernist architectural design and incorporates the statue and bell saved from the old church. Masses are offered in Polish, and many traditional Polish customs are observed by the Parish.
stmarymiddletown.com

St. Mary of Czestochowa Church, Middletown, CT (Romuald Byczkiewicz)

NEW BRITAIN

Central Connecticut State University's Polish Studies Program and the Connecticut Polish American Archives (CPAA)

The intellectual and scholarly heart of Connecticut Polonia is the Polish Studies Program and Connecticut Polish American Archives (CPAA). Founded by the late Stanislaus A. Blejwas in 1974, the Polish Studies Program has served CCSU students and the wider community with classes in Polish history and language since its founding. The CPAA, located in the CCSU's Elihu Burritt Library includes important historical materials documenting life in the Polish American community. The Archive also includes the Polish Heritage Collection of over 21,000 items. Thanks to Dr. Blejwas' diligent efforts at fundraising the second endowed chair of its kind in the country was established. Named in honor of its founder after his passing, the Stanislaus A. Blejwas Endowed Chair in Polish and Polish American Studies regularly sponsors the annual

Bust at the Connecticut Polish American Archives (Iwona Flis)

Father Jerzy Popiełuszko Monument, New Britain, CT
(Romuald Byczkiewicz)

Fiedorczyk Lecture in Polish American Studies, the Annual Milewski Lecture in Polish Studies, the biennial Godlewski Evening of Polish Culture, the Koproski Lecture on Polis Business and the Economy Series, and the Rudewicz Evening of Polish Music. There are also regular exhibitions and cultural events, a Polish Film series, musical concerts, and literary evenings.

Father Jerzy Popiełuszko Monument

Located at Walnut Hill Park at 184 W. Main Street, this memorial is dedicated to Rev. Jerzy Popiełuszko, a Roman Catholic priest and Solidarity activist who was murdered by Communist security forces in 1984. It symbolizes the universal struggle for human rights and freedom and is sometimes referred to as the Human Rights Memorial. This modernist steel sculpture was designed by Henry Chotkowski and was dedicated in 1989. Next to the monument is a granite stone with an inscription *Zło dobrem zwyciężaj* (Conquer evil with good) and a dedication.

Holy Cross Church

The founding of Holy Cross Parish was surrounded in a controversy that began in 1927, as parishioners disaffected with the leadership style of Father Lucyan Bójnowski at the Sacred Heart Church in New Britain decided to establish a new Roman Catholic parish. They petitioned the diocesan bishop and soon afterwards received approval. The church at 31 Biruta Street was completed in 1934 in the French Gothic style with a single towering steeple to the south. There is a richly carved oak Gothic altar and, on both sides of the church, a series of stained-glass windows depicting scenes from the life of Christ and Polish saints and patrons. In the back vestibule next to the icon of the Black Madonna there are two modern stained-glass windows, one depicting St. Maximilian Kolbe and the other St. Pope John Paul II. Two ministries sponsored by the Polish church continue: the former Our Lady of Rose Hill Orphanage is now a women's shelter and St. Lucian's Residence provides a home for the elderly in a historic building.

holycrosschurchnb.org

Holy Cross Church, New Britain, CT
(Romuald Byczkiewicz)

Katyń Monument
Located in the veterans' section of Sacred Heart Cemetery (662 Burritt Street), this simple black granite monument was dedicated in May of 1980, "In memory of our comrades in arms, Polish prisoners of War who were massacred by the Soviet Russia at the Katyn Forest in the spring, 1940." The Gen. Jozef Haller Post No. 111 of the Polish Army Veterans Association of America led the initiative for the monument. There is also a statue of Father Jerzy Popiełuszko in the cemetery.

"Little Poland" on Broad Street
The Broad Street area of New Britain has been the home of Polish Americans for more than a century. By the 1990s the area, considered "an ethnic neighborhood," needed revitalization. Recently arrived Polish immigrants started businesses there and neighborhood organizations joined together to push for its revitalization. In 2008, the New Britain City Council declared the Broad Street area as "Little Poland" to celebrate this revival. An annual Little Poland Street festival is held in spring while the end of summer hosts a large Dożynki Festival at Falcon Field. Once known as the Hardware City of the World, New Britain drew tens of thousands to the factories that made hardware, cutlery, bricks, and appliances. The city still has the largest concentration of people of Polish ancestry in Connecticut.

Polish Genealogical Society of Connecticut and the Northeast
This Archive and Resource Center at 8 Lyle Road contains works on Polish American family history, Polish immigration history, and unpublished community studies and commemorative booklets of Polish parishes in the northeast. The largest collection is that of gravestone inscriptions from nearly 300 cemeteries. It also houses records of Polish organizations, photographs, and a sizeable obituary collection. Researchers are welcome to use these materials. The organization began in 1984 and many documents are now available online in their database. **pgsctne.org**

Sacred Heart Church
At the heart of Broad Street (158 Broad Street) stands Sacred Heart Roman Catholic Church. The parish was organized by New Britain's Polish immigrants led by the Rev. Lucyan Bójnowski (later Monsignor) in 1895. The first church building was a small wooden structure on Orange Street, but as the number of Polish immigrants grew, by 1902 ground was broken for the present location. The church is built in the form of a Gothic cross with gray-blue granite stone on the outside, and decorated with white sand marble in the interior, which features many Polish religious symbols and decorations,

Mural of Monsignor Lucyan Bójnowski in Sacred Heart Church, New Britain, CT (Romuald Byczkiewicz)

including a painting of the Black Madonna and Our Lady of Ostrabrama high in the apse above the altar. Bójnowski also established a religious order for women, the Daughters of Mary, who served as teachers at the parochial school and who were housed in a permanent home for the order on Osgood Avenue right behind Sacred Heart Cemetery. A statue of Msgr. Bójnowski as well as one of St. Pope John Paul II are next to the church. **www.sacredheartnb.org**

Sloper-Wesoly House
This house built in a Queen Anne style in 1887, was owned by Andrew Jackson Sloper, a local industrialist and banker. In 1946, this historic house was purchased by Dr. Andrew S. Wesoly, whose medical practice served the local Polish American community. In 2000, the daughters of Dr. Wesoly donated the house to the Polish American Foundation (PAF). After extensive renovations, the house opened as the Sloper-Wesoly Immigrant Heritage and Cultural Center. In addition to serving as headquarters of PAF, the center houses Connecticut Virtuosi Chamber Orchestra and is a location of many cultural and artistic events. The Sloper-Wesoly House is listed in the National Register of Historic Places.

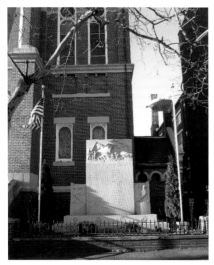

NEW HAVEN
St. Stanislaus Bishop and Martyr Church
Since 1903, St. Stanislaus has been served by the Vincentian Fathers. The present red brick Romanesque-revival church at 9 Eld Street was constructed in 1911-13, and the interior is opulently decorated in the Baroque style. In 1942-43, Vincent Mundo was commissioned to paint the interior on the theme of Poland's conversion to Christianity which includes a painting of Poland's King Władysław Jagiełło. Outside, there is a monument with a bas-relief of soldiers and sailors dedicated to the sons of the parish who died in World War II.
www.ststanislaus-newhaven.com

St. Stanislaus Church World War II Monument, New Haven, CT (Romuald Byczkiewicz)

ROCKVILLE
St. Joseph Church
St. Joseph's Parish was established in 1905 by Polish immigrants. By 1907, the large brick church building at 33 West Street and an adjacent school were constructed. The church features an arched stained-glass window with a limestone cross and a nine-foot statue of St. Joseph over the entrance. Connected to the building is a 55-foot bell tower that was designed by architect George Vuinovich and dedicated in 1958. **www.stjosephct.org**

STAMFORD
Holy Name of Jesus Church
The Holy Name of Jesus Church at 325 Washington Boulevard is considered one of the most impressive Polish churches in the state of Connecticut. The parish was established in 1903 but it was only in 1934 that the first Mass was said in the new church due to the Depression. The style of the architecture blends Romanesque and Byzantine elements. The Black Madonna icon that hangs in the church is one of the artifacts from the 1939 Polish Pavilion at the New York World's Fair.

A crest on the baldachin features the Polish and American flags. The parish is served by the Vincentian Fathers. Beside the church is a statue of St. Pope John Paul II and a unique bell that was also part of the Polish exhibit at the 1939 World's Fair and is known as "The Freedom Bell." It features images of six Polish saints, a quote from Adam Mickiewicz, images of the 19th-century national uprisings, and Queen Jadwiga. **www.holynamestamford.org**

Thaddeus Kosciuszko Monument

This monument is in the middle of the oldest part of the Polish American community in Kosciuszko Park which is the largest waterfront park in town.

"The Freedom Bell," once part of the 1939 World's Fair Polish exhibit and now outside Holy Name of Jesus Church in Stamford, CT (Romuald Byczkiewicz)

TERRYVILLE

St. Casimir Church

The St. Casimir's Society predates the construction of the church which finally occurred in 1906, after much pressure for the bishop's recognition. The white clapboard exterior belies St. Casimir's highly decorated interior that preserves many original features such as societal banners from 1901 and paintings. The church, at 19 Allen Street, is now part of St. Maximilian Kolbe Parish. **www.stmkp.org**

WEST HARTFORD

Statue of Noah Webster

Standing across from the Noah Webster Library (20 South Main Street) in Blue Black Square, this 13-foot tall, modernistic statue of Noah Webster was sculpted by the Polish American artist Korczak Ziolkowski from a single thirty-two-ton block of marble in the town where he lived for several years before moving west. (*See* Crazy Horse, SD: Crazy Horse Memorial). He donated his time to memorialize the town's most famous native son. During the construction, hundreds of local residents would come to watch him working but he offended the town people because he often carved without a shirt, with alleged profanity, and defied the Blue Laws by working at night and on Sundays. Ziolkowski maintained that he was a victim of prejudice enduring numerous ethnic slurs. When the statue was unveiled in 1942, residents discovered this message engraved on the book at the bottom right of Noah's robe: "For you I labored, not for my own day, that by the Word men should know brotherhood. My fellow men! You have not understood since each of you would go his separate way." The residents felt the artist was sending them a message about their interactions.

WILLIMANTIC

Commemorative Bench

Willimantic, which was known as the Thread City, employed many Polish immigrants in its textile industry. In 1933, the combined Polish societies built a large Polish National Home, which served as a Polonia community center until the 2000s when it was sold. It eventually became a

*Commemorative bench in
Willimantic, CT, dedicated to
the Polish citizenry of the area
(Anna Jaroszynska Kirchmann)*

Latino evangelical church and only a corner stone with the initial TK for Tadeusz Kosciuszko Club serves as a reminder about its past. In 2008, the Pulaski American Citizenship Club dedicated a commemorative bench made of Italian red marble, standing next to the entrance to the townhall (979 Main Street). The inscription reads: "Dedicated to the Polish citizenry who served the Windham area in business, industry, government and community service."

WINDSOR LOCKS
New England Air Museum
This museum recently added a permanent exhibition that commemorates Kościuszko Squadron 303. The volunteer American airmen fought bravely in Poland in 1919 against the Soviet Union and fought under the British command during World War II, helping the UK to win the Battle of Britain in 1940. An interactive kiosk highlights their bravery and flying skills, the aircraft they flew, and personal histories, and also includes the contributions of Thaddeus Kosciuszko to the American Revolution and Poland's fight for freedom during the 1790s. This initiative was sponsored by the Central Connecticut State University Polish Studies Program with contributions of panels by Poland's Institute of National Remembrance.
neam.org/pages/the-kosciuszko-squadron

*New England Air Museum,
Kosciuszko Squadron exhibit,
Windsor Locks, CT
(Mark Dillon)*

DELAWARE

WILMINGTON
St. Hedwig Church
The cornerstone of this building at 408 South Harrison Street was laid in 1904 although the church was founded in 1890. The church is neo-Gothic in style with a massive granite foundation, trimmings of cut Bedford stone and galvanized iron, and a quarry roof. It is the only church in the Diocese of Wilmington and the state of Delaware with twin towers (80 feet tall) and upon completion, it was the largest Catholic church in Wilmington. The architect was Brielmaier & Sons of Milwaukee (*see* Milwaukee, WI: Basilica of St. Josaphat; Lemont IL: Sts Cyril & Methodius Church). Stained-glass windows depict Polish saints. St. Hedwig's continues to serve as the centerpiece for the Polish community and Masses and religious events are in Polish. An annual Polish festival was begun in 1956. It was added to the National Register of Historic Places in 1982. **www.sthedwigde.org**

Thaddeus Kosciuszko and Casimir Pulaski Plaques
Kosciuszko Park (at the intersection of South Broom Street and Sycamore Street) and Pulaski Park (where Maryland Avenue and Oak Street meet), named after the Polish heroes, are less than a quarter mile apart so they are included together. Each has a historical marker honoring the namesake of the park; both were erected by the City of Wilmington. Pulaski's plaque is embedded in a tall stone wall. Kosciuszko's plaque was dedicated in 1976, the bicentennial of U.S. independence, which he fought to secure. **www.hmdb.org**

Kosciuszko Park marker, Wilmingtn, DE (Keith Smith)

DISTRICT OF COLUMBIA / WASHINGTON D.C.

WASHINGTON, D.C.

Air and Space Museum

This is easily the most popular museum in Washington with millions of visitors each year. The museum holds an exhibit of Polish interest. The Lunar Roving Vehicle, also known as a "moon buggy," used by astronauts when on the surface of the moon, was designed by a Polish engineer, Mieczysław Bekker (1905-1989). As a scientist, he was a leading specialist in theory and design of military and off-the-road locomotion vehicles and an originator of a new engineering discipline called "terramechanics." He was a professor at the University of Michigan and part of the lunar crew vehicle project at General Motors.

Lunar Roving Vehicle at the Air and Space Museum designed by Polish engineer Mieczysław Bekker (JD Hancock, photos.jdhancock.com)

Arlington National Cemetery

Though across the Potomac River from Washington D.C. in Virginia we are listing Arlington Cemetery here as it is usually a place visitors go when they are visiting the U.S. capital.

Paderewski's memorial marker, Arlington National Cemetery. His body was later moved back to Poland in 1992. (Larry Romans)

Ignacy Jan Paderewski Memorial Marker

Paderewski's remains were interred for fifty-one years (1941-1992) in the vault of the Mast of the USS Maine Memorial in Arlington National Cemetery. A plaque at the memorial to honor him is located across Arlington Memorial Bridge on the Virginia side of the Potomac River, directly outside the entrance to the USS Maine Memorial section 24 under a linden tree that is part of the memorial. Paderewski was Poland's greatest twentieth-century pianist, and he toured the U.S. extensively. He also represented Poland at the Paris Peace Conference and was instrumental in getting President Woodrow Wilson to include an independent Poland as the thirteenth point in Wilson's Fourteen Points for settling World War I. Paderewski served as premier and foreign minister of Poland in 1919 before he largely left politics and returned to music. Paderewski's body was exhumed and moved to Poland in July 1992 to a crypt in St. John's Cathedral in Warsaw after Poland regained its independence. His heart is encased in a bronze sculpture in the National Shrine of Our Lady of Czestochowa (*see* Doylestown, PA).

Grave of Brigadier General Włodzimierz Krzyżanowski

Brigadier General Włodzimierz Krzyżanowski, a Polish born nobleman, became the colonel of the 58th New York Volunteer Infantry Regiment formed from the recruits he gathered mainly in New York State to fight in the Civil War. It was listed in the official Army Reg-

Washington D.C. and Polonia
Although Washington, D.C. does not claim very many Polish American residents, there is a sizeable and culturally active Polish American community in the D.C.-metropolitan area. Many Polish Americans who have held government or government-related positions have lived there. They include: Zbigniew Brzezinski, National Security Advisor to U.S. President Carter and a top advisor to many high U.S. officials since; Jan Nowak, former head of the Polish section of Radio Free Europe and later an advisor to the Polish American Congress; Stefan Korboński, the last head of the Polish underground state in World War II; Jan Karski, Polish WWII resistance fighter and later professor at Georgetown University, who reported on the Nazi atrocities in the Warsaw Ghetto and the Holocaust in unsuccessful attempts to stop them. On November 15, 1989, Lech Walesa addressed a Joint Session of Congress, becoming the first non-head of state to do so.

The greatest importance of the capital to Poland and Polish Americans stems from its function as the national and international nexus of America. The Polish Embassy is a dynamic center of cultural activity now that it represents a free Poland. The national executive office of the Polish American Congress office is a crucial connection to the government of the U.S. The American Council for Polish Culture, an educational and lobbying organization founded in 1948, opened a Washington, DC, office in 1991.

ister as the "Polish Legion." He was a Polish American engineer, politician, and brigadier general in the Union Army and is often considered America's most decorated soldier. After the war he had governing duties in Alabama, was appointed governor of Georgia, and worked for the U.S. Treasury Department and later in the customs service in Panama and New York. He retired to San Francisco and ran a tavern where he often entertained the novelist Henryk Sienkiewicz and he also helped with the American debut of the Shakespearean actress Helena Modjeska. He was reinterned and is buried in Arlington National Cemetery, Section 1, Site 832.

Basilica of the National Shrine of the Immaculate Conception:
The Polish Chapel of Our Lady of Czestochowa

Although the Shrine is four miles from the Capitol, there is a metro stop, so it is accessible and well worth a visit. The dedication of this largest Roman Catholic Church in the Western Hemisphere took place in 1959 although it was not yet finished. The famous Polish chapel has been the focal point of many Polish and Polish-American religious and patriotic events. It contains a faithful replica done by a Polish artist of the Black Madonna, Poland's revered religious icon, and the dome has Polish saints around the Madonna. The north apse of the church has a huge mosaic of "Christ in Majesty" which may be the largest mosaic of Jesus in the world (3,610 sq. ft), and several murals (mosaic tympana with the interior of the east porch) all done

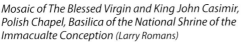

Mosaic of The Blessed Virgin and King John Casimir, Polish Chapel, Basilica of the National Shrine of the Immacualte Conception (Larry Romans)

Polish Chapel dome depicting Polish saints surrounding the Madonna, Polish Chapel in the Basilica of the National Shrine of the Immacualte Conception (Larry Romans)

Jan Henryk de Rosen (1891-1982)
Jan Henryk de Rosen, born and educated in Poland, was a muralist, mosaic and fresco artist whose works are found in at least ten states as well as in Europe. His artwork can be found in the National Shrine of the Immaculate Conception, St. Matthew Cathedral (D.C.), St. Luke in Buffalo, Grace Cathedral, Chapel of the Nativity, Epiphany Church in San Francisco. During World War I, he served in the Haller Army and was a diplomat accompanying Ignacy Jan Paderewski to the Versailles Peace Conferences. He received numerous awards from Poland, France, and Great Britain, as well as the Vatican, and taught at the Catholic University of America for the duration of World War II.

by the great Polish American artist, Jan Henryk de Rosen. In 1990 Pope John Paul II raised the status of the National Shrine to that of a Minor Basilica.
www.nationalshrine.com

Cathedral of St. Matthew the Apostle
Built in 1893, this cathedral at 1725 Rhode Island Avenue NW is the seat of the Archdiocese of Washington and is most known as the site of President John F. Kennedy's funeral. Our Lady's Chapel, in the left aisle, has a striking nine foot tall, 3½-ton Carrara marble figure of the Virgin Mary commissioned by Cardinal William Baum in 1980 and sculpted by the local Polish American artist, Gordon Kray. There is also a large bust of St. Pope John Paul II by the same artist commemorating the Pope's celebration of Mass on this site on October 6, 1979, during his first of seven visits to the U.S. Kray also sculpted a bust of St. Pope John Paul II in The Catholic University of America Law Library. In the baptistery, there are two magnificent mosaics created by the Polish painter Jan Henryk de Rosen.
www.stmatthewscathedral.org

The Embassy of the Republic of Poland

The Polish embassy (2640 16th Street NW) is a center for many functions and events: film showings, concerts, discussions, and lectures. Architect George Oakley Totten designed and completed the building in 1910. Prince Kazimierz Lubomirski, the first ambassador to the U.S. purchased it in 1919 and turned it over to the new Polish state, establishing it as one of Poland's first foreign missions after the country regained independence in 1918. In 1990, Kazimierz Dziewanowski (d. 1998), well-known author and journalist, became the ambassador of new Poland, serving until 1993. It contains paintings by famous Polish painters such as Julian Fałat and Jacek Malczewski, and Paderewski's Steinway piano that he played during his last American tour. Note the large Paderewski statue in the garden. There is also a sculpture of a Polish eagle with a crown by Andrzej Pitynski. For more information on Polish-U.S. diplomatic relations, see the Adams Morgan Heritage Trail plaque in front of the building.

Paderewski statue in the garden of the Polish Embassy in Washington D.C. (Larry Romans)

Jan Karski Memorial

Jan Karski, a Polish World War II resistance movement fighter and later a distinguished professor at Georgetown University, is remembered by a memorial on Georgetown University campus. The life-size sculpture of Karski sitting on a bench playing chess, his favorite game, was executed by Polish sculptor Karol Badyna and dedicated in 2002. It is located on Copley Lawn beside White Gravenor Hall. Born Jan Kozielewski, Karski provided eyewitness testimony on the Holocaust to the West by secretly entering the Warsaw ghetto. He was awarded the Presidential Medal of Freedom by President Barack Obama.

Memorial sculpture of Jan Karski at Georgetown University in Washington D.C. (Larry Romans)

The Kosciuszko Foundation Washington D.C. Center

Conveniently located in the Dupont Circle area at 2025 O Street NW, the KF has among its holdings and on display hundreds of paintings, prints, posters, and sculptures by Polish artists as well as books, pottery, and Polish folk crafts and costumes. In addition, this chapter hosts numerous cultural events throughout the year. It includes the Museum of Polish Art and Culture with an extensive gallery of Polish painters. The Jan Karski Room holds memorabilia related to his life and his struggle against the Holocaust. The elegant townhouse was acquired in 2010 from the National Polish Center. Formerly it was known as The American Center of Polish Culture. **www.thekf.org/kf/chapters/washington-dc/kf**

Kosciuszko Monument

Located at the northeast corner of Lafayette Park on Pennsylvania Avenue, across from the White House, the Kosciuszko Monument (dedicated by President William Howard Taft) is one of several statues dedicated to Revolutionary War heroes in Washington, D.C. The Polish sculptor Antoni Popiel (1865-1910) fashioned it as a standing portrait of Brigadier General Thaddeus Kosciuszko holding a map of the fortifications of Saratoga. His dress is that of the U.S. Continental Army

Polish Room at the Kosciuszko Foundation Center in Washington D.C. (previous page) (KF)

Kosciuszko Monument at Lafayette Park, Washington D.C. (Szczebrzeszyn CC-BY-SA-2.0)

military uniform. The inscription on the pedestal reads: "Erected by the Polish National Alliance of America and presented to the United States on behalf of Polish-American citizens, May 11, 1910."

The Library of Congress

The Library of Congress—the largest library in the world—estimates its Polish book collection at over 150,000 volumes, accessible largely through the Jefferson Building's European Division. The Manuscript Division (in the Madison Building) contains notable historical Polonia items including: the 1659 indenture of Jan II Kazimierz, King of Poland; the Acts of the Confederacy of Bar; the Charles S. Dewey Papers, part of which relate to his service as a financial advisor to Poland and director of the Narodowy Bank Polski, 1927-1930; the Kościuszko Air Squadron Records that describe this volunteer unit of American pilots serving with Polish armed forces against the Bolsheviks. The papers of American diplomats Henry White, Robert Lansing, Henry Morgenthau, Cordell Hull, and W. Averell Harriman attest to the situation in Poland during and after WWI and WWII. The Zbigniew Brzezinski Papers have restrictions, but researchers can apply through the division for access to them. Materials relating to Kosciuszko, apart from letters found in the Washington and Jefferson Papers, include a copy of his commission as the engineer responsible for the fortifications at West Point. There is a small collection of information on the construction and dedication in 1910 of the statues of Kosciuszko, in Lafayette Park and Pulaski in what is now called Freedom Plaza. The Polish Declarations of Admiration and Friendship for the United States from 1926, in 111 manuscript volumes, honoring the U.S. on its 150th anniversary and to celebrate American aid to Poland during World War I (considered one of the division's notable treasures, recently digitized and thus accessible offsite) contain signatures from more than one-sixth of Poland's then residents.

Mount Olivet Cemetery, Jan Karski Grave

Mount Olivet Cemetery, the largest Catholic cemetery in the District of Columbia, is located on a historic hill overlooking the monuments of the nation's capital. Jan Karski, born Jan Romuald Kozielewski, is buried here. Karski took part in the Resistance movement during World War II, famously being the first to report the atrocities of the German Nazi concentration camps to the Western Allies. Karski later became a professor at Georgetown University, where he taught Eastern European studies to such alumni as U.S. President Bill Clinton.

Polish Library in Washington

The Polish Library is located at 1503 21st Street, N.W. Of its over seven thousand volumes, 90 percent are in Polish (fiction, memoirs, and history). The English language collection has translations from the Polish and a section on "Poles in America." The library is located on the lower level of the same building that houses the Embassy of Poland Economic and Commercial Section.

Pulaski Statue, Freedom Plaza

The statue of Brigadier General Casimir Pulaski, at Freedom Plaza on the corner of Pennsylvania Avenue and 13th Street NW, is a heroic-sized equestrian statue over eight feet tall and shows the founder of the American cavalry in the uniform of a Polish nobleman and marshal. The names of Revolutionary War battles in which he par-

Brigadier General Casimir Pulaski statue at Freedon Plaza in Washington DC (Robert Lyle Bolton CC-BY-SA-2.0)

ticipated are carved on the pedestal. Sculpted by Kazimierz Chodziński, who also sculpted the Kosciuszko monument in Chicago, it was unveiled on May 11, 1910, the same day on which the Kosciuszko statue in D.C. was dedicated. The U.S. Congress paid for the Pulaski statue, realizing the American government's pledge in 1779 to erect a monument to the fallen revolutionary war hero. This monument is the center of many gatherings commemorating important events in Polish history.

St. John Paul II National Shrine, Washington DC (Gavin Moulton)

St. John Paul II National Shrine

Located near the Basilica of the National Shrine, this site, which had previously been the Pope John Paul Cultural Center, was turned into a national shrine after its acquisition by the Knights of Columbus. A permanent exhibit "A Gift of Love" includes papal memorabilia, interactive exhibits, and many rarely seen photographs tracing the life of the first Polish pope. The St. John Paul II National Shrine is a place of pilgrimage housing first-class relics of St. Pope John Paul II, St. Faustina, St. Maximilian Kolbe, and St. Albert Chmielowski. **www.jp2cc.org**

Washington National Cathedral

In this magnificent Episcopal Cathedral, Polish artist Jan Henryk de Rosen created the chapel of St. Joseph of Arimathea located below the crypt of the cathedral. De Rosen painted the faces of Jesus and St. Joseph of Arimathea using cathedral choirboys and staff as models. It is the only mural in the church.

FLORIDA

BROOKSVILLE
Historical marker for St. Stanislaus Church
The Diocese of St. Petersburg erected a historical marker in 2010 to outline the story of St. Stanislaus Church (14249 Citrus Way) which was originally built in 1915 by a small group of Polish farmers who had purchased land in this area of Hernando County to begin a new community. The current church from the 1930s is in the "Old Florida" clapboard style and many of the original founders are buried in the cemetery behind the church. Locally, it is known as the "once-a-year" church because Mass is celebrated in the church only on All Souls Day.

BUNNELL
Polonia Society of Korona
Established in 1982, the Society has had its own building at 2925 W. Highway 100 since 2010. They host many functions and events to further knowledge of Polish culture, traditions, history, arts, and current affairs that are open to the public. **www.poloniasocietyofkorona.com**

CLEARWATER
Polish Center of John Paul II
This Center at 1521 N. Saturn Avenue was started in 1995 as an educational and cultural institute. It sponsors Saturday language schools in Clearwater and Tampa Bay, and houses a library, senior club, film club, cabaret, and discothèque. The Polish Center houses the American Institute of Polish Culture which began in 1982. It presents artistic events, concerts, film presentations, lectures, and exhibits and sponsors the biggest Polish social event of the Tampa Bay area—the annual Polonaise Ball. **polishcenterfl.org**

Polish Center of John Paul II, Clearwater, FL (JPII Center)

Polish Missions of Florida
There are three missions in Florida that provide spiritual guidance to the Polish community:

Mercy of God Polish Mission covers the diocese of St. Petersburg and holds Polish Masses and services, and promulgates Polish Christian heritage, culture, traditions, and language through its programs since 1991. Masses are held at St. Paul Catholic Church in St. Petersburg and at St. James the Apostle in Port Richey. **www.polskamisja.org**

Our Lady of Czestochowa Mission in Pompano Beach was established in 1983. It runs a Saturday Polish school, library, gift shop, and café. Mass and activities are in Polish for their parishioners. In the vestibule there is a plaque remembering the tragic plane crash in Smolensk, and a painting of the mysteries of the rosary done by a World War II Siberian POW. The parish cultural center has a wall-sized painting that is a reproduction of Jan Matejko's "Battle at Grunwald" done in Poland. A painting of Our Lady hangs above the altar and a painting of St. Pope John Paul II given by Cardinal Dziwisz of Poland hangs in the back of the church. **www.polishchurch.com**

St. Joseph Discalced Carmelite Monastery is in Bunnell and is part of the Warsaw Province of Discalced Carmelites (**www.bunnellcarmelites.org**). **St. Mary Catholic Church**, which was founded by immigrants in 1914 and continues to hold Polish language masses, is located on the grounds of the monastery. **www.stmaryccfl.net**

GREENACRES
The American Polish Club "Sobieski"
Officially established in 1959, the present clubhouse at 4725 Lake Worth Road was constructed in 1984 after a major fire. The club runs an expansive banquet hall, sponsors the Chopin Choir, a children's dance group, a Polish language school, and maintains the John Paul II library. It also organizes the city-wide Pulaski Day Parade. Cultural events include Polish plays, concerts, and poetry readings as well as dances. **www.americanpolishclub.com**

JACKSONVILLE
Polish-American Club of Jax
Founded in 1974 by the Polish American Cultural Society (PACS), they opened a new clubhouse at 5850 Collins Road in 2013 and continue to serve area Poles in finding a home community. Members participate in the annual World of Nations Festival and teach Polish culture in the county public schools. PACS also promotes Polish information at the Mayport Naval Base Cultural Festival. PACS hosts many events ranging including Easter basket blessings, *Wigilia*, and *Opłatek*. **www.polishclubinjax.com**

Polish American Club of Miami (PACOM)

MIAMI
Polish American Club of Miami (PACOM)
Founded in 1938 with its headquarters on the Miami River on the 79th Street Causeway, the organization has been a major presence in the city. It presents cultural and social programs, hosting authentic Polish events for the promotion of cultural activities. Recently, a new cultural center at 1250 NW 22nd Avenue was designed to house the American Institute of Polish Culture, Polish American Club of Miami, Chopin Foundation of the United States, Polish American Chamber of Commerce, and the Honorary Consulate of the Republic of Poland. During construction, the club continues to meet and host events. **www.polishamericanclubofmiami.com**

NORTH LAUDERDALE
Polish American Club Polonez
One of the oldest Polish clubs in Florida, this club at 935 Rock Island Road sponsors plays, concerts, and events honoring Polish history and culture. **polishclubpolonez.com**

ST. PETERSBURG
Kosciuszko Monument
The Kosciuszko Monument in Williams Park between 4th and 3rd Streets North and between 2nd and 1st Avenues North is a gift from Americans of Polish descent to their fellow Americans.

Kosciusko Monument, St. Petersburg, FL (Polish American Society)

American Institute of Polish Culture (AIPC)

Since 1972, this Institute has promoted many cultural initiatives. The Institute translates and publishes books on Polish cultural topics, sponsors lectures at Florida International University as part of the Lady Blanka Rosenstiel Lecture series on Poland, and provides over a dozen student scholarships annually. In 1998, it spearheaded the establishment of the Kosciuszko Chair of Polish Studies at the University of Virginia, later moved to the Institute of World Politics in Washington, D.C. In 1978, Lady Blanka established an International Film Festival in Miami at which Polish films and Polish filmmakers appear annually. It will be part of the new PACOM complex in Miami (*see page 34*).
www.ampolinstitute.org

It was sponsored by the American Institute of Polish Culture (Miami and Pinellas County), American Council for Polish Culture, Kosciuszko Foundation, Polish American Engineers Association, Polonia, Inc., and numerous individual donors.

Polish American Society

In 1951, a group of Polish American retirees met to establish a place to meet others of Polish descent and enjoy the traditions of their Polish culture. In 1957, the group opened their own place at 1343 Beach Drive SE to hold dinners and dances, Christmas dinner, *Paczki* day, *Dyngus* Day, and live band performances—they claim to have the "best dance floor in the Tampa area." They are the oldest Polish society in the state.
www.polishsociety.org

St. Petersburg Polish American Society dance (Don Kohler)

Polonia, Inc.

Since 1992, this club has promoted Polish language and culture throughout the Tampa Bay area through events such as plays and visiting artists from Poland. It sponsors a Polish Saturday school in Tarpon Springs. The Club's building provides a large rental hall. It is conveniently located near the Mercy of God Polish Mission at St. Paul Church. **poloniafl.org**

SARASOTA
Polish-American Association of Sarasota

In 1975, the Association wanted to create an awareness of Polish contributions to culture and history within the broader American society. They were proud of their heritage and history and envisioned a center that would continue that spirit. They sponsor a Polish Saturday School and hold monthly meetings and events.
www.polishsarasota.org

VERO BEACH
Polish American Social Club of Vero Beach

Within a few years of its organization in 1981, this club was able to build their own hall at 7500 US-1 N for social as well as cultural gatherings. The group promotes and sponsors Polish culture and art, including Polish language classes, dances, choral, and other activities. **pacvbusa.org**

GEORGIA

AUGUSTA

Dr. Paul Fitzsimmons Eve Monument & Plaque

Born on June 27, 1806, in Forest Hall, Georgia, Dr. Paul Fitzsimmons Eve was a noted 19th-century surgeon who published an estimated 500 professional articles, edited the *Southern Medical and Surgical Journal* and the *Nashville Medical and Surgical Journal*, and served as president of the American Medical Association. While studying in Europe, Eve volunteered to provide medical services to the Polish revolutionary forces during the November Uprising against Russian control in 1830–1831. Additionally, he was also among the organizers who formed a committee in Paris to raise funds to support the Poles. The revolutionary government awarded him a Gold Cross of Merit for his service, and on the centennial of the uprising the Polish government, in cooperation with the Medical Department of the University of Georgia and the Polish Medical and Dental Association of America, funded a monument to his honor on Greene Street in Augusta, GA. There is also a marker to him erected in 1986 by the Polish Heritage Association of the Southeast on Telfair Street near the intersection of 6th Street in Augusta.

Dr. Paul Fitzsimmons Eve monument and plaque, Augusta, GA (John Dunn)

COCKSPUR ISLAND

Fort Pulaski National Monument

After the War of 1812, Fort Pulaski was planned as part of the Third System of Coastal Fortifications. Named in honor of Brigadier General Casimir Pulaski, and constructed between 1829 and 1847, Fort Pulaski was one of the most formidable coastal forts defending the United States coast at the time. Robert E. Lee was given his first assignment in 1829 to work on its construction. Seized by the Georgia militia during the secession crisis in January 1861, Fort Pulaski became a

Fort Pulaski National Monument, Cockspur Island, GA (Matthew Adams)

Confederate fort after the state seceded from the United States. During the American Civil War, the fort was retaken by Union forces in April 1862 at the Battle of Fort Pulaski. This battle was significant as it was the first battle in either North or South America to use rifled artillery. The fort was designated a national monument in 1924 and was transferred to the National Park Service in 1933. Fort Pulaski National Monument is open to the public and features a variety of historic features, including the historic fort, as well as miles of trails and wonderful views of the Savannah River and coastal wetlands.

LAWRENCEVILLE
St. Marguerite d'Youville Church
St. Marguerite Church at 85 Gloster Road NW is the head of the Polish Catholic Apostolate of the Archdiocese of Atlanta under the patronage of St. Pope John Paul II. For over thirty years Polish Masses, annual Polish festivals, and Polish Saturday schools have helped to grow the parish. An icon of Our Lady of Częstochowa is located near the main altar. The Apostolate is run by the Society of Christ Fathers for Poles Living Abroad. Also under the Apostolate is another parish about thirty minutes west, Mary Our Queen Catholic Church in Peachtree Corners. **stmdy.org**

POOLER
National Museum of the Mighty Eighth Air Force
The National Museum of the Mighty Eighth Air Force, located just ten miles west of Savannah at 175 Bourne Avenue, was constructed in 1996 and focuses on the actions of the U.S. 8th Air Force in the European Theatre of Operations during World War II. In addition to a R.A.F. exhibit, the museum also has an exhibit on the Polish Air Force (its origins and participation in World War II). The exhibit is original to the museum and the product of a request by two benefactors: Mr. Steve Rasiej and Dr. Jan Koniarek. In addition, the museum also has a display of Col. Francis S. Gabreski (displayed items donated by Mr. Jerald Kochan), the leading ace of the 8th Air Force. Gabreski is also honored with a monument at the US Air Force Academy. **www.mightyeighth.org**

National Museum of the Mighty Eighth Air Force, Pooler, GA (avgeekery)

SAVANNAH
Battle of Savannah Battlefield Park
Managed by the Coastal Heritage Society, the park encompasses a portion of the Savannah battlefield of 1779 and the reconstruction of an earthen fort near where Gen. Casimir Pulaski fought and was mortally wounded. The park has a field of tablets, set in rows under the name of the nations that participated, memorializing individuals who played a part in the Revolutionary War. For Poland, the tablets memorialize Brig. Gen. Pulaski, Brig. Gen. Kosciuszko, Capt. Zielinski, Capt. Paschke, and Feliks Miklaszewicz. The tablets were privately funded by donors and initiated by the Savannah Gen. Pulaski Committee of the American Council of Polish Culture. In the park

Battle of Savannah Battlefield Park
(Edward Krolikowski)

on Louisville Road a state historical marker, erected in 1952, marks the spot where two notable heroes of the Revolution were mortally wounded—Brig. General Pulaski and Sergeant William Jasper. Located across Louisville Road is the Savannah Visitors Center with a museum. Inside the museum are fragments of the Pulaski Monument that were replaced during its renovation.

Pulaski Monument, Monterey Square, Savannah, GA (Matthew Adams)

Pulaski Monument, Monterey Square

This monument, in Monterey Square between Taylor and West Gordon Streets, is dedicated to the memory of Brig. Gen. Casimir Pulaski, commander of the Pulaski Legion, who fought and was mortally wounded in the Battle of Savannah on October 9, 1779. Through a lottery, the city of Savannah funded the construction of a 55-foot-tall marble monument, the first one dedicated to Pulaski in the United States, in 1852. It was designed by Robert E. Launitz of New York and dedicated on January 8, 1855.

The monument was dismantled in 1995 after weathering caused serious deterioration and the restored monument was re-dedicated in October 2005. A bas relief at the base designed by Henryk Dmochowski depicts the moment of Pulaski's death. Nearby markers tell the story of Pulaski's heroism and his place as the Father of the American Cavalry.

There are memorabilia at the Georgia Historical Museum located nearby, chief among which is the ball of grapeshot which was extracted from Pulaski's fatal wound. In proximity are several notable historical markers to Gen. Pulaski, a Pulaski monument plaque which provides more detail on his heroic contributions, and information on the attack on the British lines.

IDAHO

RATHDRUM

St. Stanislaus Church

Although not a Polish parish, there is a large historical painting on the altar of St. Stanislaus Church at 812 McCartney Street depicting St. Stanislaus reaching out to Mary and infant Jesus. There is an annual Polish Festival with traditional Polish foods which attracts Polish participants from nearby Spokane. The little brick church which dates from 1900 is now part of St. George Parish.

WALLACE

North Idaho's Pulaski Trail

A four-mile round-trip hiking trail, ten minutes from downtown Wallace, is named for Ed Pulaski, whose father was born in Poland. He was an assistant ranger with the United States Forest Service based out of the mining town of Wallace and is remembered for his bravery in the wildfires of August 1910. Informative plaques along the trail delve into the history of Pulaski, the tool he designed, and the 1910 wildfires that still leave their mark on North Idaho. At trails-end there is the tunnel and commemorative markers indicating where Ed Pulaski saved all but six of the forty-five firefighters under his command by holding them at gunpoint in a mine tunnel while the fire raged around them. Due to the significance of the events, both the trail and the tunnel are listed on the National Register of Historic Places. The tool he is credited with inventing is still a principal firefighting tool; it is a combination of a mattock and an axe and referred to as a "Pulaski."

Axe belonging to Assistant Ranger Ed Pulaski of the US Forest Service, Wallace, ID, remembered for his bravery in the wildfires of 1910 (CC BY-SA 3.0)

Wallace District Mining Museum

The Wallace District Mining Museum at 509 Bank Street features displays covering more than 130 years of silver, lead, zinc, and gold production in the largest silver producing mine district in the world, of which Historic Wallace is the capital. The museum offers a 20-minute video on the history of the area, a replica of a mine tunnel, interactive displays on the Big Burn (1910 Fire), and other displays. Polish miners and their lives are represented in the displays and collections. **wallaceminingmuseum.com**

ILLINOIS

BRIDGEVIEW
St. Fabian Church
St. Fabian Parish at 7450 W. 83rd Street was established in July 1963. This heavily Polish parish is symbolic of the movement of Chicago's South Side and Southwest Side Polish community to the suburbs. While it was originally founded as a non-ethnic and territorial parish, Polish Americans have come to be a large part of the church population. St. Fabian's opened a Polish school in 1999 which teaches Polish language, customs, geography, and history. The parish celebrates seven Masses in both Polish and English every Sunday. **www.saint-fabian.org**

CALUMET CITY
St. Andrew the Apostle Church
A stone's throw from the border with Indiana, St. Andrew the Apostle Church at 768 Lincoln Avenue is a legacy of the Polish immigrants that settled in Sobieski Park at the turn of the century. Between its twin belfries is a rose window with a central medallion of the parish namesake, St. Andrew. Inside is a barrel-vaulted nave with small side aisles. The Baptismal Shrine holds an oil painting of the Black Madonna and the two bronze figures on the baptismal font are Sts. Cyril and Methodius. The Church is now part of Jesus, Shepherd of Souls Parish. **jesussheperdofsouls@archchicago.com**

CHICAGO
Agora Sculpture
This installation of 106 headless and armless sculptures by famed Polish artist Magdalena Abakanowicz sits at the south end of Grant Park. In 2006, the work was brought to Chicago on permanent loan from the Polish Ministry of Culture. The artwork gets its name from the Greek word for meeting place. The cast-iron figures are 9-ft. tall and weigh 1,800 pounds and are arranged in various groups. They are made from a hollow, seamless piece of iron that has been allowed to rust, creating a reddish appearance. Some suggest great movement, while others seem to be standing completely still. Most of them are in crowds, although some seem to be pulling away from the larger group. The artist herself donated time to build the project as did a group of artists in Poznań, Poland.

Adjacent to this installation, another project, led by the Chicago Chopin Foundation, is underway to bring a 5/8 scale replica of the famous Fryderyk Chopin monument found in Park Łazieńkowski in Warsaw. The area is landscaped so that concerts can be held in the Chopin Garden.

Association of Polish Army Veterans
The Association of Polish Army Veterans (*Stowarzyszenia Weteranów Armii Polskiej* or SWAP) building is located on the southwest corner of 48th and Wood Street just to the west of St. Joseph's. This organization served veterans of the Polish Army raised in North America during World War I. More than 750 Polish residents of the Back of the Yards volunteered for the Blue Army or Haller's Army to fight first for Polish Independence and then to secure the borders of the new Polish state.

Chopin Theater
Built in 1918 at 1543 W. Division Street, this is the only historic Polish theater building still standing in Polish downtown although the interior has been completely gutted. It now offers a variety

CHICAGO: CITY OF NEIGHBORHOODS *(see map page 289)*

Polish Downtown
The capital of American Polonia for some 75 years was on Chicago's near northwest side within a mile radius of the Division, Ashland, and Milwaukee Avenue intersection. The first permanent Polish settlement in Chicago took roots here in 1867 and was known to outsiders as "Polish Downtown." To its mostly Polish residents it was *Stanisławowo-Trójcowo*, after the two Polish Catholic parishes whose physical presence dominated the neighborhood and whose spiritual, cultural, recreational, and social organizations filled the lives of its parishioners. It was also the headquarters for all major fraternal associations, the Polish press, and numerous businesses. Nearly every Polish undertaking of any consequence in the U.S. through World War II either started in or was directed from this tight-knit neighborhood.

Polish Village/Avondale
Avondale developed northwest along the Milwaukee Avenue corridor as a neighborhood of modest, working-class homes dotted with small-scale industrial and storefront businesses. Poles leaving the overcrowded Polish Downtown moved into this mixed ethnicity area, clustering around two major Catholic churches that lent their names as part of "Polish Village" —*Jackowo* (for St. Hyacinth or *Św. Jacka*) and *Wacławowo* (for St. Wenceslaus or *Św. Wacława*). In the 1980-1990s the area spawned a lively nightlife with contemporary musicians from Poland and dancing clubs up and down the avenue. Podlasie Club is one of the notable remaining Polish club venues in the Avondale neighborhood, with more traditional Polka dancing every Saturday night. St. Hyacinth remains one of the largest Polish Catholic parishes in the country and there are still some Polish businesses, but the area has been changing. After an influx of Hispanic residents joined the mix, the area has been recently discovered by young upscale professionals.

Union Stock Yard District/Packingtown (Bridgeport, Back of the Yards)
The Union Stock Yard opened on Christmas Day 1865 in what was then the suburban Town of Lake. The livestock market's boundaries were Pershing Road (39th Street) to 47th Street and from Halsted Street to Racine Avenue. Chicago's meat packing industry located just to the west of the stockyards in the 1870s, creating Packingtown. Poles labored in large numbers in Chicago's meat industry throughout its history, but particularly between 1877 and 1960. Poles arrived in large numbers after 1880 and founded six Catholic parishes in three of the four adjacent neighborhoods: Bridgeport, McKinley Park, and Back of the Yards. These neighborhoods played important roles in the creation of a vibrant South Side Polonia.

The Union Stock Yard closed in 1971 after the major meat packers left Chicago in the 1950s and early 1960s. The Stone Gate at Exchange and Peoria remains as a monument to the workers and the industry.

Villa Historic District
With just 126 homes in Craftsman and Prairie styles from the early 20th century, this district was dubbed the "Polish Kenilworth" by *Chicago Daily News* columnist Mike Royko. First laid out by Samuel Eberly Gross in 1896, it featured lots double the typical Chicago lot size at the time, standard setbacks, and requirements to build bungalows, located on the northwest side directly north of the *Wacławowo* neighborhood . It is both a Chicago landmark and listed on the National Register of Historic Places.

OBIORCZYK·R 2019

of live theatrical productions in Polish and English. Check the website or the lobby for current shows. **www.chopintheatre.com**

Consulate General of the Republic of Poland in Chicago

This consular mission serves the largest Polish community outside of Poland. The consulate was established in 1920 with its first location at 1115 N. Damen Avenue (still standing). After several moves, in 1974 the Polish government purchased the 1916 Bernard Albert Eckhardt mansion overlooking Lake Michigan at 1530 N. Lake Shore Drive. It was designed by renowned local architect Benjamin H. Marshall and was included as a landmark in the Gold Coast Historic District in 1989. There are frequent public programs and events. **www.chicago.msz.gov.pl**

Consulate General of the Republic of Poland, Chicago, IL (Ryszard Gbiorczyk Consulate Archives)

Copernicus Monument

The Nicolaus Copernicus monument stands on Solidarity Drive close to the Adler Planetarium. It was installed in 1973 to mark the 500th anniversary of the astronomer's birth. The Copernicus Foundation of Chicago raised funds to replicate famed Danish sculptor Bertel Thorvaldsen's original 1830 monument in Warsaw, Poland, at the Palace Staszic, home of the Polish Academy of Science. The original monument was damaged in the attack on Warsaw during World War II. Although the Nazis planned to melt it down, Poles eventually recovered the sculpture, and after full repairs and conservation, it was rededicated in 1949. Sculptor Bronisław Koniuszy (1917-1986) recast the original monument for Chicago. Koniuszy served as a member of the Polish Underground Army before graduating in 1953 from the Academy of Fine Arts in Warsaw. After making the new casting, the artist shipped his 100,000-pound bronze statue on the *Zawiercie*—the first ship to travel regularly between Chicago and the Polish port of Gdynia.

Nicolaus Copernicus Monument by the Adler Planetarium, Chicago, IL (Dominic Pacyga)

Copernicus Center

The Copernicus Center at 5216 W. Lawrence Avenue was originally designed as an 1,800-seat atmospheric-style movie palace in 1930 by Rapp & Rapp. It was reborn as the Copernicus Center in 1981, complete with a "Solidarity Tower," modeled after the Royal Castle in Warsaw, Poland. The Copernicus Foundation hosts a wide variety of Polish and other ethnic programs throughout the year, and the *Taste of Polonia* outdoor festival is held on the grounds every

Tower of the Copernicus Center in Chicago modeled after the Royal Castle in Warsaw, Poland (Victoria Granacki)

Dom Podhalan / Polish Highlanders Hall, Chicago, IL (Dominic Pacyga)

Labor Day weekend. Jefferson Park is an extension of the Polish settlement that historically followed Milwaukee Avenue north through the city. St. Pope John Paul II's motorcade made its way down Milwaukee Avenue through the neighborhood on his historic visit to Chicago in 1979. The Paderewski Symphony Orchestra, founded in 1997, is a large cultural organization with its own choir and Academy of Music and holds many of its concerts here. Consult their website for events and programs. **www.copernicuscenter.org**

Davis Square Park
Davis Square Park is located just west of the former site of Packingtown and the Union Stock Yard. The ten-acre park opened in 1904 and quickly became a community center in the primarily Polish and Lithuanian section of the Back of the Yards. The fieldhouse provided a men's and women's gymnasium as well as community meeting rooms, a library, and shower rooms. It was one of the first of the Progressive Era parks built in Chicago and provided a model for the city and the nation. In December 1921 police charged a large group of Polish women and children on the edge of the park at the corner of 44th Street and Marshfield to break community support for a strike. Three Polish parishes were among the most active supporters of organizing the workers into the Back of the Yards Neighorhood Council.

Dom Podhalan / Polish Highlanders Hall
Dom Podhalan or Polish Highlanders Hall at 4808 S. Archer Avenue serves as the home of the Polish Highlanders Alliance of North America, founded in 1929 in the Back of the Yards neighborhood. The first meeting of the organization was held at Słowacki Hall (demolished) after a Mass at Sacred Heart Church (demolished). Most of Chicago's Polish Highlander or *Góral* community is concentrated on Chicago's Southwest Side and in the Southwest suburbs. The Dom Podhalan is styled in the traditional Zakopane-style of architecture. The building underwent renovation under artist Jerzy Kenar in 2005. The Dom Podhalan's restaurant *Bioło Izba* is highly recommended.

Ed Paschke Art Center
This art center at 5415 W. Higgins Avenue was opened in 2014 to preserve the work of legendary Polish American Chicago Imagist painter Ed Paschke, and to serve as an educational resource for the community. Consult their website for exhibits and programs: **www.edpaschkeartcenter.org**

Five Holy Martyrs Church

Five Holy Martyrs Church at 4327 S. Richmond Street on the southwest side of Chicago was founded in November 1908 to serve Polish families in the Brighton Park neighborhood. Polish immigrants settled in the neighborhood after 1914, when the Crane Company relocated its manufacturing plant in this area. The cornerstone of the present church building was laid on August 3, 1919 and constructed in the Spanish "mission style" according to plans drawn up by architect Arthur Foster.

Five Holy Martyrs parish was selected as the site of a Field Mass celebrated by Pope John Paul II on October 5, 1979, during his three-day visit to Chicago. More than 17,500 people attended the Mass held in the church parking lot, and the altar still stands. On January 16, 1980, part of West 43rd Street which runs along Five Holy Martyrs Church was renamed Pope John Paul II Drive. Today the parish serves both the Mexican and Polish American communities. The church celebrates Mass in English, Polish, and Spanish.

Holy Trinity Polish Mission Church

Begun as a Resurrectionist church in 1872, Holy Trinity closed, then reopened in 1893 under the Congregation of the Holy Cross and played a key role among early Polonia. The church at 1118 N. Noble Street was designed in 1906 by William Krieg in the Polish Baroque tradition. Paired towers with faithfully rebuilt copper roofs frame a central porch with huge classical columns. The hall-style interior was extensively restored from 2002-2007, and paintings were uncovered over the main altar, the choir loft, and the ceiling. Pilasters and capitals were stenciled and gilded. The stained-glass windows were installed in 1955 from designs by Irena Lorentowicz.

In winding catacombs below the altar, there is a rich collection of over 260 relics—material objects or remains from saints, including from St. Pope John Paul II and St. Faustina, as well as rocks and soil from pilgrimage sites.

Holy Trinity Polish Mission Church, Chicago, IL (Jeremy Atherton)

The Polish Mission of Holy Trinity is run today by the Society of Christ Fathers from Poland and all services are in the Polish language. They are assisted by the Missionary Sisters of Christ the King, a Polish order of religious women. The elementary school building next door, built in 1916, is now a Polish Saturday School, and the High School designed by Slupkowski and Piontek is still active. **www.htcchicago.org**

Immaculate Conception of the Blessed Virgin Mary Church

Polish immigrants organized Immaculate Conception, B.V.M. (*Kościół Niepokalanego Poczęcia Najświętszej Maryi Panny*) parish in 1882 at 88th and Commercial Avenue. The parish was eventually divided three times to form the parishes of St. Michael, St. Mary Magdalene, and St. Bronisława. The original church structure was destroyed by fire on August 31, 1894. A cornerstone of the present church was laid on November 11 of that year. For four years parishioners celebrated Mass in the basement of the unfinished building. Finally, with the arrival of Fr. Francis M. Wojtalewicz as pastor, the parish debt was paid off and work began on the superstructure of the parish church designed by Martin A. Carr. The present structure was dedicated in 1899 and the Polish iconography is present throughout. This massive church still serves South Chicago Catholics, although the ethnicity of the parish has dramatically changed since the 1960s. Mexican Americans make up most parishioners today. **church.immaculateconceptionsouth.org**

International Polka Association (IPA) Hall of Fame and Museum

Kosciuszko Monument, Chicago, IL (Dominic Pacyga)

The Polka Hall of Fame and Museum is in the century-old Polonia Grove building at 4604 S. Archer Avenue which was the site of many Polish celebrations. Polish organizations from across the South and West Sides celebrated there. The IPA celebrates Polka music in all its forms—Polish, Czech, Slovenian, German. In addition to honoring deserving personalities, the Polka Music Hall of Fame serves as a historical and educational center for polka music plus it provides an historical record of events in the polka field. The museum contains a unique collection of artifacts, sheet music, records, and memorabilia associated with polka music. The Hall of Fame celebrates people like Walter "Mały Władziu" Jagiello, Eddie Blazończyk, and Marion Lush. **www.ipapolkas.com**

Jan and Harriet Smulski House

The 1884 Wicker Park home of banker and civic leader Jan Smulski at 2138 West Pierce Avenue was designed by Fromann and Jebsen when the neighborhood was home to wealthy Germans. It is believed to be where Ignacy Jan Paderewski played the piano to a crowd from the front porch during one of his many trips to Chicago. Paderewski frequently collaborated with Smulski and the Polish National Department of America from 1910 to 1920, working for the cause of Polish nationalism. All U.S. efforts to secure freedom for Poland were coordinated from Chicago's Polish Downtown with the pair frequently at the helm. The house is part of the National Register of Historic Places and Chicago Historic Districts.

Kosciuszko Park ("Koz Park")

This eight-acre park is in the *Jackowo* part of the Avondale neighborhood. The historic fieldhouse was designed in 1916 by Albert A. Schwartz in a Tudor Revival style and has a swimming pool, gymnasium, and auditorium. The fieldhouse hosted one of the first two Polish language schools in Chicago, *Polska Szkoła im. Tadeusza Kościuszki,* as well as English language and citizenship classes, particularly for post-World War II displaced persons. **www.chicagoparkdistrict.com**

Kosciuszko Monument

On February 5, 1892, Chicago's Polish leaders organized to erect a monument in Humboldt Park to the American Revolutionary War hero and leader of Poland's struggle for independence. The equestrian statue, the work of sculptor Kazimierz Chodziński, was finally dedicated on September 11, 1904, and became an important gathering place for patriotic demonstrations during both World Wars. It provided the traditional end point for the annual Polish Constitution Day Parade, which has been observed since 1891. In 1978, the Polish National Alliance, Polish Roman Catholic Union, and Polish Women's Alliance sponsored the conservation and relocation of the monument to Solidarity Drive on Northerly Island. The groups installed a time capsule beneath the sculpture containing many documents relating to Polish history. In 2008, the time capsule was rediscovered during a roadway improvement project that required the slight relocation of the sculpture. The items from the time capsule were conserved and additional items were added and placed once again under the monument.

Polish American Association (PAA)

Founded in 1922 as the Polish Welfare Association, the PAA is a human services organization providing services to the Polish American community and others. It moved from Chicago's historic Polish Downtown to this building at 3834 North Cicero Avenue in 1955. Its five departments include education, employment, immigration, clinical services, and supportive services, and its Learning Center at 3819 North Cicero Avenue offers a diverse selection of classes. **www.polish.org**

Polish Roman Catholic Union of America &
Polish Museum of America

"Symbol of Poland Reborn" stained glass at the Polish Museum of America, Chicago, IL (PMA)

The Polish Roman Catholic Union of America (PRCUA), the oldest Polish American fraternal association in America was established in 1873 and now has 90,000 members. It remains the only Polish fraternal association still located in Chicago's historic Polish Downtown. Its headquarters building at 984 North Milwaukee Avenue was designed by John Flizikowski in 1912 and is listed on the National Register of Historic Places. **www.prcua.org**

The PRCUA headquarters building also houses the Polish Museum of America, the largest and oldest Polish museum in the United States. Founded in 1935, the Museum highlights a unique permanent collection as well as temporary exhibits, and hosts workshops and programs to preserve Polish arts, customs, and traditions. Highlights of the permanent exhibitions include personal and professional mementos of Ignacy Jan Paderewski, statesman and pianist (1860-1941), including the last Steinway he played, the pen that he used to sign the Treaty of Versailles, and the suite at the Buckingham Hotel in New York city where he died; interwar art, paintings, sculptures, and artifacts from the Polish Pavilion at the 1939 New York World's Fair which could not be returned to Poland with the outbreak of World War II. With over three hundred identified collections, the Museum's archives are a unique resource for scholars, researchers, and genealogists. Through original documents, rare maps, photographs, and diverse items, such as recruitment records of volunteers to the Polish Army in France, and collections on Kosciuszko, individuals, organizations, associations, and other notables in the Polish American community are represented by these materials. The library features a popular circulating collection and historical collections which include titles published before 1945, the Polonica Collection with nearly 4,000 items, and the Rare Books Collection, featuring publications from the 16th through 19th centuries. The oldest item, *Carminum structura* by Laurentius Corvinus (c.1465-1527), was published in Cologne, Germany, by Martin von Werden in 1508.

Polish National Alliance Building, Chicago, IL (Dominic Pacyga)

There are regularly scheduled "Meet the Author" and literary discussions, lectures on art and history, film screenings, and musical performances throughout the year, as well as the annual State of Illinois Casimir Pulaski Day.   **www.polishmuseumofamerica.org**

Polish National Alliance Headquarters
This national organization was formed in 1880 in Philadelphia and Chicago as a fraternal insurance society and remains one of the largest ethnic fraternals with 230,000 members. It was in Chicago's Polish Downtown until 1976, then relocated to its present location at 6100 North Cicero Avenue, and has always been a staunch supporter of independence for Poland. Besides insurance, the PNA also offers sports and music programs, Polish language instructions, scholarships, events, and other benefits. It publishes a quarterly magazine, *Zgoda,* for its members and has a radio station, WPNA 103.1 FM. Since 1908, it has published *Dziennik Związkowy/Polish Daily News,* the oldest Polish language newspaper in the country. It has member lodges in every state. "The Oak Prospect of Independence" (*Dębowa Aleja Niepodległości*) is an initiative to commemorate the centennial of Poland regaining its independence by planting one hundred oak trees, the first one in the PNA Gardens on the grounds and subsequent trees, with a commemorative plaque, at the PNA Polish Youth Camp in nearby Yorkville. **www.pna-znp.org**

Polish National Alliance Building
Now Studio Gang architecture offices, this art-deco-style building at 1520 West Division Street was designed by Joseph A. Slupkowski in 1937-1938 for the headquarters of the Polish National Alliance, which it housed until 1976. This building was designated a Chicago Landmark in 2014 and is on the National Register of Historic Places. Most of the interior was gutted but the historic entrance lobby and staircase remain and are accessible to visitors.

Polish Women's Alliance
The Polish Women's Alliance was founded in 1898 to help Polish women become financially secure and economically independent. Its home office was built here in 1911 and remodeled in 1933 for the first Polish Women's Congress. In 2017 the PWA merged with the First Catholic Slovak Ladies Association. Their former building is now apartments and storefront commercial, but their

extensive archives can be accessed at the Women and Leadership Archives at Loyola University in Chicago.

Pulaski Park and Fieldhouse

Pulaski Park and Fieldhouse, Chicago, IL (Chicago Park District)

In 1911 an entire block of ninety structures was wiped out for the creation of Pulaski Park built by the West Park Commission as part of the Progressive Reform Movement to serve the poor, immigrant, working classes in dense urban neighborhoods. English language and citizenship classes were featured. The site plan for the new park was by Jens Jensen of the West Park Commission, who was a renowned Prairie School landscape architect. The Fieldhouse was designed by William Carbys Zimmerman. There are two interior murals: the recently restored Proscenium Arch in the auditorium by James Gilbert, and a mural of Polish peasants on the third floor of the Tower. **www.chicagoparkdistrict.com**

Second Northwestern Trust and Savings Bank

Now City Sports, the ornate interior bank hall is partially visible in the retail store. The building at 1201 N. Milwaukee Avenue was originally Jan Smulski's Second Northwest Trust and Savings Bank designed by John Flizikowski in 1920. In 1942 Rev. Casimir Sztuczko dedicated it for the *Polish Daily Zgoda* and the offices of Alliance Printers and Publishers. The *Zgoda* started its Chicago publication in 1888 and continues to this day as the official magazine of the Polish National Alliance.

Society for Arts

This not-for-profit was founded in 1981 to promote cultural communication between Europe and the US through cinema, art exhibitions, concerts, and educational activities. It has sponsored the "Polish Film Festival in America" since 1989, which they describe as the most extensive annual showcase of Polish cinema outside Poland. The Film Festival is held for two weeks in mid-November and has shown over fifteen hundred films by filmmakers of Polish descent and hosted 600 Polish film professionals. The Society moved into this 1920 former bank building at 1112 North Milwaukee Avenue in 1994. **www.societyforarts.com**

Solidarity Drive

Solidarity Drive along the Lake Michigan lakefront which leads to the Adler Planetarium is named after the Polish trade union that brought down the Communist regime in Poland and helped end the Soviet Union. The drive's median strip contains two monumental sculptures of Copernicus and Kosciuszko, depicting Poland's contributions to science and the fight for freedom (*See* Chicago, IL: Copernicus Monument *and* Kosciusko Monument). Both honor important Polish historical figures and serve as a symbol of pride for the city's large and active Polish community. Solidarity Drive also provides one of the best views of the Chicago skyline.

"Tribute to the Past," Steelworkers Park, Chicago, IL
(Dominic Pacyga)

Steelworkers Park

Steelworkers Park is located at the former lake-front site of U.S. Steel's South Works. Many Polish Americans worked in the plant and made their home in South Chicago. Structural steel from the South Works was used in the construction of the Willis Tower (Sears Tower) in downtown Chicago. At its peak, South Works had more than 20,000 employees and covered an area of 600 acres. The mill closed in 1992 after more than one hundred years of service. In 2002, the Chicago Park District acquired the site and transformed it into an attractive landscape with natural areas and views of Lake Michigan, and in 2014 officially named it Steelworkers Park. Elements of the steel industry highlight the park, most notably a series of enormous concrete ore walls. On May 9, 2015, Mayor Rahm Emanuel dedicated "Tribute to the Past" by Chicago artist Roman Villarreal in the park. The bronze sculptural group portrays a steelworker encircled by and embracing his family. The artwork pays tribute to generations of residents of Chicago's Southeast Side, for whom life was centered around the steel industry.

St. Adalbert's Church

Polish immigrants founded St. Adalbert's Parish (*Kościół Świętego Wojciecha*) in 1874. It is the mother church of all Polish churches on the South Side and West Side of Chicago. The building on 17th Street between Paulina Street and Ashland Avenue was designed by Henry J. Schlacks and reflects Renaissance church architecture. A statue of the church's patron, the martyr St. Adalbert, stands on the massive thirty-five-ton marble altar. On the arch above the altar are inscribed the opening words of the Polish hymn *Bogurodzica* composed by St. Adalbert.

This Polish parish proved to be central to Polonia's efforts to help regain Polish independence in the pre-1914 era. Residents built Pulaski Hall nearby in 1893 (demolished) as a meeting place for political rallies and cultural celebrations. Today the parish's future is very much in doubt. Even though St. Adalbert's has continued to serve the community for over 140 years, the Archdiocese closed the parish in 2016. The St. Adalbert Preservation Society has been organized to try and save the parish and various plans have been put forward by Polonia and the present Mexican community which is undergoing gentrification. As of 2021, the Archdiocese was still trying to sell the building to developers.

St. Hedwig Church

This church at 2226 North Hoyne Avenue was designed in 1901 by Aldolphus Druiding, the same architect who created St. John Cantius Church. The front has a classical lower porch with granite columns and an upper porch with a balustrade and triangular pediment. The end towers have square bases and domed spires. The interior painting scheme is another gem by John Mallin completed for the parish's 50th anniversary in 1938. The central dome has four angels holding up a crown of thorns with a circular banner at their feet in Polish. Granite columns supporting the side aisles have small cherubic faces above. The classical main altar is topped with rows of saints in stained glass. St. Hedwig's breathtaking interior now hosts Polish and Spanish-speaking congregations, along with English-speaking parishioners drawn from the revitalization of the nearby Bucktown neighborhood. **www.sthedwigbucktown.org**

St. Hyacinth Basilica

St. Hyacinth Basilica is located in the Avondale neighborhood of Chicago at 3636 West Wolfram Street and the Avondale neighborhood is commonly referred to as *Jacko*wo (St. Hyacinth). The Basilica's glorious Polish Baroque design from 1921 by Worthmann & Steinbach uses stone, glazed terra cotta and brick on the exterior but has an unusual three-towered façade. A painting in the European Baroque tradition by Thaddeus Zukotynski dominates the interior. The crowning glory is John Mallin's 75-foot-high dome with over 150 saints, clergy, and laity. During a restoration in 2000, the figures of St. Pope John Paul II and Cardinal Glemp, Polish primate, were added. Before becoming pope, Karol Cardinal Wojtyla visited twice in 1969 and 1976. St. Hyacinth was named a minor basilica in 2003 and is one of the largest Polish parishes in the country. It contains a symbolic grave of Blessed Jerzy Popiełuszko, a Catholic priest who was associated with the Solidarity trade union and was murdered in 1984 by the Communist secret police. The icon of Our Lady of Częstochowa has crowns made from hundreds of gold chains and rings offered by the parishioners; next to this chapel there is a plaque in honor of Pope John Paul II with some of

St. Hyacinth Basilica, Chicago, IL
(Ivo Shandar CC BY-SA 3.0)

his memorabilia. Statues of Polish saints adorn alcoves. A set of bronze main entrance doors, installed in 2005, carved by Polish artist Czesław Dźwigaj, show the building of the Basilica and St. Hyacinth with Our Lady and Child. A 17-foot bronze statue of St. Pope John Paul II was erected in the parish Memorial Garden. Just inside the lobby there are two plaques (Polish and English) outlining the history of the basilica. Many concerts and Polonia events are held at the Basilica. **www.sthyacinthbasilica.org**

Replica of Kraków's 15th-century Gothic Wit Stwosz altarpiece, St. John Cantius Church, Chicago, IL (Colter J. Sikora)

St. John Cantius Church

Located at 825 North Carpenter Street, this church was built in 1898 to handle the overcrowding at St. Stanislaus Kostka. Designed by Aldophus Druiding, the exterior looks like a classical temple with round-arched doors at the base, and engaged columns that support a triangular pediment, clearly inspired by the classicism of Chicago's 1893 World's Fair. This front is flanked by different-height towers, the largest modeled after St. Mary's Church in Kraków, St. John Cantius' home city. The interior has been carefully restored and the pipe organ completely repaired. The three altars in natural wood tones with gold leaf reflect Baroque church interiors in Poland. Hidden in a rear chapel is a scale replica of Kraków's 15th-century Gothic Wit Stwosz altarpiece carved by Michal Batkiewicz in 2003. The parish has grown under the Canons Regular of St. John Cantius with services in the Tridentine rite. **www.cantius.org**

St. Joseph Church

St. Joseph Parish is in the Back of the Yards neighborhood of Chicago at 4821 South Hermitage Avenue. Founded in 1887, St. Joseph's was the first of three Polish Catholic parishes in the neighborhood. The other two, St. John of God and Sacred Heart of Jesus parishes, have been closed by the archdiocese. St. Joseph Parish is currently staffed by the Missionaries of the Sacred Heart and primarily serves the Hispanic community, but Polish and Spanish Masses are offered. The iconography depicts many Polish saints and retains much of the 1950 interior designs of John A. Mallin.

St. Mary of the Angels Church, Chicago, IL (Victoria Granacki)

During World War I, the parish was a rallying spot for Polish organizations raising money both for Polish war relief and to raise a Polish Army to fight for Polish independence. Ignacy Jan Paderewski and others gathered at this church on October 14, 1917, and at Słowacki Hall (Columbia Hall) across the street as the starting point for the parade to the International Amphitheater to present the first battle flags to the Polish Army.

Also across the street stood the Julius Słowacki Library organized in 1902 by sixteen Polish societies. It began with only thirty books but grew rapidly to become one of the largest Polish libraries on the South Side. Such libraries filled a need that at first the Chicago Public Library could not meet and they helped to provide a vibrant Polish culture in the Back of the Yards neighborhood. The building still stands but is no longer a library. **www.stjosephparishchicago.org**

St. Mary of the Angels Church

Located at 1850 North Hermitage Avenue in the Bucktown neighborhood, this is one of the most lavishly decorated churches in Chicago—a 1920 design by Worthmann & Steinbach, perhaps the grandest architects of the period. There are square towers with round arches and a large central dome alluding to St. Peter's in Rome. Grand stairs at the front entrance lead up to a portico with paired columns topped by a classical balustrade. In the interior the dome dominates the intersection of the light-filled nave and transept, and elaborate paintings by John Mallin fill the rounded barrel vaults. The mural above the altar depicts Mary with angels in heaven looking up to the Trinity. Stained-glass windows depict many Polish saints. A window opposite one of St. Francis Assisi receiving the stigmata depicts the Virgin Mary entrusting the child Jesus to St. Stanislaus Kostka. The church was threatened with demolition in 1988 but was rescued by the priests of Opus Dei and has been magnificently restored for a mixed congregation with English, Spanish, and Polish language Masses. Access through the south side door to visit the church.
www.sma-church.org

St. Mary of Perpetual Help Church, Chicago, IL (Dominic Pacyga)

St. Mary of Perpetual Help Church

St. Mary of Perpetual Help Parish opened in 1882 to serve the growing Polish community to the north of the Union Stock Yard in Bridgeport. The congregation held Mass in a frame building on the corner of Lyman and Farrell Street. A new church was built in 1885 and Rev. John Zylla served as the first resident pastor. Work began on the present magnificent church at 1039 West 32nd Street in 1889 and it opened in 1892. It is a good example of the Polish Cathedral style. By 1900 St. Mary's was a flourishing Polish parish and the community paid off its entire debt. Archbishop James E. Quigley consecrated the church building on October 24, 1903. St. Mary's played a crucial role in the Polish American response to both World Wars. Today the parish serves a very ethnically diverse population but retains much of its Polish character and iconography.

St. Mary of Nazareth Hospital

Now located at 2233 West Division Street, this hospital was first founded in 1894 by the Sisters of the Holy Family of Nazareth to care for Polish immigrants. Mother Mary Lauretta Lubowicka, the U.S. Provincial, was called the "Saint of Division Street" as she walked the streets speaking to residents in five languages. By 1902 the hospital had replaced smaller structures with a large, six story brick building on Leavitt Street. Planning for the current medical campus began in 1967 under the leadership of Sr. Stella Louise Slomka, who pledged to stay in the historic Polish neighborhood. The current Brutalist-style building opened in 1974. Linked in 2003 with nearby St. Elizabeth Hospital, which had been founded in 1884 to serve German immigrants, the two-campus complex is now known as Presence Saints Mary and Elizabeth Medical Center. There is a small historic display inside St. Mary that is open to hospital visitors and an archive which has more than a million items on the history of the "Polish Hospital." **www.presencehealth.org.**

St. Michael the Archangel Church
St. Michael Parish was founded in 1892 to serve the growing Polish community in the Bush neighborhood adjacent to the South Works. The current Gothic revival structure at the corner of 82nd Street and South Shore Drive opened in 1909 under the pastorate of Rev. Paul Rhode, who became the first Polish bishop in the United States. William J. Brinkman designed the church. The main altar is constructed of butternut and birds-eye maple wood, as are the two side altars. The communion rail is oak with a white marble top. The church houses a piano once owned by Ignacy Jan Paderewski, the famous pianist and Polish patriot. A shrine to Our Lady of Częstochowa is in the sanctuary. The stained-glass windows were made by F. X. Zettler of Munich, Germany. Of special note are the two transept windows on the east and west sides of the church. One window depicts Pentecost, the other Saint Michael the Archangel at the last judgment. The church enshrines a relic of St. Cyprian, Bishop and Martyr. The parish has been permanently closed as of November 2021 and the parishioners are lobbying for landmark status for the church.

St. Michael the Archangel Church, Chicago, IL (Dominic Pacyga)

St. Stanislaus Kostka Church
Located at 1351 West Evergreen Avenue, St. Stanislaus Kostka was the first Polish parish in Chicago, organized in 1867 and considered the "mother church" of Chicago's Polonia. Its first pastor, Rev. Vincent Barzynski of the Congregation of the Resurrection, was a powerhouse who founded twenty-three parishes in twenty-seven years until his death in 1899. Barzynski was spiritual director for Mother Mary Theresa Dudzik, who founded the Franciscan Sisters of Chicago, ministering to the poor, orphans, and elderly. One of her earliest homes for the aged stands across the street from the church at 1368 W. Evergreen Avenue. A life-size statue of her, designed by sculptor and artist Stefan Niedorezo was installed in a side chapel in 2017; another of his sculptures is found at the Franciscan Motherhouse in Lemont, Illinois (*see* Lemont, IL: Heritage Hall).

Architect Patrick C. Keely created a light brick Renaissance Revival church built from 1876 to 1881 with round-arched doorways and windows that hearken back to the glory days of the Polish-Lithuanian Commonwealth in the 16th and 17th centuries. One of the twin towers was hit by lightning and burned in 1964 and not replaced. Windows are by the noted stained glass firm, F. X. Zettler of the Royal Bavarian Art Institute of Munich. Interior painting is by Polish-born and trained painter, Thaddeus Zukotynski, with the recently restored sanctuary mural featuring St.

Stanislaus. The parish has a Resurrectionist pastor and Sunday Masses are in English, Polish, and Spanish. A Sanctuary of the Divine Mercy, based on Poland's St. Faustina Kowalska, is open 24 hours, 7 days a week for adoration. A restored memorial plaque honoring the 842 soldiers from the parish who fought for Poland's independence is located outside the church building. **www.ststanschurch.org**

St. Wenceslaus Church

Although founded in 1912 to relieve crowding at St. Hyacinth, St. Wenceslaus was one of the first Polish parishes to break completely away from the Polish Baroque style and adopt an Art Deco interior. Located at 3400 North Monticello Avenue, the present church design from 1940 was by the resolutely Americanizing Cardinal George Mundelein's favorite architectural firm, McCarthy, Smith and Eppig. The soaring front façade with gable peak is marked with a very tall, round-arched recess having three sets of entry doors at the base and a tall, square tower, with its hexagonal cap. There is a Purgatorial Shrine by Polish painter Jan Henryk de Rosen inside. The church is filled with depictions of Polish saints and folkloric motifs, but it is much more subdued in comparison with Chicago's more well-known Polish cathedrals. It is administered by the Congregation of the Resurrection and the parish is now combined with St. Viator Parish. **www.stviatorparish.org**

St. Stanislaus Kostka Church, Chicago, IL
(Dominic Pacyga)

Tribune Tower

Embedded into the base of the Tribune Tower located at 435 Michigan Avenue in downtown Chicago are 149 fragments of famous buildings, structures, and landmarks from around the world, including one of Wawel Castle in Kraków. Visitors can view these as they walk around the perimeter of the building. **chicagoarchitecture.org**

CICERO

St. Mary of Częstochowa Church

This parish was founded by Polish Catholics in 1895 who had settled in the industrial suburb of Cicero. In 1903, the Western Electric Company plant opened and quickly became the area's largest employer. Over the years, the Western Electric Company provided jobs for thousands of immigrants of many nationalities. In June 1916, the parish broke ground on the current Gothic structure at 3010 48th Court that was dedicated by Archbishop George W. Mundelein in 1918. The towers of this church rise 200 ft. (61 m.) above the ground. The beautiful Gothic altars, pulpit, and a communion rail were all crafted in Italy of Carrara marble and date from 1927. Atop the main altar is a copy of the "Black Madonna." Shrines to Our Lady of Guadalupe and Our Lady of Ludźmierz are recent additions and celebrate the traditions of the parishes numerous Mexican

Stained glass at the Resurrection Cemetery Mausoleum in Justice, IL (Ewa Barczyk)

American and Polish Highlander parishioners. St. Mary of Częstochowa offers Mass in Polish, Spanish and English and is currently home to 1,450 families. **stmczcicero.com**

DUBOIS
St. Charles Borromeo Church

In the early years after its establishment in 1868, the congregation of St. Charles Borromeo was largely German, but increasingly became Polish. Father Joseph Ceranski was appointed as the first Polish pastor in 1898 and led the parish through a period of expansion culminating in the construction of the present church at South 3rd Street in 1908. This massive church stands in contrast to the modest size of DuBois. Father Ceranski was inspired to recreate the design of St. Stanislaus Kostka Church in St. Louis, supposedly drawing the plans himself. The twin steeples reach a height of 116 feet, lending the nickname, "cathedral of the prairie." The church is filled with dozens of beautiful stained-glass windows, many of which depict Polish saints such as St. Stanislaus, St. Hedwig, St. Casimir, St. Hyacinth. The most unique one depicts the attack on the Monastery of Our Lady of Częstochowa. **scbc.worthyofpraise.org**

Stained-glass window at St. Charles Borromeo Church, DuBois, IL (Parish)

JUSTICE
Resurrection Cemetery

Resurrection Cemetery was founded in 1904 by the Polish and Czech communities of Chicago's Southwest Side. The spectacular mausoleum, which contains 10,000 crypts, was designed by the firm of Harley, Ellington, Cowin, & Stirton of Detroit (known today as Harley Ellis Devereaux). It is not only wrapped in columns but also in 22,000 square feet of stained glass, the single largest stained-glass piece in the world. The images depicted are not only of classic biblical imagery but also contain representations of dinosaurs, guided missiles, bombers, and atomic explosions. The first floor of the mausoleum portrays Polish and Polish American Catholic history through various forms of art. The cemetery also includes a striking shrine, Shrine of St. John Paul II, honoring a thousand years of Polish Christianity designed by Bert Gast and dedicated in 1969. Karol Cardinal Wojtyła (St. Pope John Paul II) officially opened and blessed the "Millennium Shrine." In front of the shrine, a 20-foot-tall bronze statue of St. Pope John Paul II designed by Teresa Clark is visible on an 86,000-pound block of black granite. The cemetery is popularly known as the home of the hitchhiking ghost Resurrection Mary, a young girl reportedly killed in an accident along Archer Avenue. Resurrection Cemetery and Mausoleum are open daily.

LASALLE
St. Hyacinth Church
The stately clocktower steeples of St. Hyacinth make this Gothic church a town landmark. The congregation was established in 1875 and the current red brick structure was completed in 1892 to plans by George P. Stauduhar. Across the street from the church is the St. Hyacinth school, with its stunning trefoil pediment. The school building has recently been converted to apartments. Each year a Mass is celebrated in Polish to honor the heritage of the parish. **www.lasallecatholic.org**

LEMONT
Sts. Cyril and Methodius Church
Located at 608 Sobieski Street in the Jasna Gora subdivision of Lemont, Sts. Cyril and Methodius was founded in 1884. The growing church members built the present Romanesque structure in 1929 to a design by Erhard Brielmaier & Sons, the firm that famously designed Milwaukee's St. Josaphat Basilica. Inside, a shrine to the Black Madonna was unveiled in 1999 with several relics; the ornate icon was made for the parish by Hinsdale artist Zygmunt Kimel. Polish artist/architect Andrzej Urbanczyk designed a new grotto that features the statue of St. Pope John Paul II praying to Mary in front of a piece of stone cut into the shape of the map of Poland. Carved into the stone are a cross and the Pope's apostolic motto: "Totus Tuus." Polish Masses and celebrations of Polish religious and historical events are held. The church hosts a weekly Polish school and the Polish Club of Lemont. **www.stcyril.org**

Heritage Hall of the Franciscan Sisters of Chicago
This Franciscan congregation was founded in 1894 by Polish-born Josephine Dudzik, who is now up for sainthood—a statue of her designed by sculptor and artist Stefan Niedorezo is found in the Administration Building as well as at St. Stanislaus Kostka Church (*See* Chicago, IL: St. Stanislaus Kostka Church). As the congregation grew, it focused on educating Polish youth in elementary and secondary schools; starting orphanages; care of sick in hospitals and nursing homes; pastoral, parish, catechetical and prison work; and later mission work in Mexico. Heritage Hall was opened in 1992 to document this order with such a rich history and so many contributions to the Chicago Polonia community. The Sisters saved documents, books, articles, letters, and photographs relating to their foundation and growth ranging from 1894 to the present and these make up the rich archives. A permanent exhibit highlights the history of the sisters. Not only is Heritage Hall an archive of the ministry of the congregation, but it is also a place for meditation. Heritage Hall is in the Our Lady of Victory Convent of the Franciscan Sisters of Chicago at 11400 Theresa Drive in Lemont, Illinois, fifty miles southwest of Chicago and thirty miles northeast of Joliet. **www.chicagofranciscans.org/history/heritagehall**

NILES
St. Adalbert Catholic Cemetery
This cemetery at 6800 North Milwaukee Avenue is named for one of the patron saints of Poland and dates to 1872. It served as a burial ground for many Polish parishes in the area.

Katyń Memorial Monument
This monument was designed by Chicago artist Wojciech Seweryn and dedicated in 2009 by Cardinal Józef Glemp, primate of Poland, to honor the 22,000 Polish officers (including Seweryn's father) who were massacred at Katyń by the Soviets during World War II. A towering black granite cross with a bronze statue of St. Mary holding one of the victims is located at the foot of the cross. An inscription reads: monument in honor and memory "Golgota of the East." There are also two bronze reliefs graphically depicting the horrors of the mass executions.

Tragically, Seweryn died with Polish President Lech Kaczynski and numerous other notables in a plane crash near Smolensk, Russia, in 2010 while in route to observe the 70th anniversary of the Katyń Massacre in Russia. A new 10-foot black granite monument was erected next to Seweryn's Katyń Memorial, which lists the names of the victims of the plane crash; it was organized by the Alliance of Polish Clubs of the USA.

Katyń Memorials, St. Adalbert Cemetery, Niles, IL (Kasia Trznadel)

World War I Memorial
To the right of the entrance, an obelisk honors Polish Americans who fought and lost their lives on the battlefields of France in World War I. The monument was erected by the Polish American mothers and fathers of the Gold Star Society, consecrated, and unveiled on July 4, 1928. The obelisk, which lists the names of the soldiers, is surrounded by statues representing four armed services in which Polish Americans served: Army, Marines, Navy, and Haller's Army.

World War I Memorial, St. Adalbert Cemetery, Niles, IL (American Legion)

Maryhill Catholic Cemetery & Mausoleum
Maryhill Cemetery at 8600 North Milwaukee Avenue was consecrated in 1961 as a successor to the older and large St. Adalbert Cemetery.

Polish Veterans Memorial
The 1975 Polish Veterans Memorial is dedicated to the Polish soldiers who fought for freedom in many wars but could not return to their homeland. There is a large mosaic of Our Lady of Częstochowa and Jasna Góra at the entrance to the mausoleum area.

St. Pope John Paul II Sculpture
A 32-foot-tall obelisk on a 4-foot by 4-foot base honoring St. Pope John Paul II was dedicated in 2014 to commemorate the Pope's canonization. It is constructed of Barre Gray granite from Vermont. Its four sides feature detailed Venetian glass mosaics—known as "smalit"—which were handcrafted in Venice. Two of the sides in-

Polish Veterans Memorial, Maryhill Catholic Cemetery, Niles, IL (Victoria Granacki)

clude mosaic renderings of the pope's 1979 visit to Chicago, the third and fourth sides are adorned with mosaic renderings of Our Lady of Częstochowa and the Virgin of Guadalupe. It is installed in a new section of Maryhill.

SKOKIE
Jan Karski plaque
A plaque dedicated to Jan Karski is found at the Ferro Fountain of the Righteous at the Holocaust Museum and Education Center at 9603 Woods Drive. The Polish community hosts a commemorative ceremony on the anniversaries of his death. Karski had visited Chicago several times during his life. The ceremony remembered his efforts to stop the Holocaust of European Jews by risking his life by getting into the Warsaw ghetto and a concentration camp. As a courier for the Polish Government in Exile, he met with President Roosevelt and reported to the British government, describing the horrors of the extermination of the Jews. In 2020 on the 20th anniversary of his death, the Polish delegation renamed a part of Milwaukee Street near the Copernicus Center in Chicago "Jan Karski Way."

New Gračanica Monastery, Third Lake, IL
(Sdancuo CC BY-SA 4.0)

THIRD LAKE
New Gračanica Monastery
Although it is a Serbian Orthodox Monastery built in 1984, New Gračanica's Polish connection lies in its 1995 frescos by Polish American iconographer Fr. Theodore Jurewicz. The project was executed over three years and covers the entirety of the church interior in Byzantine-style decoration. The paintings are true fresco, meaning they were painted directly onto wet plaster, making the accomplishments of Fr. Jurewicz even more impressive. The church itself, at 35240 West Grant Avenue, is a replica of a medieval original in Kosovo. **newgracanica.org**

WILLOW SPRINGS
Pulaski Memorial
A rectangular granite tablet was erected by the American Legion in honor of Casimir Pulaski in the parking area of Pulaski Woods in the South Palos Trail System, Forest Preserves of Cook County, south of Wolf Road, between 107th Street and 95th Street. Polish organizations hold an annual ceremony here on the first Monday of March, which is Pulaski Day in Illinois.
www.legion.org/memorials/242231/brigadier-general-count-casimir-pulaski-memorial

INDIANA

EAST CHICAGO
Thaddeus Kosciuszko Park and Monument
This statue memorializing Brigadier-General Thaddeus Kosciuszko (1746-1817) is the focal point of a city park that also bears his name. The monument was erected by local citizens of Polish heritage in 1939 to honor his services and devotion to the cause of American Independence. Kosciuszko Park is located one block south of St. Stanislaus Church (808 W. 150th Street), the first Polish parish established in 1896. The City of East Chicago hosts Kielbasa Fest, an annual celebration of Polish culture and food, at the park in August.
www.facebook.com/pages/Kosciuzko-Park/149699775042453

Thaddeus Kosciuszko Monument, East Chicago, IN (Ronald Trigg)

Whiting Pierogi Fest
Next door to Hammond, Whiting is located two miles from the southside of Chicago and attracted Polish workers to the Standard Oil Refinery plant. The annual fest is held downtown and spans three days during the last weekend of July, drawing over 300,000 attendees from around the globe. Locals dress up as Mr. Pierogi, the Buscias, Miss Paczki, or Pieroguettes and join in the wacky fun featuring lots of polka music, food booths, pierogi toss contests. The fest was even featured by Oprah.
www.pierogifest.net

HAMMOND
Casimir Pulaski Park and Monument
This monument to General Casimir Pulaski (1747-1779) stands in the Hammond city park bearing his name. Pulaski distinguished himself on the battlefields at Brandywine and in the Carolinas, and in October 1779, he died of wounds received at Savannah. Pulaski Park is in a traditionally Polish neighborhood of Hammond. The monument was erected in 1997 by the city's park department and citizens of Polish descent. The flags of Poland and the U.S. are displayed at the site.

St. Casimir Church
Established in 1890, with the current church at 4340 Johnson Avenue dedicated in 1924, St. Casimir was the first Polish parish in Lake County, Indiana. Located in a heavily industrial belt along the southern shore of Lake Michigan, Hammond and adjacent communities offered jobs in the steel, oil, and manufacturing sectors that attracted thousands of Polish immigrants in the decades

St. Casimir Church, Hammond, IN (Ronald Trigg)

Shrine of our Lady of Częstochowa, Merrillville, IN (Ronald Trigg)

surrounding the turn of the 20th century. Polish-language Mass is still said on Sundays. Above the altar, there is a painted statue of St. Casimir. There are stained-glass windows of St. Casimir (near the confessional) and St. Stanislaus Bishop & Martyr. A painting of our Lady of Częstochowa by a parishioner is in a Marian side altar.

MERRILLVILLE
Shrine of Our Lady of Częstochowa
Located on the grounds of one of the four American religious communities founded by the Polish Province of the Society of the Divine Saviour, the shrine houses a large replica of the "Black Madonna," the holiest icon in Poland. The original, protected at Jasna Gora in Poland's mountainous south since the 14th century, is said to have been painted by St. Luke the Evangelist and is credited with numerous miracles. The Salvatorian Fathers installed the replica at Merrillville in the early 1980s. Before leaving Europe, it was personally blessed by Pope John Paul II, a statue of whom now stands outside the shrine. The focal point of the newly constructed church is the huge (8ft x 12ft) painting of Our Lady of Częstochowa by Włodek Koss of the Koss Family Artists of New York. The Polish Community of Chicago conducts a 33-mile walking pilgrimage to the shrine every August for the Feast of the Assumption of the Blessed Virgin, replicating a similar trek that occurs annually in Poland. The shrine and its surrounding picnic grounds are open to the public. Other attractions periodically presented here are a Panorama of the Millennium, which celebrates the history of Christianity in Poland, and an exhibit about the life of St. Pope John Paul II. Polish-language Mass and confessions are available. **www.salwatorianie.us**

MICHIGAN CITY
Friendship Botanic Gardens: Ignacy Jan Paderewski Monument, Polish Garden, Polish Heritage Festival
The Paderewski monument is located at the Friendship Botanic Gardens. The bust of the Polish statesman, piano virtuoso, and composer is the work of the noted Italian-born sculptor Dora Natella. The slightly larger-than-life bust was unveiled on May 20, 2018, and sits atop the pedestal of the original bust created by Robert Allen Wilcox (1903-1977), sponsored by the Paderewski Society of Michigan City, and dedicated in a major ceremony in 1950. The new Paderewski bust is the centerpiece of the Polish Garden, part of the Friendship Botanical Garden (originally called

Paderewski monument in the Polish Garden, Friendship Botanic Gardens, Michigan City, IN (Janusz Duzinkiewicz)

International Friendship Garden). In addition to the Paderewski bust, the evolving Polish Garden includes native Polish plants and "Florek," a statue of the storks so common to Poland. The Friendship Botanic Gardens are also the venue of the annual Polish Heritage Festival in mid-September. The Paderewski bust, Polish Garden, and Polish Heritage Festival are funded and maintained by the Heritage Association of Michigan City founded in 2012.

Carmelite Shrine, Munster, IN (Ronald Trigg)

MUNSTER
Carmelite Monastery and Shrine

The Discalced Carmelite monks, displaced from their native Poland during World War II, came to America in 1949 to serve the pastoral needs of the Polish American community throughout northwest Indiana and the Chicago area. Their monastery at 1628 Ridge Road features a church with an exhibit hall dedicated to St. Pope John Paul II and the Miraculous Statue of Our Lady of Ludźmierz; the Our Lady of Ostrabrama chapel; the St. Raphael Kalinowski Polish Saturday School; and a banquet hall. The gardens are home to many statues of Polish saints; the Marian Grotto; the Stations of the Cross; the chapel of Our Lady of Mercy; the Highlanders' Chapel *(Góral)*. Activities throughout the year include Polish Highlander Masses and picnics, among the most popular being the Anniversary of Pope John Paul II's Pilgrimage to Ludźmierz held in June, and the Solemnity of Our Lady of Ludźmierz (Queen of the Polish Highlanders) held in August. Guests are welcome every Sunday from Easter to November 1st; call before visiting on weekdays or to organize a group tour or pilgrimage. **www.carmelitefathers.com**

Mural in St. Mary's Church apse depicting Our Lady of Częstochowa surrounded by nine Polish saints, Otis, IN (Ronald Trigg)

OTIS
St. Mary's Church

The small LaPorte County farming community of Otis was the first place in Indiana to attract a sizeable number of Polish immigrants. Poles from New York and other points to the east began arriving in the late 1850s via the railroad that went through town. These early arrivals had their roots primarily in small villages around Poznań, Poland. Most worked as farmhands, lumberjacks, and railway laborers, earning money which eventually allowed them to purchase land and start their own farms. By 1872 enough Polish settlers had arrived to form their own parish, and permission to do so was obtained from the Diocese of Fort Wayne. The following year, St. Mary of Czestochowa Parish (as it was originally called) was established at 101 North Church Street. It was the first Polish parish in Indiana. The state's first Polish school was also here. A cemetery adjacent to the church contains the remains of many of the original settlers, as well as several generations of their descendants. A mural above the tabernacle depicts Our Lady of Częstochowa surrounded by nine Polish saints, including St. Stanislaus of Cracow, St. Andrew Bobola, St. Josaphat, and St. Kinga. **www.dcgary.org/parishes/stmary_otis.htm**

Polish Worker's home, South Bend History Museum, South Bend, IN (Ronald Trigg)

SOUTH BEND
Polish Worker's Home / Dom Robotnika

Located on the grounds of the South Bend History Museum at 808 West Washington Street (facing Thomas Street, just opposite the museum entrance), the Worker's Home (*Dom Robotnika*) is an 1870s-era house where employees of the Oliver Chilled Plow Works lived until the 1980s. It was moved to its present site in 1992. The modest, simply designed house memorializes the lives

of Polish working-class families in the mid-20th century. The 1,200-square-foot dwelling has seven rooms. The furnishings, household appliances, and decorative pieces all reflect the fashion of the 1930s. The exhibit is child-friendly; visitors are encouraged to touch the items on display. Guided tours of the home are conducted daily and can be scheduled at the museum desk.
www.historymuseumsb.org/see-do/historic-house-2

St. Casimir Church
This parish was founded by Polish immigrants in 1898, in the center of a neighborhood that initially was Polish and has been staffed by the Congregation of Holy Cross since its inception. The church at 1302 West Dunham Street is Romanesque architecture with the traditional Polish style of red brick exterior. In the apse above the tabernacle, St. Casimir is depicted to the left of Christ and St. Stanislaus Kostka to the right. The stained-glass windows were crafted by Columbia Plate Glass Window Co. of Milwaukee, and many depict Polish saints including St. Casimir, St. Stanislaus, St. John Kanty, St. Hyacinth, St. Stanislaus Kostka, St. Hedwig, St. Bronislawa, Blessed Chester. The crest at the east vestibule door says *Boże Zbaw Polskę* (God deliver Poland) and in Latin "Queen of Poland Pray for us Jesus Mary." Outside on the grounds around the church, there is a statue of St. Casimir, and in the transept of the front of the church building is a statue of St. Stanislaus Kostka. The three bells in the tower are named Stanisław, Kazimierz, and Antoni.
www.stcasimirparish.net

St. Hedwig Church
St. Hedwig Church at 331 South Scott Street was established in 1877 to serve the large numbers of Polish immigrants who came to South Bend from the 1870s through the turn of the 20th century. They were part of a wave of Poles coming to urban centers in the East and Middle West seeking work. The biggest employers in South Bend at the time were the Studebaker Brothers Carriage Works, the Singer Sewing Machine Company, and the Oliver Chilled Plow Works. Eventually Poles came to represent a sizeable portion of the city's population, and three more Polish parishes were established: St. Stanislaus (415 Brookfield Street), St. Casimir (1302 W. Dunham Street), and St. Adalbert (2420 W. Huron Street). A plaque on the front of the church records its beginnings: "Saint Hedwig Roman Catholic Church. Founded by Polish Immigrants in 1877."
www.sthedwigsb.org

WARSAW
General Tadeusz "Thaddeus" Kosciuszko Marker
A historical marker, erected in 2014, is located on the north side of the Kosciusko County Courthouse on Main St. The inscription outlines his heroic achievements and ends with the famous quote from Thomas Jefferson: Dedicated to Freedom for All *"He is as pure a Son of Liberty as I have ever known."* A large portrait of Kosciuszko hangs in the Council Room of City Hall.

Historical marker outside Kosciuszko County Courthouse in Warsaw, IN (Ronald Trigg)

66

IOWA

POLISHVILLE
Polishville Community Center and Cemetery

Polish immigrants settled close to rural Germanville (near Brighton) in the late-19th century where they formed their own St. Mary of the Immaculate Conception Parish and began holding Masses in 1882. Intermarriage led to the end of the parish in 1945. The church building burned to the ground in 1971 and the Polishville Community Center (1345 Tamarack Avenue), built in 1988, stands on the site and includes the Esther Johanna Peck Museum which holds artifacts from the church. The community center hosts Polish dances, bazaars, and other events from time to time. Next door is the Polishville Cemetery, a small picturesque burial ground of many members of the Polishville community.

SIOUX CITY
Pulaski Park

The meat-packing industry began slaughtering animals in the Sioux City stock yards near the Missouri River in the 1880s. This industry drew Polish immigrants around 1905 to what became known as "The Bottoms." They built a small wooden church, St. Francis, which hosted a PNA lodge and other Polish organizations. In 1914, Polish immigrants increasingly moved up the hill to the more affluent Morningside neighborhood. This residential area is still known as Polish Hill although local residents use an ethnic slur instead. During the 1920s, the Polish community declined with many residents moving to Detroit and other cities for factory work. As a cattle market, Sioux City declined in the 1980s but exists on a much smaller scale and many Poles still work in the meat-packing house. The remnants of the stockyard buildings can be found at 1951 Leech Ave. "The Bottoms" or the Stock Yards neighborhood still contains other buildings of a similar era and a memorial marker to the early immigrants. Although the Polish parish closed in 1998, one of the lasting legacies of the Polish American community is Pulaski Park just off Highway Business 75.

Polishville Cemetery, Polishville, Iowa (Stephen Leahy)

KANSAS

KANSAS CITY

St. Joseph Church

St. Joseph Church was founded in 1887 to minister to the large number of Slavic Catholic immigrants who settled in the Kansas City area, drawn by the prospect of employment in the local meat packing industry and rail yards. Before long, it became a parish closely identified with Polonia within the district commonly called "Polish Hill." The present two-towered Romanesque structure at 811 Vermont Avenue dates from 1921-1922. In recent decades, the neighborhood changed from Polish to largely Spanish-speaking, and St. Joseph's became part of a merged All Saints Parish. The building retains some of the original interior decoration and exterior elements with inscriptions in Polish. All Saints Parish continues to hold an annual "Polski Day" event on the first Saturday in May. **www.allsaintsparishkck.org**

Strawberry Hill Museum and Cultural Center

This sprawling Queen Anne structure, situated on the crest of a hill overlooking the Missouri River at 720 North 4th Street, houses a museum devoted to the immigrant heritage of Kansas City, Kansas. Originally a private residence built in 1887, then operated for many years as an orphanage, the building was acquired in 1988 by the Strawberry Hill Ethnic Cultural Society and converted into the present museum. The predominant ethnic character of the neighborhood was historically Croatian, and Poles are one among many nationalities and cultures represented in the exhibits of the museum. Of greatest interest are relics related to St. Pope John Paul II, including

St. Joseph Church cornerstone, Kansas City, KS (Ewa Barczyk)

Strawberry Hill Museum & Cultural Center, Kansas City, KS (Ewa Barczyk)

the air travel bed he used in flight for pilgrimages to the United States in 1979, 1987, and 1995. A gift shop offers numerous items with Polish motifs. **www.strawberryhillmuseum.org**

LEAVENWORTH
St. Casimir Church

St. Casimir's is a historically Polish Catholic church at 715 Pennsylvania Avenue that dates from the late-19th century. By the 1890s a significant number of Polish immigrants, many from West-phalia Germany, had settled in Leavenworth, drawn by the prospect of work in recently opened coal mines. St. Casimir's parish was founded in 1889 to serve their community, and the present church building was dedicated in 1894. Renovated numerous times over the years, the structure retains little of its original character other than stained-glass windows with Polish inscriptions and symbols, an icon of Our Lady of Częstochowa, and a large statue of St. Casimir within the al-tarpiece. There is a historical plaque on the west side of the church giving the history of the found-ing of the parish. Now part of a merged Sacred Heart/St. Casimir parish, the church continues to hold occasional events that evoke its Polish heritage. **www.shsc.org**

KENTUCKY

LEXINGTON
Lexington Cemetery

Thomas Lewinski, a nationally noted architect, arrived in Lexington in 1842. Born in England to a Polish father, he attended a Roman Catholic seminary to become a priest, but later served as a soldier in the British Army and eventually taught at the University of Louisville. He was a colleague of Cassius Marcellus Clay and joined in his anti-slavery endeavors. He designed his house, and a plaque outlines the history of Clay Villa mentioning Lewinski. In 1848 Lewinski designed Christ Episcopal Church and many plantation homes in the Greek revival style which are on the National Register of Historic Sites. He designed the cornerstone for a massive monument to Henry Clay, the "Great Compromiser" begun in 1857 and finished in 1861 in the Lexington Cemetery where Lewinski is buried as well in Section J, Lot 101.

Henry Clay monument by Thomas Lewinski in Lexington Cemetery, KY (Long Hunter)

LOUISIANA

GIFT OF
THE ARCHDIOCESE OF NEW ORLEANS
AMERICAN ITALIAN CULTURAL CENTER
BLESSED BY POPE FRANCIS   DEDICATED BY
IN SAINT PETER'S SQUARE   ARCHBISHOP GREGORY AYMOND
NOVEMBER 15, 2017   JANUARY 7, 2018
NEW ORLEANS TRICENTENNIAL

NEW ORLEANS
Statue of St. Pope John Paul II in
Cathedral-Basilica of St. Louis King of France

The Basilica contains an outdoor chapel with a marble statue of St. Pope John Paul II which is a frequent stop for Polish American tourists. The 6-foot-tall, approximately 5,000-pound statue by sculptor Franco Alessandrini was blessed by Pope Francis in St. Peter's Square in Vatican City and dedicated January 2018. It is a gift from the Archdiocese of New Orleans to the residents for the city's tricentennial. The statue commemorates Pope John Paul II's visit to the city in 1987 which made history as he was the only sitting pope ever to walk the streets of New Orleans. The St. Louis Cathedral is one of the major landmarks of the city overlooking Jackson Square and is the oldest Catholic cathedral in continual use in the United States. **www.stlouiscathedral.org**

The statue commemorating Pope John Paul II's visit to New Orleans in 1987, in Cathedral-Basilica of St. Louis King of France (Camille Shaw)

MAINE

PORTLAND
St. Louis Church
A composite church-school brick building was constructed in 1924 on land purchased in 1915 at 279 Danforth Street. This humble Catholic church continues to serve as a touchstone for the Poles in Maine as it is the only one in the state that has Mass in Polish and where Polish traditions are observed, such as Easter basket blessings. **portlandcatholic.org/saint-louis**

RUMFORD
Edmund Muskie Memorial
Born to Polish immigrants in the mill town of Rumford, Edmund Sixtus Muskie served as United States Secretary of State under President Carter. He also served in the U.S. Senate (1959-1980), was the first Catholic governor of Maine (1955-1959), and ran as the Democratic Party's vice-presidential nominee in the 1968 presidential election. In addition to this monument in his hometown, the University of Maine's School of Public Service in Portland bears his name as a tribute to his impactful career as a statesman.

Edmund Muskie Memorial in his birthplace, Rumford, ME (Christopher Siuzdak, J.C.L.)

MARYLAND

ANNAPOLIS JUNCTION
National Cryptologic Museum
The National Cryptologic Museum at 8290 Colony Seven Road contains a wealth of artifacts chronicling the history of cryptology and its use in intelligence and counterintelligence activities. These include information on notable people, events, explanations of techniques, and examples of the machines and devices used in various eras. One exhibit is dedicated to the Polish cryptologists who broke the German Enigma code machine prior to World War II and shared their achievement with the British and French intelligence services. This coup was critical to the Allied victory. **national-cryptologic-museum.business.site/#gallery**

BALTIMORE
Holy Cross Polish National Catholic Church
Holy Mother of Unceasing Help Polish Independent Church was founded in 1898 after four years of conflicts with Holy Rosary Church over possession of church property. With the help of Father Walenty Gawrychowski, dissatisfied members established an initial 451-member congregation. It was not until 1913 that the parish aligned with the Polish National Catholic Church of America and changed its name to Holy Cross. The exterior side of the Church at 208 South Broadway has a plaque in Polish and English and inside near the entrance there are two plaques about the founders and one about Bishop Hodur in Polish. Polish language banners adorn the church. The congregation holds an annual Polish bazaar and celebrates Polish customs. **www.holycrosspncc.org**

Exhibit dedicated to the Polish cryptologists who broke the German Enigma code, National Cryptologic Museum, Annapolis Junction, MD (James Pula)

Holy Rosary Church
In December 1887, Holy Rosary became Baltimore's second Polish Church. By 1920, the congregation exceeded twelve thousand and a new church was built in 1927 by Monsignor Stanislaus Wachowiak at 408 South Chester Street. The Romanesque church is 200 feet long and 100 feet wide with seating for two thousand. The exterior is granite with two towers 125 feet high. When built, it was

Holy Cross Polish National Catholic Church, Baltiimore, MD (Anthony Monczewski)

Baltimore's Polish Wall Street

The larger commercial banks were reluctant to loan money to Polish immigrants to buy houses because the majority were laborers prone to periods of unemployment. As a result, Building and Loan Associations were formed beginning in 1889 with Sobieski First Polish American Building and Loan Association. At their peak there would be fourteen banks, some organized within the Polish Catholic parishes.

By 1925, ten of the twelve then existing banks were located within a block or two of Broadway and Eastern Avenue, thus the area became known as the "Polish Wall Street". The creation of these building and loans allowed Baltimore Poles to have a higher rate of homeownership than many other ethnic groups. You can still see the names of many of the banks on the building facades as you walk around.

the largest church in the Baltimore archdiocese. After the parish became the Archdiocesan Shrine of Divine Mercy in 1993, Rev. Ronald Pytel was healed in the church. This was the second miracle for St. Faustina Kowalska. Rev. Pytel said Mass with Pope John Paul II for her canonization in 2000. The church remains as Baltimore's center of Polish religious, cultural, and social life serving a Polish-speaking and non-Polish congregation. The Fathers of the Society of Christ serve the parish. Pope John Paul II visited the parish when he was cardinal and again as pope. Relics of St. Faustina, St. Pope John Paul II, and Bl. Michael Sopoćko are in the church. It is the only church in the city that still has Masses in Polish.

Holy Rosary Church, Baltimore, MD (Anthony Monczewski)

National Katyń Memorial

The Katyń Memorial is Baltimore's tallest sculpture and commemorates the almost 22,000 Polish officers and intellectuals murdered in 1940 by the Soviet Union. The 44-foot-tall bronze memorial was created by sculptor Andrzej Pitynski as a representation of an eagle rising from the flames of war. It sits in the middle of the Katyń traffic circle in the Harbor East neighborhood atop a stepped-waterfall base. Multiple figures within the flames of the gold-leaf sculpture represent the doomed officers and Polish military heroes that include Poland's first king Bolesław Chrobry, Thaddeus Kosciuszko, Casimir Pulaski, and King Jan III Sobieski. The memorial was dedicated in 2000 and a Remembrance Ceremony is held yearly in April. **www.katynbaltimore.org**

Polish National Alliance – Council 21

The first PNA Lodge in Baltimore was organized in 1886 to sponsor commemorative events, celebrations, and amateur theatricals to preserve the history and culture of Poland. In September 1907, the National Convention was held at the Broadway Institute with delegates from across the

Pope John Paul II Prayer Garden, Baltimore, MD (Thomas L. Hollowak)

United States and Canada. An outcome of the meeting was renewed efforts that led to the erection of monuments to both Pulaski and Kosciuszko in Washington D.C.

Council 21 meets in the building that was formerly Holy Rosary School at 1627 Eastern Avenue. The Henryk Sienkiewicz Library, named after the Polish Nobel laureate, is on the second floor. The facility includes a lounge, hall and meeting rooms for entertainment, Polish language and cooking classes, book club gatherings, and Polish movies. Both the Krakowiaki and Ojczyzna dancers hold public performances in the building.

Pope John Paul II Prayer Garden

The centerpiece of this downtown garden at 1 West Franklin Street is a seven-feet-tall bronze statue commemorating the 1995 arrival of Pope John Paul II in Baltimore sculpted by Joseph Sheppard. The garden features plants, shrubs, and trees specifically chosen for their relation to the Bible, Pope John Paul II, or the local area. Stainless steel bands embedded in the wall bear the symbols of Christianity, Islam, and Judaism. A mural on a side wall includes flowers traditionally associated with the Black Madonna and a quote by St. Pope John Paul II.
www.archbalt.org/te-archdiocese/pope-john-paul-ii-prayer-garden/

Polish National Alliance–Council 21, Baltimore, MD
(Thomas L. Hollowak)

Pulaski Banner, Maryland Center for History & Culture

During his stay in Baltimore, Casimir Pulaski visited Bethlehem, Pennsylvania, where he received a banner for his legion from the Order of Moravian Nuns. After Pulaski's death, the cavalry banner was brought to Baltimore by Pulaski's friend and aide, Captain Paul Bentalou. The banner is in the permanent textile collection of the Maryland Center for History & Culture at 610 Park Avenue. In 1976, the Polish Heritage Society of Maryland commissioned Sister Irene Olkowski of the Polish Order of Sister Servants of Mary Immaculate to make a replica of the banner based on the original. This replica is also a part of the Historical Society's permanent collection. (*See also* Bethlehem, PA: Sisters House) **www.mdhistory.org/museum**

Pulaski Monument

The General Casimir Pulaski Monument was unveiled on October 14, 1951, in South Patterson Park at Eastern Avenue and Linwood Avenue to several thousand Polish Americans. Sculpted in bronze bas-relief is a dynamic Casimir Pulaski leading a cavalry charge at the siege of

Pulaski Monument in Patterson Park
(Anthony Monczewski)

Savannah followed by his aide Paul Bentalou. The sculpture depicts great energy and movement with horses and men moving forward. The monument is 16 feet high, 33 feet across, and 5 feet thick.

St. Casimir Church

St. Casimir Church at 2800 O'Donnell Street earned an award as the Best Architectural Religious Monument built in Baltimore in 1926. The parish was founded in 1902 in Canton, an area of industrial growth and affordable row homes that was ideal for immigrants to live and work. Fr. Benedict Przemielewski became the second Franciscan pastor in 1920 and designed the church. The structure is 225 by 70 feet with seating for fourteen hundred. The exterior has Indiana limestone. The façade is 80 feet from base to gable and flanked by two 110-foot towers. The main altar is a replica of Donatello's altar in the Basilica of St. Anthony in Padua. The church interior has murals that depict the triumph of the Franciscan Order, growth of the Catholic Church in America, and development of Catholicism in Poland. The windows tell the story of the spiritual triumph of Poland with images of heroes and heroines of the Church of Poland. **www.stcasimir.org**

DUNDALK

Four Polish Cemeteries on German Hill Road

1. **Holy Rosary Cemetery**, the oldest Polish cemetery, was acquired in 1889 and a 32-foot-high cross was placed in the center of it. The first pastor, Father Piotr Chowaniec, known as the Missionary of Minnesota, was buried beneath the cross.

Pulaski Brigade Memorial in Holy Rosary Cemetery

Erected in 1958, the Pulaski Brigade Memorial pays tribute to its deceased members. Three flags—United States, State of Maryland, and Poland—are markers to the location of the monument. The Pulaski Brigade began at a group meeting in a home in 1908 to organize a drum corps around Holy Rosary Church known as the Pulaski Brigade Drum, Fife and

Pulaski Brigade Memorial, Holy Rosary Cemetery, Dundalk, MD (Anthony Monczewski)

Bugle Corps. It was reorganized as a military unit equipped with rifles and sabers and their purpose was to serve the church in many ways. Each year members performed memorial services for deceased members at the monument. Members were required to be buried in their uniforms. The Pulaski Brigade lasted until the late 1980s when the last member died.

2. Holy Cross Polish National Catholic Cemetery was dedicated on July 24, 1898, following the dedication of the church earlier in the day. The **National Catholic War Veterans Monument** commemorates members of Pioneer Post Number 1 whose members served either in World War I or World War II. The members names are inscribed on the monument and includes a Ladies Auxiliary.

3. Sacred Heart of Mary Church Cemetery started in 1925. Between 1917 and 1918, 305 men from Baltimore volunteered to serve in the Polish Army in France also known as both Haller's Army and the Blue Army. Thirty-three women also joined as a Women Volunteer Ambulance Corps. A recruitment station was opened at the Polish Falcon Hall on Fleet Street. After the war only seventy men returned to Baltimore, seventy-three were killed in action, and sixty remained in Poland. It is believed all the women returned. The **Polish Army Veterans Monument** is in Section C or "St. Stephen." Surrounding the monument are buried twenty of

Polish Army Veterans Monument, Sacred Heart of Mary Cemetery, Dundalk, MD (Thomas L. Hollowak)

those who served in the Polish Army in France. The large **Father Stanislaus Wikarski Memorial** was erected by his parishioners since he was the moving force behind the establishment of Sacred Heart of Mary Church and Cemetery.

4. Christ Lutheran Polish Cemetery acquired property next to Holy Cross Cemetery in 1926. The parishioners at the Polish parishes, St. Athanasius and St. Adalbert, used nearby Holy Cross Cemetery in Anne Arundel County for their burials.

SILVER SPRING
Our Lady, Queen of Poland and St. Maximilian Kolbe Church
This church at 9700 Rosensteel Avenue contains first class relics of St. Pope John Paul II, St. Maximilian Kolbe, and St. Faustina Kowalska. It was established as a national parish in 1983, to serve the Archdiocese of Washington. The current dual parish was erected thanks to the intervention of St. Pope John Paul II with the cardinal-archbishop of Washington. He requested that a Polish mission church be established, and the subsequent archbishop raised it to a full parish. Since the Polish community took over an existing 19th-century church, the external marks of the Polish community are limited to an icon of Our Lady of Częstochowa, a painting of St. Maxmilian Kolbe,

Villa Anneslie, Towson, MD (PNAF)

and a banner depicting St. Pope John Paul II. The church actively holds Polish traditional devotions and observes national holidays such as Polish Constitution Day and hosts a Polish language school. **www.parafia-dc.org**

TOWSON
Villa Anneslie
The origins of Villa Anneslie (529 Dunkirk Road) can be traced to Lord Baltimore who granted a tract of wooded land to Govane Howard. Although the original house burned sometime in the 18th century, the stone cottage and courtyard enclosure wall on the Villa grounds are what remains from the original manor. In 1850 Frederick Harrison purchased additional land to build Villa Anneslie as a country home for his family. The house was designed by the architect John Rudolph Niersee.

The current owner, Dr. Roger Chylinski-Polubinski, purchased the estate in 1972 as headquarters for the Polish Nobility Association of America Foundation. It was formed by nobility and ex-officers after the Polish uprising of 1830 to re-establish the monarchy but now activities are primarily devoted to genealogical and heraldic research. The home and gardens have hosted visiting nobility, receptions, and community concerts. The organization helps individuals with research on Polish-Lithuanian heraldic information and then registers and issues certificates to successful PNAF Heraldic Name Search Applicants. Their website has extensive historic photos and issues of their journal *White Eagle*. Villa Anneslie was listed on the National Register of Historic Places and the Maryland Historical Trust in 1977. Access is by appointment only. **www.pnaf.us**

MASSACHUSSETTS

ADAMS

St. Stanislaus Kostka Church

The spires of turn-of-the-century St. Stanislaus Church at 25 Hoosac Street tower over the small valley that nestles Adams. Although it is one of the best preserved and mostly lavishly decorated Polish churches in New England, the survival of St. Stanislaus can be credited to the tenacity of its parishioners. After the local diocese closed the church in 2009, parishioners held a three-year prayer vigil outside the barricaded church and finally the Vatican intervened to reopen the church. Every surface of the vaulted interior is covered in paintings of Polish saints or biblical scenes. A curiosity of the church is the c.1950 stained-glass window featuring Archbishop Jan Cieplak with Lenin, Trotsky, and Stalin. This Polish bishop was sentenced to death in a sham trial but managed to secure permission to come to the United States and briefly visited St. Stanislaus. The parish's elementary school across the street utilizes its original building with its name engraved in Polish above the entrance.
adamscatholicchurches.org/st-stanislaus-kostka-church

AMHERST

Polish Archives at the University of Massachusetts Libraries

The University of Massachusetts Libraries contains over 160,000 items concerning Polish topics. Polish American Archival documentation has been collected since 1985. The University Archive is a depository of almost 10,000 items about church histories and jubilee catalogs, personal documents of Polish families, old photos, records of fraternal organizations, newspaper clippings, memories, diaries, audio tapes, and similar material. Also gathered are the records of several large manufacturing companies that employed many Polish immigrants at the turn of the century. The archives include the Polish American Collection, Polish Architecture and Folk-Art Photograph Collection, Polish Genealogical Society of Massachusetts Collection, Polish Jubilee Catalogs and Souvenirs, Polish Soldiers Relief Correspondence and Polish Women's Club of Three Rivers Records. Also available are such unusual items as the Michael Kislo notebooks of folk poems and drawings, the Edward Borkowski diary (written when he was ninety-nine years old), the Lesinski collection of more than two hundred postcards and photographs, the Jozef Obrebski "Polesie" papers and photographs, and the St. Kazimierz Society records from the years 1904-1919. For hours and additional information contact the Slavic and European librarian. **www.library.umass.edu**

Our Lady of Częstochowa Church, Boston, MA (Gavin Moulton)

BOSTON

Our Lady of Częstochowa Church

The unquestionable heart of Boston's Polish Triangle is Our Lady of Częstochowa on the South Side at 655 Dorchester Avenue. Though established as the first Polish parish in Boston in 1893, it has survived many changes. At the behest of railway companies in 1899, the original structure was turned around

Boston's Polish Triangle

Since the late 1800s part of Boston on the South Side has been synonymous with Poles, so much so that an entire district just south of the Andrews T-Stop is known as the Polish Triangle. Visitors to the Polish Triangle will find a Polish deli and restaurant nearby (Café Polonia, famously visited by Guy Fieri). Each year a Polish Festival is hosted here at the beginning of May by the **Polish American Citizens Club** located at 82 Boston Street (www.polishclubboston.com) just down the street from Our Lady of Czestochowa Church. The Club was established in 1923 and today has a vibrant young membership of recent Polish immigrants. One monument of note in the Triangle is the 1963 Pulaski statue just in front of the Polish Club.

and moved due to changes in the street plan. Today's white clapboard structure with a large reproduction of the Black Madonna above the entrance dates only to the 1970s when a fire destroyed much of the previous church. In contrast to the somber exterior, the inside of the present church features colorful patriotic murals with angels and famous Polish saints. **www. ourladyofczestochowa.com**

The Partisans Sculpture

A 23-foot-high and 33-foot-long sculpture by the Polish American sculptor Andrzej Pitynski can be found near the Convention Center next to the World Trade Center T station. This modern aluminum sculpture, executed in 1979, depicts five riders and their gaunt horses, symbolic of the Polish anti-communist underground fighters who fought against the communist takeover of Poland after World War II. The horsemen have their heads bowed and carry their spears on their backs, conveying the themes of crucifixion and sacrifice. It is dedicated to freedom fighters worldwide.

The Partisans Sculpture, Boston, MA (Kraktraffic CC BY-SA 4.0)

Tadeusz Kosciuszko Statue
In the Boston Public Garden (Boston Commons) there is a statue of General Tadeusz Kosciuszko, the Revolutionary War hero. Boston's statue was erected to commemorate the 150th anniversary of Kosciuszko's enlistment into the American Revolution Continental army. The work was completed by Theo Ruggles Kitson. This bronze creation portrays the general in military attire, holding plans for the yet to be built West Point Academy. He stands at the Boylston Street entrance to the Boston Public Gardens, within viewing distance from the state house. Funds for its development were raised by Poles and Polish Americans throughout New England.

Statue of Tadeusz Kosciuszko, Boston Public Garden, Boston, MA (Kenneth C. Zirkel)

CAMBRIDGE
Tadeusz Kosciuszko and Kazimierz Pulaski Markers
Two stone markers with brass plaques with inscriptions are found on the Cambridge Commons: one is dedicated to Kosciuszko and the second to Pulaski. They were erected in 1934 by Cambridge Citizens of Polish Extraction.

Kosciuszko and Pulaski markers, Cambridge, MA (Bill Coughlin)

CHELSEA
St. Stanislaus Bishop and Martyr Church
The largest Polish church in Eastern Massachusetts, St. Stanislaus Bishop and Martyr at 171 Chestnut Street, has a Romanesque brick façade with two twin towers. The parish built the current structure after the 1908 Chelsea fire turned the building and much of the city to ashes. The new church was designed by noted ecclesiastical architect Edward T.P. Graham, who worked on projects throughout the Northeast and as far west as Ohio. Inside, the tripartite altar features a central statue of the church's patron, St. Stanislaus Kostka. Sadly the parish closed as of August 30, 2020, when the final Mass was said there, but is open for special commemorations.

The nearby 1931 **Pulaski Monument** sits in front of the county courthouse and was constructed at the initiative of St. Stanislaus parishioners.

CHICOPEE
Holy Mother of the Rosary Polish National Catholic Church
Like many older Polish National Catholic churches, Holy Mother of the Rosary first separated from the Roman Catholic Church and became an Independent Catholic Church in 1897 and later joined the Polish National Catholic Church in 1912. The church was one of the founding organizations of the Kosciuszko Foundation (*See* New York City, NY: Kosciuszko Foundation) established by one of its parishioners, Dr. Stephen P. Mizwa. His grave is located in the parish cemetery which dates back to 1897. The parish at 26 Bell Street still celebrates Polish religious customs and Polish themed events. **hmrpncc.org**

*Polish Center of Discovery & Learning,
Chicopee, MA (John Skibiski)*

Polish Center of Discovery & Learning

In 1999, a former brick library building on the campus of Elms College was transformed into the Polish Center of Discovery and Learning. Beginning with Polish immigration to the American colonies, the Center illuminates the succeeding four centuries of Polish life in Europe and America including everything from the reconstruction of a country cabin to military flags and newspapers. A unique strength of the collection is its gallery of traditional Polish folk clothing, with over sixteen regions represented. For visitors, residents, and Elm College students, the calendar of year-round events, lectures, and classes helps to keep Polish heritage alive in Western Massachusetts. The center also houses the Polish Genealogical Society of Massachusetts. **www.polishcenter.net**

Dom Narodowy Polski / Polish National Home, Chicopee, MA (Frank Szelag)

Polish National Home / Dom Narodowy Polski

The Polish National Home (PNH) is a five-story masonry building at 144 Cabot Street with steel I-beam framing. It was constructed from 1912-14 in the Georgian colonial revival style and has been changed little since then. It is on the National Register of Historic Places. The PNH was organized as a fraternal service organization catering to the needs of the local Polish immigrant and Polish-American communities. Chicopee had seen an explosive growth in its Polish population as Chicopee's textile industry employed most of the Polish immigrants. The main building provided social meeting spaces, a library, and assembly hall. The adjacent brick building was built in 1924, designed by local architect George Dion, to provide athletic facilities for the members' use. The PNH was significant as a focus of social life for Chicopee's Polish population for many years. Today the buildings house the Polish National Home Café and units of affordable housing known as "Dom Narodowy Polski Apartments." **www.dompolski-apts.com**

St. Stanislaus Bishop & Martyr Basilica

Since its establishment in 1891, this parish community has been served continuously by Polish or Polish-American priests. The present church at 566 Front Street was constructed in 1908 and named a minor basilica in 1991 by St. Pope John Paul II. The connection to ancestral culture can be seen throughout the cathedral-like brownstone basilica in the Baroque revival style. The wooden altar, sculpted by Francis Szumal, features a central icon of Our Lady of Częstochowa flanked by statues of saints. On the nave ceiling, there is a large painting of St. Stanislaus in the center surrounded with stained-glass clerestory windows of portraits of nine Polish saints including Blessed Salomea, St. Adalbert, and St. Hedwig. The church was built with donations from Polish laborers working for low wages in the dangerous conditions of local cotton mills. Weekly Mass is in Polish. **www.ststansbasilica.org**

EASTHAMPTON
General Casimir Pulaski Monument
This 1929 Pulaski Monument stands over six feet tall and was installed in Pulaski Park on the 150th anniversary of the death of General Pulaski. Reflecting traditional Polish iconography, there is a white eagle and olive branches underneath the Polish and American flags etched into the granite slab.

FALL RIVER
Kosciuszko Square Monument
The Kosciuszko Square monument stands in a small triangle at the intersection of South Main, East Main, and Hamlet Streets, in a historically Polish neighborhood. This monument was first dedicated in 1950, and a special plaque concerning the Revolutionary War general was installed forty years later on the 173rd anniversary of Kosciuszko's death. The monument is 22 feet tall, very ornate, and a focal point of Polish American cultural activity in Fall River.

HOLYOKE
Pulaski Park
Designed by the landscape designers Olmstead Brothers, who did hundreds of urban parks, Prospect Park was built around a bend in the Connecticut River at the turn of the century. In recognition of the growing Polish population in the surrounding neighborhood, the park was renamed after General Casimir Pulaski in 1939 and a small monument to him was installed.

General Casimir Pulaski Monument, Easthampton, MA
(John Skibiski)

Kosciuszko Square Monument, Fall River, MA
(John Skibiski)

Bread and Roses Heritage Festival / Everett Cotton Mill Strike
When the Everett Cotton Mill reduced their wages, Polish women in the textile town of Lawrence began what would become one of the world's most influential and famous strikes. The textile strike of 1912 is known as the "Bread and Roses" strike, a reference to the workers' twin demands for higher wages and higher quality of life. What began with Polish women at the Everett Cotton Mill eventually spread to over 25,000 workers across the city. The strikers organized across ethnic boundaries and kept a nine-week strike during a bitterly cold winter. The strike was successful and resulted in wage increases of 5 to 25 percent not just in Lawrence, but across New England. The mills are still standing along with the Lawrence Heritage Park Visitor Center which has exhibits about the history of Lawrence. Each year since 1986 on Labor Day, the Bread and Roses Heritage Festival commemorates this history and the Polish culture through music, theater, dance, and art.
www.breadandrosesheritage.org

LUDLOW
Polish American Citizens Club
Since 1914, this club at 355 East Street has promoted political discussions and promotes Polish heritage through various events. The club serves meals and has a full bar with polka dancing on the weekend. **pacc-ludlow.com**

MARBLEHEAD
General Casimir Pulaski Monument
On July 23, 1777, Casimir Pulaski arrived in Massachusetts to aid the struggling American revolutionary soldiers. A small bronze plaque placed in 1989 close to the intersection of Front Street and Fort Sewall Terrace commemorates the spot where the General stepped onto American shores.

NORTHAMPTON
Grave of a Polish Exile, Bridge Street Cemetery
The Polish exile August Antoni Jakubowski was a son of the romantic poet Antoni Malczewski. He was a young revolutionary who participated in the Polish insurrection of 1831. After the failed revolution, he came to the United States as an exile in 1834. He learned English and authored a book, *The Remembrances of a Polish Exile,* and taught French at Miss Dwight's Seminary in Northampton. At the age of twenty-one, he died from what likely was tuberculosis of the spine. Being penniless, he was buried in a pauper's grave in Bridge Street Cemetery (156 Bridge Street) with a special gravestone purchased by his students.

Pulaski Monument, Northampton, MA
(John Skibiski)

General Casimir Pulaski Monument
The Pulaski Monument in Pulaski Park commemorates the famous general with a medallion of his likeness sporting a feather in his cap. The granite monument was constructed by the town's Polish citizens in 1929 and sits on Main Street between City Hall and the historic Academy of Music Theater.

St. Valentine's Polish National Catholic Church
Dedicated by Bishop Hodur himself, St. Valentine's is a small brick church at 127 King Street that was built in 1931. Inside, a trefoil arch above the apse proclaims *Chwała Na Wysokości Bogu,* or Glory to God in the Highest. Just over the lettering of the arch is a painting of the symbol of the Polish National Catholic Church with its characteristic book, cross, sun, and palm. Bilingual Mass is celebrated along with yearly Christmas carols in Polish and commemorations of Constitution Day. **stvalentinespncc.com**

SALEM
St. John Paul II Shrine of Divine Mercy
The Shrine, formerly known as St. John the Baptist Church, at 28 St. Peter Street promotes devotion to Divine Mercy which is closely identified with the Polish Pope. The shrine displays a reliquary with the blood of St. Pope John Paul II given by Poland's Cardinal Dziwisz. The parish holds Polish Masses and actively promotes Polish religious traditions and sponsors an annual Polish Festival.

   The Stefan Starzynski Polish Legion of American Veterans (PLAV) Post #55 has its building nearby and provides food, drinks, and entertainment. **www.jpiidivinemercyshrine.org**

St. Joseph Hall, Salem Maritime National Historic Site
Although most often associated with the colonial-era witch trials, Salem is also home to a sizeable Polish community. One of the first Poles in Massachusetts was Hugh Laski (Laskin) who came to Salem in 1637. Today the story of the city's Poles is on permanent display in the first-floor windows of St. Joseph's Hall, a mutual aid building from 1909 that is now the headquarters for the Salem Maritime National Historic Site. The photographs on display offer a look into the rich cultural and culinary traditions of Salem's Polonia—Easter banquets, grand weddings, and ceremonies of the "Hussars" paramilitary drill team. Derby Street, where the hall is located, was for many years an ethnically Polish neighborhood next to the city's docks. Workers settled here due to proximity to the leather and textile plants. Low wages and automation led to the 1933 Pequot Mills strike, a wildcat strike led by Polish women who felt the union did not advocate for their interests. The Naumkeag Cotton Mill as it was formally known is closed, but the building survives at the Shetland Office Park. **www.nps.gov/sama/index.htm**

THREE RIVERS
Sts. Peter and Paul Church
The roots of Sts. Peter and Paul Church are with the St. Joseph Men's Society of Thorndike that was founded in 1895. The new church at 2267 Main Street opened in 1905 in Four Corners, a location equidistant from the four nearby villages where Poles lived. Although the wooden church's exterior is in a staid New England colonial style, the interior is an exuberant Baroque style. In 1954, the church was redecorated and altars were donated by the Rosary Sodality and St. Joseph Society. The present altar for Our Lady of Częstochowa was created in 1976 and several years later in 1980 the Divine Mercy Grotto was constructed. A unique feature of the parish is that many of its historic societies, established over a century ago, continue to operate. In 2009, the parish merged with St. Anne's to form Divine Mercy Parish at the site of Sts. Peter and Paul. There are Masses in Polish and English. **www.churchofdivinemercy.org**

TURNERS FALLS
Chapel of Mary Queen of the Polish Martyrs of World War II
Located in St. Mary's Cemetery on Turners Falls Road, the chapel was constructed in 2012 in the style of the Polish highlander carpentry. It was designed by Fr. Charles DiMascola and modeled after the Jaszczurówka Chapel in Zakopane, Poland. The chapel was funded and built by 88-year-old Our Lady of Częstochowa parishioner Lawrence Krejmas. Its centerpiece is an icon of Our Lady of Częstochowa with the martyrs of World War II depicted underneath her mantle.

Our Lady of Czestochowa Church
The first Polish Mass was celebrated in Turners Falls in 1909, although Poles have been present in the town since 1885. Fr. Franciszek Chałupka, who was one of the most important religious figures in early New England Polonia, oversaw the establishment of the church in 1912 shortly before his death. A new Gothic church at 84 K Street was constructed for the congregation in 1929 and designed by architect Donat R. Baribault. Polish traditions continue at the parish with *Gorzkie Żale* during Lent and Forty Hours Devotions held in September. An ornate icon of Our Lady of Częstochowa is in the large altarpiece behind the main altar.

Nearby, two parish societies hold monthly meetings in their own halls which also have a bar and clubhouse: **St. Stanislaus Society Hall** was founded in 1911 as Lodge 549 of the Polish Roman Catholic Union of America, while **St. Kazimierz Society Hall** was established in 1904 by thirty families with the intention of creating a Polish church. The Societies' archives from 1904-84 are held at the special collections of the University of Massachusetts at Amherst.

St. Joseph Basilica, Webster, MA
(Christopher Siuzdak, J.C.L. & Mary Castellano)

WEBSTER
St. Joseph Basilica

St. Joseph Basilica was the earliest church constructed by Polish immigrants in New England; it was founded in 1887. Since then, the community had experienced growth culminating in the erection of the current magnificent brick church in 1954 at 53 Whitcomb Street. The contributions of the church to Polonia were recognized in 1998, when Pope John Paul II, whose statue is seen on a pedestal outside, recognized it with the title of Basilica. The school is run by the Polish order of Congregation of the Felician Sisters, and it was their first missionary establishment. There is a Polish Saturday School, and Masses and services in Polish as well as an annual Polish Festival. **saintjosephbasilica.com**

WORCESTER
Our Lady of Częstochowa Church

In 1894, Poles and Lithuanians in Worcester joined together to form St. Casimir's Church. As the Polish population grew, another church became necessary. Fr. Moneta, a priest from Orchard Lake, was dispatched and the congregation purchased property for a new church, Our Lady of Częstochowa (34 Ward Street). The St. Francis of Assisi and St. Michael the Archangel Societies formed in 1896 and 1898, respectively, and were essential to the growth of the parish. Their prominent role is reflected in donations of side altars featuring their patrons. The church venerates a first-class relic of St. Maximilian Kolbe in a side chapel and many Polish saints are represented in stained-glass windows, among them St. Pope John Paul II, St. Maximilian Kolbe, Our Lady of Ostrabrama. Famous visitors to the church include Ignacy Jan Paderewski, General Józef Haller, General Thaddeus Bór-Komorowski, Poland's last pre-war prime minister Stanisław Mikołajczyk, and President Harry Truman. The church continues to sponsor a Polish school.
www.olcworcester.com

MICHIGAN

ANN ARBOR

Copernicus Center for Polish Studies, University of Michigan

The Copernicus Center for Polish Studies offers lectures, symposia, and films that are accessible to the public. The Center also offers mini-courses, Polish language instruction, undergraduate and graduate student fellowships, study abroad opportunities, and an annual newsletter (*Koperni-kana*). The Center has close collaborations with numerous educational and cultural institutions in Poland, including universities in Gdańsk, Kraków, and Warsaw, as well as POLIN: The Museum of the History of Polish Jews and the Adam Mickiewicz Institute. Together with the University's Jean & Samuel Frankel Center for Judaic Studies, the Center offers a rich array of lectures, symposia, films, and other events to which the public is invited. They also offer courses in Polish studies. **ii.umich.edu/polish/about-us.html**

BAY CITY

St. Stanislaus Kostka Church

Our Lady of Częstochowa is a Roman Catholic parish that highlights the shared Polish heritage of Bay City's South End. The parish combines two historic parishes, representing over 125 years of Catholic tradition: St. Stanislaus Kostka and St. Hyacinth. The neo-Gothic Church of St. Stanislaus Kostka at 1503 Kosciuszko Avenue, which is the parish church and parish center, features a shrine and stained-glass window to the church's namesake and has a shrine to Our Lady of Częstochowa. The Polish refugees who escaped from the Prussian dominated part of Poland settled here and in 1874 formed a society under the patronage of Saint Stanislaus Kostka and then built a wooden church in 1874. It was replaced with the current large church which was dedicated in 1892. As the parish continued to grow, it purchased additional land and dedicated a new church and school in 1907, naming it after another Polish saint, St. Hyacinth. St. Stanislaus is recognized as a state historical site and a plaque in front of the church gives its history.

St. Stanislaus Kostka Church, Bay City, MI (OLC Parish)

In 2014, as part of the Saginaw Diocese plan, St. Stanislaus Kostka and St. Hyacinth parishes merged into the new combined parish of Our Lady of Częstochowa, which continues to honor their heritage with Mass in Polish and an annual Polish Festival. The Tri-City Polish Heritage Society is affiliated with the parish. **www.baycityolc.com**

DECKERVILLE

Białowieża Scout Camp of General Kazimierz Pulaski

Located near Lake Huron, Białowieża is a large 92-acre camp with buildings dedicated in 1964 to create space for camp activities for Polish Scouting. The camp is named after the famous national park

Białowieża Scout Camp, Deckerville, MI (Teresa Wiacek)

Cross Village's Legs Inn

Located on a bluff overlooking the wide expanse of Lake Michigan at 6425 North Lake Shore Drive, Cross Village's Legs Inn is a lovely restaurant, bar and music venue that was built by Polish immigrant Stanley Smolak in the late 1920s and opened in the 1930s. Stanley immigrated to the U.S. from Kamionka, Poland, in 1912 and worked in Detroit and Chicago auto plants before he moved to Cross Village, Michigan, in 1921. The interior of the restaurant is full of wood and stone carvings that are the original work of Stanley Smolak, and the Legs Inn gets its name from all the old stove legs that adorn its front roofline. It caters to tourists from all over the Midwest, and since its opening, it has become one of the iconic Michigan eateries, a must stop for all northern Michigan visitors. Operated today by George Smolak (Stanley's nephew) and George's wife, Kasia, the Legs Inn is open from mid-May to mid-October and is famous for its Polish cuisine as well as draft Polish beers. **www.legsinn.com**

(Marian Krzyzowski)

in Poland, a UNESCO World Heritage site, with primeval forests and the world's largest population of European bison.

The Polish Scout movement came to the state in the 1950's with post-war immigrants and they wanted to find a secluded area for scouting events. Over the years tens of thousands of scouts from all over the world have come together here. In addition to scouting activities, various Polish organizations hold retreats, meetings, and seminars. Many Polish families have bought lots in the immediate vicinity, forming a community of scouting enthusiasts and supporters.

DETROIT

Kosciuszko Statue

This large bronze equestrian statue of Tadeusz Kosciuszko located in the downtown area near the MGM Grand Hotel was a gift from Poland to the city of Detroit. It was cast in Poland and then dedicated in 1978 in honor of the American Bicentennial. It is a replica cast of the statue at the Wawel Castle in Kraków, Poland, which was created by Leonard Marconi.

Kosciuszko statue, Detroit, MI (Leonard Kniffel)

Mother of Divine Mercy Parish:
The Sweetest Heart of Mary and St. Josaphat Churches

Located half-a-mile apart, the Sweetest Heart of Mary Church (4440 Russell Street) and St. Josaphat Church (715 East Canfield Street) were built in 1893 and 1901 respectively, when the Polish community in Detroit was rapidly growing. After World War II, freeways cut through the

St. Josaphat Church with Sweetest Heart of Mary Church in background, Detroit, MI (Alina Klin)

neighborhoods and started the process of the depopulation of the city, which intensified after the Detroit riots of 1967. Both churches experienced dwindling numbers of parishioners but survived the parish closings during the 1990s. The two parishes merged into the new Mother of Divine Mercy Parish in 2013. At present over 90 percent of the parishioners live in the suburbs, while approximately 30 percent of them are of Polish descent.

St. Josaphat Church's focus is the High Altar Tabernacle with three shields behind it that represent the partitions of Poland. An Our Lady of Częstochowa icon, which touched the original icon in Poland, has hung above the altar since 1900. Two murals in the front of the church are called the "Miracle on the Vistula" and "Prayer Pilgrimage to Częstochowa."

A plaque on the front of The Sweetest Heart of Mary Church tells the history of the church whose stained-glass windows won awards at the 1893 Chicago Columbian Exposition. The annual Sweetest Heart of Mary Pierogi Festival is the biggest parish social event, bringing in thousands of people from all over metropolitan Detroit, as well as from out of state.
www.motherofdivinemercy.org

Nicolaus Copernicus Monument
A large bronze bust on a marble pedestal, sculpted by Ferenc Varga, was dedicated in 1973 to commemorate the 500th anniversary of the birth of Polish astronomer Nicolaus Copernicus. It stands next to the large and impressive Detroit Public Library at 5201 Woodward Avenue.

Nicolaus Copernicus monument, Detroit, MI (John Bukowczyk)

Detroit Cigar Factories

Polish women were the backbone of Detroit's once prosperous cigar industry. However, they were often paid less than half of their male counterparts and faced sexual harassment and poor working conditions. This led to a first strike in 1916. In February 1937, after wages were slashed during the Great Depression, the majority-women workers held a 66-day sit-down strike that was inspired by the UAW strike in Flint. The network of the Polish neighborhood and shared language helped the women to organize, utilizing the Dom Polski as a center, and benefitting from the skill of Polish trade unionist and future state senator Stanley Nowak. The police responded to the strike harshly. The women persevered and in conjunction with the UAW held the largest rally in state history on March 24, 1937, at Cadillac Square, with some estimates at 250,000 attendees. The workers formed their own cigar union in May after the end of the strike. Two factories from the era survive: San Telmo Manufacturing Company No. 2 (5715 Michigan Ave.) that was built in 1910 and designed by Albert Kahn, currently housing a community health clinic; and the Mazer-Cressman Factory (5031 Grandy St.) presently a building of the Department of Human Services.

Polish Heritage Room at Wayne State University

The Polish Heritage Room, one of fourteen Wayne State University Ethnic Heritage Rooms, is located on the ground floor of Alex Manoogian Hall. Most of the room's artwork and furnishings were made in Poland, including: a marble and granite mosaic depicting kings of Poland; the metal relief tribute to Nicolaus Copernicus; the wooden ceiling depicting King Jan III Sobieski and his generals; stained-glass windows with portraits of Maria Skłodowska-Curie, Casimir Pulaski and Thaddeus Kosciuszko; and tapestries with the Black Madonna of Częstochowa, a white eagle, and the Wawel Sigismund Chapel. The newest additions to the room are a case dedicated to Polish American musician Ted Gomulka, and a portrait bust of Marie Skłodowska-Curie, sculpted by

Evelyn Bachorski-Bowman. The Sculpture, commissioned by WSU and with a gift from Steven and Linda Plochocki, was installed in the room in 2018. The room was dedicated May 3, 1986. Professor Wiktor Zin, a Polish architect designed the room. The Polish Room now serves as a student study lounge.

Tapestries, Polish Heritage Room at Wayne State University, Detroit, MI (Alina Klin)

General Casimir Pulaski Heritage Monument

Erected in the downtown area at the intersection of Washington Boulevard and Michigan Avenue by the Central Citizens Committee, this monument was dedicated in 1966 for the 400,000 Americans of Polish descent living in the Detroit Metropolitan area with a Pontifical Mass celebrated by Stefan Cardinal Wyszynski, Primate of Poland.

St. Albertus Church

The church of St. Albertus Parish (4231 St. Aubin), the oldest Polish parish in Detroit, was finished in 1885 and includes Polish iconography. In 1990, the parish was closed due to the depopulation of the city, and since 1991 St. Albertus Church has been in the care of the Polish American Historical Site Association (PAHSA), which purchased the church along with the parish buildings from the Archdiocese of Detroit for a symbolic $1.00, saving them from demolition. Although the church does not provide regular weekly services, PAHSA volunteers, in cooperation with the archdiocese, organizes unique events in the church every month. In addition to masses and lenten prayers, *Gorzkie Żale*, which are said in English with Polish music, they also hold special dinners, picnics, Polish Christmas Eve midnight mass (*Pasterka*), and a festive Polish heritage mass with a procession and attended by Polish dance schools in October. **www.stalbertusdetroit.org**

St. Francis D'Assisi Church

St. Francis is a Baroque church at 4500 Wesson Street constructed of Malvern brick from 1903-05 and designed by architect Henry Engelbert. On the pediment above the entrance is a Polish eagle, flanked above on either side with emblems representing Ruthenia and Lithuania. The interior is remarkably well-preserved with an altar that is a smaller version of the church's façade, historic lighting, and the original floors. The church recently celebrated its 125th anniversary and many Polish customs such as making *chruściki, Gorzkie Żale,* and blessing Easter baskets are practiced. Private tours of the church are available by prior arrangement with the parish office. Since 2013 this parish has been part of a joint parish with St. Hedwig Parish (*see below*).
www.stfrancis-sthedwig.org
toursh.stfrancis-sthedwig.org/default.htm#second *(for a virtual tour)*

Pulaski Heritage Monument, Detroit, MI (Alexander Clegg)

St. Hedwig Church

As the Polish population of Detroit expanded, it was necessary to construct a church in the vicinity of St. Francis d'Assisi. The present St. Hedwig Church at 3245 Junction Street was built in a Romanesque style from 1911-1916 and designed by Harry J. Rill. There are two soaring clock towers and a central niche with a statue of St. Hedwig on the façade. The vaulted interior has the original *Scagliola* high altar made by the Daprato Altar Company which includes a statue of St. Hedwig. The intricate stained-glass windows include several Polish saints including St. Casimir, Blessed Bronisława, and Mother of God of Tarnów. There is a more recent mural of St. Maximilian Kolbe. The parish was served by the Franciscans for over eighty years and is now joined with St. Francis D'Assisi Parish (*see page 91*). **www.stfrancis-sthedwig.org** **toursh.stfrancis-sthedwig.org/default.htm#second** (*for a virtual tour*)

St. Hyacinth Church

Located in the Poletown neighborhhood of Detroit at 3151 Farnsworth Avenue, St. Hyacinth's was established in 1907. The present Byzantine-Romanesque-style church was built from 1922-1924 and was intended to be the grandest church in the city. It was designed by Donaldson and Meier architects in a style inspired by the pastor's visit to the new Cathedral of St. Louis and the interior of Sts. Peter and Paul Church in Oberammergau, Germany. Paintings of Polish saints adorn the central apse. In 1988, St. Hyacinth was listed in the State of Michigan's Historical Site Registry. A large historical plaque on the outside of the church outlines the history of the Polish community in the founding of the parish. In 2001 as part of celebrations of Detroit's tricentennial, local artist Dennis Orlowski painted a mural in the back of the church displaying six historic Polish churches of the area and Polish customs such as *Wigilia*. Polish religious customs continue to be celebrated. **sainthyacinth.com**

St. Hyacinth Church, Detroit, MI (Colter J Sikora)

St. Stanislaus Bishop and Martyr Church

St. Stanislaus Parish was established in 1898 and the present Baroque church at 5818 Dubois Street was built from 1911-1913, measuring 190 feet by 95 feet. The architect was Harry J. Rill, who also designed St. Hedwig's. Two resplendent towers feature open arches with a dodecagonal domed metal lantern. Over the years projects such as the construction of I-94 and demolition of the Poletown neighborhood damaged the social fabric that sustained the church, leading to its closure in 1989. Since the closure, the building has housed another congregation, but it is currently vacant. The immense architectural value of the complex was recognized with the designation of the St. Stanislaus Historic District on the National Register of Historic Places in 1989.

St. Stanislaus Bishop and Martyr Church, Detroit, MI (Andrew Jameson)

West Side Dom Polski

The Dom Polski at 3426 Junction Avenue is an icon of west side Detroit's Polonia. It served as a social and cultural hub from the early 20th century throughout the 1960s. Built in two stages, in 1916-1917 and 1925, the building was designed by Polish-born architect Joseph Julius Gwizdowski. It boasted an auditorium with galleries, a seating capacity of 1,000, and a fully equipped stage. The rear portion of the building, consisting of three levels of office space, was dedicated on July 5, 1917. The remainder of the structure was completed in 1925. For decades, it was considered the pride of Junction Avenue. The second cornerstone of the Dom Polski reads *Jedność i zgoda to siła nasza* (Unity and Harmony are Our Strength). A pair of Ionic columns support a portico frieze above the Dom Polski's doors, which bears the inscription *Dom Polski z jedność towarzystw* (loosely translated, Dom Polski United Societies).

*West Side Dom Polski, Detroit, MI
(Laurie E. Gomulka Palazzolo)*

   The West Side Detroit Polish American Historical Society was responsible for obtaining a listing for the west side Dom Polski in the National Register of Historic Places in 2006.
www.detroitpolonia.org *(menu>significant sites>West Side Dom Polski)*

St. Stanislaus Church, Dorr, MI (Rossograph CC BY-SA-4.0)

DORR
St. Stanislaus Church

This small country church at 1871 136th Avenue was constructed by Polish and Kashubian farmers in 1892. The foundation was made from local field stones and the bricks were carted on sleighs by horses from a brickyard about eighteen miles away in Hamilton. Stained-glass windows were added in 1910. However, the roots of the parish date to 1876 when the St. Stanislaus and Rosary Societies were formed. The parish school was served by Felician sisters for slightly over a century and remains active. In the interior, there are three altars: a central altar with a statue of St. Stanislaus and side altars dedicated to the Virgin Mary and the Sacred Heart. Historic banners of the St. Stanislaus and Holy Rosary Sodalities from 1876 are displayed. The grave of noted Polonia author Fr. Stanislaus Iciek is in the surrounding cemetery. Every year, in mid-August, the Polish Festival attracts visitors from around the country. St. Stanislaus is now part of a joint parish with Sacred Heart Parish in Allegan.
st-stanschurch.net

Hamtramck

Hamtramck, Michigan, is a 2.2-square-mile city surrounded by the city of Detroit. Originally a farming community, Hamtramck was changed forever when it became the site of the Dodge main auto plant in 1914. Tens of thousands of immigrants from all over the world flocked here for work. Until the 1990s Hamtramck was dominated demographically and politically by Poles. Despite an increasingly diverse population, including many Muslims from Yemen and Bangladesh, signs of Polishness are still apparent throughout the city. This includes churches, institutions (such as the Polish American Congress-Michigan Division and the Piast Institute),

veterans' groups (such as Polonia, Polish Village, and just over the Detroit border Krakus), bars, bakeries, and grocery stores. The Polish language is still spoken on Hamtramck's streets and at its businesses. A walk around Hamtramck will also reveal Polish street names, public monuments, and murals, including the Kraków mural at Pope Park and the Polish Highlander mural at Joseph Campau and Evaline Streets. Renowned for its Pączki Day festivities, the city also holds an annual Labor Day Festival that includes a Polish Day Parade.

One of the murals in Hamtramck, MI
(Karen Majewski)

HAMTRAMCK
Piast Institute

The Piast Institute at 11633 Joseph Campau Avenue is a non-profit founded by Dr. Thaddeus Radzilowski and Ms. Virginia Skrzyniarz in 2003. It is one of the few brick-and-mortar think tanks in the country devoted to the research of Poland and Polish-American affairs. The Piast

Institute maintains an extensive archive of books, photos, and publications related to Poland, as well as many documents and artifacts documenting the history of Hamtramck and surrounding areas. The Piast Institute commits its resources to creating seminars, publications, and research on Poland and Polish-Americans.

The Institute is housed in the historic Pieronek Photo Studio which was established by Paul Pieronek shortly after his immigration from Poland in 1906 and relocated to Hamtramck in 1923. Paul Pieronek and his family captured photographically the many

Pieronek Photo Studio/ Piast Institute, Hamtramck, MI
(Alexander Clegg)

people and places of Hamtramck and Detroit throughout the 20th century, documenting Hamtramck's rise as a city of immigrants. His photography includes some of the earliest photographs of an urbanized Hamtramck and is of crucial importance to the area's history. The studio closed in 2002, and the building was donated to the Piast Institute in 2007. Pieronek's photographs and materials are preserved and maintained by the Piast Institute. **piastinstitute.org**

St. Florian Church

St. Florian Church at 2626 Poland Street is Hamtramck's cathedral, visually dominating the landscape and providing a cultural anchor for the city's Polonia. The original church was dedicated in 1909. But as the growing auto industry attracted tens of thousands of Polish immigrants to the city, architect Ralph Adams Cram designed a new building in the Gothic style. *American Architect* magazine named it "best new church building" of 1929. Cardinal Karol Wojtyla of Kraków, the future Pope John Paul II, celebrated Mass at St. Florian in 1969.

St. Florian today is served by the Society of Christ order of Polish priests (as is Our Lady of Częstochowa in suburban Sterling Heights). In addition to regular Polish Masses, this very active parish supports a Polish language school, folk dance ensemble, and contemporary Catholic music group, as well as numerous dances and festivals throughout the year. In the church hall a large mural by Dennis Orlowski chronicles the history of Poland.

St. Florian Church, Hamtramck, MI (Karen Majewski)

Joining St. Florian Parish to serve the Polish religious community in this 2.2-square-mile city are St. Ladislaus (now a chapel of St. Florian), Our Lady Queen of the Apostles, and Holy Cross Polish National Catholic Church. **www.stflorianparish.org**

St. Pope John Paul II Statue

In a small city park at Belmont Street, and Joseph Campau Avenue in Hamtramck's central business district stands a 10-foot bronze statue of Karol Wojtyła, St. Pope John Paul II. Erected in 1982, the statue and its 18-foot base were created by sculptors Ferenc Varga and Bruno Nowicki. Flanking the statue is a large mural depicting Kraków's Main Market Square by resident artist Dennis Orlowski. The Pope himself passed by the statue on his way to conduct Mass in Hamtramck in 1987. (A smaller monument to the Pope's visit stands at the corner

St. Pope John Paul II statue and mural depicting Kraków's Main Market Square, Hamtramck, MI (Karen Majewski)

Mural depicting Poles at Hamtramck Historical Museum, MI (Karen Majewski)

of Jos. Campau and Hewitt Streets.) Early on, the statue was the subject of disputes over its legal ownership and financing. But at home in "Pope Park," it has become a site for public events, including recitations of the rosary, historical commemorations, and community rallies.

Hamtramck Historical Museum

Housed in the city's first department store building at 9525 Joseph Campau Avenue, the Hamtramck Historical Museum opened in 2013. Although it represents all aspects of Hamtramck's history and ethnic makeup, visitors will find a treasure trove of Polonian artifacts, documents, and exhibits, reflecting the fact that, until recently, the city was dominated demographically and politically by Poles. The museum is a destination for tour groups, hosts regular lectures, workshops, and presentations, and contains a small gift shop.

Basilica of St. Adalbert, Grand Rapids, MI (Barbara Rylko-Bauer)

A mural depicting Hamtramck's major ethnic groups, including Poles, wraps around the museum's walls. Among other topics, recent events have focused on local Polish immigrant photo studios, Hamtramck's historically vibrant bars and nightclubs, and World War II as experienced by city residents. In addition, the museum has offered *pisanki* (decorated Easter eggs) workshops attended by a cross-section of Hamtramck's ethnic groups. Permanent exhibits depict local businesses, home and family life, political figures, cultural events, and other aspects of life in this working-class immigrant community.

The Hamtramck Historical Museum is open to the public. Access can also be arranged by request at the adjacent Polish Art Center during regular business hours. **hamtramckhistory.com**

GRAND RAPIDS
Basilica of St. Adalbert

The St. Adalbert Aid Society was started in 1872 to help newly arrived Polish settlers with housing and employment. As the number of settlers grew, they built a small wooden church in 1881.

Grand Rapids Polish Casinos and Halls

There are fourteen Polish and Lithuanian halls, dating back to the late 1800s or early 20th century, within a five-mile radius of downtown Grand Rapids and many are in historically interesting buildings. They welcome members and visitors and maintain lively social activities: dinners, outings to Polish American Day at a Detroit Tigers game, Polish cooking classes, and sponsorship of Pulaski Days. For example, St. Adalbert's Aid Society (5th St. Hall)

began in 1872 to support new Polish immigrants and to build the Church. It is now also called a casino as is the building at St. Isidore Church that houses the "Diamond Hall," reflecting how important bingo was for socializing and fund raising. Outside the building, there is a Pulaski Memorial. The former Polish Armory is now the "Sixth Street Hall." The Halls offer a way of maintaining these architectural traces of the Polish American past. For more information, see: **polishheritagesociety.com/polish-lithuania-halls**

St. Isadore Casino with Pulaski Memorial to the left, Grand Rapids, MI (Barbara Rylko-Bauer)

This was the oldest Polish parish in Grand Rapids. Expansions were made to the church as the Polish population continued to grow. In 1892, the Aid Society constructed the St. Adalbert Meeting Hall, which is still in use today. The current limestone church at 654 Davis Avenue NW was constructed between 1907 and 1913. It has a Romanesque Revival edifice with a Byzantine dome. In 1980, the church was elevated to the status of a minor basilica, the first in the state of Michigan. As a reference to the ethnic background of the original founders of the parish, there are five windows in the apse depicting Polish saints: St. Hyacinth, St. Casimir, St. Adalbert, St. Stanislaus Kostka, and St. Hedwig. It is now linked with St. James Church, a historically Irish parish. Nearby is the St. Adalbert Casino built in 1892 which is still in use today. **basilicagr.com**

Polish Falcons Hall

The Polish Falcons Aid Society Grand Rapids chapter, whose motto is "First to fight, first to help out," was founded in 1927 to help Polish immigrants new to the city find work in the furniture factories and gypsum mines, and places to live in the surrounding neighborhood. PFAS helped the large influx of immigrants assimilate, as they did not speak English and were Catholic whereas the city's leadership was Dutch Protestant. At the time, the building at 957 Fulton Street W was in the heart of the old Polish neighborhood, and everyone would walk to the Hall to socialize and hold meetings. In its heyday, during the 1940s through the 1970s, the PFAS of Grand Rapids had more than four hundred members, but as Poles moved out to the suburbs, the building deteriorated, as did the neighborhood. In recent years, a community effort raised funds and renovated the building, which continues to serve as a welcoming place and a supporting organization for its community members. Every August, volunteer members of the PFAS help to organize and staff the annual Dozynki Polish Harvest Festival (sponsored by the Polish Heritage Society) in downtown Grand Rapids, as well as promote Pulaski Days.

Sacred Heart of Jesus Church

This parish owes its origins to the settlement of Polish immigrants in the southwest part of Grand Rapids in the late 1800s, many of whom worked in the local gypsum mines. It was the third such Polish-speaking community of faith in the city. The founding parish priest, Father Ladislaus Krakowski, along with his fledgling community, grew the parish. In 1904, a school, convent, and church complex were dedicated. The original church was replaced with the current building at 156 Valley Avenue SW in 1920, built in the style of Rome's Basilica of St Paul Outside the Walls. **sacredheartgr.org**

Sacred Heart of Jesus Church, Grand Rapids, MI (Mark Levandoski)

St. Isidore the Laborer Church

Polish immigrants also settled in the northeast side of Grand Rapids, finding work in the large brickyards located there. For some years, they and their children walked the three miles to St. Adalbert for church and school, but eventually they formed a building committee and in 1897 work began on a new church, St. Isidore's, on Diamond, near Flat Street. The naming of this church was the center of controversy. Bishop Henry Richter was a German immigrant and proponent of assimilation and felt that parishes should be named after general saints, rather than ethnic-specific saints. The Polish people in the Brickyard neighborhood, under the direction of Father Simon Ponganis, picked St. Stanislaus. However, on the day of the blessing of the cornerstone, Bishop Richter named the church St. Isidore. Within a few years, a larger church was constructed at 628 Diamond Avenue NE and dedicated in 1917. The parish casino building from 1904 still stands near the church. **saintisidorechurch.org**

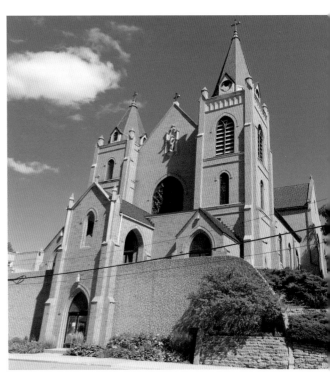

St. Isidore the Laborer Church, Grand Rapids, MI (Barbara Rylko-Bauer)

Stanley Ketchel Memorial

Grand Rapids native Stanley Ketchel (*né* Stanisław Kiecal), the son of Polish immigrants, became a boxing prodigy and held the world middleweight championship title from 1908 until 1910, when he was murdered by gunshot at age 24. Known for his ferocious fighting style that won him the nickname "The Michigan Assassin," he is ranked among the greatest of middleweights. Ketchel is now enshrined in the International Boxing Hall of Fame. There are three memorial sites to Ketchel in his hometown: his gravesite is found in Holy Cross Cemetery, marked by a prominent stone; a plaque in his honor is located at the intersection of Stocking Avenue and 3rd Street; and since 2015 a statue of Ketchel, sculpted by Ann Hirsch, has stood at 438 Bridge Street.

Stanley Ketchel Memorial, Grand Rapids, MI (Mark Levandoski)

KINDE
St. Mary of Czestochowa Church
Although it was built in 1932, St. Mary's (as it is popularly known) at 1709 Moeller Road has a remarkable resemblance to Polish Romanesque churches, with detailed brickwork and a metal lantern over a central tower. This style is owed to Fr. Henry Podsiad, who oversaw its construction. The parish was established in 1902 by Poles looking to have a parish of their own, but who lived in the area since the 1850s. There is a historic marker in front of the church, and it is now one of several worship sites for Annunciation of the Lord Parish.
www.annunciationofthelordparish.weebly.com

LIVONIA
Presentation of the Blessed Virgin Mary Convent and Felician Heritage Center
The Romanesque Presentation of the Blessed Virgin Mary Convent on the campus of Madonna University, with an austere central chapel, was built as the headquarters for the growing Presentation province of the Felician Sisters in 1936. It is one of the ninety convents that were constructed by the order throughout the United States in their mission to serve Polish immigrants. At its height, over eight hundred sisters lived at the convent, and it remains the center of the order outside of Poland. In addition, the campus houses Madonna University, a hospital, senior housing, a high school, hospice, and retreat center all sponsored by the order.

St. Mary of Czestochowa Church, Kinde, MI (Kathy Garmon)

Following the consolidation of all the North American provinces, the sisters' archives will be centralized at the Felician Heritage Center, part of a new admissions building at Madonna University. The centerpiece of the facility is a stained-glass window with the Felician symbol surrounded by the names of the former provinces. **www.madonna.edu**

ORCHARD LAKE
Polish Institute of Culture and Research at Orchard Lake
Originally known as the "Polish Seminary," and then Orchard Lake Schools, this institute currently consists of two main institutions: St. Mary's Preparatory High School and The Polish

Auschwitz Concentration Camp Uniform PASIAK from Auschwitz at Orchard Lake (OLS)

Mission. The third component, Sts. Cyril & Methodius Seminary, founded by Fr. Józef Dąbrowski in 1885, closed at the end of the 2021-2022 academic program.

The campus also includes: The Polish American Liturgical Center, The Center for Studies and Research on Polish Culture, The Chapel of Our Lady of Orchard Lake, The John Paul II Center (established in 1978), and an Archdiocesan Shrine of St. Pope John Paul II. The Polish Mission oversees the archives and library collection belonging to the campus library and museum. The most valuable collections include manuscripts of various personalities and royal letters, especially that of King Jan Kazimierz Vasa to Anna Bordins from 1660. The main part of the collection is memorabilia from World War II, donated by veterans from the 2nd Corps of the Polish Armed Forces, the Home Army (AK), and prisoners of concentration camps. A separate department of the museum is a gallery of paintings, among which are works of outstanding Polish artists such as Juliusz Kossak, Jacek Malczewski, Julian Fałat, Zofia Stryjeńska, Tadeusz Styka, and Jan Komski. The museum also features the Polish Panorama—an interactive display that depicts 106 notable figures in Poland's history, dating from the establishment of the Polish state to modern times. A 6-foot bronze monument to General Józef Haller, a Polish World War I hero, a gift from the Polish government, was installed on campus in 2021 adjacent to the Art Gallery. In conjunction with this, a new monument and headstones are installed at the campus Holy Sepulchre Cemetery to honor fifty-nine Polish American Veterans who fought in Haller's Blue Army.
www.polishmission.com

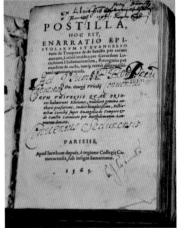

Orchard Lake Polish Institute liturgical book from 1565 (OLS)

POSEN

St. Casimir Church

Polish immigrants arrived in the Presque Ile area in the 1870s from the Prussian partition. The local towns (Posen, Pulaski, Krakow) reflect a strong Polish influence. St. Casimir's started from humble roots in a c.1879 log cabin and today has a modern building constructed in 1972 at 10075 M-65. A Polish inscription over the altar reads "My house is a house of prayer," referencing Isaiah 56:7. A stained-glass window and statue of St. Casimir are found in the church.
www.stcasimir-stdomic.org

Posen Potato Festival

Posen's signature event is the Posen Potato Festival, a celebration of the area's most prosaic, but delicious product. It is held each year the weekend after Labor Day and includes Polish food and dance.

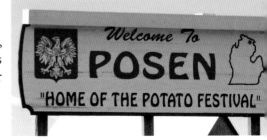

Parisville, Michigan

There is some debate on whether Parisville, Michigan, or Panna Maria, Texas, is the oldest permanent Polish settlement in the United States, but we will leave that for historians to settle. Both early communities were founded around the same time. Parisville is in Huron County in northeast Michigan. Pomeranian Poles came to Michigan directly from Poland through Canada in the 1850s-1860s and settled in Paris, later renamed Parisville. A sparse group of Poles (who used the term Polanders) came to Huron County as early as 1848 and the Parisville mission had its beginning in 1852 according to several documents. The first church, St. Mary's Church, was a log chapel built by Fr. Kluck in 1857 on the spot where the present Blessed Virgin shrine now stands. A fire in 1881 destroyed most of town but spared **St. Mary's Catholic Church**, now part of St. Isidore Parish (along with St. Patrick Church). In 1899, while Fr. Leopold Moczygemba served at Parisville, he invited the Felician nuns to run a Catholic school there. He is best known as the founder of the Panna Maria settlement in Texas, thus another connection between these two earliest Polish settlements.

Old Polish settlers' cabin, Parisville, MI (St. Mary Church)

The town's heyday was in the 1920-30s with many Polish-owned businesses and dance halls. A massive fire in 1974 destroyed the historic church and only the bell and chimney remain. Just north of the church, there is a Polish settler log cabin from 1875, which is considered by the locals as one of the oldest in the United States. A plaque installed in 2021 by the Polish Genealogical Society of Michigan honoring the immigrants who made the area one of the oldest Polish villages in the United States and the oldest in Michigan is located across from the 1876 Parisville Hotel. **www.angelfire.com/mi3/ancestry/church.htm**

STERLING HEIGHTS

Our Lady of Częstochowa Church

Part of the archdiocese of Detroit, this Polish Pastoral Mission was founded in 1979 and is served by the Society of Christ order of Polish priests. A large icon of Our Lady hangs on the altar and a chapel to St. Pope John Paul II is found to the right of the altar. The parish sponsors a Saturday Polish language school and a song and dance troupe. Polish Mass and celebrations of traditional Polish holydays are observed. The parish participates in the annual American Polish Festival held at the nearby American Polish Century Club. **www.parisholc.org**

TROY

American Polish Cultural Center

The Center was established in 1985 by the American Polish Cultural Society and houses the National Polish American Sports Hall of Fame and Museum (*see page 102*) as well as a restaurant and bar serving Polish cuisine. The Society provides scholarships and recognition awards and is involved in numerous charitable, literary, educational, and social events promoting awareness of Polish and Polish American contributions. The building itself at 2975 East Maple Road is interesting in that it was built with materials from across America and Europe and features ornate interior woodwork from many prominent residences, such as the Rockefeller Family estate. **www.americanpolishcenter.com**

National Polish-American Sports Hall of Fame and Museum

The National Polish American Sports Hall of Fame and Museum was founded in 1973 to honor and recognize outstanding American athletes of Polish descent, both amateur and professional. It was first housed at Orchard Lake Schools until it outgrew the space and relocated to its current location at 2891 East Maple Road, which is in the American Polish Cultural Center. It now honors over 150 inductees with an outstanding collection of historic artifacts on display. Many of the items are one-of-a-kind. The museum houses plaques and memorabilia of athletes of Polish heritage who, in their time, gained fame and glory in a variety of professional and amateur sports. The first inductee was Stan Musial and new members are elected to the Hall of Fame each year. Visitors can see uniforms and sports equipment from famous Polish American athletes such as Mike Krzyzewski, Whitey Kurowski, and Ted Marchibroda, as well as a football signed by Bob Skoronski, Vince Lombardi, and other members of the 1967 Super Bowl I Champion Green Bay Packers. **www.polishsportshof.com/about/museum**

WYANDOTTE

Our Lady of the Scapular Church

Our Lady of the Scapular Parish was established on August 1, 2013, out of the merger of Our Lady of Mount Carmel (1899 - 2013), St. Helena (1925-2013), and St. Stanislaus Kostka (1914-2013) Parishes. Polish Catholics came to Wyandotte as early as 1870 and formed the St. Stanislaus Kostka Society to preserve their Polish heritage, eventually building the parish of Our Lady of Mount Carmel in 1899 in the northwest part of town. Since English was not their first language, they referred to their parish as "*Matka Boża Skaplerzna*" which translates to Our Lady of the Scapular, the current name of the combined parishes. As the Polish community continued to grow, another Polish parish was built in 1914 in the northeast part of the city (Ford City neighborhood), St. Stanislaus Kostka, and with time a third Polish church, St. Helena, was established on the south side of the city. Today the three communities have come together as a single Polish Personal Parish within the original church building at 976 Pope John Paul II Avenue, which is architecturally considered in the Polish cathedral style commonly seen in other midwestern Polish churches. The church is adorned with paintings of Our Lady of Częstochowa, St. Pope John Paul II and statues of other Polish saints. There are Polish Masses, a Polish festival at the end of August, and The Polish Heritage Group is a cultural association affiliated with the parish which holds classes promoting Polish heritage. **ourladyofthescapular.org**

PRCUA #162 Sacred Heart of Jesus Society

Boasting the nation's premier polka jukebox, Wyandotte's PRCUA chapter at 1430 Oak Street sponsors many community events such as Christmas *kolędy*, and a folk dancing troupe in addition to maintaining a banquet hall and lounge. It was founded in 1902. **www.prcua-wyandotte.com**

MINNESOTA

BROWERVILLE
St. Joseph Church
Established in 1885 by Silesian immigrants, this Baroque church at 720
North Main Street was built in 1908-
09 and designed by Victor Cordella. A
square tower with four saints supports
an octagonal lantern with a copper
onion dome that reaches seventy feet.
Since 1980, the church has been part
of Christ the King Parish. The sculptor and Prix de Rome winner, Joseph
Kiselewski, was born in Browerville
and designed the grotto by the rectory.
The entire complex is listed on the National Register of Historic Places. The
tower is a replica of the Kraków Wawel
Cathedral with the addition of emblems of the Polish eagle on each side
to identify it as a Polish church.

DELANO
St. Mary of Czestochowa Church
This church was built by a growing Polish farming community and dedicated
in 1884. It was designed by Polish-born
Victor Cordella. In the early 20th century, the town was also named Czestochowa but later became part of Delano.
The original wooden structure burned,

St. Joseph Church, Browerville, MN (Michael Retka)

and the existing brick building at 1867 95th Street SE was erected in 1914. The parishioners were
able to save the large painting of Our Lady of Częstochowa that still hangs above the altar. Occasional Polish pilgrimages are held here. **stmarydelano.org**

DULUTH
St. Mary Star of the Sea Church
As the Polish population of Duluth grew, St. Mary Star of the Sea was established in 1883—the name
referencing Duluth's position on Lake Superior and its significant role as a port city. In 1906, after a
fire destroyed the first church, a brick Neo-Gothic structure with a central tower was constructed
at 325 East 3rd Street. In 1907, the Rev. Kamil Sierzputowski left with much of the congregation to
found St. Josaphat PNCC which resulted in a brief closure of the church. The large transept stained-
glass windows depict scenes from the life of Christ. Other windows depict Polish saints such as St.
Casimir and historical figures such as King Jagiełło and his wife Queen Jadwiga. The Rosary Society,
which helped to establish the church, remains active. **www.stmarystaroftheseaduluth.com**

Victor Cordella

Victor Cordella was born in Krakow, Poland, in 1872 to an artisan family. He designed over twenty-seven churches in the United States, of which more than twenty survive as active parishes, plus schools, homes, rectories, orphanages, and commercial buildings throughout Minnesota. One church is now a performing arts center. His focus was on Polish Roman Catholic congregations, especially in Minneapolis and rural areas. His first major Polish Catholic church was St. Casimir's in St. Paul, modeled after churches in Krakow and Lvov, where he studied architecture and design. Cordella also built churches for the Carpatho-Rusyn Orthodox, Byzantine Greek Catholic, Slovak and Ukrainian communities in Minnesota and northwestern Wisconsin. The exteriors of his churches were often an ornate combination of Baroque and Renaissance styles, dubbed the Polish Cathedral Style in the U.S. On the interior, a large central barrel vault with vaulted side aisles was a plan favored for many of Cordella's churches. St. Mary of Czestochowa in Delano, Minnesota, is an example of his signature single-spire design and use of Corinthian columns. Cordella designed his own single-family home along Bassett Creek in Minneapolis, and he is buried at Old St. Mary's Cemetery in Minneapolis. Holy Cross Church in Minneapolis, built in 1927, was the crowning achievement of his career. *The map gives a visual overview of this important Polish American architect.*

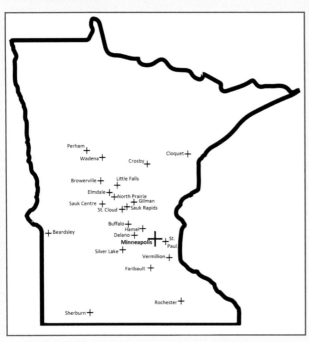

Victor Cordella Polish churches in Minnesota (Michael Retka)

GNESEN

St. Joseph Church

The township of Gnesen was named after the first Polish capital, Gniezno, and settled by Prussian Poles who arrived in the 1860s. A log cabin church was constructed in 1874 on donated land. The present clapboard church at 6110 Church Road was built in 1900. The magnificent wooden interior has survived, and the church is a well-preserved example of the many rural Polish churches that were common across Minnesota and Wisconsin. The church is now administered by St. John the Evangelist in Duluth.

LITTLE CANADA

The Polish American Cultural Institute of Minnesota

The Polish American Cultural Institute of Minnesota (PACIM) is a non-profit organization at 93 West Little Canada Road promoting Minnesota's three centuries of Polish-American heritage. The Institute has extensive library resources, offers numerous on-line classes, publishes a newsletter, maintains social media, and sponsors live events such as festivals, author readings, a book club, and exhibits that highlight Polish history, culture, and language. **www.pacim.org**

LITTLE FALLS
Our Lady of Lourdes Church

Designed by Victor Cordella, the altar in this church at 208 West Broadway resembles the one in St. Anne Church in Kraków. The church was founded in 1917 by Polish settlers and the nearby cemetery includes the early settlers. There is a shrine to Our Lady of Częstochowa. **www.littlefallscatholic.org/**

Our Lady of Lourdes Church, Little Falls, MN (Michael Retka)

MINNEAPOLIS
Holy Cross Church

The Articles of Incorporation for the Church of the Holy Cross (*Bazylika Świętego Krzyża*) were signed in 1886 whereas the cornerstone for the present structure of the church at 1621 University Avenue NE was laid on July 4, 1927. Holy Cross Church is considered the most impressive church designed by Victor Cordella in the Romanesque style with a classical interior. The church includes large paintings of St. Pope John Paul II and St. Faustina flanking the altar, and statues of Mary Queen of Poland and King Jan III Sobieski. An area is dedicated as a memorial to the victims of the Katyń massacre. Sunday Mass is the only Polish-language Mass in the Archdiocese. The parish sponsors a Polish Saturday school and many Polish lectures and events.
www.ourholycross.org

Holy Cross Church, Minneapolis, MN (Kryssy Pease)

University of Minnesota Immigration History Research Center

The Immigration History Research Center Archives (IHRCA) is in the University of Minnesota Libraries inside the Elmer L. Andersen Library. This research collection will be of interest to students of Polish American history and is open to the public. The hundreds of manuscripts

The Gray Samaritans in 1920, from University of Minnesota Immigration History Research Center, Minneapolis, MN (IHRCAimage 000402)

and archive collections document Polish migration to North America. These include records of community and fraternal organizations as well as personal papers of a variety of Polish Americans. Strengths include sources on the settlement of displaced persons and the ethnic press. The Polish American-related print collection includes over five thousand general and rarer books, and many hundreds of serials produced by the Polish American diaspora, including an especially rich collection of newspapers. **www.lib.umn.edu/ihrca**

PERHAM
Perham Performing Arts Center
The former St. Stanislaus Church, designed by Victor Cordella, now houses the Perham Performing Arts Center at 101 5th Street NE. The parish was established in 1884 and closed in 2009, due to the shortage of priests. The present structure dates from 1922 and has a particularly beautiful tower with metal lantern and a niche containing a statue of the patron. Since its repurpose as a performing arts center, plays, concerts, and community events have been held here.

ST. CLOUD
St. John Cantius Church
St. John Cantius was established in 1895 as a national parish for Poles from the Prussian partition. The church at 1515 North 3rd Street was built in 1901 in brick on a granite foundation. A domed metal lantern with a cupola surmounts the central tower. A statue of the patron of the parish is displayed and a stained-glass window with the coat of arms of Our Lady of Częstochowa is located above the entrance doors. The parish remains active and ministers to the community in downtown St. Cloud. **www.stjohncantius.org**

ST. PAUL
St. Casimir Church
St. Casimir Parish was established in 1892 as large companies and several railroads were arriving in the area, increasing the number of Poles in St. Paul. In 1888, they organized themselves into a society named St. Casimir Prince and a committee was formed to collect funds for a church building. As the parish grew, a new church in the Romanesque and Beaux Arts style at 934 Geranium Avenue East was dedicated in 1904. A school, convent, and rectory were added over the years. The choir still includes Polish hymns in Masses for special feast days. The windows and statues include Polish saints, including one of St. Casimir. It is on the National Register of Historic Places. **www.stcasimirchurch.org**

St. Adalbert Church
The first Poles came to St. Paul around 1842 from Wisconsin drawn to the manufacturing and meat packing jobs. St. Adalbert Parish was the genesis of the urban Polish settlement in the Twin Cities. The church at 265 Charles Avenue was built in a new-Gothic style in 1910 after the congregation had worshipped in several smaller churches. The parish flourished under the guidance of Rev. Dominic Majer, who was the first Polish priest to be made a prelate in the United States. He was active in efforts to promote the Polish Catholic Church and steer a course between competing factions in America's Polish Catholic churches and there is a bust of Majer inside the church. An iconic stained-glass window is found on the east side that has the symbols of the three lands of historic Commonwealth of Poland: the horseman symbolizing Lithuania, Archangel Michael symbolizing Ukraine, and the White Eagle of Poland.

SOBIESKI
St. Stanislaus Church

As the Polish population of Morrison Country grew, St. Stanislaus Parish was established in 1884. The present church at 9406 Church Circle was dedicated in 1897 and features two large towers and detailed brickwork. The original lanterns have since been replaced with steeples. In 1916, the village was renamed after King Jan III Sobieski. According to local lore, Jan Matejko painted the altarpiece. **www.triparishcatholiccommunity.org**

WILNO
St. John Cantius Church

The town of Wilno was laid out in 1883 on land provided by the Chicago and Northwestern railroad to create a Polish settlement. The community was formed as part of a planned effort between the railroad and leaders of Polish National Alliance (PNA), with the cooperation of the Catholic Church. St. John Cantius Church was established in the town in the same year through the efforts of Rev. R. Byzewski of Winona, who was born in the Kashubian regions of Poland, and Bishop John Ireland of St. Paul. By 1891, the town was centered around St. John Cantius Polish Catholic Parish and School at 3069 Kowno Street. It also had a post office with a small reading room, carpenter, general store, saloon, and wagonmaker. Legend has it that when the railroad attempted to buy land for right-of-way, two Wilno farmers refused the amount offered and the railroad was built through what became the town of Ivanhoe instead. The town remained a tiny Catholic settlement. The Church of St. John Cantius is now part of the Christ the King Parishes. The church went through major restorations and renovations in 2021. **www.christthekingafc.com**

WINONA
Basilica of Saint Stanislaus Kostka

A historic Polish parish was established in Winona on April 2, 1871. It served as the religious and civic center for Winona's numerous Kashubian Poles. By 1895, the community outgrew the original church building and St. Stanislaus Kostka erected a large Romanesque building in the Polish Cathedral style, to serve a much larger number of Polish/Kashubian worshippers. The church at 625 East 4th Street was designed by the same architects as Sacred Heart-St. Wenceslaus Church in nearby Pine Creek (*see* Pine Creek, WI). The stained-glass windows are dedicated to various saints and devotions particularly cherished by Kashubian Poles. In 2011, it was elevated as a minor basilica and is on the National Register of Historic Places. Some of the Basilica's original furnishings, along with many furnishings preserved from other churches in the diocese, can be viewed at the nearby Polish Cultural Institute and Museum.

Basilica of St. Stanislaus Kostka, Winona, MN (Ewa Barczyk)

https://ssk-sjn.weconnect.com

Polish Cultural Institute and Museum of Winona, MN (Anne Gurnack)

Polish Cultural Institute and Museum of Winona

The founder of the institute, Father Paul Breza, purchased an old lumber mill in downtown Winona in 1976 and diligently turned it into a museum which houses both important Polish and Kashubian artifacts, heirlooms, and photographs and publishes a newsletter. The Madry and Bronk families are believed to be the first Polish arrivals in Winona around 1859, which had a population of 2,500 around that time. They were followed by thousands of other Kashubians who emigrated from Bytów and other northern towns in the occupied Polish countryside in search of farmland. The Museum at 102 Liberty Street set out to preserve what remains of the history of these early settlers. The Museum takes up the first floor of the main building and contains several separate exhibits depicting the history and culture of the Kashubian Polish immigrants to Winona. Adjacent to the Museum building is the former Schulz House which now serves as a Heritage House for the Polish community. It has the décor of a Polish house one hundred years ago. Two murals found on the buildings depict Winona's Kashubian Polish heritage. There is a well-stocked gift shop. The center sponsors a large annual festival, *Smaczne Jabłka* ("tasty apples"), which attracts Poles from the surrounding area. (*See also entry under* Pine Creek, WI, *which is across the river and shares a Kashubian heritage.*) **polishmuseumwinona.org**

St. Casimir Church

Saint Casimir Parish was opened on Christmas Day 1905 as a sister parish to St. Stanislaus Kostka Church. The people who founded Saint Casimir Parish were previously members of that parish until 1905 when Saint Stanislaus started a drive for funds to construct a new and larger school building. There was a feeling among the people of Polish origin in the west end of the city that they should have their own church and school rather than contribute to a new building in the east end, and thus they started St. Casimir Church at 626 West Broadway. The cornerstone was laid in July of 1905, the combination church and school building were completed, and Father Jakub Pacholski celebrated the first Mass in this building on Christmas Day that same year. The church is now part of the Cathedral of the Sacred Heart Parish. **cathedralwinona.org**

MISSISSIPPI

(Chillin662 CC BY-SA 4.0)

KOSCIUSKO
Kosciusko Museum and Visitors Center

Kosciusko, Mississippi, is named after the famed Polish and American patriot and war hero who was the youngest general in Washington's army, and the city maintains this museum dedicated to Kosciuszko. The honor of giving the young settlement a name belonged to William D. Dodd, the first representative of Attala County in the State Legislature of Mississippi. Dodd's grandfather had served with General Thaddeus Kosciuszko in the Revolutionary War, and both were active in the siege of Fort Ninety Six in 1781 in South Carolina (See Ninety Six National Park & Star Fort, NC). When he proposed the general's name to the Legislature, he inadvertently omitted the "z," but the correct spelling of the name is present in the appellation of the Kosciuszko Heritage Foundation.

The Kosciusko Museum and Visitors Center at 101 Natchez Trace Parkway opened in November 1984. The mix of exhibits about local history and lore and exhibits about Kosciuszko are an indication of how the Polish and American patriot has become a natural and permanent part of the cultural and historical consciousness of this very American town. The Center, built and maintained by donations from citizens and friends of Attala County, is located at the geographical center of Mississippi. The memorabilia and exhibits concerning General Kosciuszko are certainly worth seeing. (The town is also well known as the birthplace of Oprah Winfrey.)

Redbud Springs Park

This park, created during America's bicentennial year of 1976, is located on the original Natchez Trace. Several points of interest in the park include a dirt mound with dirt taken from Kraków, Poland, and a statue of General Tadeusz Kosciuszko. The monument was created by Tracy H. Sugg, who also created a life-size bronze bust of Kosciuszko in the library at West Point, NY. The Kosciuszko Museum and Visitors Center is nearby.

Kosciuszko statue sculpted by Tracy H. Sugg, Redbud Springs Park, Kosciusko, MS (Tracy H. Sugg, www.tracyHsugg.com)

PINE RIDGE
Fauntleroy gravesite, Pine Ridge Presbyterian Church Cemetery

Cedric E. Fauntleroy was the American leader, along with the founder Capt. Merian C. Cooper, of the Kościuszko Squadron that took part in the Polish-Soviet War in 1920. During World War I, he had been a member of the Lafayette Escadrille, a famous French squadron of fighting planes made up largely of American pilots. One of the first to sign up for the Polish front as a volunteer right after November 11, 1918, to fight against the Bolsheviks, he was joined by other American pilots who formed the Kościuszko Squadron. The squadron later served in World War II using the same logo with Kościuszko's cap and sabers on their planes as Fauntleroy's group. He died in 1963 and is buried in a modest grave in Pine Ridge Cemetery. (There is a monument to the American pilots of the Kościuszko Squadron at the cemetery in Lviv (Lwów), Ukraine.) There is an on-going campaign to raise funds to give Fauntleroy recognition by erecting a monument at his Mississippi gravesite. He kept a detailed logbook of the Kościuszko Squadron, and the two-volume set is now at the Library of Congress.

MISSOURI

PACIFIC
Black Madonna Shrine and Grottos
A site of pilgrimage and prayer maintained by the Franciscan Missionary Brothers of the Sacred Heart of Jesus, the Black Madonna Shrine and Grottos are set in the Ozark hills. After this Franciscan community arrived in Missouri from Poland in the 1920s, one of them, Brother Bronisław Łuszcz, began construction of the Shrine, and continued work on it, singlehandedly and without the aid of power tools, until his death in 1960. Largely carved out of tiff rock, the Shrine, an open-air chapel, and seven grottos connected by a walking trail, became a place of pilgrimage, and remains so to this day. It remains largely in its original state, apart from the chapel, reconstructed after its destruction by an arson attack in 1958.
www.franciscancaring.org/blackmadonnashri.html

PULASKIFIELD
Pulaskifield, located in Capps Creek Township, is an unincorporated community originally known as Bricefield but renamed by the proud Polish settlers in honor of their fellow countryman Gen. Casimir Pulaski. Sts. Peter and Paul Church was established there in 1892 and has a cemetery with tombstones of the original settlers. Most of the immigrants who settled the farms came from Prussian Poland after the Frisco railway was extended into southwest Missouri and cheap land was offered for sale to immigrants. The parish held an annual celebration called the *Uczta* (Feast) and visitors from surrounding areas came to experience the Polish food, games, and dancing. There is a Pulaskifield Polish Historical Society whose webpage has more information on the history of the community.
www.pulaskifieldhistoricalsociety.org

ST. LOUIS
Cathedral Basilica of St. Louis
The cathedral, at 4431 Lindell Blvd., was completed in 1914 and is known for its large mosaic installation, which is one of the largest in the Western Hemisphere. The main dome's Old and New Testament biblical scenes were done by Polish artist Jan Henryk de Rosen (John De Rosen) and is recognized as one of his crowning achievements. On the side lawn of the church, a 14-foot-high contemporary welded steel sculpture titled "Angel of

Cathedral Basilica of St. Louis (Fr. Joe Laramie, S.J.)

Harmony" by Polish-born sculptor Wiktor Szostalo was installed in 1999. The winged angel with African American features is standing behind three children of Hispanic, Asian, and European features, playing a song of peace on their instruments. The sculpture emphasizes a theme of harmony, peace, and racial justice. There is also an outdoor statue of St. Pope John Paul II along with a plaque commemorating his visit in 1999. Below the cathedral, the Mosaic Museum contains some artifacts from the Pope's visit. On display are the throne he sat on during Mass, the stole he wore, and the needlepoint prie-dieu he knelt upon in the basilica. **http://cathedralsl.org**

St. Agatha Polish Church
Although the parish dates to 1871, it was designated the only official Polish Catholic parish in St. Louis in 2005, and is now under the direction of the Society of Christ Fathers for Poles Abroad. It had originally been founded as a German parish. The church building at 3239 South 9th Street dates from 1885 and showcases an icon of Our Lady of Częstochowa at the front of the church, banners in Polish, and a painting of St. Pope John Paul II, after whom the Polish Saturday school is named. Masses are in Polish and frequent lectures are held on Polish history and culture. Polish religious events are observed. A plaque on the outside of the church notes the historic landmark designation of the building. **www.polishchurchstlouis.org**

St. Stanislaus Kostka Polish Catholic Church, St. Louis, MO
(Neal Pease)

St. Stanislaus Kostka Polish Catholic Church
Now an independent church, St. Stanislaus Catholic Parish was founded in 1880 to serve the growing Polish immigrant community of St. Louis. The present church structure at 1413 North 20th Street, reflecting the "Polish Cathedral" style, dates from 1891. While renovated numerous times over the years, the interior retains much of its Polish themed decoration and inscriptions. Michael Olszewski of St. Louis created the stained-glass windows in 1928, labeling all the saints in Polish. In the 1980s, the parish became involved in a bitter dispute with the Archdiocese of St. Louis that began over issues of parish government and led to the excommunication of the pastor of St. Stanislaus and members of its lay leadership, as well as suppression of the parish. Due to a legal settlement reached in 2013, St. Stanislaus now continues as a self-governing, self-proclaimed "Polish Catholic" religious community, but is not affiliated with the Roman Catholic Church. **www.saintstan.org**

Stan Musial Statue
The statue of "Stan the Man" Musial stands in Stan Musial Plaza outside the St. Louis Cardinal's Busch Stadium. Stanisław Franciszek Musiał ranks among the brightest stars in the history of baseball and is regarded as the greatest American athlete of Polish descent. He made his debut with the St. Louis Cardinals in 1941 and spent his entire career with that

team, playing primarily as an outfielder and first baseman. He won election to the National Baseball Hall of Fame and in 1973 the National Polish-American Sports Hall of Fame named him its first inductee (see entry under Troy, MI).

Stan Musial statue, St. Louis, MO (Ann Riley)

MONTANA

BUTTE
Memorial Plaza
Memorial Plaza sits at the top of Granite Mountain in Butte as a remembrance of a hard rock mining disaster on June 8, 1917. It is still the deadliest one in the U.S. with an estimated 168 victims of a terrible fire deep down a mine shaft on a hill called Granite Mountain. Around the surrounding wall of the monument, flags of various nationalities are affixed representing the workers killed. Many of the mine workers among the largely Roman Catholic immigrants who worked in the hottest and most dangerous copper mines were Poles. The Anaconda Copper Mining Company, which consolidated earlier mining companies, dominated Butte. Many of the original homes and shops are still standing but Holy Savior Church and most of the Polish neighborhoods were swallowed up in later years by the Berkeley Pit mine. The Polish workers were at the forefront of the strikes at the time which sometimes turned violent. Butte experienced martial law from 1914 to 1921, the longest attempt in the United States to quell a labor unrest spurred by the difficult and dangerous working conditions. These events are documented at the World Museum of Mining in Butte: **miningmuseum.org**.

Butte holds the 3-day annual Montana Folk Festival in July with Polish folk groups and Polish food among the ethnicities represented.

WIBAUX
St. Philip Church
This Catholic church that served the Polish community is located at 61 Lancaster Road about fourteen miles southeast of town in an unincorporated area referred to as the Town of St. Philip. The opening of homesteads at the turn of the nineteenth century brought Polish settlers from Minnesota, Warsaw, and Minto, North Dakota. The first Mass was celebrated with the homily in Polish in 1910. The church was named in honor of St. Philip since a major local donor was Philip Wicka and the community expanded with many Polish owned businesses. The parish cemetery has the graves of the early settlers.

Wibaux Museum
The Wibaux Museum at 112 East Orgain Avenue has exhibits and a collection of photos about early Polish settlers, mainly homesteaders from Minnesota and North Dakota who followed the railroad, arriving largely around 1909-10.

Wibaux "Ski" Festival
The town of Wibaux holds an annual "ski" festival in the summer to celebrate the preponderance of townspeople with Polish names. The event includes Polka music and eastern European foods.

NEBRASKA

ASHTON
Polish Heritage Center
Founded in 1997, this museum at 120 Howells Avenue is devoted to the history, culture, and genealogy of Polish immigrants in Nebraska. Poles began arriving in rural central Nebraska in the 1870s as recruits in an organized initiative of the Polish Roman Catholic Union to develop farming colonies there. The original settlement of three hundred Polish families took root and, along with Czech and German arrivals, did much to shape the character of the region; as of 2010, thirty percent of the population of Sherman County, in which the town of Ashton is located, is of Polish descent. The museum preserves artifacts of the farming community and the gift shop offers Polish-themed clothing and curios.

Ashton Polish Heritage Center, Ashton, NE (APHC)

An annual Polish Heritage Festival is held in August in collaboration with St. Francis Church at 200 West Carleton Street which still holds a Polish Mass and a Polish Steeplechase between the steeples of St. Francis and Our Lady of Mt. Carmel in Paplin.

BELLEVIEW
St. John Kanty Cemetery
This cemetery was founded in 1923 by the members of three predominantly Polish Roman Catholic parishes in South Omaha—Immaculate Conception, St. Francis of Assisi, and St. Stanislaus. St. John Kanty, a patron saint of Poland and Lithuania, was selected as the patron of the cemetery. Most burials at St. John's are Polish. Of special note is the World War I memorial honoring local Polish immigrants who volunteered in World War I in both the U.S. forces and with Haller's Blue Army to help Poland regain independence. The monument,

St. John Kanty Cemetery, Belleview, NE (Nancy Schlesinger)

dedicated May 30, 1931, includes a cannon with markings indicating that it likely was manufactured in France for use in World War I. On one side of the four sided cannon base, there are two military medals. The *Krzyż Żołnierzy Polskich z Ameryki*, "Cross of Polish Soldiers from America" bears the image of a crowned eagle and denotes the locations of four major battles in which Polish volunteers distinguished themselves. On this same side is the medal for the Veterans of Foreign Wars of the United States, and below these two medals is an acknowledgment to Polish organizations and patrons. The second side of the marker lists the names of the Nebraska volunteers to the Allied Army of World War I. The cemetery includes an outdoor altar where, every Memorial Day, the local Polish American community gathers for an open-air Mass to remember its loved ones buried at St. John's.

FARWELL
St. Anthony of Padua Church
St. Anthony of Padua Church is the oldest Polish Catholic church in Nebraska, founded in 1877. The present church building was moved by horse and wagon in 1925 to the current site at 103 Kearns Avenue, which was an area then known as New Posen, a settlement sponsored by the Polish Roman Catholic Union of Chicago. It is now a mission of Sts. Peter and Paul Church in nearby St. Paul, so Masses are only said about once a month, including Christmas Eve midnight Mass, along with sacramental events such as First Communions and Confirmations.

LOUP CITY
St. Josaphat Church
St. Josaphat Church was founded in 1881. An earlier church building, erected in 1908, featured stained-glass windows commemorating the area's mostly Polish families. These windows were salvaged and installed in the current church at 704 North 9th Street, dedicated in 1972.

The "Polish Capital of Nebaska"
For many years Loup City has proclaimed itself the "Polish capital of Nebraska" due to its significant Polish population. The city has a white eagle from the Polish coat of arms in the town square (7th and O Street) and stages Polish Days, an annual community event, on the first weekend of June.

OMAHA
Immaculate Conception Church
Founded in 1898, Immaculate Conception Catholic Church became the leading historically Polish parish of Omaha. By the turn of the 20th century, the city had become home to the largest Polish settlement on the Great Plains, drawn by plentiful employment opportunities in the meatpacking, stockyard, smelting, and rail industries. Built in 1926, the present Romanesque church at 2708 South 24th Street remains a landmark in the traditionally Polish South Omaha district. The church was added to the National Register of Historic Places in 1998. Since 2007, it has been entrusted to the Priestly Fraternity of St. Peter for celebration of the traditional Latin Tridentine Mass. **www.latinmassomaha.org**

Pulaski Park
This two-acre park at 4065 G Street was acquired by the city of Omaha in 1923 and name Pulaski Park at the urging of Polish residents in the neighborhood. It includes playground equipment, a baseball field, and a basketball court. In 2009, the city updated the park with an interpretive panel telling the story of Polish immigrants and their contributions to the development of South Omaha as well as Casimir Pulaski's contributions to American history. At the northwest corner of the park is a memorial to General Pulaski, established by private funding from the Polish community.

St. Stanislaus Church

Founded in 1919 by Polish immigrants, this church at 4002 J Street was built in a basilica architectural style in 1955. A large stained-glass window depicts St. Stanislaus as well as a statue from the original church. A silk banner with St. Stanislaus hangs from the choir loft, a tapestry of St. Faustina and a large icon of the Black Madonna adorn the side wall. Paintings of newer Polish religious figures, such as Fr. Popiełuszko, are found along the nave. The parish runs an annual city-wide Polish Festival the third weekend in August, a Polish Heritage Mass, and a Harvest Dinner in October, and special ethnic celebrations at Christmas and Easter, such as *Kolędy, Opłatek,* and Easter basket blessings. Although Masses are in English, they do include Polish hymns. St. Stanislaus was a recipient of the 2010 City of Omaha Mayor's Historical Grant and erected a permanent monument on site honoring Polish settlements in South Omaha.

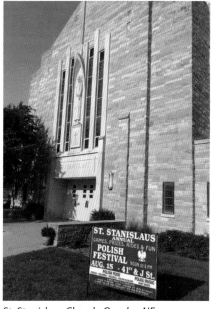

St. Stanislaus Church, Omaha, NE
(Nancy Schlesinger)

PAPLIN

Our Lady of Mount Carmel

The location of this church was former-ly called Choynice, so called because the area reminded the Polish settlers of their hometowns of similar names. Polish settlers came here in 1883 but the settlement did not prosper because the railroad was not laid nearby as planned. Today there are several farms, a fellowship hall, cemetery, and the his-toric church from the late-19th century which is being cared for by the Friends of Paplin who hold occasional fundrais-ers and services to preserve and restore the church. When the archdiocese first attempted to decommission it in 1974, the strong-willed residents protested and changed the church locks so the bishop could not enter. It was closed in 1987 but the Friends group is working hard to keep "The Little Church that Could" open for future generations.

Our Lady of Mount Carmel Catholic Church, Paplin, NE
(Nancy Schlesiger)

PAPPILON

Polish Home Omaha

The Polish Heritage Society of Nebraska runs the Polish Home at 201 East First Street, which promotes Polish heritage and culture to the Omaha area since 1933. The Polish Home relocated from its original site in South Omaha to nearby Pappilon. The Society sponsors scholarships, Pol-ish films, Polish dinners tours of Polish sites, sale of Polish foods, Polish cooking classes, and an annual *Wigilia* dinner. Frequent pop-up exhibits on Polish heritage highlight the history of the Polish community. **www.polishhomeomaha.org**

TARNOV
St. Michael Church
This church, founded in 1880 and replaced in 1900 with the current building, is on the National Register of Historic Places and boasts that it is the first Polish Catholic parish which is still operating in Nebraska. The land on which the complex stands was donated by Frank and Sophia Paprocki, immigrants from Tarnov, Poland. The old school is now the Social Hall and Museum with artifacts of the early Polish farming community. The old Rectory is rented out for gatherings or overnight stays. St. Michael's complex includes many gardens, Our Lady of Lourdes grotto which commemorates local soldiers who served in World War I, and walking paths. In 2019 St. Michael's became part of a new parish cluster of St. Francis Parish. The church continues Polish traditions such as Easter basket blessings. **www.tarnov.org**

NEVADA

LAS VEGAS
Our Lady of Las Vegas Church
Located at 3050 Alta Drive, this main parish for the St. John Paul II Polish Apostolate was established in 2012 by Bishop Joseph Pepe to serve the spiritual and pastoral needs of Polish-speaking Catholics by providing Masses in Polish. Pastoral care is provided by the Society of Christ Fathers. The parish hosts a large annual Polish Festival, a Corpus Christi procession, and sponsors the St. John Paul II Polish School. **ollvchurch.org**

St. Joan of Arc Church
The oldest Catholic church in Las Vegas was erected in 1908 and rebuilt in 1940. It is the secondary parish of the Las Vegas Polish Apostolate which also provides Mass in Polish. Above the side altars are images of Our Lady of Czestochowa and Divine Mercy Jesus. Located in downtown Las Vegas at 315 South Casino Center Boulevard, the parish is designated as a National Catholic Historical Site. **st-joanlv.org**

Joan or Arc Church, Las Vegas, NV
(Victor Barczyk)

Polish Social Club of Las Vegas
This Polish social club became a meeting place in 1968 to promote and preserve Polish heritage and culture through cultural, educational, and social events including appearances of the local Polish choir and Polish dance group *Piast*. **www.pasclv.org**

NEW HAMPSHIRE

CLAREMONT
St. Joseph Confraternity
This parish at 60 Elm Street was founded in 1922 to serve Polish immigrants after land for the parish was purchased by the Kosciuszko Society. Originally the church was named Our Lady of Ostrabrama (a famous shrine to her is in Vilnius, Lithuania, which is where many parishioners were from). It was renamed St. Joseph in 1923. The Polish American Heritage of Claremont is very active in the parish and has been celebrating Polish American Heritage Month since 1984, and holds *Dożynki*, Polish cooking classes, and other cultural events.

MANCHESTER
Holy Trinity Polish National Catholic Cathedral
This church was established in 1915 to serve Polish-speaking immigrants coming to work in the mills since the late 1800s. Originally, dissident members of the earlier Roman Catholic parish of St. Hedwig's split off and began construction of Holy Cross Church which was the forerunner of today's Holy Trinity Cathedral at 166 Pearl Street. In 1930, it aligned itself with the Polish National Catholic Church (PNCC) of Scranton, PA, and renamed itself as Holy Trinity Church. It was elevated to a cathedral in 1952. The Frédéric Chopin Choir sings at Masses and Polish heritage activities are still maintained. **holytrinitypncc.org**

Holy Trinity Polish National Catholic Cathedral, Manchester, NH (John Trombetta)

Pulaski Monument in Pulaski Park, Manchester, NH (John Trombetta)

Casimir Pulaski Monument, Pulaski Park

Pulaski Park at 128 Bridge Street was created by the Works Progress Administration as part of Franklin Delano Roosevelt's New Deal program during the Depression. The large bronze equestrian monument in the center of Pulaski Park was created by local sculptor Lucien Hippolyte Gosseline and was dedicated in August 1938, following a parade of thousands of participants. It underwent a massive restoration, completed in 2020, to bring it back to its original condition.

St. Hedwig Church

This church at 147 Walnut Street was founded in 1902 by Polish and Lithuanian immigrants and still maintains its Polish identity. The church has large stained-glass windows of Our Lady of Częstochowa and St. Hedwig, and a painting of St. Pope John Paul II. The parish celebrates many Polish religious customs such as an annual *Wigilia* dinner and holds a Polish Fest in conjunction with Pulaski Day. The old cemetery is nearby in Bedford and has the graves of many of the original Polish founders. **www.sainthedwignh.org**

Stained-glass window of Our Lady of Czestochowa, St. Hedwig Church, Manchester, NH (St. Hedwig Church)

NEW JERSEY

BAYONNE

General Casimir Pulaski Memorial Plaque

In the entrance hall of Bayonne High School's General Pulaski Wing (30th Street entrance) one finds a memorial plaque declaring that the General Pulaski Wing of Bayonne High School, by resolution of the Bayonne Board of Education dated November 29, 1979, is dedicated to General Casimir Pulaski, "fearless fighter in the cause of freedom in the American Revolutionary war." The plaque, an initiative of the Polish American Congress, Bayonne Chapter, and the Polish American Community of Bayonne, was unveiled on October 7, 1984. In addition to the above text, the plaque includes a relief of General Pulaski, his dates of birth and death, as well as a summary of his contributions to the cause of liberty during the American Revolutionary War.

Maria Skłodowska Curie Monument

Within the courtyard of the historic main branch of the Bayonne Public Library at 697 Avenue C stands a bronze bust of Maria Skłodowska Curie. The Polish-born two-time Nobel laureate is portrayed with both Nobel medals around her neck. Unveiled in 1987, thanks to the efforts of the Polish American Heritage Committee of Bayonne, NJ, the monument was created by Polish American sculptor Andrzej Pitynski. The following is inscribed on the monument's pedestal: "Maria Skłodowska Curie (1867-1934) – Scientific Genius – Discoverer of Radium and Polonium – Twice Nobel Laureate – Polish Patriot – Presented to the City of Bayonne by the Polish American Community – Erected 1987." The monument is accessible during working hours when the library is open.

Maria Skłodowska Curie Monument, Bayonne, NJ
(Matthew Stefanski)

Our Lady of Mount Carmel Church

Our Lady of Mount Carmel (OLMC) was established by Polish immigrants on January 25, 1898. While in its early years the parish was beset by divisions, it would go on to become one of the largest Polish parishes in the United States. The current church at 39 East 22nd Street, the parish's third house of worship, was constructed in 1909-1910 and designed by New York architects Robert J. Reiley and Gustave E. Steinback. It is Romanesque in style with Gothic ornamentation. The church building was blessed by Bishop Paul Rhode, the first Polish bishop in America, and was consecrated on October 16, 1917.

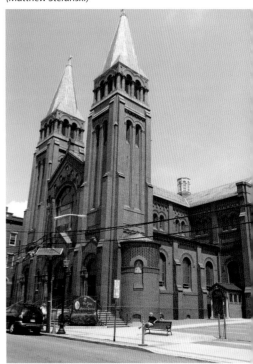

Our Lady of Mount Carmel Church, Bayonne, NJ
(Matthew Stefanski)

The church contains a hand-crafted wooden side altar dedicated to Our Lady of Częstochowa, and a bronze statue of St. Pope John Paul II, as well as two towering works of art by renowned Polish painter Adam Styka: the Good Shepherd and the Assumption Dogma.

In 2016 the parish merged with Our Lady of Assumption and the previously joined St. Michael's & St. Joseph's parishes to form St. John Paul II Parish, with OLMC church serving as the parish's main house of worship. The parish has been administered by Salvatorian Fathers since 2016 and offers Masses in English, Polish, and Italian. **http://johnpaul2parish.com**

Polish American Home

The Polish American Home at 27-31 West 22nd Street was incorporated in 1927 and exists in its original location to this day. The Polish American Citizens Club, once the largest organization in the city, was a driving force behind the establishment of the Polish American Home, so that the numerous Polish societies and organizations of Bayonne—at one point numbering seventy-five—would have a common meeting place. The Home was expanded in the 1930s and again in 1957. The Home hosts various cultural, educational, and civic undertakings for the Polish community including the annual commemorations of the 3rd of May Polish Constitution Day and festivities following the New York City General Pulaski Day Parade in October. There is a large bar with food open to the public.
polishamericanhome.com

Polish American Home, Bayonne, NJ (Matthew Stefanski)

Plaque at Kosciuszko Fortifications, Billingsport, NJ (James Pula)

BILLINGSPORT
Kosciuszko's Fortifications

In August 1776 the Continental Congress was concerned about the safety of its meeting place in Philadelphia because the Delaware River provided a direct route to the city for the powerful Royal Navy. To defend against this, the Pennsylvania Committee of Safety hired Thaddeus Kosciuszko, newly arrived in North America, to design fortifications along the river south of the city. The first fortifications he planned were at Billingsport on the New Jersey side of the river. The defenses also included a sunken obstruction of log boxes filled with stones so they would sink and fitted with pointed logs designed to tear into the bottoms of any ships attempting to pass the barrier. Although none of the original fortifications exist, the area is listed as a National Historic Site and there is a plaque commemorating the Polish engineer. (*See also* **Red Bank**, NJ.)

BOUND BROOK

St. Mary of Czestochowa Church

Organized in 1914 on the initiative of the St. John's Polish Catholic Organization, the present St. Mary's church at 201 Vosseller Avenue was built in 1919 from local stone. The central altar features the eponymous icon flanked by angels. There are weekly Masses in Polish, and *Gorzkie Żale* devotions are held in Lent. The parish school hosts Polish Saturday school sponsored by the Polish Falcons. **www.stmarys-boundbrook.com**

CAMDEN

Cooper's Ferry

There is a historic sign in Johnson Park on the Rutgers University Camden campus in front of the Cooper Branch Library marking the site of Cooper's Ferry, where a skirmish between Pulaski's forces and the British forces occurred during the Revolutionary War. At the time the British were occupying Philadelphia and Pulaski came with a group of cavalry to help push the British back across the Delaware River. **johnson-park.camden.rutgers.edu**

St. Joseph Church

St. Joseph Church at 1010 Liberty Street is an example of Polish Mannerist-inspired architecture in America. The central tower is patterned on the clock tower of Poznań Town Hall, designed by Bonawentura Solari in the late-18th century. Architect George I. Lovatt designed the church in 1913 and also worked extensively in Philadelphia to serve the needs of rapidly expanding Catholic parishes. The pre-Vatican II interior is unusually well-preserved. The name of St. Joseph was likely inspired by St. Joseph's Church in Philadelphia where the presence of Polish-speaking Jesuits attracted many early families to the parish. A unique feature is the mechanical *szopka*, or Nativity scene—the parish believes it is the only one of its type in America with moving figures. Polish Mass is celebrated every Sunday. **www.stjosephscamdennj.org**

Oil Workers Strike of 1915
Constable Hook

In 1915, due to increased demand from World War I, Standard Oil was making record profits. However, these gains were not shared with company workers, who were forced to toil harder to meet the increased orders. Combined with dangerous conditions and low pay, a group of primarily Polish workers went on strike in July 1915. Soon workers at the Tide Water Refinery on Constable Hook joined the strike. Standard Oil responded violently by hiring armed guards. Four Polish strikers were killed. After resuming work, an additional strike occurred to demand an 8-hour day and fair compensation. Constable Hook remains an industrial district with several oil refineries and visitors can learn more about the area's history at the Bayonne Museum at 229 Broadway.

CLARK
Polish Cultural Foundation
The Polish Cultural Foundation at 177 Broadway was incorporated in 1973 with the purpose to enrich both American and Polish cultures through national, social, educational, scientific, and cultural. It consists of over 40,000 square feet of floor space in three interconnected buildings containing offices, classrooms, meeting rooms, and program facilities with a large capacity auditorium. It houses the **Skulski Art Gallery** which exhibits local, national, and internationally renowned artists; the **Marjanczyk Library** with over fifteen thousand books and publications; and the Polish Supplementary School. The Foundation administers an adult Studies Program featuring Polish language courses, art and music instruction, and hosts the Clark chapter of the Polish Scouts. Annually, it hosts numerous concerts, lectures, social and ethnic commemorative, and heritage events. It is home for the **Polish Athletic Club of the USA** which sponsors Olympic-style events for members of all ages and participates in the games sponsored by the Polish government every four years. **www.polishculturalfoundation.org**

CLIFTON
St. John Kanty Church
The organization of this parish began in the 1920s as the local Polish community increased. In 1935, the Franciscan Order was entrusted with the parish and oversaw construction of the present Romanesque church at 49 Speer Avenue. During the dedication of a statue of St. Maximilian Kolbe in 1982, Franciszek Gajowniczek, whose life was saved by Kolbe's sacrifice, attended. There are Masses in Polish each week and Polish religious and cultural events are observed. **www.saintjohnkanty.org**

EDISON
Marie Curie-Skłodowska Monument
The bronze image of Marie Curie was cast by Slawomir Mielesko and sculptor Henry Koszalka executed the bas-relief stand to replace an earlier monument which has fallen into disrepair. It was rededicated in 1993 by the Polish American Congress/New Jersey Division and is in Roosevelt Park near the police station with a marker that tells about the nearby tree dedicated to the Polish scientist.

Marie Curie Skłodowska monument, Edison, NJ
(Howarthe CC BY-SA 3.0)

ELIZABETH CITY
St. Adalbert Church
Industrial work, especially at the Singer Manufacturing Company, best known for their sewing machines, and Standard Oil refinery, brought legions of Polish immigrants to Elizabeth. The city's first Polish church at 250 East Jersey Street was built in 1905-06 as a combination school-church building, but due to growth in the community it became inadequate. An expansion in 1911 added side aisles to the main nave. The interior was painted in 1935 by Brooklyn artist Henry Niemczynski. On the main altar, a central statue of the Sacred Heart of Jesus is flanked by St. Adalbert and St. Joseph. The church has relics of St. Adalbert on display. More recent additions

to the church include the mural and statue of St. Pope John Paul II and a chapel to our Lady of Częstochowa. **www.stadalbert.us**

St. Hedwig Church

With its church office and chapel fittingly situated on Polonia Avenue, St. Hedwig Church at 600 Myrtle Street is one of the few Polish-American Art-Deco churches. It was built in 1926 and designed by Norwegian immigrant architect William L. Finne. A monumental ceramic statue of St. Hedwig adorns the entrance portico. Terracotta tiles decorate the upper edge of the façade and lower windows of the belfry, forming a cross on the latter inscribed "PAX."
www.sainthedwignj.org

HACKENSACK

St. Joseph Church

St. Joseph is a small church at 460 Hudson Street that was built in 1909 by workers after finishing their shifts in nearby industries. Prominent organizations in the parish's history include the St. Joseph Sokol, St. Cecilia Choir, and Sodality of Our Lady. The church was extended in the 1940s to meet the needs of the growing congregation. Many of the stained-glass windows depict Polish saints. Daily Polish Masses are said. Traditions such as the blessing of homes in January and blessing of food at Easter remain active. **www.stjosephsnj.org**

HAMILTON TOWNSHIP

Grounds for Sculpture

Seward Johnson, a sculptor and philanthropist, envisioned a public sculpture garden and museum that would make contemporary sculpture accessible to all. Grounds for Sculpture at 80 Sculptors Way opened to the public in 1992. The Park is exhibiting nearly three hundred works and special exhibits. Magdalena Abakanowicz's *Space of Stone* was one of the commissioned works for the park. Her other works here include *Sage, Sage B, and Hand Like Tree: Cecyna.* Spatial experience is an essential part of her work with themes of isolation, anonymity, obedience, and oppression. A work by Andrzej Pitynski, *Space, Conquer or Die: Swiatowid,* is on display. It reflects the struggle for freedom that permeates much of his work and has its origins in both the personal and national struggles that he witnessed. **groundsforsculpture.org**

HARRISON

Our Lady of Czestochowa Church

Our Lady of Czestochowa at 115 South 3rd Street is a three-story church and school combination built in a neo-Gothic style. Polish Bishop Ignatius Dubowski, who escaped the Soviet Union, dedicated the church's cornerstone in 1923. Polish traditions are celebrated. The interior is painted with biblical scenes and the altar feature an icon of Our Lady of Częstochowa.
www.olczestochowa.com

JERSEY CITY

Katyń Memorial

Sculptor Andrzej Pitynski's graphic representation of a soldier stabbed in the back with a bayonet commemorates the 1940 Katyń Massacre perpetuated by the Soviet Union against thousands of Polish military officers and intellectuals. Dedicated in 1991, it is prominently located on the Jersey City waterfront with a height of almost forty feet with the cast bronze statue weighing six tons on a 120-ton granite base. In May 2018, during commercial development, local officials attempted to relocate the statue. Following outcry by Polonia organizations, who had not been consulted, and objection by the Polish government that culminated in the visit of Polish president Andrzej Duda to the site, the municipality backed down and the statue remains in its original site. Buried within the granite base is soil taken from the forest where the atrocities were committed.

Our Lady of Czestochowa Church

Like many other immigrant congregations, the growing Polish Catholic community of the now historic Paulus Hook neighborhood bought a Protestant church for their new parish. That 1831 church at 120 Sussex Street, with a spectacular granite façade, was adapted to a Catholic space by architect Louis H. Giele and dedicated in 1905. Inside a large icon of Our Lady of Czestochowa is enshrined on the main altar. It is unclear whether the namesake icon was commissioned in Warsaw specifically for the new church, or transferred from the mother parish, St. Anthony of Padua, which also served the early Polish community in downtown Jersey City. The historic icon has been installed since the establishment of Our Lady of Czestochowa. **www.olcjc.org**

St. Anthony of Padua Church

From its humble beginnings in 1882, St. Anthony of Padua's congregation peaked with 10,000 members due to vigorous immigration. As it was the first church for Poles in New Jersey, St. Anthony of Padua has played an important role in the area's Polish culture, evinced in its place on the

Katyń Memorial by Pitynski, Jersey City, NJ (Marcin Tatjewski)

National Register of Historic Places. The current structure at 330 6th Street, with its soaring central bell tower, was built in 1894, but a disastrous fire in 1895 destroyed the church's interior. The crucifix survived unscathed and has since been hailed as miraculous. In the 1930s, new marble altars featuring mosaics of St. Hedwig and St. Adalbert, as well as a mosaic baptistery (now a chapel to St. Maximilian Kolbe) were installed. **www.saintanthonyjc.com**

White Eagle Hall

The White Eagle Hall at 337 Newark Avenue, built at the initiative of the Franciscan Fr. Boleslaus Kwiatowski in 1910, was recently converted to a concert venue. Two stained glass ceiling medallions embrace Polish musical history, commemorating the renowned composer Frédéric Chopin and Metropolitan Opera singer Marcella Sembrich. **www.whiteeaglehalljc.com**

LODI

Felician Sisters Convent Chapel

The convent of the Felician Sisters in Lodi is located at 260 South Main Street on the campus of Felician University, which was founded by the sisters as Immaculate Conception Normal School in 1923. Their historic chapel features a Gothic wood-carved altar and a painting of the Immaculate Conception. On the back wall is an icon of Our Lady of Częstochowa.

MANVILLE
Sacred Heart Church

Now part of Christ the Redeemer Parish, the original Sacred Heart Church at 98 South 2nd Avenue was built in 1919, designed by architect Henry Swartza. There are Masses in English and Polish, and the parish celebrates traditional Polish holydays, *Gorzkie Żale* during Lent, Easter basket blessings, *Opłatek*, an annual Polish Festival, and *pierogi* dinners. **www.ctrmanville.com**

NEWARK
St. Casimir Church

Known as the "Basilica of the Ironbound" for its magnificently decorated sanctuary, St. Casimir at 91 Pulaski Drive was the second Polish church in Newark, built by the expanding population of Galician immigrants. The construction and decoration of the church lasted from 1917-25 and was done in a Renaissance design by architect Joseph A. Jackson. The portrait of St. Casimir is operated on a pulley system and can be interchanged with a jeweled portrait of Our Lady of Częstochowa. Each of the great window bays is dedicated to an important Polish city. A painted ribbon below the St. Casimir window proudly proclaims "Polonia Semper Fidelis." More recent additions to the church, two murals flanking the altar depict the Thirteen Martyrs of Pratulin and the Massacre of Nowogrodek. The church is on the National Register of Historic Places. Polish traditions are observed such as *Pasterka* (Midnight Mass) and *Kolęda* (Blessing of the Homes). **www.stcnewark.com**

St. Stanislaus Bishop and Martyr Church

A Gothic church with a central steeple and elaborate spires, St. Stanislaus B&M at 146 Irvine Boulevard was built in 1901, six years after the parish was formed. After threats of demolition in the 1980s, the parish regrouped and worked to save and preserve the historic church. A new main altar was erected to Our Lady of Częstochowa with a large painting placed above the altar, and twelve new chasubles from Poland were obtained. The church is part of the Polish Apostolate of Newark and is the second largest Polish parish in Newark. There are paintings of St. Pope John Paul II and stained-glass windows with Polish saints.

PASSAIC
Holy Rosary Church

The second Polish church in Passaic, Holy Rosary Church at 6 Wall Street was historically important. Founded by mostly Galician and Cracovian immigrants in 1913, over the years it has welcomed luminaries such as painter Wojciech Kossak and opera singer Adam Didur. Holy Rosary later hosted Archbishop Jan Feliks Cieplak, who after fleeing Soviet persecution made his headquarters at the parish for several months before his death in 1926. The church continues to have a strong Polish identity as the Diocesan Shrine of Saint John Paul II, and through its Polish school and yearly Pulaski Day parade. **www.holyrosarypassaic.org**

Passaic Textile Mills Strike of 1926

Industrial growth in Passaic attracted thousands of Poles and other European immigrants. However, dangerous conditions, 10-hours days, and unfair wages remained serious issues. These tensions culminated in the 1926 Passaic Textile Strike. Of the 15,000 workers who went on strike from January to November, Poles had the greatest participation of any ethnic group. Workers produced *The Passaic Textile Strike: The Battle for the Life of the Workers that Make the Cloth That Clothes You,* a film that focuses on the plight of fictional Polish workers Stefan and Kada Breznac. Several of these textile mills are extant, including the Botany Worsted and Dundee Textile plants.

Polish Peoples' Home
As opposed to individual halls for each Polonia organization, the Polish Peoples' Home at 1 Monroe Street was built to house the myriad associations of Polish Passaic ranging from the mainstream PRCUA and PNA to the lesser-known Society of Archbishop Jan Cieplak, Society of Polish Workers, and Maritime Society. Another group housed there, the Arfa Girls Choir, played an important role in promoting Polish music, participating in radio broadcasts and producing recordings, even broadcasting with the Office of Information during World War II. The Home hosts Polish musicians, concerts, Polish film series, and other Polish events.

St. Joseph Church
Founded in 1892, St. Joseph Parish is the mother church of Polish Catholicism in Passaic and the surrounding suburbs. The church at 7 Parker Avenue is a 1901 red-brick building featuring a tall central steeple and rose window. A medallion with the Holy Family crowns the apse, dating from the interior painting of the church in the 1930s. **www.stjosephrcpassaic.org**

Sts. Peter and Paul Polish National Catholic Church
Founded in 1890, this church at 126 River Drive stands on land once occupied by Gen. George Washington and Casimir Pulaski during the Revolutionary War in 1776. Until 1902, the church building was a Dutch Reformed Church. A historical marker was erected in 1976 outside the church which details the history of this location and the church. The Moniuszko Choir, named after the Polish composer Stanisław Moniuszko, accompanies Masses. **www.sspeterandpaulpncc.org**

PATERSON
Pulaski Monument
Unveiled for the 150th anniversary of Casimir Pulaski's death in 1929, the Pulaski Monument is in Eastside Park at the intersection of East Park Drive and East Side Park Road. The sculptor was the Italian immigrant and Paterson resident, Gaetano Federici. The statue depicts Pulaski in a military uniform atop a granite pedestal with a plaque featuring the Polish and American eagles. It was a gift from Americans of Polish descent of Paterson.

PENNSAUKEN
Kosciuszko and Pulaski Monuments
In 1936 the Polish community in Camden dedicated a monument to Casimir Pulaski. When Camden's Pulaski Park was designated to be the site of a new medical school in 1982, the monument was relocated through fundraising efforts of the South Jersey Division of the Polish American Congress, the Polish Army Veterans Post 121, and the Polish American Citizens Committee to Cooper River Park in Pennsauken on North Park Drive near Route 130. Two years later, a new

Pulaski Monument, Paterson, NJ (Poles in America)

monument to Thaddeus Kosciusko was dedicated. Both monuments have busts on top of pedestals measuring fourteen feet in total height. The two monuments were joined in 1995 by a new monument dedicated to Polish American veterans of St. Joseph Roman Catholic Church (*see* Camden, NJ) who were killed in World War II.

PERTH AMBOY
Kosciuszko Monument
One of the first monuments to Thaddeus Kosciuszko built by Polish Americans, Perth Amboy's memorial was dedicated in 1894 to commemorate the 100th anniversary of the 1794 Kosciuszko Rebellion. The original monument was temporary and was replaced with a terracotta bust situated on a short column. It sits in front of the school next to St. Stephen Church (*see entry below*).

St. Stephen Church
The first wooden church and school of this parish were built by Polish immigrants in Perth Amboy. The present church at 490 State Street was constructed between 1915-19 in a Gothic style by Philadelphia-based architect, E.F. Durang and Son and was one of the largest in the city. A notable feature of the church is its belltower with gargoyles made locally. Several of the ornate stained-glass windows depict Polish saints. There is a side altar dedicated to St. Pope John Paul II with a painting and relics. To the right of the main altar, a Marian altar contains a replica of the Black Madonna. The church is now part of St. John Paul II Parish along with three other churches under the care of the Redemptorists from Warsaw. Masses and Polish holyday celebrations are in Polish.
www.johnpaulsecond.com

Stained-glass window in St. Stephen Church, Perth Amboy, NJ (JPII Parish)

RED BANK
Fort Mercer
During the American Revolution, after Thaddeus Kosciuszko designed defenses at Billingsport along the Delaware River to prevent the British navy from reaching Philadelphia by water, the Pennsylvania Committee of Safety assigned him to plan Fort Mercer upriver at Red Bank. An earthen fortification surrounded by a ditch and log stockade, it was placed opposite Fort Mifflin on the Pennsylvania side of the river so British ships attempting to pass

between the two would face a crossfire. Today at the Red Bank Battlefield Park on Hessian Avenue along the Delaware River, the remains of some of the earthworks are visible along with recovered artifacts and a plaque commemorating Kosciuszko as the fort's military engineer. (*See also* Billingsport, NJ.)

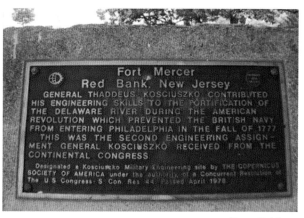

(James Pula)

SAYREVILLE
St. Stanislaus Kostka Church
The local clay deposits and brick industry that helped create Sayreville's Polonia are reflected in St. Stanislaus Kostka Church at 225 MacArthur Avenue. Bricks and land for the church were donated by the Sayre Fisher Brick Company for its construction in 1914. The architect was William Endelbrock. Inside, the left altar features a jewel-encrusted screen over the Our Lady of Częstochowa icon and iconography of Polish saints adorn the walls. The church maintains its strong Polish identity with Polish hymns and Polish religious customs, and sponsors a Polish language school. **www.sskparish.org**

SOUTH RIVER
St. Mary of Ostrabrama Church
St. Mary's Polish Church at 30 Jackson Street was built from 1903-1908 in granite stone. The architect, Henry Dandurand Dagit, had worked extensively in Philadelphia and became the prime architect for the Diocese of Trenton. The church's spire is a nod to a style popular in Central and Eastern Europe. Its interior is lavishly decorated, with trompe d'oeil coffers on the ceiling. An icon of St. Mary of Ostrabrama adorns the central altar and one of Our Lady of Częstochowa hangs on the left side. The parish changed its name to St. Mary of Ostrabrama in the 1990s to reflect the origin of its founders. **www.stmarysr.org**

TRENTON
Holy Cross Church
The founding pastor of Holy Cross Church was Fr. Valentine Swinarski, a bishop-designate in Poland who left for America after the Russian government refused to recognize his appointment. He also founded the first Polish newspaper in Trenton. In the early years, many members of the congregation worked at the cable and wire factory of John Roebling, the designer of the Brooklyn Bridge. Their hard work culminated in 1910 in the construction of the present magnificent church at 201 Adeline Street which was dedicated by Polonia's first bishop, Paul Rhode. The interior has seen extensive additions with paintings by Jozef Mazur in the 1920s. A Fatima grotto was built in 1957. The parish has merged with St. Stanislaus Parish and is now known as Divine Mercy Parish.

Pulaski Plaque at Old Barracks Museum
Organized by the Daughters of the American Revolution at the turn of the century on the grounds of the last standing barracks of the era dating back to 1758, Old Barracks Museum at 101 Barracks Street is open year-round and offers many interactive displays and rotating exhibits. There is a plaque dedicated to the contributions of Casimir Pulaski during the Revolutionary War. **www.barracks.org**

St. Hedwig Church

St. Hedwig Parish was established in 1904 as the city's third Polish church after the work of several organizations including the Casimir Pulaski Society. The present Baroque church at 872 Brunswick Avenue was constructed in 1924. In the interior there is a mural with prominent Polish saints at the altar of Our Lady of Częstochowa and a second mural highlighting Polish history. St. Hedwig sponsors a Polish school and holds services for Polish religious and cultural events including masses in Polish. A bronze bust of Fr. Jerzy Popiełuszko with a rope tied around his neck on a granite pedestal, created by Polish-born sculptor Andrzej Pitynski, was dedicated in 1987 in memory of Rev. Henry Schabowski, a pastor at St. Hedwig. It is inscribed in Polish and English and stands to the right of the church entrance. On the left side, a large bronze statue of St. Pope John Paul II greets visitors. Nearby is the historic, but now disused, Kosciuszko Hall (at Ohio Avenue and North Olden). **sainthedwigparish.com**

WALLINGTON

Most Sacred Heart of Jesus Church

After the 1937 split of the Archdiocese of Newark and the Diocese of Paterson, the need for a Polish church in Wallington was acutely felt. The polyglot Fr. Alexander Fronczak was essential in the organization of the parish which met in a house, municipal hall, and converted store—ringing a bell lent by the local firehouse—before building the current church at 127 Paterson Avenue designed by Anthony DePace. Delayed by World War II, the church was not constructed until 1947 and it was not until 1955 that the upper church was finished. The church is in an elegant art-deco style. Polish Masses, Polish feast day celebrations such as Corpus Christi, and a Polish Saturday School are held here. There is an outdoor shrine with a large bronze statue of St. Pope John Paul II. The parish also sponsors the Wallington Pulaski Parade Committee. **mshchurch.com**

Transfiguration of Our Lord
Polish National Catholic Church

This church at 135 Hathaway Street opened in 1925 and continues to hold weekly Masses in Polish and hosts the Polonia Choir. It offers a hall rental and holds traditional Polish ceremonies such as *Święconka*. **www.transfigurationpncc.org**

Bronze bust of Fr. Jerzy Popiełuszko by Pitynski at St. Hedwig Church, Trenton, NJ
(Polish Arts Club of Trenton)

Most Sacred Heart of Jesus Church, Wallington, NJ
(Parish)

NEW MEXICO

LOS ALAMOS
Immaculate Heart of Mary Church (IHMCC)
The Catholic presence here goes back to when the government established Los Alamos Scientific Laboratory in 1943. Masses were held in a theatre until 1946 when IHMCC was established at 3700 Canyon Road. The small Polish community began a campaign in 2010 to build a memorial to St. Pope John Paul II. A statue was made in Poland and dedicated on May 1, 2011, in the presence of the Polish couple who designed and created the statue along with representatives from the Polish Consulate. The statue is just north of the main church and provides a quiet place to sit and meditate. **ihmcc.org**

PUERTO DE LUNA
First Court House of Guadalupe County
Constructed of red cut stone, the courthouse stands on land donated by Alexander Grzelachowski. When the New Mexico Legislature formed the new County of Guadalupe in 1891, Grzelachowski persuaded the legislature to make Puerto de Luna the county seat. Grzelachowski became probate judge in 1893 and occupied an office in the courthouse. In 1902, the county seat was moved to Santa Rosa and the empty courthouse became a school. Today, it is a private residence.

Our Lady of Refuge Church
This church served the large Grzelachowski family, and he is buried in the cemetery. The church, built in 1892, has a dome in the quasi-Byzantine style, but the windows have elements of Moorish architecture. It is an active parish today.

Alexander Grzelachowski
Historic Puerto de Luna was the center of Alexander Grzelachowski's enterprises in the 19th century: merchandising, cattle, and sheep ranching. Grzelachowski was born in Poland in 1824 and came first to Ohio and then the New Mexico Territory in 1851 as a priest in several parishes. Grzelachowski spoke fluent Spanish, and his parishioners called him Padre Polaco, the Polish Father. He left the priesthood to begin a mercantile business, went back to serve as a chaplain in the Union Army and after the war left the priesthood again and got married. He ran the local post office, and served as San Miguel county's justice of the peace.

Billy the Kid and the man who sought to capture him, Sheriff Pat Garrett, both used to stop in Puerto de Luna and visit Padre Polaco. While in custody after being captured by the sheriff, Billy the Kid ate his last Christmas dinner at Grzelachowski's home. But Grzelachowski's most important contribution to New Mexico history took place at the Battle of Glorietta on March 18, 1862, which was the decisive Civil War battle in the West. He saved a Union force from capture by the Confederates and thus ensured the Union victory at Glorietta.

His combined old store and home was a centerpiece of the town and is now on the National Register of Historic Places. After all the Grzelachowski descendants had left, the building continued as a home until 1970. Since then, it has served as a warehouse and is succumbing to decay but is still standing. The town has a historical marker mentioning Grzelachowski.

Alexander Grzelachowski's home in Puerto de Luna, NM (cc0 1.0 Ammodramus)

NEW YORK

BOLTON LANDING

Marcella Sembrich Opera Museum & Memorial Studio (*The Sembrich*)

Polish-born soprano Marcella Kochanska Sembrich made her American operatic debut in 1883 at the Metropolitan Opera in New York having already had great acclaim throughout Europe. She founded the vocal departments at the Juilliard School in New York and the Curtis Institute of Music in Philadelphia, where her fellow-Pole Josef Hofmann was the director. Working with Ignacy Paderewski during the World War I era, she was an active philanthropist and founded the American Polish Relief Committee to send money and supplies to Poland. The operatic diva had a music studio on Lake George at 4800 Lake Shore Drive which now houses a museum, *The Sembrich*, that opened to the public in 1937. On display are such artifacts as portraits, autograph scores, objects of art, trophies, and various costumes that document the rich contributions of Sembrich to the opera. Occasional performances are still given on the original Steinway. The museum is open only from July through Labor Day during which time an annual musical festival is held. Sembrich's papers and letters are available for researchers at the New York Public Library for Performing Arts in New York City. **thesembrich.org**

BUFFALO

Adam Mickiewicz Library and Dramatic Circle

This is the oldest secular Polish American organization still operating in Buffalo and is considered one of the most important cultural landmarks of the Polonia neighborhood. Named after the Polish poet Adam Mickiewicz, the Circle began producing amateur theatricals in 1895. The library at 612 Fillmore Avenue has over four thousand books and over four hundred handwritten scripts for Polish plays. Performances of plays as well as readings of Polish poetry are held frequently. It is a long-standing tradition to read the Preamble of the Polish Constitution of May 3 at the Library and raise a toast to that momentous event that was the ratification of the revolutionary document. Although a members' social club, a nominal fee gets you access to the lively lounge and restaurant with an authentic Polish vibe, and the cultural events are open to all.

Assumption of the Blessed Virgin Mary Church

By 1882, a small Polish colony was formed in the Black Rock area of Buffalo around jobs in the railroad and shipbuilding industries. The cornerstone of the church was laid in 1888. They also built a school and formed many societies including a youth group—the Polish Cadets (*see* Buffalo, NY: Polish Cadets). In 1914 a larger brick and stone church was built at 435 Amherst Street through the labor of parishioners with over fifty stained-glass windows and reflecting "Old World" architecture with 170-ft. twin towers topped with 7-ft. crosses. It is Romanesque in spirit and of cathedral proportions, designed by Karl and William Schmill, C.J., and no effort was spared to build a flawless church with the skills available at the time.

The majestic, solid, fireproof church originally seated sixteen hundred people and is built of a unique tapestry-type brick. The varied colored brick is of a style known as "Norman" brick. The sanctuary was redecorated by artists Michael Baranowski and Józef Sławiński from Poland. A variety of liturgical symbols highlighting five scenes from the life of Blessed Virgin Mary, created in sgraffito, were Sławiński's first work. The parish still hosts Polish dinners and an annual Polish Carnival. **assumptionbuffalo.org**

Black Rock Historical Museum

The city of Buffalo sits as the gateway to the Great Lakes. It has long been the center of migration for people from many countries. From the late 1870s into the early 1900s, Buffalo became home to a wave of Polish immigrants. Most familiar is the enclave of Poles who lived in the area called the East Side. Lesser known but equally important is a second enclave called Black Rock. Poles who settled in Black Rock were largely from the province of Galicia. They came for work in the factories and quickly established churches, civic organizations, bakeries, and butcher shops as part of the community fabric. Catholic bi-lingual schools and churches were the heart of the community. Much of the Polish heritage and its history can be found in collections, photos, and exhibits at the Historical Museum at 436 Amherst Street. **www.BlackRockHistoricalSociety.com**

Chopin Monument

The monument in honor of the Polish pianist and composer Frédéric Chopin was created by artist Jozef Mazur in the 1920s and presented to the city of Buffalo by the Chopin Singing Society in June 1925. The bust sits on a granite pedestal with two bronze plaques. It was originally located in front of the Buffalo Museum of Science but now stands on the front lawn of Kleinhan Music Hall at the south end of Symphony Circle.

Corpus Christi Church

To accommodate the rapidly growing Polish immigrant community of Buffalo, Corpus Christi Parish was established in 1898, just minutes away from St. Stanislaus Parish. It was the first home of the Polish Franciscan Fathers (O.F.M. Conventuals) established by Rev. Jacek Fudzinski. The upper walls of the church at 199 Clark Street above the center aisles are adorned with six large Madonnas that are reproductions from famous Marian shrines in Poland. Murals above the center entrance to the interior of the church and pictures of saints over the arches were done by the artist-painter Marion M. Rzeznik. In 1931, Corpus Christi Parish began hosting "The Father Justin Rosary Hour" radio program which reached millions of listeners and is commemorated with a plaque on the outside of the church. (*See* Hamburg, NY: Franciscan Friars Convent where it operated until 2020.) According to the plaque, the radio program is the "oldest continuing hour-long religious network program in the Polish language in the world." Corpus Christi also hosts the "Dożynki Polish Harvest Festival," in

Polonia Trail: Western New York State Trail of Polish Heritage Sites

The Western New York State Trail of Polish Heritage Sites is an excellent interactive digital resource for historical Polonia sites at **poloniatrail.com**. It includes almost one-hundred churches, society homes, scouting sites, and monuments such as the monument to Copernicus in North Tonawanda. The pictures have links with more detailed information on each location. The trail goes from Buffalo to Niagara-on-the-Lake, through Niagara Falls, Fredonia, Olean, and Albion with many towns in between. It includes interesting historical tidbits like the Duffy Silk Mill Strike and famous Poles who visited the towns, such as Helena Modjeska, Marie Curie, and Ignacy Jan Paderewski. Some of the sites are no longer active or have since been demolished but played a significant role in the region. Each site includes photos, and a bibliography, trail directory and trail map of the region, plus a detailed map of the historic Polonia district of Buffalo. This initiative was sponsored by the Polish American Congress of Western New York.

August, a centuries-old Polish tradition celebrating the harvest season which takes place in September. During the Christmas season it hosts a Polish traditional *Wigilia*, or Christmas Eve dinner. **corpuschristibuffalo.org**

Józef Sławiński in Buffalo

Józef Sławiński, a Polish born muralist who trained in Italy, settled in Buffalo in 1964. His works adorn multiple buildings in Buffalo and across the country. He has been compared to the Mexican muralist Diego Rivera, who worked in a variety of mediums, including fresco, hammered copper, scratched tempera, mosaics, and wrought iron. His most common medium was sgraffito, a subtractive technique in which he created four layers of colored cement which had to be etched while still wet. In addition to those murals mentioned in the specific sites, there is a magnificent color copper etched mural of the first ruling prince of Poland, Mieszko I, in St. Joseph Cathedral in Buffalo. Buffalo City Hall has a large copper etched wall mural commemorating the massacre at Katyń, which was unveiled on the 40th anniversary of the event. His art is scattered in fifteen locations in the Buffalo/Niagara area and these websites provide more detail: **info-poland.icm.edu.pl/exhib/s/index.html and buffaloah.com/a/archs/slaw/slaw.html**

Fronczak Room (SUNY Buffalo State College)
Established in 1970, this archive is a part of the Archives & Special Collections of the E.H. Butler Library thanks to a generous donation by the Fronczak Family. It is a repository of official documents, manuscripts, flyers, photos, paintings, World War II memorabilia, and materials relating to Polonia in Western New York, along with publications of local Polish churches and organizations. It also holds extensive materials on Dr. Francis E. Fronczak, community activist for Polish independence and Polish War Relief, as well as Dr. Walter M. Drzewieniecki, who established the College's East European and Slavic Studies Program and was a founder of the Polish Cultural Foundation. **library.buffalostate.edu/archives/fronczak/home**

Historic Polonia District
Two miles from downtown Buffalo, there is a Polonia neighborhood with cultural and architectural landmarks that still have visible signage including Dom Polski (which welcomed Helena and Ignacy Paderewski and Gen. Joseph Haller and hosted many Polish organizations, became the Polish Cultural Center, and now is the Matt Urban Center), St. Adalbert Basilica, the Polish Union's former headquarters and Polish Army Veterans Assoc. Post 1, both on Fillmore Street. Buffalo has a rich Polonia history as it was the founding city of the Polish American Congress in 1944 and is the home of the Polish Union of America, founded in 1890, and is the largest Polish fraternal headquartered in New York state.

Buffalo claims to be the Dyngus Day capital of the world with one of the largest Dyngus Day celebrations the week following Easter, with activities taking over Buffalo's Polonia District. The festivities kick-off with a parade on Easter Monday marching down Broadway and Fillmore Avenue. Scattered throughout the Polonia District are food tents with pierogi, and people dressed in their best Polish-pride attire hitting one another with pussy willows. Tours of the area are available on the link below. **www.forgottenbuffalo.com/historicpoloniadistrict.html**

International Railroad Bridge
On Unity Island Park (formally Squaw Island) along the Niagara River, one can see a railroad bridge connecting the island to southern Ontario, Canada. This bridge, opened in 1873, is a remarkable engineering feat, accomplished under the supervision of the Polish immigrant, Sir Casimir Gzowski (1813-1898). On November 3, 1873, it opened for travel and quickly became one of the most used entry points between the United States and Canada.

Józef Sławiński Mural, SUNY Buffalo State College
The historic concrete sgraffito mural is on the outside of the north wall of the E.H. Butler Library, 1300 Elmwood Avenue in Buffalo. The plaque below the piece reads "Joseph Calasanctius (1557-1648) surrounded by the children of the world's first free public school he founded in Rome in 1597." A local Polish immigrant, Józef Sławiński, created the mural in 1967. Sławiński, born in 1905 in Poland, made the Buffalo area his home in 1964. In 1967, Piarist Priests commissioned Sławiński to create the 18-by-12-foot mural to commemorate the 350th anniversary of the founding of the Piarist order. The piece was originally located on the Graycliff estate, designed by Frank Lloyd Wright. In 2005, thanks to the Polish Arts Club of Buffalo, the mural underwent restoration and was relocated to Buffalo State College where students and the public can admire it. Sławiński was on the faculty so it was a homecoming of his art.
poloniatrail.com/location/joseph-slawinski-home

(left) Józef Sławiński mural, SUNY Buffalo State College, Buffalo, NY (Jacquie Pason)

Józef Sławiński mural, Erie County Medical Center, Buffalo, NY (PAC)

Józef Sławiński Mural, Erie County Medical Center

A 21-foot-long mural in the entrance lobby of the medical center at 462 Grider Street is one of Józef Sławiński's most iconic works. The mural was commissioned by Erie County in celebration of Buffalo Polonia's centennial in 1973. It depicts individuals and institutions that played a significant role in the development of the Polish American community in America and Buffalo from different waves of immigration in the first one-hundred years.

Pulaski Statue

In front of the Ellicott Square Building at 283 Main Street, there is a large bronze statue of General Pulaski sculpted by Kazimierz Danilewicz in 1979. On the black granite base of the statue it reads, "General Kazimierz Pulaski Hero of Poland and the United States of America." On one side, there is a dedication in Polish and the English translation is on the opposite side, "A gift from the people of Poland to the people of the United States of America commemorating 200 years of American Independence." It is located only a few blocks from where the Polish American Congress was established in the now demolished War Memorial Auditorium. **buffaloah.com/a/pulaski/cp.html**

Pulaski statue, Buffalo, NY (Jacquie Pason)

Poland's Contribution in World War II Memorial

This memorial, located on Marine Drive in the Buffalo & Erie County Naval Military Park, was erected in 2002 by the SPK (*Stowarzyszenie Polskich Kombatantów* / Polish Veterans of World War II) Post 33. It was designed by Michael Angelo and sculpted by H.A. Gomez with a White Eagle coat of arms and Polish soldiers in action. It is dedicated to the members of the Polish Armed Forces, listing major battles where Poles fought bravely on the Western Front (Narvik, Tobruk, Normandy, Battle of Britain, Monte Cassino, Ancona) and in Poland as members of the Underground Army during the Warsaw Uprising.

The Polish Cadets

The Polish Cadet Society, established in 1899, originally served as a men's club for Polish immigrants. The Cadets helped advocate for Polish citizens living nearby, as well as provide a central meeting place for the immigrant community. It has since evolved to host Polish cultural and social events, such as Dyngus Day. The historic building at 927 Grant Street, designed by local architect W. Zawadzki, was constructed in 1913 and includes the Cadets Federal Credit Union and a library.
www.polishcadetsofbuffalo.com

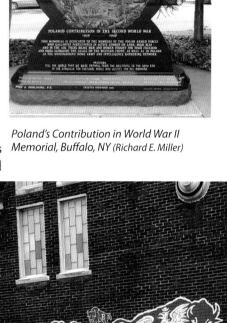

Poland's Contribution in World War II Memorial, Buffalo, NY (Richard E. Miller)

Polish Room (SUNY at Buffalo)

This collection is open to the public and is in the Lockwood Library (Room 517), on the North Campus of SUNY Buffalo. It includes over 12,000 volumes on Polish related topics as well as art and theater productions, films, and some *Solidarność* (Solidarity) documents. The room was established in 1955 when a thriving Polish American community coordinated by the Polish Arts Club wanted to preserve their heritage. The owners of Sattler's Department Store donated twenty-one Polish royal documents, the cornerstone of the collection. They are original parchments in Polish and Latin signed by Polish kings spanning 1515 until 1722. It also includes four original stained-glass medallions honoring important Polish cultural figures, one by local artist Josef Mazur depicting Marie Curie. SUNY Buffalo also has another Polish connection with a major academic building named for Francis E. Fronczak (*see* Buffalo, NY: Fronczak Room). **library.buffalo.edu/polish-room**

Decree signed by King Jan III Sobieski 1682 at Polish Room, SUNY at Buffalo, NY

Polish Cadets building, Buffalo, NY (Jacquie Pason)

St. Adalbert Basilica

St. Adalbert Basilica, located at 212 Stanislaus St., was founded in 1886 as the second Polish church in Buffalo and was designated a basilica in 1907, the first in the U.S. The original wooden altar was broken into seven

Chopin sgrafitto mural by Józef Sławiński, Villa Maria College, Buffalo, NY (Villa Maria College)

side altars and replaced with an immense marble one that has the Polish eagle at the top right under the crown and by St. Adalbert's statue. One of the chapels holds an icon of Our Lady of Częstochowa that was on display at the Pan American Exhibition in 1901. It includes symbols of Lithuania referencing the joint commonwealth. Jozef Mazur paintings from the 1920s—oil on canvas—are found on the walls; he repainted the dome in the 1940s (using his wife's face for the angels surrounding the dome). The left wall has a gallery of paintings of more contemporary Polish saints such as Maximilian Kolbe. The basilica parish merged with St. John Kanty Parish and was designated an oratory and remains open for tours and Masses on special feast days and celebrations. **http://saintadalbertbasilica.org**

St. Stanislaus Bishop and Martyr Church

To accommodate the influx of Polish immigrants in the late 19th century, Reverend Dean John Pitass began construction of St. Stanislaus Church in 1873. A marker to the left of the entrance states, "First Polish colony settled here in 1873." This church at 123 Townsend Street not only serves as a religious center, but also as the first communal, cultural, and recreational gathering place for Polish immigrants of the surrounding area. St. Stanislaus was vitally important in establishing a strong, thriving Polish district in the east side of Buffalo, known as the Polonia district. The shrine of St. Pope John Paul II includes a large statue as well as his relics. A side chapel is dedicated to Our Lady of Częstochowa. Iconography includes many Polish saints in vivid stained-glass windows and paintings by Jozef Mazur. Mass is available in Polish. The Parish holds various events throughout the year, such as a celebration of Poland's independence, an annual *Jasełka* (Nativity play), hosting Polish musical concerts, and sponsoring a Polish Saturday school. The "*Polska Czytelnia,*" the oldest Polish library in the U.S., established in 1889, has a collection of over eight thousand Polish materials in the parish's Pitass Center. **www.ststansbuffalo.com**

Villa Maria College

In 1987, a statue of St. Pope John Paul II was unveiled at Villa Maria College in front of the auditorium entrance, facing Pennock Place. The Western New York area has over 350,000 Polish Americans, many of them very conscious and proud of their heritage, so the public fund drive for the monument was hugely successful. The College itself is steeped in Polish American tradition and was a natural location for the statue honoring one of Poland's greatest sons. The campus includes the mother house for the Polish Felician Sisters, an order that operated most of the Catholic schools in Buffalo's Polonia and had ministries in New England and the Mid-Atlantic states. The Provincial Convent Building houses the Felician Sisters' Archives, Immaculate Heart of Mary Province and a Heritage Room of artifacts and documents related to the religious order which is open to the public.

A special collection in the college library contains three thousand volumes in the Polish language, with a focus on literary and historical subjects relating to Poland. The campus also has two large sgraffito murals done by Polish-born artist Józef Sławiński: Chopin and Copernicus. The Buffalo suburb of Cheektowaga, where the college is situated, holds an annual summer Polish Arts Festival in the town park.

COHOES

Peebles Island State Park Revolutionary War earthworks

Kosciuszko Entrenchments, Peebles Island State Park, Cohoes, NY (James Pula)

When American forces were retreating before the advance of a British army under Gen. John Burgoyne in the fall of 1777, Col. Thaddeus Kosciuszko was assigned to halt their march by constructing field fortifications on Peebles and Van Schaick Islands at modern-day Cohoes, New York, north of Albany. Today, surviving portions of the breastworks constructed on Peebles Island under the engineer's direction can still be seen, a very rare instance of Revolutionary War earthworks that still exist. A marker erected by the State Education Department identifies the location in the Peebles Island State Park. Entrance to Peebles Island State Park is at 1 Delaware Avenue North. West of Cohoes along the Mohawk River stands the Kosciuszko Bridge (coordinates 42.79152°N - 73.76146°W). Located between exits 7 and 8 on Interstate 87, the structure is two arch bridges, side-by-side, accommodating six lanes of traffic connecting the towns of Colonie in Albany County and Halfmoon in Saratoga County. The town of Cohoes has many buildings on the National Register of Historic Places, including the downtown.

EAST MEADOW

Polish Freedom Fighters Memorial Marker

A marker on Park Boulevard north of Route 24 was dedicated in 1979 by the American Polish Council of Long Island as a 40th anniversary tribute to Polish freedom fighters who made the supreme sacrifice in World War II during the invasion of Poland in September 1939. It also includes a statement in remembrance of the Katyń Massacre.

ELMIRA
Kopernik (Copernicus) Plaque
St. Casimir's Polish Arts Club of Elmira sponsored this plaque in honor of Nicolaus Copernicus
(Mikołaj Kopernik) at the intersection of Davis
Street and Millard Street near Pulaski Park, which
was dedicated on May 4, 1980. There is also an earlier plaque in honor of the Polish astronomer and
clergyman who formulated the heliocentric model
of the Universe erected by the city in 1972.

Kopernik plaque, Elmira, NY (Bria Scott)

GLEN COVE
Marker to Polish American Freedom Fighter
Erected in 1982 by the Polish American War Vet-
erans of Glen Cove, this marker is a tribute to those Polish American Freedom Fighters who
lost their lives in World War I and II. It is located at the intersection of School Street and Forest
Avenue.

HAMBURG (Athol Springs)
Franciscan Friars Conventual of the Our Lady of the Angels Province
Located just outside Buffalo on Lake Erie are two chapels decorated with sgraffito murals of Polish and Polish American history by Józef Sławiński and Jan Henryk de Rosen. The Father Justin
Rosary Hour, the oldest Catholic radio program in Polish in the world until 2020, was produced
at St. Francis High School, located on the grounds of the friary, and founded by Fr. Justin Figas.
(*See also* Buffalo, NY: Corpus Christi Church.) The broadcasting studio contains several religious
art works, including paintings by Jan Gross and hammered copper murals by Józef Sławiński.

LANCASTER
Holy Mother of the Rosary Polish National Cathedral
In 1995, this contemporary church at 6298 Broadway replaced the original cathedral located at Sobieski and Sycamore Streets in Buffalo's east side where it served the people for a hundred years. It
is a contemporary structure that evokes the wooden churches of the *Góral* region. It incorporated
many of the original stained-glass windows of saints, statues, the original cornerstone, and other
furnishings of the original building blended with new carvings and images. The six original Cathedral bells were recently installed in a beautiful bell tower. **www.holymotheroftherosary.org**

NEW YORK CITY: BROOKLYN
Our Lady of Consolation Church
Founded in 1909, this church at 184 Metropolitan Avenue is presently under the guidance of Salvatorian priests. Inside the church there is a life-size wood statue of St. Pope John Paul II carved
in Trebnica, Poland. In 2011, the parish unveiled a plaque on the outside walls of the church in
memory of the 96 Polish citizens killed in the Smolensk plane crash in 2010 as well as the Katyń
Forest massacre in 1940. Masses and events are mostly in Polish, including Polish religious obser-
vations such as *Boże Ciało, Gorzkie Żale, Jasełka, Pasterka*. **www.olcny.org**

Our Lady of Czestochowa & St. Casimir Church
The parish of St. Casimir was established in 1875 to serve the Polish community. It merged with

Artifacts at the Piłsudski Institute of America, New York, NY (Małgorzata Skrodzki)

Our Lady of Czestochowa Parish in 1980 and the St. Casimir church building was converted into The Paul Robeson Theatre. Our Lady of Czestochowa Church was established in 1896 and the current building at 183 25th Street dates to 1904. It was designed in the Gothic style and constructed of stone and brick with stained-glass windows depicting Polish saints and a bronze statue of St. Pope John Paul II in front of the rectory. Polish Masses and observances of Polish holidays continue to this day. **olcbrooklyn.org**

The Piłsudski Institute of America

The Józef Piłsudski Institute of America was founded on July 4, 1943, in New York at the initiative of Americans of Polish descent and wartime refugees from Poland. Among the founding members, there were several Polish-American activists: Franciszek Januszewski, Maksymilian Węgrzynek, and Lucjan Kupferwasser. The Institute derived from the tradition of the Institute for Research in the Modern History of Poland established in 1923 in Warsaw.

The Piłsudski Institute is a not-for-profit research and education institution for Polish and East-European history and culture. Its activities play a vital role in the study of contemporary history and in projecting the image of Poland in America.

The Institute located at 138 Greenpoint Avenue in Brooklyn has one of the largest archives concerning Poland—about one million seven hundred thousand pages of documents—which translates into 200 meters of shelf space. The most valuable part of the Institute's documents is the Belvedere Archive, saved from burning Warsaw in September 1939. These materials are a significant resource for researchers working on the issue of Poland's borders between 1918-1922. The bulk of the collection, however, are materials generated and collected in the United States, documenting the activities of Polonia over a period of several decades. These include files of politicians, diplomats, and high-ranking military officials. In addition, the Institute possesses archives of important Polish organizations such as the Committee for the National Defense in America.

There are rare and valuable artifacts belonging to officers serving in the Polish Legions during the years of 1914-1916 and during the Polish-Soviet war from 1919-1922. The book collection consists of around 23,000 thousand publications which are listed in the online catalog and the Institute has been digitizing its archives to preserve them and deliver online access to the public.

The gallery holds paintings donated mostly from collections by Aleksander Mełeń-Korczyński and Janina Czermańska with over two hundred oil paintings, watercolors, drawings, and sketches. Most are by eminent Polish artists, among them Jan Matejko, Juliusz Kossak, Leon Wyczółkowski, Aleksander Gierymski, Jacek Malczewski, and Stanisław Wyspiański.

The Institute offers programs open to the public with special programs like documentary film screenings, meetings with historians and book presentations. **www.pilsudski.org** (in Polish)

Kosciuszko Monument, Greenpoint, Brooklyn, NY (Wojtek Maslanka)

GREENPOINT NEIGHBORHOOD of BROOKLYN
Kosciuszko Monument
A new monument was dedicated to the Polish War hero, Tadeusz Kosciuszko in the park under the Kosciuszko Bridge at the intersection of Meeker Avenue & Apollo Street. The bronze bust was created by the artist Marian Szajda and stands on a tall granite pillar along the East River.

The Polish & Slavic Center
The Polish & Slavic Center at 176 Java Street in the Greenpoint neighborhood of Brooklyn is a non-profit social and cultural services organization founded in 1972 with the headquarters in New York City primarily serving the Polish American community. With about forty thousand members, it is the largest Polish American organization on the East Coast and serves the entire Polish and Slavic community with programs for children and seniors, and special programs dedicated to help with immigration status and English language education. The idea to establish the Polish & Slavic Center originated in the mid-1970s with Reverend Longin Tolczyk, who was working at that time among Polish American immigrants in New York City. Throughout the year, the Center provides programs, art exhibits, concerts, and other events and has a dining facility and publishes a Polish language quarterly. On the centenary anniversary of the Independence of Poland, a commemorative plaque of Ignacy Jan Paderewski (by Andrzej Renes) was unveiled on the front of the building which also has a bust of Frédéric Chopin. **www.polishslaviccenter.org**

Other Points of Interest in Brooklyn's Greenpoint
The Greenpoint area, which had been a large thriving Polish community in Brooklyn, is changing dynamically, with new modern buildings and less Polish American presence. It lies directly across from the UN Headquarters overlooking the East River. There one finds the Kurier Plus Gallery (headquarters of Weekly Kurier Plus publication), the Józef Piłsudski Institute, and several Polish restaurants and shops.

Polish & Slavic Federal Credit Union (PSFCU)
The Polish & Slavic Federal Credit Union was established in 1976 by the founders of the Polish & Slavic Center led by Rev. Longin Tolczyk. The founders wanted to help immigrants who, upon arrival in New York City, wanted to buy houses in the Greenpoint neighborhood of Brooklyn but were turned down by the banks. In 1981, PSFCU purchased a building at 140 Greenpoint Avenue which serves as its headquarters. The walls of the great hall are decorated with enlarged reproductions of sketches by the famous Polish painter Jacek Malczewski. The Credit Union currently has nineteen branches in New York City and elsewhere, allowing it to serve about 100,000 members. PSFCU is currently the largest ethnic credit union in the United States. **en.psfcu.com**

Reverend Jerzy Popiełuszko Memorial
In Father Popiełuszko Square (McCarren Park at Bedford Avenue and Lorimer Street) there is a granite bust of the martyred priest who died in 1984 as a hero of the *Solidarność* (Solidarity) movement in Poland. This solid granite monument was commissioned by the Polish American Congress, Southern New York District, and unveiled October 21, 1990. The bust seems to be emerging from a rough-hewn block appearing to be enshrouded in a map of Poland. The statue was beheaded by Communist sympathizers in November 1990 but has since been restored and the monument is well taken care of by the Polish American community.

Jerzy Popiełuszko Memorial, Greenpoint, Brooklyn, NY (Malgorzata Skrodzki)

NEW YORK CITY: MANHATTAN

Consulate General of the Republic of Poland

This residence on Madison Avenue and 37th, also known as Karski Corner, is one of the most outstanding examples of New York-style in residential architecture—Beaux-Arts. The building was built by architect C. P. H. Gilbert over one hundred years ago for Captain Joseph Raphael De Lamar, one of the richest New Yorkers at the turn of the 20th century. In 1975, the building was added to the register of monuments of New York; it was preserved in its current form due to the efforts of its host, the Polish Consulate General in New York. A copy of the Washington D.C. sculpture of Jan Karski, the World War II underground courier, sitting on a bench is in front of the Consulate on the 37th Street side (*see* District of Colombia: Georgetown University). The Consulate also has a collection of Polish paintings and sculptures, including a Polish eagle carved by Andrzej Pitynski. The Consulate sponsors exhibits of Polish artists, concerts, films, and events open to visitors.

Consulate General of the Republic of Poland, New York, NY (Ewa Barczyk)

Ignacy Jan Paderewski Artifacts and Memorabilia in New York City

This great pianist and statesman lived in New York for many years and gave numerous concerts at Carnegie Hall. His last residence was at nearby Buckingham Hotel (today the **Quin Hotel**), at 101 West 57th Street, where a commemorative bronze marker was unveiled on November 17, 1991, the 50th anniversary of his death. The marker was donated by two musicians, Raphael Castoriano and Voytek Matushevsky. Paderewski died at the hotel on June 29, 1941. The manager of the hotel at the time, Mr. Benjamin Shapiro, allowed Paderewski's body to lie in state in the very room he had occupied while visiting New York City. For the next two days thousands of New Yorkers were able to pay last respects to the Polish musician and statesman before he lay in state at the Polish Embassy in Washington, D.C. Next door, **Steinway Hall** houses several memorabilia of the great Polish artist, including a bronze sculpture by American artist Malvina Cornell Hoffman entitled "Paderewski the Statesman" (1922). Upon seeing it in Hoffman's studio, Paderewski approvingly called it "a portrait of my inner self lost in my music." The bust has been in the rotunda of Steinway Hall since 1926 along with other exhibits and memorabilia relating to renowned pianists, among them a paper mask by Władysław Benda (1940) representing Paderewski's face, several paintings, medals, documents and other memorabilia, as well as vintage Steinway Piano advertisements from 1926 depicting "Ignace Jan Paderewski" painted by "Zuloaga" for the "Steinway Collection."

In Tompkins Square, near St. Stanislaus Bishop & Martyr Church, a red oak was planted in 1941 (replaced with a new tree in 2019) that is officially known as the Paderewski Tree. A plaque by the tree, which begins with a quote from Paderewski, gives an extensive biography of his accomplishments.

The Kosciuszko Foundation

The Kosciuszko Foundation (KF) is one of the greatest American success stories in the field of public service and cultural activity. It was founded in 1925, as a memorial to Thaddeus Kosciuszko, by Stefan Mierzwa, who arrived from Poland as a teenager and received scholarships to both Amherst College and Harvard University. Upon graduating, Mierzwa raised $5,000 for the Polish American Scholarship Committee, later to become the Kosciuszko Foundation. The foundation is a monument to Mierzwa's desire to give Polish Americans the opportunity to better themselves through education. Since its founding, the KF has been promoting closer ties between Poland and the US though educational, scientific, and cultural exchanges. In 1945, the KF purchased the Van Alen Mansion at 15 East 65th Street for its headquarters which was designed in 1916 by renowned architect Harry Allan Jacobs, well known for his fashionable homes designed in historic styles. He made it to be a near-copy of a Regency-period mansion on St. James Square in London. The three-story limestone building houses the administrative offices of the Foundation, a library and large archive. The art gallery contains an extensive collection of Polish art including works by Jan Matejko, Jacek Malczewski, Jan Styka, Józef Brandt, and Olga Boznanska. It also has a vast array of memorabilia and other pieces of art, like prints and notably a collection of rare masks by Władysław Benda. The Foundation offers a rich program of cultural events to promote Polish culture including author evenings, lectures, concerts, films, and art shows. **www.theKF.org**

The Kosciuszko Foundation building, New York, NY (Ewa Barczyk)

Marie Skłodowska Curie tablet

Located in City Hall Park, across from the Woolworth Building on lower Broadway, the bronze tablet on a plinth says it was a gift of the Polish American Children of New York City on November 7, 1934, to commemorate the 67th anniversary of the birth of the Polish scientist.

The Polish Institute of Arts and Sciences of America (PIASA)

The Institute was founded in 1942 by Oskar Halecki, Bronisław Malinowski, Jan Kucharzewski, Wacław Lednicki, Wojciech Swietoslawski, and Rafal Taubenschlag to assure the continuity of Polish culture and learning during World War II. Its founders were Polish scholars and members of the pre-World War II Polish Academy of Sciences. Its purpose was to preserve for future generations Polish scholarship and culture as a center of learning devoted to the advancement of knowledge about Poland and Polish America. Since 1986 its national headquarters has been a five-story townhouse at 208 East 30th St. in the Murray Hill section of Manhattan. The building houses not only administrative and editorial offices, but also a specialized reference library and rich archives. It also has an art gallery and small lecture hall where exhibits and lectures are organized. The archival collections include manuscripts, correspondence, diaries of many prominent Polish politicians, scholars, and artists, along with maps and sound recordings. An original plaque designed by Polish artist Greg Gustaw, commemorating the poet Cyprian Norwid and the years he spent in New York City (1852-53), was unveiled in October 2015 by the main entrance to the Polish Institute. The Institute's library as well as its art collection are available to the public. **www.piasa.org**

Original plaque designed by Polish artist Greg Gustaw commemorating the poet Cyprian Norwid, PIASA, New York, NY (Iwona Flis)

Polish Army Veterans Home Association of America and Polish Military Heritage Museum of New York

The Polish Army Veterans' Association of America (PAVA) is the world's oldest independent, self-help organization of former Polish soldiers operating continuously since 1921. Its headquarters is in Manhattan in the "Polish Veterans' Home" at 119 East 15th Street which also houses the organizational archives and a museum. PAVA engages in publishing activities, among them the monthly publication of *Weteran* (The Veteran)—the oldest Polish magazine of its kind in the world.

The Polish Military Heritage Museum of New York was established at the Polish Veterans' Home in 1996 under the auspices of the PAVA Foundation to preserve and exhibit items related to the military service of Polish Americans. On exhibit are items related to the "Blue Army" that fought for Poland's independence during World War I, mementos from the interwar years, and a large collection related to the Polish Armed Forces in the west during World War II. The museum also contains archives related to the military service of Polish Americans. Throughout the year, the museum organizes special displays and other activities involving Polish military themes. The exhibited objects date back to the recruitment of Polish volunteers from the United States and Canada, as well as to the Army of Poland in France from 1917-1919. The museum exhibits the banners of PAVA, posters, paintings, and documents as well as World War II memorabilia. Particularly interesting is the collection of uniforms, armaments, and military equipment. PAVA archives contain the richest collection of documents in America illustrating the life of Polish veterans in this country from 1920 to present day. **pava-swap.org** (in Polish)

Rose Hill Kosciuszko Marker

The marker is at 2nd Avenue and East 22nd Street. When this area was the estate of Gen. Horatio Gates (Battle of Saratoga, 1777), General Thaddeus Kosciuszko stayed here with his friend and former commander in 1797. Here he received well-wishes for his daring and gallant services during the American Revolution. The plaque was erected in 1997 by Epiphany Parish, the Knights of Lithuania, the Kosciuszko Foundation, and the Pilsudski Institute in his honor.

St. Clement Church

St. Clement Church is a remnant of the forgotten and lost story of a Polish community in New York City. Located in the Hell's Kitchen neighborhood, it was founded in 1909 for Polish Roman Catholics in west Manhattan. With the gradual change in neighborhood demographics to a more affluent population in the mid-20th century, the congregation dwindled and after construction of the Lincoln Tunnel led to the relocation of many of the church's parishioners, the parish was closed in 1971. Since 1984, the church building at 410 West 40th Street has been occupied by Metro Baptist Church. The Gothic-style church building maintains many of its beautiful historic features. The sanctuary still has the ceiling murals and windows of its Polish-Catholic origin. The main hall preserves five (among nine) stained-glass windows with original Polish imagery and inscriptions, e.g., *Boże zbaw Polskę* (God save Poland) under a picture of the Polish coat of arms (Crown and Pogoń). **mbcnyc.org**

St. Patrick's Cathedral Polish Chapel

St. Patrick's Cathedral, New York, NY (Ewa Barczyk)

Inside St. Patrick's Cathedral (on 5th Avenue between 50th and 51st Streets) there is a Polish chapel dedicated to Our Lady of Częstochowa in the left nave. The altar is made of white marble and is shaped in Gothic-style matching the design of the whole church. At the center of the chapel there is a copy of the well-known image of the "Black Madonna," painted by Anna Torwirt, artist of Torun, and blessed by Pope John Paul II.

Under the altar's tabletop there are two inscriptions: on the right side, "Our Lady of Czestochowa, pray for us"; and on the left, *Matko Boża, Królowo Polski, módl się za nami* ("Our Lady, Queen of Poland, pray for us").

The chapel was funded by the Polish American community to commemorate the 50th anniversary of the National Shrine of Our Lady of Czestochowa in Doylestown, PA, and the 25th anniversary of John Paul II's papacy. A bust of Pope John Paul II is mounted in the vestibule above the 5th Avenue entrance. This and three other sculptures representing popes who visited New York City and its Cathedral were created by the artist Carolyn Palmer to memorialize these historic visits, as well as their significance to the cathedral, the city, and the generations of people. Pope John Paul II visited New York City twice, in 1979 and 1995. Every year, the Polish community gathers for notable events at the Cathedral: the Pulaski Day Parade Mass, a celebration of Polish heritage in the U.S. held in October, and a commemorative concert in honor of Pope St. John Paul II, usually held in April. **www.saintpatrickscathedral.org**

St. Stanislaus Bishop and Martyr Church

St. Stanislaus Bishop and Martyr Church was established in 1872 and has been on its present site at 101 East 7th Street since 1901. During the 42-year pastorship of Msgr. Felix Ferdinand Burant, the church became the center for religious and patriotic activities for the Polish community. The first Pulaski Day parade started from the church. In 1986, the Pauline Fathers assumed oversight

St. Stanislaus Bishop & Martyr Church, New York, NY

of the parish. Completely renovated, it is the only Polish Roman Catholic church in Manhattan and the oldest Polish church in the Archdiocese of New York. On June 23, 1991, the Monument of St. Pope John Paul II was erected in front of the rectory. In the church itself there are two large paintings by Adam Styka: "The Assumption" and "The Ascension." Over the decades, the parish hosted many prominent Poles, among them Ignacy Paderewski, General Józef Haller, General Władysław Sikorski, and Lech Wałęsa. The parish runs an active Saturday Polish language school. **www.stanislauschurch.us**

United Nations Headquarters: Copernicus Bust and "Sleeping Child" Stained Glass

At the main entrance to the Dag Hammarskjold Library at the United Nations Headquarters, there is on permanent display a bust of Nicolaus Copernicus (1473-1543), the famous Polish astronomer. It was a gift from Poland to the U.N. in 1970. This piece, carved from a block of Finnish granite, was created by internationally recognized Polish artist Alfons Karny (1901–1989). The base of this figurehead was made by stonecutter Z. Debniak. The then Secretary-General of the UN, U Thant, said: "Copernicus was one of those rare, brilliant individuals who extend the frontiers of knowledge for mankind. All of us at the United Nations will draw inspiration from the universal message which he brings to us."

The stained-glass wood-framed window "Sleeping Child," on permanent display in the hall between the Chambers of the Security and Trusteeship Councils, is based on the motifs of a drawing by the famous Polish artist Stanislaw Wyspiański (1869-1907). This piece of art is a gift to the U.N. from the people of Poland in honor of the proclamation by the General Assembly of 1979 as the International Year of the Child. It was created by Józef Olszewski of Warsaw, one of the prominent Polish stained-glass artisans, in cooperation with his wife, Alicja, from a design by Polish painter Halina Cieślinska-Brzeski of Kraków. The wooden frame of the stained glass was hand-carved by another artist, Zygmunt Dzierla.

Władysław II Jagiełło Statue

The towering equestrian monument of Władysław Jagiełło, a 14th-15th century King of Poland

"Sleeping Child" window,
United Nations Building,
New York, NY
(Chester Karkowski)

and Grand Duke of Lithuania, is in Central Park, near 5th Avenue and 79th St. It depicts the Battle of Grunwald in 1410 when the king raised the two swords given to him in surrender by the Teutonic Knights. The bronze statue, executed by Stanislaw Ostrowski, originally stood in front of the Polish Pavilion at the New York World's Fair (1939-40) but remained in the U.S. due to the outbreak of World War II and has found permanent residence in New York. The statue was presented to the City of New York by the King Jagiełło Monument Committee, with support from the Polish government in exile in July 1945.

NEW YORK CITY: QUEENS
St. Adalbert Church
Begun in 1891, St. Adalbert Parish, at 52-29 83rd Street in the Elmhurst neighborhood of Queens, is the oldest Polish parish in Queens and the fourth oldest in the New York City area. The current brick church was erected in 1949. The iconography includes depictions of Polish saints. Polish Masses and religious events are celebrated. **www.adalbertchurch.org**

NEW YORK CITY: STATEN ISLAND
Generals Kazimierz Pulaski & Tadeusz Kosciuszko tablet
Located in Silver Lake Park on Forest Avenue at Duer Lane, this large bronze tablet on a stele is dedicated to both Polish American heroes. It was erected in 1926 on the 150th anniversary of the Declaration of Independence by the Polish American citizens of Richmond County, New York, in memory of Kosciuszko and Pulaski as a token to their service to the cause of the American colonists.

Jagiełło Monument in Central Park,
New York, NY (CZmarlin CC BY-SA 4.0)

NEW YORK MILLS
Sacred Heart of Jesus Polish National Catholic Church
On the corner of Main and Walcott Streets is the Sacred Heart of Jesus PNCC, which was founded in January 1923 by its first pastor, Reverend F. J. Kłosiński. The parish property, which used to be an Episcopal Church, was dedicated in September 1925. The parish had a White Eagle group, a benefit society, and a children's society. It had a school with almost one hundred students, who studied the catechism and Polish language. It also sponsored scouting activities, summer picnics, a basketball team, dances, camping outings, the Frederic Chopin choir, and other forms of social activities. The interior is decorated with elaborate wood carvings and the side altar contains a picture of the Black Madonna. The parish is now known as Sacred Heart of Jesus–Holy Cross Parish. **www.sacredheartofjesus-holycrosspncc.com**

St. Mary, Our Lady of Czestochowa Church
Popularly known as St. Mary's, this church and its accompanying school is located on a hill off Main Street. It celebrated its first Mass on January 3, 1911. The school officially opened in September 1912, when three Felician nuns came from Buffalo. Early in its history, a women's organization, the Sacred Heart of Jesus Society, was established to purchase a statue of St. Mary for the parish, a statue of Casimir

Sacred Heart of Jesus PNCC, New York Mills, NY (Cheryl Pula)

New York Mills
New York Mills is situated in the Mohawk Valley of Upstate New York, just outside of the city of Utica. It is a "mill town," having had several textile mills during its history. Those mills attracted numerous Polish immigrants to settle in the village. Indeed, for many decades, the predominant ethnic group in residence in New York Mills was Polish. Located near the famous Erie Canal, the village was incorporated in April 1922, though the area was settled before that, as the textile mills were important at least beginning in the 1820s. The village is home to several parks including Pulaski Park, a historical society, several churches, and Hapanowicz Meat Market, known throughout central New York for its homemade Polish delicacies.

The Bell Monument, the brainchild of Reverend Walter Madej, a native of Poland, is in Pulaski Park on Main St. Dedicated July 8, 2000, in memory of Polish immigrants who labored in the town's textile mills. The bell originally hung in the tower of Number 2 mill and told Polish workers when to go to work, lunch, and end the workday, and for decades also signaled the 9 PM curfew for village children. From 1952-1993, it was installed in the steeple of Sacred Heart of Jesus Polish National Catholic Church. The Bell Monument represents the town's respect for work and family values. The copper bell rests on a rock base in the shape of a ship, symbolizing the pilgrimage of Polish immigrants seeking a better life in this country. The granite was donated from a quarry twenty miles away, and rocks at the monument's base are from the foundation of the original mill. Above the bell are copper wings, a protective canopy representing how the town has protected its families and co-workers. The second Saturday of July each year is the community's annual Bell Festival.

St. Mary, Our Lady of Czestochowa Church, New York Mills, NY (Cheryl Pula)

Pulaski in Utica, and to aid orphans in Poland. The men also had a social group, St. Casimir's Polish Men's Society which is still in existence. A large painting of Our Lady of Częstochowa was done for the church by Stanley Borowiec in 1982. The outdoor Stations of the Cross resemble Polish wayside shrines known as *kapliczki*. Today the church has a popular festival at the beginning of August, which is open to the public, featuring Polish cuisine, various forms of entertainment, and village hospitality. It is now the Sacred Heart and St. Mary Parish.
www.sacredheart-saintmary.org

Bell Monument in memory of Polish Immigrants who labored in the town's textile mills, New York Mills, NY (Cheryl Pula)

NORTH TONOWANDA
Our Lady of Czestochowa Church
This parish was founded in 1901 but the current church at 57 Center Avenue dates from 1928. There are stained glass windows designed by Buffalo artist Joseph Mazur in the nave of the church. In 1966 the Grotto Garden was added and dedicated to Our Lady of Częstochowa. The parish installed a new altar which is a replica of the original one on the back altar. A Shrine to Our Lady of Częstochowa was added in 1983. The parish hosts an exceedingly popular pierogi-making ministry that meets weekly. **nt-olc.org**

PORT WASHINGTON
The Polish American Museum

The Polish American Museum was founded in 1977 and officially opened a year later. In January 1982, it moved to its present location at 16 Belleview Ave. The founders of the museum—Chester Wrobel, Dr. Raymond Adamczak, and Julian Jurus—intended to create a center dedicated to Polish history and culture with a focus on the contribution of Poles and Polish Americans to the U.S., its society and history.

The Museum houses collections donated by Mieczysław Haiman, Edward Pinkowski, and Henry Archacki, among others, and includes

Polish American Museum, Port Washington, NY (Czeslaw Karkowski)

artifacts, displays, paintings, documents, maps, and various memorabilia as well as photographs illustrating the achievements of people of Polish heritage who have made lasting contributions to Poland, America, and humanity. The Museum, a one-story brick building, formerly the Port Washington Public Library, contains ten exhibit rooms devoted to specific topics, a research library, and a sizeable lecture hall, as well as administrative offices. The exhibition rooms are decorated by many paintings, drawings, and photographs by Polish artists. It sponsors art expositions, auctions, stamp and coin exhibitions, concerts and recitals, films, literary workshops, field trips, lectures, and seminars, all with education in mind about Poland, Polish heritage, and the history of Poles in America. **www.polishamericanmuseum.com**

POUGHKEEPSIE
General Casimir Pulaski Monument
This statue of Pulaski was erected in 1940 by the Polish American Citizens of the town in Pulaski Park, the site of the annual Pulaski Day parade. The bronze bust atop a granite pedestal is at the intersection of Washington Street and Taylor Avenue.

Pulaski monument, Poughkeepsie, NY (Michael Herrick)

RIVERHEAD

St. Isidore Church and Polish Town

Polish Town is a neighborhood settled by Polish farmers to work the rich soil on the eastern parts of Long Island at the beginning of the 20th century. By 1895, they created a Polish fraternity called *Towarzystwo Polskie Rzymsko—Katolickie Bratnie Pomocy pod Opieką św. Izydora, Patrona Rolników* (The Polish Roman Catholic Society of Fraternal Assistance under the Patronage of St. Isidore, The Patron of Farmers). In 1906, they built a church of wood with twin spires which underwent massive reconstruction in 1955. St. Isidore Church at 622 Pulaski Street, the oldest Polish Roman Catholic Church on Long Island, became the focal point and spiritual heart of the little community known as Polish Town (an area of approximately fifteen blocks which includes residential, commercial, and industrial properties). A large icon of the Black Madonna hangs near the altar. Masses in Polish and celebrations of Polish religious customs are part of parish life. Community functions are held at the Riverhead Polish Hall which was incorporated in 1907.
www.saintisidoreriverhead.org / www.polishtownusa.com

ROCHESTER

Casimir Pulaski and Thaddeus Kosciuszko bust and plaque

The Monroe County Hall of Justice at 99 Exchange Boulevard houses two Polish memorials, both presented by the Polonia Civic Centre. A bust of Kosciuszko was erected in 1970 and a plaque dedicated to Pulaski, which hung originally in the Pulaski library, was moved to the Hall in 2002.

The Polish American Citizens' Club

Opened in 1914, the Polish American Citizens' Club is the last of several Polish clubhouse buildings in what was known as "Polish Town," the neighborhood along Hudson Avenue radiating from St. Stanislaus Church. You can still see streets with distinctive Polish names and buildings that once housed Polish organizations and churches that have left the area or closed. The former Dom Polski now houses a business; the Polish Falcons Hall, the original St. Casimir Polish National Catholic Church, and its Polish National Home are now Protestant churches, but the historical buildings remain standing, with the Polish names visible. Also standing, now empty, on the southwest corner of Hudson Avenue and Norton Street is the former General Casimir Pulaski Library building.

St. Casimir's Polish National Catholic Church Cemetery

The cemetery of St. Casimir's PNCC (established in 1908 and now closed) can still be visited through an entrance behind the car dealership located in front of the cemetery located off Hudson Avenue near the Route 104 Expressway. Although the location is now near a busy intersection, when the land was purchased it was a peaceful plot outside city limits. The cemetery has approximately five hundred graves and is the final resting place of many of the parish's founding members.

Stained-glass window, St. Casimir's PNCC, Rochester, NY (St. Casimir PNCC)

St. Stanislaus Kostka Church

The first wooden chapel for this parish was built in 1890 and then a more grandiose brick church in 1909 at 34 St. Stanislaus Street. As Polish immigrants began buying housing plots in the neighborhood, the streets around the church were christened St. Stanislaus, St. Casimir, Kosciuszko, and Sobieski. The church, designed in the Romanesque Revival style of red pressed brick with distinctive domed steeple reminiscent of church spires

St. Stanislaus Kostka Church, Rochester, NY (James Buhlman)

in Poland, is a locus of Rochester Polonia. The original cornerstone is still located in the parish rectory yard. The high altar has wood carved statues of St. Stanislaus Kostka, St. Wojciech, and St. Jadwiga of Śląsk. The mural across the sanctuary dome, by Buffalo artist Joseph Mazur, depicts eighteen saints, kings, and beatified persons who appear in the history of Catholicism in Poland and Eastern Europe: King Mieczysław I, King Bolesław, St. Andrzej Bobola. More recent immigrants initiated a shrine of Our Lady of Czestochowa and St. Pope John Paul II in 2008 to celebrate the centennial of the Church. On the altar there is a first-class relic of St. Pope John Paul II given to the parish by Cardinal Stanisław Dziwisz, Archbishop of Krakow. The relic is a small piece of cloth from one of the Pope's cassocks. Worship services include Masses in both English and Polish. Polish language instruction is available through the parish and and the parish gives assistance to local charities and causes in Poland. Local community organizations, such as the Polonia Civic Center, Polish National Alliance, Lodge 512, Polish Scouting, Polonia Civic Center, and the Polish National Alliance, hold activities on the parish grounds. An annual Polish festival draws many visitors. **www. saintstanislausrochester.org**

Skalny Center for Polish and Central European Studies (University of Rochester)
Established through a generous grant from the Louis Skalny Foundation, a Polish-born local businessman who valued education, the Skalny Center for Polish and Central European Studies is housed within the Department of Political Science with a focus on Poland. The program offers programs and initiatives in advanced research, undergraduate education, and commu-

Sgraffito of Nicolas Copernicus on interior wall of Kearney Hall at St. John Fisher College, Rochester, NY (James Buhlman)

nity outreach, with an opportunity to study in Kraków at the Jagiellonian University. For the community, the Center presents lectures on topics of Poland and Eastern Europe, concerts of Polish music, and a Polish film festival with many invited presenters from Poland. There is also an annual Skalny lecture.

www.sas.rochester.edu/psc/CPCES

Skalny Welcome Center of St. John Fisher College and Polish Heritage Society

The Polish Heritage Society of Rochester, which has an office at St. John Fisher College, was established in 1919 as the Polish Peoples Home (*Dom Ludowy*) to promote Polish heritage, traditions, and culture. It actively sponsors lectures, presentations, art workshops, exhibits, musical performances, and college scholarships, including a summer program of Polish Language and Culture at Toruń University. The Polish Heritage Society also supports events at the Skalny Center at the University of Rochester (see above).

The Skalny Welcome Center at St. John Fisher College was funded through the generosity of the Skalny Foundation, which also provides scholarships. A sgraffito of Nicolas Copernicus, commissioned by the Rochester Polish Arts Group and created in 1966 by Józef Sławiński, is located on the exterior north wall of Kearney Hall at the college.

www.polishheritagerochester.org

SOUTHAMPTON
Our Lady of Poland Church

A Polish immigrant named Francis Kruszewski moved from Riverhead with his wife Regina and settled in Southampton in 1890. He was one of the founding members of the Polish community and parish in Southampton, so that Polish immigrants would not have to travel the long distances to Riverhead for Polish Mass. The church at 35 Maple Street opened in 1918 and quickly established Polish organizations and societies to sup-

Our Lady of Poland Church, Southampton, NY (OLP Archives)

port the growing community of mainly farmers. Relics of St. Pope John Paul II are located beside the painting of the saint that flanks the right side of the altar and a large painting of Our Lady of Częstochowa is found on the other side. Today, there are daily Polish Masses and a Polish choir sings each Sunday. The church has undergone major renovations but retained the architecture of the original church. The wooden structure is reminiscent of chapels in Polish mountain towns. **www.olpchurch.org**

STILLWATER
Saratoga National Historic Park

In 1777, British General John Burgoyne led a large army south from Montreal aiming for Albany, New York, where he planned to meet another British army moving north from New York City. The goal was to separate the New England colonies, which the British believed to be the source of the rebellion, from the rest of British North America so they could be isolated and defeated. After capturing Fort Ticonderoga (*see* New York: Ticonderoga), Col. Thaddeus Kosciuszko, chief engineer of the American army, received orders to delay Burgoyne's movement south. By felling trees across the road, destroying dams, and creating other obstructions to inhibit the enemy's pursuit, he was able to delay the British for over four weeks.

Kosciuszko Monument, Saratoga National Historic Park, Stillwater, NY (James Pula)

Kosciuszko then selected a position at Bemis Heights that he fortified to give defensive advantages to the American army when the British continued their advance. After two attempts to overcome the colonial forces, Burgoyne was eventually surrounded and forced to surrender his entire army of nearly six thousand troops on October 17, 1777. The battle changed the course of the American Revolution, persuaded France and Spain to come to the aid of the Americans and made independence a reality. General Gates commented that "the great tacticians of the campaign were hills and forests which a young Polish engineer was skillful enough to select for my encampment."

There is a monument to Kosciuszko erected by the Polish American residents of Albany, Amsterdam, Cohoes, Schenectady, Troy, Watervliet, and vicinity at Stop 2 on the Saratoga National Historic Park battlefield tour road. The Visitor Center contains a timeline of the war (which includes artifacts), some battle models, a fiber optic light map, and a film. Kosciuszko is mentioned in the timeline, movie, and map. An interpretive talking marker on Kosciuszko is located on the battlegrounds. The Park is open year-round; battlefield tours are available from April 1 to December 1.

SYRACUSE
Basilica of the Sacred Heart of Jesus

Sacred Heart of Jesus Parish was established in 1892 as the first Polish parish in the diocese and a small wooden church was built. It later became the mother parish for others. St. Adalbert, the oldest Polish Society in Syracuse, was key to the establishment of the parish. The congregation soon outgrew the small church, and the new pastor, Rev. Rusin, initiated a new building. Since carpentry was his hobby, he worked on the church himself and there are stories that he went around to the various saloons and homes to beg for nickels and dimes to support construction. The parishioners dug the foundation to save money and the 210-foot twin-towered Gothic-style church at 927 Park Avenue was dedicated in 1910. The main bronze doors include a stained-glass insert of St. Maximilian Kolbe, the east door has a symbol of Blessed Angela Truszkowska, foundress of the Felician Sisters and repeating panels around the church include the Polish eagle. Stained-glass windows depict several other Polish saints. In recognition of the parish's contributions, Pope John Paul II designated it a basilica in 1999. Relics of St. Andrew Bobola, St. Casimir, and St. Stanislaus Kostka are located inside altars. On the rectory side of the building there is a statue of St. Faustina Kowalska. Bilingual Masses continue to be celebrated as well as Polish memorial events.

Pulaski Park, directly across from the Basilica, contains an obelisk erected in 1949 to commemorate Polish-American veterans of World War II, Korea, and Vietnam. **Kosciuszko Park**, directly to the west of Pulaski Park, contains a monument to Polish American veterans of World War I. **sacredheartbasilicasyr.org**

The de Ropp Polish Art Collection at Le Moyne College

The de Ropp Polish Art Collection is located at the Noreen Reale Falcone Library of Le Moyne College and has been on display since 1958. The collection was commissioned and later donated by Baron Stefan de Ropp, former Commissioner General of the Polish Pavilion of the 1939 New York World's Fair, and later an adjunct professor at Le Moyne College. He commissioned artists of the Brotherhood of St. Luke in Poland, a group of painters who adhered to the pre-Raphaelite school, to create seven large murals depicting pivotal events in Polish history. They were painted on wood in tempera reminiscent of medieval

Mural from the New York World's Fair at Le Moyne College, Syracuse, NY (Le Moyne College)

paintings and considered the jewels of the 1939 World's Fair. There are also four prize-winning tapestries, designed by Mieczysław Szymanski and executed by the Lad Workshop under the leadership of Maria Łomnicka-Bujakowa, celebrating the life of King Jan III Sobieski of Poland. They were first displayed at the 1937 Paris exhibition in the Polish Pavilion Hall of Honor. Because World War II broke out the same year the World's Fair opened, the artifacts could not go back, and after the war Poland was under the control of Soviet Russia so it was decided that the exhibit materials be dispersed throughout the United States (see entries for Chicago, IL: Polish Museum of America; and New York City, Manhattan: Władysław II Jagiełło Statue). Check website for more historical information and exact locations for visits, and whether the collection is still at the College—there have been protracted negotiations for their return to Poland. **resources.library.lemoyne.edu/arts/de-ropp-polish-art-collection**

Polish Home and Basilica of the Sacred Heart, Syracuse, NY
(Robert Synakowski)

Syracuse Polish Home / Dom Polski

The Syracuse Polish Home at 915 Park Avenue was established in 1919 as a club and community center, and offers and supports cultural events. It sponsors a Polish Saturday School and supports the annual Polish Festival. A wide assortment of traditional Polish meals is available for guests. There is a library and an archive with important resources of Syracuse Polonia. Post 1 of the Polish American Veterans of World War I was folded into the Polish Legion of American Veterans (PLAV), which now operates out of the Syracuse Polish Home. **syracusepolishhome.com**

Transfiguration of Our Lord Church

This parish at 740 Teall Avenue was established in 1911 to serve the Polish community. It still offers cultural events in addition to its spiritual mission, including hosting Polish dinners, pierogi-making events, and *Opłatek*. On the grounds one can find a large statue of St. Maximilian Kolbe, with the arms of the Blessed Mother around him, which was dedicated in 1990. Nearby is the outdoor shrine of Our Lady of Częstochowa. **http://transfigurationsyr.com**

TICONDEROGA

Fort Ticonderoga

In the late summer of 1777, when Gen. Horatio Gates was named commanding officer of the American army defending the route from Montréal to Albany, Col. Thaddeus Kosciuszko accompanied him as chief engineer. Gates sent him to inspect the defenses of Fort Ticonderoga. Foremost among several suggestions he made for their improvement was that Sugar Loaf Hill (modern Mount Defiance) be fortified to prevent the British from placing artillery on its height overlooking the fort. The local commanders ignored the advice and when the British arrived, they did exactly as Kosciuszko had predicted. In a major colonial disaster, the fort fell within three days along with large amounts of arms, ammunition, and supplies.

Today, Fort Ticonderoga houses a museum and archive. Entering, one passes a plaque with

Kosciuszko's name, though misspelled, listed among distinguished Revolutionary era people who passed through the gate. The museum contains several artifacts related to the Pole including prints and paintings donated by Count Alexandre Orlowski. These include an oil on canvas depiction of the Kosciuszko monument at West Point, an oil on canvas bust depicting Kosciuszko wearing the Polish Order of Virtuti Militari and the American Badge of the Society of the Cincinnati, three engraved etchings of Kosciuszko, two lithographs, and a watercolor. Collections are available to researchers in the Thompson-Pell Research Center at the fort, includ-

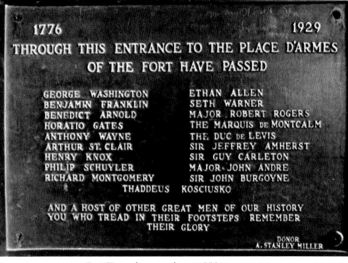

Fort Ticonderoga plaque, NY (James Pula)

ing the Orlowski Collection. The fort is open to the public daily and has frequent reenactments and special events. **www.fortticonderoga.org**

UTICA
Brigadier General Casimir Pulaski Monument
Erected in 1930, the Casimir Pulaski Monument stands at the corner of Memorial Parkway and Oneida Street. The ten-feet-by-four-feet bronze statue was created by Joseph P. Pollia. There is an annual wreath-laying ceremony at the Memorial. Not too far from the memorial are Route 5, Route 8, and Route 12, known locally as the North-South Arterial. In recent years, the roadway was renamed the Casimir Pulaski Highway in honor of the general.

Kopernik (Copernicus) Statue
Across Genesee Street from the Munson-Williams-Proctor Institute in Utica is the statue of Mikołaj Kopernik (Nicholas Copernicus). It was funded through private donations, made mostly by Polish Americans and local businesses. The statue of the astronomer is made of bronze, mounted on a granite pedestal. It is fifteen feet tall and surrounded by a small city park. Being in a park, it is accessible twenty-four hours a day, seven days a week. The statue was sculpted by Bogdan Chmielewski, cast in Poland, then brought to the United States. Julian Noga, a local monument dealer, designed the base. It is inscribed, "Mikołaj Kopernik, Polish Astronomer, 1473–1543. By reforming astronomy, he initiated modern science."

Casimir Pulaski Memorial, Utica, NY (Cheryl Pula)

Utica, New York

Utica is in Oneida County, on the banks of the Mohawk River, approximately one-hundred miles west of Albany and fifty miles east of Syracuse. With a population of 62,235, it is the tenth most populous city in the state. Originally a Native-American settlement around 4000 BC, it was home to the Mohawk, Oneida, and Onondaga tribes. It later became Old Fort Schuyler, an English town, and early on attracted European settlers during and after the Revolutionary War. Many came to work in the textile mills in the city and surrounding areas, and represented several ethnicities, including Polish, Welsh, English, Italian, and Germans. Through the years many Polish immigrants settled in what is now west Utica. It became known as a "melting pot," welcoming refugees after both World Wars. It was an important stop on the famous Erie Canal, which aided in its industrial development. The city was also crucial in the abolitionist movement during the Civil War, as the first meeting of the New York State Anti-Slavery Society was held there. Utica is also an educational center, boasting Utica College, the Mohawk Valley Community College, and SUNY Polytechnic Institute in nearby Marcy.

The Polish Community Club

Kopernik Cultural Center and Polish Community Club, Utica, NY (Cheryl Pula)

Many Polish immigrants came to the central New York area in the early 1900s, including the Mohawk Valley. They wished to establish a cultural center in Utica for social activities. In 1910, Reverend Ludwik Muszynski, pastor of Holy Trinity Church, suggested a Polish Home. In response, many individuals donated money to finance such a meeting place. That was the beginning of the Polish Community Inc., also known as the Polish Home and today known as the Polish Community Club. Under its first president, Adam Idzikowski, it was incorporated in 1911, and encourages good citizenship, and hosts activities on national, religious, political, and patriotic themes. Located at 810 Columbia Street in Utica, the Club is home to the Kopernik Memorial Association and the White Eagle Society. Each week on Thursdays the Club has a Polish dinner featuring Polish foods which is open to the public. **pccutica.com**

Kopernik Cultural Center

This Center, founded in 1990, is in the Polish Community Club at 810 Columbia Street (*see above*). It was established by the Kopernik Memorial Association which was founded in November 1972 by Julian Noga, who at the time was president of Utica's Polish Community Home. One of the Association's first concerns was the upcoming 500th anniversary of the birth of astronomer

Nicolaus Copernicus (Mikołaj Kopernik). They established a fund-raising committee and erected a statue of the Polish scientist in Utica (*see above*). Today, the Association has many activities, including the sponsorship of a *Wigilia* supper during Christmas, awarding college scholarships to deserving students, and sponsoring concerts. Open to the public, the Center includes a library with books and materials pertaining to Polish themes and changing displays of art works.

Holy Trinity Church

Holy Trinity Parish (1206 Lincoln Avenue) was founded in October 1894, when eighty-two families contributed $79 each toward the establishment of a church to serve Polish immigrants in the Utica area. In 1889, they established the St. Stanislaus Society, the foundation for the future parish and church. To this day, this saint's statue and picture are in Holy Trinity's sanctuary. The first Polish pastor was Father Szymon Pniak, who celebrated his first Christmas Mass there in 1886. Holy Trinity Parish was legally incorporated in 1897 and the cornerstone for the church was laid in July 1906. Impressed with the design of the church made of granite with twin 80-foot-tall Gothic spires, several other parishes in Central New York and Syracuse copied the design, so Holy Trinity is also nicknamed the "Mother of Many Daughters." It remains the largest Polish parish in the area.

Holy Trinity Church, Utica, NY (Cheryl Pula)

A statue commemorating the canonization of St. Pope John Paul II stands across from Holy Trinity Church. Nearby is the Polish Veterans' World War II Association Post No. 13. **www.holytrinityutica.com**

VESTAL

Kopernik Observatory & Science Center

This center, named for Mikołaj Kopernik (Nicolaus Copernicus) has been one of the best-situated and best-equipped public observatories in the northeast United States for over forty-five years. It offers public programs on a wide range of science and engineering topics and after the programs, the public can view the night sky through the Observatory's professional telescopes. Visitors can examine a replica of Kopernik's notebook where he proposed the heliocentric model of our solar system. The Center has a STEM-themed playground where children can learn about the science or engineering theory behind the structures or activities on which they are playing. **www.kopernik.org**

WEST POINT
United States Military Academy

During the American Revolution, George Washington called West Point "the most important Post in America." The engineer assigned to fortify this crucial location in 1778 was Col. Thaddeus Kosciuszko. When completed, professional military engineers regarded it as far ahead of its time in anticipating modern concepts of defense in depth. Portions of his original works of Fort Clinton, Fort Putnam, and Redoubt Number 4 can still be seen today.

Kosciuszko Statue: Located on the northeast end of the famous plain where cadet reviews are held overlooking the Hudson River, the Corps of Cadets dedicated the Kosciuszko monument in 1828, the first such commemorative marker to be placed at West Point. In 1913 Polish American donors placed a statue atop the original memorial column. A short walk to the west of the statue along Cullum Road lies the remnant of "The Great Chain" the engineer installed across the Hudson to interrupt British shipping.

Kosciuszko Garden: Below the plain, on the cliffside leading to the river, is Kosciuszko's Garden where he sought solace in his off-duty hours. Access requires descending a stairway located behind Cullum Hall. Walk south from the Kosciuszko Monument to Cullum Hall where a sign points the way. Benches are available in the garden to rest before scaling the stairs back to the plain. There is also a spring that was active when the engineer used the garden but has since been turned into a more modern fountain.

Kosciuszko statue and Kosciuszko Garden, West Point, NY (James Pula)

West Point Library: A bust of Kosciuszko by sculptor Tracy H. Sugg resides in the Academy Library in Jefferson Hall at the south end of the plain at the junction of Cullum Road and Jefferson Place. *(See Kosciusko, MS, for another statue by Sugg.)*

West Point Museum: The museum contains a sword attributed to Kościuszko bearing the inscription "Draw me not without reason, Sheathe me not without honor." It also contains some prints and a signed letter. The museum is located outside the south gate to the Academy at 2110 New South Post Road.

YONKERS
St. Casimir Church

This church at 239 Nepperham Avenue continues to celebrate traditional Polish Masses, holy days, and cultural events. Poles settled here for work in factories but would travel to New York City to have weddings, baptisms, and other sacraments in Polish. In 1900, St. Casimir began construction of a local Polish church which was completed three years later. In 1970, the parish initiated a Polish language school. The main altar contains an icon of Our Lady of Częstochowa as well as murals depicting Polish history. **www.casimir.church**

St. Casimir Church, Yonkers, NY (Edyta Grzelakowska)

NORTH CAROLINA

CASTLE HAYNE
St. Stanislaus Church
Polish immigrants arrived in 1907 just outside of Wilmington and built a church which was considered a mission church of St. Mary's in Wilmington until 1933. The present church at 4849 Castle Hayne Road was built in 1998 and includes paintings of St. Stanislaus Kostka (acquired in 2008) and Our Lady of Częstochowa. Since 1998, November has been the time for polkas and Polish food for the annual Polish festival and during the year Polish dinners can be found at the parish. The cemetery has many of the original settlers' graves. **www.ststanislauscatholic.org**

RALEIGH
St. Joseph Church
St. Joseph Church at 2811 Poole Road shares its early history with an African American community and characteristics of blended faiths are apparent in this building. St. Joseph is the first site at which Polish Mass was said in North Carolina. This church has the distinct honor of being a Shrine of Our Lady of Częstochowa—an icon of the Black Madonna was given to the church by Polish immigrants Danuta and Jan Adam in 1987. The image was blessed by Pope John Paul II at the Vatican in 1990 and weekly novenas are said at this shrine. The altar of the church was designed by Piotr Nowak and constructed by the Polish community and dedicated by Bishop Zygmunt Zimowski in 1988. There are Stations of the Cross inscribed in Polish which were acquired from a Polish church in Lorain, Ohio, when it was being consolidated with another parish. Masses in Polish are arranged several times a year here and in Saint Julia's Church in Silver City, NC. Polish traditions are continued such as Easter basket blessings. **www.saintjosephraleigh.org**

The Raleigh Paderewski Festival
Held annually in Raleigh since 2014, The Paderewski Festival celebrates the legacy of Ignacy Jan Paderewski while bringing nationally and internationally acclaimed pianists to the NC Triangle region. During the November festival week, performances are given in concert halls around the area. Programs have included music by Paderewski, Chopin, and other composers of their period.

Between 1917 and 1939 Paderewski played four concerts in Raleigh. His relationship with North Carolina resident Josephus Daniels was an important link to President Woodrow Wilson's ear. Paderewski's first Raleigh performance on January 23, 1917, took place the day after Woodrow Wilson delivered a speech that called for the re-creation of an independent Poland upon the end of World War I. A Steinway piano signed by Paderewski on May 10, 1924, and presented to Paderewski's wife's secretary is at the home of the Honorary Consul of the Embassy of Poland, Alvin Mark Fountain, who is also the organizer of the Festival. **paderewski-festival.org**

The Polish-American Club of The Raleigh Triangle co-sponsors this festival as well as organizing and sponsoring Polish holiday celebrations, lectures and social events. They run a Saturday Polish School and coordinate a scholarship program. **www.polamrtp.com**

J.S. Dorton Arena (Paraboleum Nowickiego), Raleigh, NC (Peg Cieslak)

Holy Name of Jesus Cathedral

A statue of St. Pope John Paul II adorns a niche in the right transept of this new cathedral at 715 Nazareth Street, one of the five largest in the U.S., dedicated in July 2017. The figure of the pope, as well as the figures of other saints in the transepts along both sides of the nave, were carved in the studios of Ferdinand Stuflesser in Ortisei, Italy. **holynamecathedralnc.org**

J. S. Dorton Arena ("Paraboleum Nowickiego")

Designed by Maciej Nowicki, the Dorton Arena located on the North Carolina State Fair Grounds was the first structure in the world to use a cable-supported roof system. The 7,600-seat arena, which opened in 1952, was the predecessor of today's domed stadiums. Nowicki, who was educated at the Warsaw Polytechnic in the 1930s and taught in the underground university during World War II, became an internationally recognized architect. He executed his designs for this arena from 1948-1950. Architects and students in the field continue to study this innovative design today. The saddle-shaped roof is supported by only a network of wire cables regarded as revolutionary, allowing for unobstructed seating. His wife, architect Stanislawa Sandecka, aided the arena's completion after her husband's death in a plane crash, by interpreting the building designs as construction progressed. The Dorton Arena was added to the National Register of Historic Places on April 11, 1973. It was recognized as a National Historic Civil Engineering Landmark in 2002. Nowicki's influence can also be seen in the United Nations Building in New York—he was selected to be the Polish representative on an international team of architects and planners for the project. As the UN project ended, Nowicki accepted a position as the Acting Head of the Architecture Department in the School of Design being organized at North Carolina State College. A collection of Maciej Nowicki's drawings are catalogued at the North Carolina State University School of Design.

NORTH DAKOTA

GRAFTON
Walsh County Heritage Village
This Heritage Village at 800 West 12th Street is a collection of historic building and artifacts which were moved here to re-create early settlers' lives. Special attractions include a furnished farmhouse, farm buildings, and artifacts of a Polish farmer, Sig Jagielski, a country church, a log cabin, and a taxidermy shop. Jagielski's farm was originally at nearby Jugville and it was transported to the historic village. A plaque honors the contributions of "Uncle Sig." **walshhistory.org**

Log cabin at Walsh County Heritage Village, Grafton, ND (Walsh County Historical Society)

MINTO
St. Joseph Chapel
This roadside chapel, reminiscent of Polish countryside chapels, was built in 1907 by Joseph Kosmatka, a Polish farmer and carpenter, in a composite Colonial Revival, Stick and Late Gothic Revival style of architecture. The wood frame wayside chapel is in Pulaski Township, just ten miles south of Grafton and five miles east of Warsaw on then-owner Joe Wosick's farm on land donated for the purpose. It is a small structure, eight feet by eight feet, with just enough room for an altar, a priest, and two altar boys. It is on the National Register of Historic Places because of its significance to the Polish community which began settling in the area in the early 1870s; the priest would use this chapel to pray for a good harvest and bless the crops. This Polish custom has continued annually since the construction of the chapel.

Walsh County Historical Museum
This museum at 323 Third Street offers three stories of displays of artifacts that have been donated by area families with new items continually being added. The Museum recaptures the era of the homesteaders from the mid- to late-nineteenth century. Although a heavily Norwegian community, there were close to 10 percent Polish settlers, mainly on the rich farmlands around this Great Northern Railroad town site. **www.walshhistory.org/historical-museum**

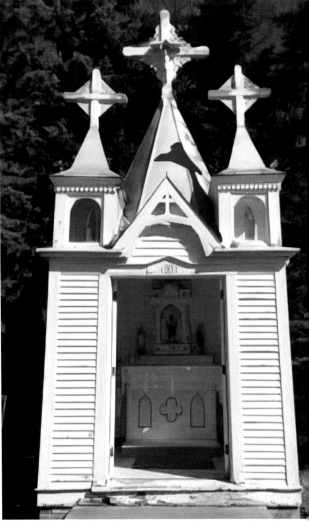

St. Joseph Chapel, Minto, ND (Lady Amanda)

WARSAW
St. Stanislaus Church and Historic District

This historically Polish neighborhood and Catholic Church was placed on the National Register of Historic Places in 1979. Immigrant Poles began settling as farmers in rural Walsh County in North Dakota in the 1870s, and the village of Warsaw remained mainly Polish well into the 20th century. St. Stanislaus Parish was founded in the 1880s, and the present church was dedicated in 1901. Polish saints are represented in windows and statues, including an elaborate icon of Our Lady of Częstochowa in the foyer. Regarded as a fine example of Gothic Revival architecture, it is familiarly called "The Cathedral on the Plains" and is the northernmost Polish Catholic church in the United States. St. Stanislaus continues to observe Polish customs and holidays. In 1976, St. Stanislaus Parish erected a Bicentennial Pioneer Monument on the church grounds in conjunction with the national bicentennial to commemorate the early Polish settlers. **www.sh-ss.org**

St. Stanislaus Church, Warsaw, ND (Neal Pease)

OHIO

BEREA

Berea Sandstone Quarries Historical Marker
Poles settled in Berea in the late 1860s and many were employed in the stone quarries. The plaque located adjacent to Coe Lake Park documents their history in this region.

St. Adalbert Church
St. Adalbert Parish was organized in 1873 for the Polish stonecutters and is the oldest Polish parish in Ohio. The original church was adorned with hand-cut altars from Poland which were then used in the new church built in 1937 at 66 Adalbert Street. Stained-glass windows depict Polish saints including St. John Kanty, St. Casimir, St. Hyacinth, and St. Andrew Bobola.
www.saintadalbertparish.org

CLEVELAND

Church of the Immaculate Heart of Mary (IHM)
This church was stablished in 1894 as an independent Polish Catholic Church after a schism between the pastor of St. Stanislaus, Rev. Anton Francis Kolaszewski, and the diocese over the Poles demanding more say in the governance of the church. When a new pastor was installed at St. Stanislaus, the congregation "welcomed" him with broomsticks, resulting in a huge brawl. But in 1908, IHM rejoined the Cleveland diocese. In 1914, a new church at 6700 Lansing Avenue was designed by a prominent Polish architect, Anthony F. Wasielewski, who during his career designed and built three dozen churches in the U.S., including a cathedral in Oklahoma. The parish is proud of the beautiful stained-glass windows which reflect Polish saints and themes: the Childrens' Offering Window shows a Polish village in the background, the Poland in Chains Window includes the city of Warsaw, others highlight St. Adalbert and King Boleslaus.
www.immaculateheartchurch.org

Church of the Immaculate Heart of Mary, Cleveland, OH (Mary Erdmans)

Warszawa Historic District of Cleveland

In the late 19th century, there were three Polish neighborhoods in Cleveland: Warszawa, Poznan, and Kantowa (Tremont). The construction of the Ohio & Erie Canal and later railroads led to industrial and commercial growth, including the establishment of steel mills. This prompted a large influx of European immigrants. The Polish immigrants built the cottages typical of the neighborhood as well as churches and national halls, most of which still serve the community. The concentrated Polish community gave the South Broadway area of the neighborhood the nickname of "Warszawa," which was the largest and most institutionalized neighborhood for the city's Polish immigrants. It is now also known as Slavic Village. The Warszawa Neighborhood District includes four blocks of East 65th Street between Fleet and Baxter Avenues, and one block of Forman Avenue east of 65th Street. The community continues to work hard at preserving its unique character, identity, and flavor.

John Paul II Polish-American Cultural Center

This Center at 6501 Lansing Avenue was established in 2001 to promote Polish traditions, language, history, literature, arts, and education. A museum attached to the Center includes exhibits on Polish military history, folklore, Solidarity, Paderewski, and Cleveland Polonia. There is a permanent gallery displaying original paintings, reproductions, and sculptures by Polish artists or artists dealing with Polish subjects, as well as a rotating gallery. A library and archives documenting Polonia in Ohio is open to all researchers. There are ongoing lectures, musical events, parades, festivals, film series and classes. Their website has useful resources.
www.polishcenterofcleveland.org

Polish Garden at Cleveland Cultural Gardens

The Polish Garden is one of forty nationality gardens in the Cleveland Cultural Gardens located along Martin Luther King and East Boulevards. One of the oldest, the Polish Garden was dedicated in 1934 and includes sculptures of Frédéric Chopin, Nicolaus Copernicus, Maria Skłodowska Curie, Adam

Mickiewicz, Henryk Sienkie-wicz, Ignacy Paderewski, and Pope St. John Paul II (this newest statue was erected May 18, 2019, and created by sculptor Andrzej Pitynski). There is an octagonal fountain decorated with allegorical figures that represent music, literature, science, and astronomy in the center of this garden. The fountain was dedicated to the daughter of 16th-century poet Jan Kochanowski. It is a beautiful place to sit and relax with shady and well-maintained landscaping.
www.clevelandculturalgardens. org/gardens/polish-garden

*Bust of Chopin in Polish Garden
at Cleveland Cultural Gardens, OH
(Mary Erdmans)*

St. Casimir Church, Cleveland, OH (Mary Erdmans)

St. Casimir Church

Founded in 1891, St. Casimir Church at 8223 Sowinski Avenue was built in 1914 in the Polish neighborhood known as Poznan. The now-demolished White Motor Company plant was nearby and attracted Polish immigrants to this neighborhood, which has street names like Pulaski and Kosciuszko. The church is in the Polish Cathedral-style with Romanesque additions. An icon of Our Lady of Częstochowa, brought from Poland, is in one of the side altars. Images of Polish saints adorn the church apse.

There is an interesting history of the closing of the parish in 2009 and subsequent appeals to Rome and daily vigils and singing of Polish hymns in front of the fenced-off church until 2012 when the parish was reopened and over one thousand people attended the first Mass. St. Casimir Parish continues to have bi-lingual Mass on Sundays, celebrate major Polish religious and national holidays, and host an annual Polish festival in July. **www.stcasimir.com**

St. John Cantius Church

St. John Cantius Parish was founded in 1898 in what would be called the "Kantowa" neighborhood after the parish (the area is now called Tremont). Most of its families moved here to be close to the steel mills. A new church, at 906 College Avenue, was built in the Polish Cathedral-style in 1925 as the parish continued to grow. There is a large St. Pope John Paul II statue and a painting of Our Lady of Częstochowa inside the church. Polish Masses continue to be held weekly as are observances of traditional Polish religious customs. The parish hosts the annual Tremont Polish Festival on Labor Day weekend. **www.stjohncantiuschurch.org**

Shrine Church of St. Stanislaus Bishop and Martyr

St. Stanislaus Parish was officially founded in 1873. It has been the center of the community known as Warszawa Historic District (*see sidebar, page 171*). When the church at 3649 East 65th Street was completed in 1891, it was one of the largest Victorian Gothic churches in the United States. An award-winning restoration of the church was completed in 1998 and guided tours are available for groups. The stained-glass window in the choir loft depicts St. Stanislaus raising a dead man. A side altar holds icons of Our Lady of Ostrabrama in Vilnius and Our Lady of Częstochowa. Another altar is dedicated to St. Pope John Paul II with an icon from Poland depicting him with St. Stanislaus. Relics of St. Stanislaus from then Cardinal Wojtyła in 1969, and two relics of St. Pope John Paul II—his miter as Bishop of Kraków and a piece of the cassock he was wearing in 1981 when he was shot in Vatican City—are located in a side shrine. A new shrine was just installed dedicated to Divine Mercy with images of St. Faustina and St. Pope John Paul II.

The Polish Women's Alliance of America conducts a Polish language school for learners of all ages from preschool to adults and includes classes in language, culture, and music. In the summer, the annual Polish Festival is held. **www.ststanislaus.org**

Tadeusz Kosciuszko Statue

This statue, in Wade Park on the west side of the Cleveland Museum of Art, was dedicated on May 7, 1905. Rev. Kolaszewski, pastor of St. Stanislaus Church in Cleveland at the time initiated the installation. The eight-foot statue situated on a twelve-foot stone pedestal was created by sculptor Gaetano Trentanove, the same artist who produced the Milwaukee, Wisconsin, monument (*See* Milwaukee, WI: Kosciuszko Monument). The memorial was

Statue of Kosciuszko in Wade Park, Cleveland, OH (Mary Erdmans)

funded by Clevelanders of Polish descent at a cost of $9000 and sponsored by the Polish National Alliance of America. It portrays the decorated military engineer in a military uniform holding a sword in a design noticeably different from the one in Wisconsin.

DAYTON
St. Adalbert Polish Church
The cornerstone of St. Adalbert Church was laid on September 4, 1904. A new larger church was built in 1967 at 1511 Valley Street with unique stained-glass doors: the center two doors show male and female figures in native Polish dress against a background of red and white, the Polish colors. The greeting on these windows is: *Niech Będzie Pochwalony Jezus Chrystus Na Wieki Wieków. Amen.* (Praised be Jesus Christ for ever and ever. Amen). The church was added to the National Register of Historic Places in 1991. Polish traditions currently practiced include *Wigilia*, sharing the *opłatek*, midnight Mass with *kolędy, Gorzkie żale*, and *Święconka*.

DUBLIN
Thaddeus Kosciuszko Park
This park dedicated to General Kosciuszko in May 2012 is part of the land originally given to Kosciuszko by the American government as a payment for his contribution to the Revolutionary War. The "Kosciuszko Lands," originally five hundred acres, are east of the Sciota River down to the Delaware County Line. He was also given $15,000 for his services in the Revolutionary War. The park includes an educational trail about Thaddeus Kosciuszko. **dublinohiousa.gov/parks-open-space/thaddeus-kosciuszko-park**

St. Adalbert Polish Church door, Dayton, OH (Mary Erdmans)

Northern Boundary of Kosciuszko Lands Marker
A historical marker (dedicated April 27, 1980, by PNA Lodge 2422) is at the northern boundary of the lands on the eastern border of Jack Nicklaus's Muirfield Village Golf Course where the annual Memorial Tournament is held. It is along the north-south road just east of the course. The historical marker is near a large boulder that is believed to mark the northern boundary.

Polish Village Parma
This business district in Parma, Ohio, with public spaces and businesses promotes Polish traditions and food. A non-profit organization was established to restore this historically Polish area located along Ridge Road from Pearl Road to Thornton Avenue. Polish Village holds the following annual events: Polish Constitution weekend organized by the Ohio chapter of PAC since 1948, Taste of Polish Village, and Pączki Day. The city is located on the southern edge of Cleveland and experienced a population growth after World War II of primarily Poles and other Eastern Europeans moving from Cleveland. **polishvillageparma.org**

Poland, Ohio
Poland, a village located seven miles southeast of Youngstown, was first known as Fowler's Place after Jonathan Fowler and his family, the first colonists to settle there. For years after the Revolutionary War, there was a feeling of gratitude and respect for those who had come from other countries to assist in the cause of freedom. The people of Fowler's Place had the desire to honor the two Polish foreign heroes, Kosciuszko and Pulaski, and so as not to slight either man, decided to name their community Poland after their country of birth.

GARFIELD HEIGHTS
Marymount Hospital
Marymount Hospital at 12300 McCracken Road was established in 1949 and operated by the Polish Felicians. Founders included Felician Mother Mary Theobold, Warren Chase, Chester Jablonski, and Edmund Lewandowski, and it was supported by the estate of Frances Tetlak. The Virgin Mary Statue (1950) was designed by Mother Mary Theobald and Sister Mary Xavier and stands in front of the hospital.

POLAND
Peterson Park
Peterson Park is designed with pergolas, arches, and statues to honor Poland. The Park was dedicated in 2006. The bronze statue of Casimir Pulaski and Tadeusz Kosciuszko, "American Freedom Fighters," was designed by the local artist Tom Antonishak. The statue was moved in June 2011 from Krakusy Hall in Youngstown, Ohio (now closed) to its current location. It is said that this is the only park in the United States that has both Kosciuszko and Pulaski in one statue. A monument to Polish veterans of World Wars I and II was also rededicated here on June 25, 2011, from its original home of four decades outside a Polish American hall on Youngstown's South Side.

American Freedom Fighters statue, Peterson Park, Poland, OH (Tom Antonishak)

TOLEDO
Kuschwantz Polish neighborhood marker
Kuschwantz ("cow's tail") was a vibrant Polish neighborhood in the late-19th century and a historical plaque tells the story of the community and its most prominent church. Today the community is known as Kwanzaa. The institutional cornerstone of this community, St. Anthony's Church (establish 1894, closed 2005), was slated for demolition in 2018 but efforts are now underway to save the structure and as of publication, it was being repaired and redeveloped. Construction of St. Anthony Church began in 1890 and it became the second Polish church built in Toledo and became known as the "mother" church for the local Polish community serving as many as eight

thousand parishioners prior to the 1970s. For more information about Polish Toledo see: **www.polishtoledo.com**

Polish Community in Toledo Historical Marker

This marker, located on Warsaw St., highlights the history of Poles in the area. The first wave of Polish immigrants arrived in Toledo beginning in 1871. Most were Roman Catholics escaping oppression in Prussian Poland. The first formal association of the Toledo Polonia occurred on October 16, 1875, when twenty-five families formed St. Hedwig Parish on that saint's feast day. By 1900 Toledo had become a center of Polish population in America, and many Poles found work here in the growing glass and automobile industries. The reverse side of the marker outlines the history of St. Hedwig Parish.

Sts. Hedwig & Adalbert Church

St. Hedwig, the first Polish parish in Toledo, opened in 1875 in the Lagrange Street district (aka Lagrinka) and has served as the heart of Toledo Polonia. The original church was replaced by the larger current church at 2916 Lagrange Street in 1892. Once the Poles outgrew this parish, in 1907 St. Hedwig's launched another parish, St. Adalbert at 3233 Lagrange Street. Since 2010, both function together as one parish. There is a large statue of St. Pope John Pauk II in front of St. Adalbert and both churches have statues of Polish saints.

In 1916, the Order of the Sisters of St. Francis designated the first St. Hedwig building as its motherhouse, directed by Mother M. Adelaide Sandusky, O.S.F. (1875-1964). This community, now located in Sylvania, was initially devoted to training teachers for Polish parishes throughout the Midwest. **www.stadalbertsthedwig.org**

YOUNGSTOWN

Our Lady of Częstochowa Shrine

With the consolidations of parishes, the "Polish Youngstown" Polonia spearheaded a fundraising initiative to guarantee that Poles would have a chapel dedicated to the beloved Polish Madonna. The belltower baptistry at St. Columba Cathedral at 159 West Rayen Avenue was selected to be a shrine to Our Lady. Dedication of the shrine took place in 2012 followed by a month-long commemoration. St. Stanislaus Kostka Parish gifted their large mosaic of Our Lady for the chapel.

Polish Youngstown

Polish Youngstown, a non-profit since 2008, has been working to bring back Polish traditions that were forgotten as the Polish population moved away and Polish parishes closed. It functions as an umbrella organization linking and uniting Polonia of the Youngstown area. They offer Polish language classes, lectures, movies, cooking classes; they have organized bus trips to celebrate Dyngus Day in Buffalo or Pączki Day in Hamtramck; and they were integral to the creation of the Slavic collaboration that created the Simply Slavic festival. The group was instrumental in relocating the "American Freedom Fighters" monument to nearby Poland (see Poland, OH: Peterson Park) and raising funds for the Shrine at the Cathedral. **polishyoungstown.org**

OKLAHOMA

MOUNTAIN PARK
Camp Radziminski Marker

This historical marker commemorates a short-lived military outpost named in honor of a Polish-born soldier who served in the U.S. armed forces. Charles (né Karol) Radzimiński arrived in America as a political refugee after the failed Polish "November Uprising" of 1830-1831 against Russian rule and became an officer in the United States Army. He fought with distinction, along with other Polish volunteers, in the Mexican War, and subsequently contributed to exploration and mapping of Oklahoma, Texas, and the new U.S.-Mexico boundary. After he died in 1858, "Camp Radziminski" was founded in his name with the intention of serving as a base in the Indian wars, but it was soon abandoned, and nothing remains of it. The marker stands to the north of Mountain Park, two miles from the site of the camp.

Camp Radziminski marker, Mountain Park, OK (hmdb.org)

OREGON

PORTLAND
Polish Hall / Polish Library Building Association (PLBA)

The PLBA has represented and organized the Portland area Polish community since the start of the 20th century. It built the current Polish Hall at 3832 North Interstate Avenue in 1912. Previously, Polonia met in a building on the Williamette River called "*Biały Orzeł*" (now the McMenamin Brew Pub and Restaurant) ongoing back to 1892 when the first PNA group was formed. The current Polish Hall hosts lectures, musical events, meetings, and Grandpa's Café and Deli, which serves and sells Polish cuisine. PLBA sponsors the Polish Cultural Enrichment Program (Polish Saturday School) begun in 1994 at St. Stanislaus Church which is next door and includes classes for adults and children, a Polish folk-dance group, plus many cultural events. In 1995, the annual Polish Festival was launched and is touted as the largest Polish event in the northwest region. It runs each September over several days in conjunction with St. Stanislaus Parish.
portlandpolonia.org

St. Stanislaus Church

The cornerstone for this church was laid July 4, 1907, to serve the needs of Poles and other Slavic groups and it is the only Polish church in Oregon. The church is located at 3916 North Interstate Avenue, north of downtown in the Overlook neighborhood, close to the railyards, warehouses,

PLBA Polish Hall, Portland, OR (PLBA)

and port where Poles found work. The parish went into a decline as Polish immigrants moved away but had a resurgence beginning in the 1950s with the influx of many post-World War II immigrants. Another wave of immigrants, the post-Solidarity activists, reinvigorated the parish with permanent Polish priests from the Society of Christ for Poles Living Abroad. The Parish is also a home for the Croatian community. Masses are said in Polish, English, Latin, and Croatian.

To celebrate the 33rd anniversary of St. Pope John Paul II's pontificate inauguration, the parish dedicated a statue of the Pope made by a local polish artist, Bruno Drozdek. The church has been placed on the City Register of Historical Sites. **www.ststanislausparish.com**

White Eagle Saloon and Hotel
Early in its history, the White Eagle at 836 North Russell Street was known as the B. Soboleski & Company Saloon. The original saloon was established in 1905 in an 1880s wood-framed structure at this location. The present simple brick two-story structure was completed in 1914, replacing the old commercial building. Opened as a watering hole for Polish immigrants, the White Eagle is one of the last echoes of Old Portland's working-class history, as well as its rock 'n roll counterculture of the 1970s and 80s. It also is alleged to have some great ghost stories. **www.mcmenamins.com** (*click on Pubs & Restaurants*)

PENNSYLVANIA

Pulaski & Lafayette Monument, Brandywine Battlefield Museum, Chaddsford, PA (Staury01 CC BY-SA 4.0)

BETHLEHEM
Sisters' House Historical Marker
In 1778, Brig. General Pulaski received an embroidered silk banner for his cavalry from the Order of Moravian Nuns living in the Sisters' House for offering protection during the American Revolution. He carried the crimson banner into battle with him until his death in Savannah. A state historical plaque identifies the house where the banner was created, which is located near the Moravian Cemetery on West Market Street at 50 West Church Street. The original banner is in Baltimore and was memorialized in Henry Wadsworth Longfellow's "Hymn of the Moravian Nuns of Bethlehem." (*See* Baltimore, MD: Pulaski Banner, Maryland Center for History & Culture)

CHADDS FORD
Brandywine Battlefield Museum
The battle of Brandywine was fought around the creek near Chadds Ford, on September 11, 1777, during the American Revolution, between the American Continental Army of General George Washington and the British Army of General Sir William Howe. It was the largest single-day land battle in the war although it ended in defeat for the Americans. As Washington's army retreated, General Casimir Pulaski defended Washington's rear allowing him to escape. The Brandywine Battlefield Museum in the 52-acre park honors Pulaski's contributions in saving the Continental Army and markers in the vicinity of the battlefield mention Pulaski. A monument honoring both Lafayette and Pulaski is located in the Battle of Brandywine Cemetery. The first Saturday in March the museum celebrates Casimir Pulaski Day. **brandywinebattlefield.org**

CARNEGIE
All Saints Polish National Catholic Church
Dissenters from the Immaculate Conception Church (first Polish parish in Carnegie) established the Holy Family PNCC in 1918 and finished

Polish Pennsylvania Historical Markers
Throughout Pennsylvania there are sixteen historic markers that chart the stories of Polish Americans. Approximately half are dedicated to military history, from the role of Pulaski's cavalry at the Battle of Brandywine to the site where Paderewski rallied recruits for Haller's Army. Others are related to industrial history and strikes. Go to the following website for more information and locations: **www.poles.org/DB/Pol_Museum/Pol_Markers/Markers_desc.html**

construction in 1921 on the impressive red brick church at 500 5th Street. The founding bishop of the PNCC, Francis Hodur, presided over the dedication ceremonies. With a name change in the 1930s, the parish switched from Holy Family to All Saints. Characteristic activities such as the Polish Festival remain active. **www.allsaintspnccpa.org**

CONSHOHOCKEN
St. Mary Church
After a merger of parishes in 2014, the future of this historic 1950 stone Gothic church at 140 West Hector Street was unclear. However, the St. Mary Polish American Society and the Priestly Fraternity of St. Peter successfully petitioned for the church to become the home of the Latin Mass in the Archdiocese of Philadelphia. Since then, the church has operated as a quasi-parish. The Polish American Society has ensured that Polish liturgical traditions continue, such as weekly devotions to Our Lady of Częstochowa and *Święconka*. A painting of Our Lady of Częstochowa is found on the wall near the altar. **www.stmarypolish.org**

DICKSON CITY
Visitation of the Blessed Virgin Mary Church
Visitation of the Blessed Virgin Mary is a Romanesque church that robustly maintains a Polish identity. The church at 1090 Carmalt Street was designed by Hancock Architects in 1909 and the next-door parish school was later added by architect Alexander Prawdzika. Further embellishment occurred in 1959 for the jubilee with paintings by Victor Zucci and Son. On the sides of the nave, angels hold scrolls inscribed with ten titles in Polish from the Litany of the Blessed Virgin. The rose window above the Blessed Virgin Mary altar features a shield commemorating the dates of Polish uprisings in 1794, 1830, 1848, and 1863. Of the four bells, "Maria" is the largest at fifteen hundred pounds. Customs such as the Forty Hour Devotion and *Święconka* baskets blessed for Easter remain vibrant. Each year, *Boży Grób* (God's Grave)—an elaborate display including a life-size statue of Jesus laying in the tomb—is displayed after the Good Friday service. **www.vbvm.org**

DOYLESTOWN
The National Shrine of Our Lady of Czestochowa
The chief catalyst of the creation of this Shrine was Rev. Michael Zembrzuski, a Pauline priest, who came to the U.S. with a copy of the icon of Our Lady of Częstochowa to establish a shrine like the one in Poland. In 1955, a small wooden barn chapel (now located in the cemetery) was dedicated.

The National Shrine of
Our Lady of Czestochowa,
Doylestown, PA (Shrine of OLC)

Below: Mściciel Sculpture at
National Shrine, Doylestown,
PA (Kuryer Polski)

A much larger church at 654 Ferry Road was designed by the architect Jerzy George Szeptycki and erected in 1966 on the 1,000th anniversary of Poland's Baptism. Many consider The Shrine the spiritual capital of Polonia. There are many mementos, plaques, and inscriptions commemorating events in the religious, cultural, and historical life of Poland and the Polish American community. Stained-glass windows depict the history of Christianity in Poland and in the United States. There are thirty paintings, most of them by the Styka family. The heart of the great Polish virtuoso and statesman Ignacy J. Paderewski is enshrined in the Church in an urn by sculptor Andrzej Pitynski.

The cemetery is guarded by an imposing sculpture of a "winged" hussar *Mściciel* (Avenger) which was sculpted by Andrzej Pitynski commemorating Poland's greatest battles as well as the massacre in 1940 by the Soviets of Polish soldiers in Katyń. Because of the numerous graves of Polish veterans and prominent Polish Americans such as Adam Styka, the cemetery is often called "The Polish Arlington." On Labor Day weekend, the Pauline Fathers put on a Polish Festival that draws large crowds. **www.czestochowa.us**

ERIE
Holy Trinity Church
Replacing the earlier church from 1903, the current Romanesque church was built in 1940 and was designed by architect G.W. Stickle. The exterior masonry is made of yellow-hued stone and the interior has a strikingly modern series of white concrete arches with red soffits that evoke the Polish flag. The parish has a resident Polka band and Polish dance group, and the Polish Women's Alliance of America chapter has continued its activities since the beginning of the parish. Each summer on the fourth weekend in August, a *Zabawa* Polish festival is hosted. The parish continues to function as a "national" parish (i.e., one without geographical boundaries) but it shares functions with St. Stanislaus Parish (*see next page*). **www.holytrinityrc.org**

St. Hedwig Church

Now an alternate worship site for St. Stanislaus Parish (*see below*), St. Hedwig is a Tudor Gothic church designed by Pawel Rys with Polish-inflected decorations. It is located in the historic East Bayfront neighborhood at 521 East 3rd Street. The focal point of the church is a silver and gold icon of Our Lady of Częstochowa and a litany of Polish saints in a medieval style. The icon of Our Lady of Częstochowa was produced in Poland by a contact of Msgr. Francis Robaczewski, the founding priest of the parish, and imported in 1941. The Polish inscription under the icon means "Under your protection." The stained-glass windows—another European import—were manufactured by Joseph Herzig of Munich in 1934. The parish, along with the other Polish churches of Erie, greatly contributed to St. John Kanty College, which closed in the 1980s and was demolished in 2010. The statue of the eponymous saint that graced the entrance to the campus has been transferred to St. John Cantius Church in Philadelphia. **www.sainthedwigparisherie.org**

St. Stanislaus Church

The oldest Polish parish in Erie, St. Stanislaus Church at 516 East 13th Street is an example of the Polish cathedral style. It is 66 feet wide by 147 feet long, with two 135-feet steeples. The design by J. Frank was influenced by Richardsonian Romanesque architecture and constructed beginning in 1896. Side altars with classical pediments contain Polish inscriptions translating as, "Heart of Jesus Have Mercy on Us" and "Mother of Christ, Pray for Us." An annual Corpus Christi Day procession started in 1902 has continued to the present. In recent years, several local parishes have been consolidated under St. Stanislaus, including St. Hedwig and Holy Trinity. **www.ststanserie.org**

GETTYSBURG

Polish Legion Marker at Gettysburg National Military Park

Among the thousands of men who fought during the crucial battle that helped to save the Union was Col. Włodzimierz Krzyżanowski, who led a brigade through three days of deadly combat. On July 1, 1863, he fought a costly delaying action north of town where two monuments are of interest to visitors of Polish heritage. Both memorials are located north of town along Howard Avenue. One is a plaque erected by the National Park Service to commemorate

Polish Legion Monument, Gettysburg National Military Park, Gettysburg, PA (James Pula)

his brigade's location on the first day. The other was erected by the state of New York to honor one of his regiments, the 58th New York Volunteer Infantry. Known as the "Polish Legion," it contained a mixture of Poles, Germans, and other European immigrants. On the second day of the battle, Krzyżanowski led the Polish Legion and the 119th New York Infantry in a counterattack that helped save the crucial Cemetery Hill position south of town and prevent a Union defeat. Although there is no specific marker to the colonel or his troops there, it is worth the time to stop atop Cemetery Hill to see where this crucial action took place.

GLEN LYON
St. Adalbert Church
Now one of three worship sites for the Holy Spirit Parish, St. Adalbert Church at 31 South Market Street was built in 1914 following a fire that destroyed the previous 1889 structure. St. Adalbert is an attractive brick church with an elaborate altar and neo-Renaissance interior that features several religious murals.
www.holyspiritparishnepa.org

HARWOOD
Lattimer Workers Massacre Plaque
Located on PA Route 924 and 2nd Street in Harwood, this marker was placed in 1997 thanks to research and effort by Edward Pinkowski, founder of Poles in America Foundation, at the site where the workers' march began. (*See* Lattimer, PA, *for another memorial to the Lattimer workers' massacre.*) The plaque reads: "Near here at Harwood, on Sept. 10, 1897, immigrant coal miners on strike began a march for higher wages and equal rights. Unarmed, they were fired upon at Lattimer by sheriff's deputies. Nineteen marchers – Polish, Slovak, and Lithuanian – were killed. The majority of the dead were buried in St. Stanislaus Cemetery, Hazleton."

Lattimer Massacre plaque, Harwood, PA (Peter Obst)

Miracle of the Bells
Glen Lyon was fictionalized as Coaltown, USA, in the acclaimed 1948 film *Miracle of the Bells*. The film is based on the bestselling novel by Russell Janney and tells the story of the Polish-born actress Olga Treskovna, whose character was based on the life of Anna Trotzski (variant spellings Trocki or Trochi)—a Polish American actress from Glen Lyon. As Trotzski's career progressed, she changed her name to Olga Treskoff and produced plays with her lover Russell Janney. Olga died from cancer when she was forty-six. Her funeral was held at St. Michael church in Glen Lyon, and she was buried in the local cemetery. Russell Janney visited the cemetery in Glen Lyon after her death and authored the novel based on the actress's life. It quickly became a bestseller, and a studio acquired the film rights for which Ben Hecht wrote the screenplay. The film reflects some aspects of Polish coal miner's culture, including the folk song "Ever Homeward" performed partially in Polish by Frank Sinatra. This song was in turn broadcast by the US Department of Information to Poland on January 31, 1981, as part of the "Let Poland Be Poland!" show following the imposition of martial law.

JOHNSTOWN

Monument to the Workers Killed in the Rolling Mill Mine Explosion

On July 10, 1902, one of the deadliest mine explosions in U.S. history occurred in Johnstown. Forty parishioners from St. Casimir Church were killed, along with seventy-two other miners. As St. Casimir Church was not yet complete, the funerals were held at the nearby St. Stephen's Slovak Church. In 1903, St. Casimir's Lodge dedicated a monument in the miners' memory in the parish cemetery. It is constructed of stone with a large cross and lists the names of each of the forty killed miners.

St. Casimir Church

Located at the edge of the Conemaugh River, St. Casimir's was once the mother church for Poles in central Pennsylvania. However, in 2009 when the six ethnic parishes of Johnstown merged into one, the church closed. Construction on the Romanesque church designed by Walter Myton began in 1901 but would not be finished for another five years as forty parishioners were killed in the 1902 Rolling Mill mining explosion. A stained-glass window depicting St. Barbara, patron saint of miners, was donated in memory of the explosion victims. The steelworkers sponsored a window for St. Florian, who was burned on an iron grate. The property at 500 Power Street is now being redeveloped as Casimir Cultural Center as part of the Cambria City Historic District. After the church mergers, a historic walking tour of the city's architectural heritage was organized by The Steeples Project and can be viewed online. More information about the Polish community and work in the mines and steel mills can be viewed at the **Heritage Discovery Center** at 201 6th Avenue. In the Ethnic Social Club at the Center, there is a restored 1940s bar from the West End Polish Citizens Club. **www.jaha.org/attractions/heritage-discovery-center**

St. Casimir's Polski Dom

The Polski Dom at 306 Power Street, with a frescoed second-floor ballroom, was built in 1915 and designed by architect Walter Myton, who had previously been commissioned for St. Casimir Church. As many visited the club after a day in the mines, the first floor had showers for members to remove layers of soot. At present, a popular bar and billiards room operates on the first floor.

Rolling Mill Mine explosion monument, Johnstown, PA
(Gavin Moulton)

St. Casimir's Dom Polski, Johnstown, PA
(Gavin Moulton)

LARKSVILLE
St. John the Baptist Church
The present church at 126 Nesbitt Street was constructed in a Spanish Gothic style in 1920. To the right of the altar, there is a painting of St. Faustina. In 1930 the 3,015-pound church bell arrived via Chicago from Poland, where it was cast in the Silesian industrial town of Bielsko-Biała. The parish has occasional Masses in Polish and an active weekly pierogi-making group. **stjohnslarksville.org**

LATTIMER
Lattimer Coal Miner Massacre Memorial
In memory of the miners, the majority being Polish, killed during the Lattimer coal mine strike of 1897, an eight-foot-tall rough-hewn shale boulder with a bronze pickaxe and a shovel attached to it were placed on the location where strikers from the Lattimer coal mine were killed at the fork of Main Street and Back Street. The boulder is adorned with a bronze plaque that describes the massacre and lists the names of the men who died at the site. It is locally referred to as the "Rock of Remembrance" or the "Rock of Solidarity." A plaque outlining the history of the event is located next to the monument. (*See* Harwood, PA, *for another plaque related to the massacre.*)

MCKEESPORT
Holy Family Polish National Catholic Church
Holy Family PNCC was established in 1921 and the present church at 1921 Eden Park Boulevard—with a striking stained-glass façade and triangular form—was designed by Pittsburgh-based architect Charles Pepine and built from 1966-68. There are four bells in the exterior carillon, two called Franciszek and Thaddeus, named after the PNCC bishops Franciszek Hodur and Thaddeus Zielinski. The parish sponsors the Lajkoniki Dance Ensemble and events such as *Gorzkie Żale* services. **www.hfpncc.org**

MINERSVILLE
St. Stanislaus Kostka Church
The beginnings of this parish date to 1903, but the present brick church at 120 Oak Street—designed by Louis H. Giele—was built in 1913. Fr. Zmich imported the three altars from Poland around 1920, along with the carved confessional and vestments case. The main altar has a plaque showing St. Stanislaus Kostka being comforted by the Blessed Mother. After the economy began to recover, decoration of the parish was completed in 1936, with paintings by Paul Daubner, an artist from Hungary, and installation of twenty-two stained-glass windows. The parish was consolidated twice recently, becoming part of St. Matthew the Evangelist Parish in 2008, and then in 2020 incorporating into Holy Family Parish. **www.minersvillecatholic.com**

NANTICOKE
St. Mary of Częstochowa Church
A Renaissance revival church built in red brick, St. Mary's at 1030 South Hanover Street was one of four Polish churches in Nanticoke and is now the alternate worship site for St. Faustina Parish, which consolidated all the city's Catholic churches, including the closed St. Stanislaus Church which serves as a secular gathering place. The church's architects appear to have been Reilly and Schroeder, a local firm. A unique feature are two shields over the side entrances, one featuring the emblem of the 1864 January uprising, with the symbols of Poland, Lithuania, and Ruthenia. Fixtures from the closed churches have been installed at Holy Trinity Church (520 South Hanover Street), the main worship site for St. Faustina Parish. **www.nanticokecatholic.com**

NATRONA
St. Ladislaus Church
St. Ladislaus Church at 48 Spruce Street is an impressive Italianate structure with a large dome that can be seen throughout the surrounding neighborhood. The parish was established in 1893 and the present building constructed in 1903-1904. Later additions include stained-glass windows from the local Dlubrak Studio added in the late 1960s and paintings commemorating the parish jubilee in 1968. Two windows on either side of the altar are most noteworthy—one depicts a modern interpretation of Our Lady of Orchard Lake considered the "Queen of Polonia" and the other is of Our Lady of Częstochowa. The church has survived multiple mergers and is now part of Guardian Angels Parish. **www.guardianangelspgh.org**

PHILADELPHIA
Abakanowicz's *Open Air Aquarium* Installation
Just south of the Benjamin Franklin Bridge, at 717 S. Columbus Boulevard, in front of The Residences at Dockside on Penn's Landing, is a statuary space featuring Polish sculptor Magdalena Abakanowicz's *Open Air Aquarium*. Unlike her rusty headless manikins in Chicago, this display is playful, featuring thirty unique brushed stainless-steel fish shapes set up on 12-foot-tall metal poles.

Abakanowicz's Open Air Aquarium, Philadelphia, PA (PIA)

Associated Polish Home
The Associated Polish Home, in Northeast Philadelphia at 9150 Academy Road, is the hub where Poles of Philadelphia meet and hold their events. The Home hosts many Polish cultural organizations including the Polish Heritage Society of Philadelphia, a chapter of the Kosciuszko Foundation, Adam Mickiewicz Language School, Marcella Kochanska Female Choir, the Polski Uniwersytet Ludowy lecture group, PKM Dance Ensemble, the Adam Mularczyk Theater Group, the Polish Families Association, and the Gazeta Polska Club. On the main floor is a ballroom with a stage and an excellent dance floor. Located downstairs is the *Piwnica u Dziadka* (Grandpa's Cellar) bar and musical club. The Polish Home is open for various events and patriotic anniversaries. A schedule is posted on their website. **polishhome.com/main**

The Balch Institute, Historical Society of Pennsylvania
The Balch Institute documents the histories and experiences of over sixty ethnic groups in the United States. In 2002, the Historical Society of Pennsylvania at 1300 Locust Street merged with the Balch Institute and acquired its holdings, including manuscripts, images, and other records. the collection contains records of Polish American societies, Polish American Congress (PA), Polish churches in the surrounding states, a large photographic collection of the Polish community as well as records of the newspaper *Gwiazda*. **hsp.org/about-us/the-balch-institute**

Polish Philadelphia Map
Because Philadelphia is home to so many different organizations, mementos and places that relate to the Polish presence there, only the most significant items are included in our list. Those who would like to see more "Polish places" in Philadelphia (and in a fifty-mile radius around center city) plotted on a map with access links with additional information are welcome to visit the **www.poles.org** website and click "Polish Philadelphia Map" in the side menu on the left of the Poles in America Foundation site.

Ralph Modjeski Commemorative Marker

Ralph Modjeski (Rudolf Modrzejewski 1861-1940), son of actress Helena Modjeska, who performed in Philadelphia many times at the Walnut Street Theater, was one of America's great bridge builders. He interned with George Morison, one of America's best bridge engineers. Later, he started the firm of Modjeski and Masters going on to build four bridges in the Philadelphia area, over forty nationwide as well as many in Europe. In the Philadelphia area he built the Benjamin Franklin Bridge, the Tacony-Palmyra Bridge, and two bridges on Henry Avenue. His other major projects included the Thebes Bridge at Thebes, Illinois; Quebec Bridge on the St. Lawrence River; the Trans-Bay Oakland-San Francisco Bridge; the Huey P. Long Bridge in New Orleans; and the Government Bridge (Arsenal) over the Mississippi linking Davenport and Rock Island. During a lengthy career he introduced many advances in the design of long steel truss and suspension bridges and was one of the first engineers in the United States to build large structures of reinforced concrete. He received many awards for his work including the Franklin Institute Franklin Medal (1922), the John Fritz Medal (1930), and the Washington Award (1931) given for his contributions to transportation through superior skill and courage in bridge construction and design. The firm he founded continues to design and build bridges, maintaining the legacy he established. The Polish Heritage Society of Philadelphia led the initiative to dedicate an official marker to Modjeski on 6th and Race St. by the Benjamin Franklin Bridge.

Polish stamp depicting Ralph Modjeski and the Benjamin Franklin Bridge in Philadelphia (Peter Obst)

Benjamin Franklin Bridge

The Benjamin Franklin Bridge is a major crossing of the Delaware River at mid-town Philadelphia. This pioneering steel suspension bridge was designed and engineered by Ralph Modjeski (*see sidebar above*). Modjeski spent several years in Philadelphia while the bridge was being built. It was completed in 1926 and opened during the American Sesquicentennial celebration with President Calvin Coolidge in attendance. Modjeski also completed the Tacony-Palmyra Bridge farther north on the Delaware River and a majestic concrete arch bridge on Henry Avenue, spanning the Wissahickon Creek ravine.

Casimir Pulaski Statue

The cavalryman hero of the American Revolution, General Casimir Pulaski, was honored in Philadelphia with a bronze figure, in the statuary gallery called the Terrace of Heroes. It is located on the west side of the Philadelphia Museum of Art on the mall between the museum and the Azalea Garden. Retired General William M. Reilly left in his will a sum of money to erect statues of Generals Richard Montgomery, Friedrich von Steuben, Marquis de Lafayette, and Casimir Pulaski. He wanted to honor the great Revolutionary War volunteers from Poland, Ireland, Germany, and France. The bronze of Pulaski, created by sculptor Sidney Waugh, was dedicated in 1947.

Polish Districts of Richmond and Bridesburg
Located along a stretch of US 95 north of center city Philadelphia are the Polish districts of Brides-burg and Richmond. Its most Polish landmark is **St. John Cantius Church** at 4415 Almond Street. Built of red brick, with two spires, it has been a center for the local Polish community. There are also Polish businesses in the nearby commercial strip.

A much grander church is **St. Adalbert's Church** at 2645 East Allegheny Avenue. It is built of cut stone and has twin spires and interiors typical to the Polish Cathedral style of architecture. While the church is still strongly identified as a place for Polish Catholics where one can hear Mass in the Polish language, it now serves a diverse community. Along Allegheny Ave. there are many Polish businesses, restaurants, food shops, bakeries, travel agencies, and a Polish bookstore. At the far eastern end of Allegheny Avenue is a park dedicated to General Casimir Pulaski. It is located on a small pier that juts out into the Delaware River. **stjohncantiusparish.org / stadalbert.org**

Centennial Fountain
More popularly known as the Catholic Fountain because it was built in 1876 for the Centennial Exhibition by the Catholic Total Abstinence Union of America, the fountain is located in West Fairmount Park at the crossing of the Avenue of the Republic and States Drive. The fountain is 100 feet in diameter and 35 feet tall. Embedded in the fountain's perimeter wall are the medallion heads of seven patriots and supporters of the American Revolution. Two of the medals represent Generals Kosciuszko and Pulaski.

Church of the Gesu
This church is run by the Jesuit Order and is part of the St. Joseph's Preparatory School complex at 1733 West Gerard Avenue. Although not usually opened to the public, it serves as a chapel for the adjacent school and is used for special occasions. Embedded in its sanctuary wall is a painting of the Blessed Virgin Mary painted by the celebrated Polish artist Jan Styka (1858-1925). While still a student of Poland's greatest artist, Jan Matejko, he painted this canvas in 1883. The canvas was sent to America to be part of the Chicago World's Columbian Exposition of 1893, but then it disappeared, next surfacing in the Gesu Church in 1897.

Kopernik (Copernicus) Monument
The Toruń Triangle, at 18th Street and Benjamin Franklin Parkway across the street from the Kosciusz-ko Statue and opposite the Cathedral of Sts. Peter and Paul, is a small park with a memorial to Mikołaj Ko-pernik (Nicolaus Copernicus), the Polish astronomer. Numerous Polish groups and local art organizations worked under the auspices of the Kopernik Quin-centennial Commemorative Committee to erect the statue in 1973. Dudley F. Talcott of Farmington, CT, the sculptor, chose an abstract form with which to represent the man through his revolutionary idea. The heliocentric system discovered by the astronomer is shown as a stainless-steel ring sixteen feet in diameter which symbolizes the orbit of the earth; in the center

Kopernik Monument in Toruń Triangle Park, Philadelphia, PA (PIA)

there is a disc, which represents the sun at the center of the solar system. The sun and earth's orbit are supported on a steel angle which represents the primitive instruments with which Copernicus was able to successfully verify his theory. The monument is 24 feet in height. **www.associationforpublicart.org/artwork/kopernik/**

Kosciuszko National Memorial

On August 18, 1797, Kosciuszko's ship docked at Philadelphia, while guns in the forts that he had built on the other side of the Delaware River in New Jersey during the Revolutionary War boomed in salute. His house at 301 Pine Street is important not just as Kosciuszko's last place of residence in the United States, but as the place where he formulated his unprecedented last will and testament that designated money for the liberation and education of slaves. The house was built as a boarding house in 1775 and Kosciuszko lived there from November 1797 to May 1798. By the 1960s the building was to be demolished, but Philadelphia historian Edward Pinkowski authenticated the historical importance of this building. In 1970, Philadelphia

Kosciuszko National Memorial, Philadelphia, PA (Krystyna Matusiak)

industrialist and philanthropist Edward J. Piszek purchased the property and donated it to the U.S. government. After testimony before the United States Congress, the house was renovated into the Kosciuszko Memorial under the U.S. Park Service, which also administers Independence Hall and other historical sites within the city.

Today, this museum contains an interesting collection of mementos, works of art, and documents relating to Kosciuszko. A copy of his will is there, as well as a re-creation of the room he occupied, containing the various pieces of furniture he used. **www.nps.gov/thko**

Kosciuszko Statue

A 20-foot-high cast-bronze sculpture of General Tadeusz Kosciuszko stands on the southwest corner of 18th Street and Benjamin Franklin Parkway. This monument is a gift from the people of Poland to the people of America on the 200th anniversary of American independence and was dedicated on July 3, 1979. The Philadelphia Polish Heritage Society, headed by City Councilman Joseph Zazyczny, funded the pedestal and moved the project to completion. It was sculpted by artist Marian Konieczny. **www.associationforpublicart.org/artwork/general-tadeusz-kosciuszko**

Mother with Twin Infants Sculpture

Created by artist Henryk Dmochowski Saunders, this is a beautiful sculpture depicting a young mother holding two babies in her arms. It is in Section 7, Lot 375 of the Laurel Hill Cemetery at 3822 Ridge Avenue in Philadelphia. Dmochowski was a professional, well-known sculptor, who had come from Poland and settled in Philadelphia. The death of his young wife in childbirth prompted him to create this white marble tribute to his deceased family. After the monument was erected in 1858, Dmochowski returned to Poland, where he took part and was killed in the January Uprising in 1863.

Piasecki Historical Marker

On Callowhill Street (between 18th and 19th Streets) is an official Pennsylvania Historical Commission marker commemorating a son of Polish immigrants who wrote an entire new chapter in the history of aviation by developing and flying the second helicopter in the U.S. and the world's first tandem rotor helicopter. Frank N. Piasecki (1919-2008) founded Piasecki Aircraft Corp, now a division of Boeing, and was awarded the National Medal of Technology.
http://www.polishcultureacpc.org/Piasecki/

Polish American Cultural Center

Located in the heart of Philadelphia's Historic District at 308 Walnut Street, this museum was dedicated in August 1988 at a ceremony attended by John Cardinal Krol of Philadelphia and Vice President George Bush. The museum features portraits of famous Poles, including St. Pope John Paul II, Lech Walesa, Frédéric Chopin, and Ignacy Paderewski. A portrait of Casimir Pulaski and paintings of the Jamestown Polish settlers were executed by local artist Walter Cichocki. Beneath the portraits are display cases which contain related mementos and artifacts. Two of the display tables, recognizable by their supporting eagle legs, are from the Polish Pavilion at the 1939-1940 New York World's Fair. Other displays are devoted to Polish arts and crafts, including straw art and paper cut outs. The museum also includes displays of Polish jewelry and native clothing and tools from various regions of Poland. There is a gift shop with Polish books and mementos.
www.polishamericancenter.org

Polish American Cultural Center, Philadelphia, PA (PIA)

Polish Posters Collection at Drexel University

Westphal College of Media Arts & Design at Drexel University holds one of the largest collections of Soviet-era Polish posters in an institution in the U.S. The Frank Fox Polish Poster Collection of around 2,500 Polish posters that range in date from the 1930s through the 1990s was acquired in 2007, and the Kenneth F. Lewalski Polish Poster Collection of 140 posters was acquired between 1960 to 1990. These collections feature some unique and rare posters.

Elsewhere on the Drexel campus, there is an official marker dedicated to the Polish American engineer and inventor, Walter Golaski (1913-1996), class of 1946, who perfected the Dense Knit Dacron Vascular Prosthesis, the first practical artificial blood vessel replacement.
https://drexel.edu/westphal/academics/undergraduate/graphic-design/polishpostercollections

Sister Cities Park and John Paul II Plaques

Beside the Toruń Triangle at 1723 Race Street stands the Roman Catholic Cathedral Basilica of Sts. Peter and Paul. On October 3, 1979, the Philadelphia Archbishop, John Cardinal Krol, hosted a visit by Pope John Paul II. A great outdoor Mass was celebrated on a multi-story altar built over the fountain in the center of Logan Circle. To record this significant event, a bronze plaque with a bas relief of St. Pope John Paul II was placed in the vestibule of the cathedral. A similar plaque was placed on a stand beside the walkway on the northeast side of the fountain by the Knights of Columbus.

A green space between the cathedral and Logan Circle is named Sister Cities Park and commemorates the international Sister Cities Program and Philadelphia's partnership with eleven international cities including Toruń, Poland. This is marked on the fountain in the center of the park and on the stone bench that surrounds the fountain.

PITTSBURGH

Immaculate Heart of Mary Church

Easily one of the most visible landmarks in the Allegheny River valley, the dome and towers of Immaculate Heart of Mary Church at 3058 Brereton Street mark the center of the neighborhood of Polish Hill. The isolated area, dug into the slopes between the Strip District and Middle Hill District, used to be called Herron Hill until 1970 when it was renamed Polish Hill. Unofficially, it had been known by this name for decades before. The booming population of Polish immigrants grew large enough in 1895 that the community requested from the bishop their own parish, separate from St. Stanislaus in The Strip. That request was granted, and the new church was completed in 1905. Ohio-based architect William P. Ginther designed the church, using the Polish Cathedral style common to the era, but also drawing inspiration from St. Peter's Basilica in Rome. The parish lays claim to being the first in the United States to have the Divine Mercy Novena. A relic of St. Pope John Paul II is in the Divine Mercy side altar. Regular Masses in Polish and holiday-specific Polish traditions, such as Easter basket blessing, are offered at Heart of Mary.

Immaculate Heart of Mary Church, Pittsburgh, PA
(Alexander Kirchmann)

Polish Falcons of America Nest 8

Located in Pittsburgh's Southside neighborhood at 60 South 18th Street, the red and white painted building is the home of Nest 8, the Pittsburgh chapter of Polish Falcons of America. The fraternal organization was founded in Chicago in 1887, and in 1912 was unified with Polish American societies around the country, when the headquarters was moved to Pittsburgh. Currently the headquarters is in a nondescript office building elsewhere, but the life of the society is at Nest 8. The nest is active and provides a social venue for regular events including watch parties for sports,

Remnant of Forbes Field outfield wall

Forbes Field, in the Oakland section of Pittsburgh, was built in 1909, and was one of the first concrete and steel stadiums in the country. It was the home of the Pittsburgh Pirates until June 1970.

Baseball fans with a keen sense of the history of the American national sport will know that one of the greatest endings to a World Series took place there. But for those interested in Polish Americana, that exploit is linked with Bill Mazeroski, a slick-fielding second baseman who grew up in Witch Hazel, OH, a coal-mining town close to Wheeling, West Virginia. Maz came up to the plate at Forbes Field in the last of the ninth of Game 7 of the 1960 World Series. The game with the Yankees was tied. Mazeroski, not known for his power, drove a fastball over left fielder Yogi Berra's head, and well over the 406-foot sign painted at the base of the brick outfield wall of the 51-year-old park. A celebration ensued as the stunned Yankees looked on, and the Pirates had their first World Series title in 35 years. Mazeroski became a hero to the Steel City, and especially to its Polish American working-class fans.

The left outfield wall still stands in tribute to the field itself and one of the most historic plays in baseball. A plaque marks the location where the ball cleared the wall, located on the campus of the University of Pittsburgh, near Posvar Hall, off Roberto Clemente Drive.

Forbes Field Wall and Plaque, Pittsburgh, PA
(daderot)

bingo, live music, dances, food trucks, tailgates, picnics, and potlucks. Holidays are celebrated in traditional Polish style, and events around Christmas and Easter attract the wider city community. Nearby is a historic plaque marking the site of a speech by Ignacy Paderewski on April 3, 1917, to delegates of the Polish Falcons to begin a recruitment of a Polish army in the U.S. to fight in Europe for an independent Poland. **www.polishfalcons.org**

St. Adalbert Church

As the last active Catholic parish on the South Side of Pittsburgh, St. Adalbert's has collected a variety of statues and relics from the seven former churches of the neighborhood. The combined parish is now known as Mary Queen of Peace Parish. St. Adalbert Church at 160 South 15th Street remains a magnificent sanctuary with interior walls painted in a soft pink. The church was constructed in the Romanesque style in 1889 and can seat over one thousand people and is filled with Polish iconography. Polish traditions continue such as the blessing of Easter baskets. The five bells— Ladislaus, Anthony, Adalbert, Joseph and Casimir—were cast in 1892 by the McShane foundry in Baltimore. **www.princeofpeacepittsburgh.com**

St. Stanislaus Kostka Church
In the middle of the constant construction and weekend deluge of shoppers in
the Strip District stands an active Catholic
church at 57 21st Street, listed on both the
U.S. National Register of Historic Places
and the Pittsburgh History & Landmarks
Foundation (PHLF). The congregation of
St. Stanislaus Kostka was formed in 1873
and the church constructed in 1891, when
almost a third of residents in the Strip District had been born in Poland. German
American architect Frederick C. Sauer designed the church, among many others for
ethnic communities around Western Penn-

St. Stanislaus Kostka Church, Pittsburgh, PA (Alexander Kirchmann)

sylvania, and St. Stanislaus is recognized as a "prime" example of the Polish Cathedral style. Some
of the ornament of St. Stanislaus was lost in the devastating 1936 flood, and other renovations
occurred over time. On September 20, 1969, Cardinal Karol Wojtyła visited the church to pray
and the location where he knelt is marked with a memorial. The windows are Munich glass from
the Royal Bavarian Art Institute and include depictions of Polish saints.

University of Pittsburgh — Allen Hall
On the façade at the entrance to this historic building, which is the main building of the Physics
and Astononomy Complex, hangs a plaque honoring Marie Skłodowska Curie who was granted
an honorary degree of Doctor of Law in 1921. The plaque was proposed by the Committee of
Central Council of Polish Organizations of Pittsburgh on the centennial anniversary of her birth
and was unveiled by then Cardinal Wojtyła of Kraków.

**University of Pittsburgh — Polish
Nationality Room at the Cathedral of
Learning**
Known to University of Pittsburgh
students as "Cathy," the Cathedral of
Learning is a 535-foot-tall Gothic Revival tower completed in 1937 at the
heart of the Oakland neighborhood's
main campus at 4200 Fifth Avenue. The
Cathedral is in reality a secular class-
room building, the tallest education
building in the western hemisphere.
Arrayed around the ground floor are
functional classrooms decorated in
the historical styles of dozens of different nationalities. The effort was led by
University of Pittsburgh Chancellor Dr.
John G. Bowman, who wanted to con-
nect the university to its residents and
their European immigrant roots. The

*Polish Nationality Room at the Cathedral of Learning,
University of Pittsburgh, PA (University of Pittsburgh)*

nineteen rooms were completed after halting fundraising efforts in 1957, and in 1987 new rooms were added on the third floor, reflecting new sources of immigration to the U.S. and the city.

The Polish Room was dedicated in 1940 and is inspired by the Renaissance Wawel Castle in Kraków. The wood-beam ceiling was painted by a Polish artist using egg tempera paints in a 16th-century style. A Jagiellonian globe replica, a portrait of Copernicus, windows inlaid with coats of arms, and an original score of Paderewski's only opera, *Manru,* complete the decorations.

READING
Polish American Cultural Center
Founded in 1992, the Berks County Polish American Heritage Association maintains a rotating exhibit on local Polish American culture in the Polish American Cultural Center at the Goggle-Works Center for the Arts at 201 Washington Street. Each year, a new exhibit is curated and in the past, these have included wedding customs and traditional garments. Additionally, the group sponsors a scholarship contest and regular cultural events, workshops, tours, and other Polish American initiatives. **www.berkspaha.org**

St. Mary Church
St. Mary Church at 250 South 12th Street replaced the original church from 1888. It was designed by Philadelphia-based architect E.F. Durang and completed in 1900. The Gothic church was re-painted by Henry Niemczynski & Sons, who added murals of Polish saints above the altar: St. Stanislaus Bishop and Martyr, St. Andrew Bobola, St. Casimir, and St. Stanislaus Kostka. St. Mary's is the starting point for two Polish congregations of women religious in the United States: the Bernardine Sisters (whose headquarters are at nearby Alvernia University) and Little Servant Sisters of the Immaculate Conception, arriving in 1894 and 1926 respectively. Polish Mass is said on the fourth Sunday of each month. In 2016, it merged into St. Catherine of Siena Parish.
www.stmaryrdg.com

SCRANTON
Anthracite Heritage Museum
The Pennsylvania anthracite industry employed 90 percent of the Polish immigrants who came to Pennsylvania at the turn of the 20th century. The Anthracite Heritage Museum, located at 22 Bald Mountain Road in McDade Park in Scranton, Pennsylvania, serves the educational needs of the public regarding the story of hard coal mining, its related industries, and the immigrant culture of northeastern Pennsylvania. The Museum tells the story of the people who came from Europe to work in the anthracite mining and textiles industries. On a tour of the facility visitors will experience the lives of proud people who endured harsh working conditions yet carved out communities filled with tradition. The diverse collection highlights life in the mines, mills, and factories. Visitors are welcomed into the families' homes and neighborhoods with a moment of reflection in the kitchen, a visit to the pub, or a seat in a local church.
www.anthracitemuseum.org

Kosciuszko statue, Scranton, PA
(William Fisher, Jr.)

Kosciuszko and Pulaski Statues
In front of the Lackawanna County Courthouse at 200 North Washington Avenue within 500 feet of each other are two statues of the Polish heroes of the American Revolutionary War: Thaddeus Kosciuszko and

Casimir Pulaski. The Pulaski statue was constructed in 1973 on a granite base by the Pulaski Memorial Committee of Lackawanna County. Dedicated in 1998, the Kosciuszko Monument was cast by local artist Lawrence Alan Dutcher.

Sacred Hearts of Jesus and Mary Church

After worshiping at a German parish for a number of years, the Poles of Scranton established their first Catholic church in 1885. The desire to have an independent church remained a major theme. The second pastor, Fr. Aust, was regarded by parishioners as too Prussian, and this is one of the factors that led to the formation of an independent Polish church: the Polish National Catholic Church (PNCC), just a block away (*see below*). The present church at 1217 Prospect Avenue was built from 1904-08. Architecturally, it is in an elaborate neo-Renaissance style. Above the side altars is a fresco of Our Lady of Ostrabrama. The church is now a worship site for St. Paul of the Cross Parish. **stpaulofthecrossparish.org**

St. Stanislaus Polish National Catholic Cathedral (PNCC)

Scranton is the national seat of the PNCC in America. The PNCC was founded on March 14, 1897, after a split with the Roman Catholic Church due to resentment of the Polish clergy and parishioners with non-Polish hierarchy over parish financial and land ownership issues. The breakaway church became a symbol of the desire among Polish immigrants to run their own church affairs and worship in their own language. The parish assembly elected Franciszek Hodur, a Polish-American Catholic priest, as its pastor and built a new independent church. Hodur was quickly excommunicated by the Roman Catholic Church and he then organized and consolidated other independent churches into the PNCC and was elected its bishop in 1904. Outwardly, it retained most Roman Catholic practices and beliefs, except for its refusal to recognize the authority of the pope. Other PNCC practices anticipated changes by the Second Vatican Council including use of a vernacular liturgy and the facing of the priest toward the congregation during Mass. The first Mass in Polish was celebrated here in 1901 although the current red brick Greek Revival-style church at 529 East Locust Street was not built until 1925-26. The stained-glass windows include Polish national poets such as Adam Mickiewicz and Juliusz Slowacki and Polish saints, St. Kinga and St. Stanislaus Kostka. The Cathedral is now the seat of the central diocese of the PNCC which stretches from Albany to Washington DC and serves around 25,000 members. A plaque on the outside of the church lists all the founding members of the church from 1896-1897. St. Stanislaus is a building of immense historic importance in the religious history of Polish Americans.

On the next block the Polish National Union, a fraternal benefit society founded by Hodur in 1908, has a gift shop open to all. Its membership is over 25,000 in one hundred locations. **saintstanislauspncc.org**

St. Stanislaus PNCC Cemetery

In the St. Stanislaus PNCC Cemetery, about one mile away from the Cathedral, is a historical marker about Prime Bishop Franciszek Hodur and his mausoleum. A few steps away is another marker and statue dedicated by the members of St. Stanislaus in 1933.

(left) St. Stanislaus Polish National Catholic Cathedral, Scranton, PA, the national seat of the PNCC in America (Tomdobb CC-BY-SA 3.0)

SHENANDOAH
Greater Shenandoah Area Historical Society Museum
Located in a historical (1860s) building at 201 South Main Street, this museum has an ethnic room with collections of documents, photos, and other Polish and other ethnic group artifacts documenting the community. The Poles settled here for mining beginning in the 1870s and established several churches, of which only St. Stanislaus is still open. Although mining is no longer the industry, the town is rebounding and becoming known as the Ethnic Food Capital of Pennsylvania. Mrs. T's Pierogi is located here and produces over half a million pierogi a year and the town boasts of several Polish sausage shops.

Polish American Fire Company #4
Though it is the only Polish American Fire Company in the country, Company #4 is just one of five all-volunteer stations in Shenandoah. It was founded in 1915 by a group of young Polish men who were not allowed to join the other "American" fire companies. Over the years, with help from the pastor of St. Stanislaus parish, the company was able to acquire equipment and a new building. The historic station at 115 West Centre Street was built in 1921 and continues to serve as the home for the organization. Annual block parties or bazaars are held with Polka music and food.

Polish American Fire Co.#4 emblem, Shenandoah, PA (PAFC)

St. Stanislaus Church
In 2014, Divine Mercy Parish was formed from the consolidation of seven parishes in Shenandoah. The congregation utilizes the St. Stanislaus site at 108 West Cherry Street, a Polish church established in 1898 with many icons and statues of Polish saints. Across town, the fate of the Polish church of St. Casimir at 229 North Jardin Street remains unclear although it is open for select services. The parish also hosts the Fr. Walter Ciszek Prayer League and associated museum, an organization dedicated to promoting the canonization of the Polish American Jesuit who spent many years in Russian gulags after being accused of serving as a Vatican spy during his missionary activities.
www.dmparish.com

WARMINSTER
Moland House
On the National Register of Historic Places, Moland House, from c. 1750, was rented by George Washington in August 1777 for thirteen days and was his headquarters for a while where he conducted a Council of War on August 21st. Many generals were invited to meet with Washington, including Count Pulaski. A plaque was erected in 1947 which states "... Count Casimir Pulaski of Poland met Washington for the first time. An experienced military commander, Pulaski was later appointed Brigadier General of mounted troops and is remembered as the 'Father of the American Cavalry.'" The museum at 1641 York Road is run by the Daughters of the American Revolution and open to the public. **www.moland.org**

WAYMART
Spojnia Farm
Located in the mountains above the Lackawanna Valley, Spojnia Farm was originally a place of retreat for Bishop Franciszek Hodur, the founder and first bishop of the PNCC, where he wrote *Apocalypse or the Revelation of the XXth Century*. At one point the facility at 611 Honesdale Road housed the Spojnia Manor Home for the Aged, and then was repurposed as the Waymart Church. Today, the property houses the Bishop Hodur Retreat and Recreation Center.

WILKES-BARRE
Polish Union Building
The Polish Union Building at 53 North Main Street #2 in downtown Wilkes-Barre was built in 1936 in the art-deco style. Polish American architect Joseph E. Fronczak designed the structure which features bas-reliefs; above the central entrance a sculpted Polish eagle is flanked on both sides by American eagles. The building was originally constructed for the eponymous fraternal insurance company, Polish Union of the USA, which merged with the First Catholic Slovak Ladies Association in 2017.

Wilkes University: Polish Room
Designed in the Zakopane region style by Stefan Mrozewski, this room is dedicated to the memory of Polish settlers in the Wyoming Valley since 1856. A plaque in the room honors the settlers' contributions to mining and farming in the region. The room is located on the second floor of the Farley Library and has been operated by the Polish Room Committee, a community non-profit group, since 1950. The first president of the university was inspired to open the Polish Room after he visited the Nationality Rooms at the University of Pittsburgh which also has a lovely Polish room. The room contains many cultural artifacts fostering an appreciation of Polish heritage such as furniture in the Góral tradition, kilims, map of Poland by Ortelius (16th c.), paintings and lithographs, folk costumes, and a set of goblets from Wawel in Kraków. The Polish room has been affiliated with several publications on Poles in the region that can be found on the website. Visitors should call to make an appointment. **www.wilkes.edu/polishroom**

RHODE ISLAND

CENTRAL FALLS
St. Joseph Polish Church

The first Polish people who came to Central Falls settled on High Street where the parish is located. Since there was no church to fit their cultural needs, on November 11, 1900, they organized themselves into "St. Joseph's Brotherly Aid Society" and began the process of starting a new Polish parish. Construction began on a church in 1905. In 1915, a new and bigger church at 391 High Street was built in the Gothic Revival style for the growing parish; the main altar, still used today, was purchased from another parish in town. In commemoration of the 75th anniversary of the parish and the 600th anniversary of Our Lady of Częstochowa at Jasna Góra, Poland, Pope John Paul II gave the pastor a ceramic bas relief of Our Lady of Częstochowa. An icon of Our Lady of Częstochowa, which was painted in Poland, touched to the miraculous painting at Jasna Góra, and later blessed by Pope John Paul II, was added in 1982 and now hangs above the main altar. On the outside wall of the church, there is a plaque titled *Golgota Wschodu* (Golgotha of the East) remembering the suffering of Polish citizens under Nazi and Soviet occupation. Polish feast days are observed, Masses are in Polish, and an annual fall Polish festival is held.

St. Joseph Polish Church, Central Falls, RI (Joan Tomaszewski)

COVENTRY
Our Lady of Czenstochowa [sic] Church

By 1905, as the Pawtuxet Valley of Rhode Island was populated with increasingly more Polish immigrants, Bishop Rev. Matthew Harkins determined a Polish-speaking church was warranted. The church at 445 Washington Street, completed in 1907, was established to meet the needs of the growing Polish community. On the outside the church is a white, wooden structure whereas the in-

Polonia in Rhode Island

Polish immigrants entered Rhode Island in three waves: around 1900, following World War II, and again in 1989 after Poland regained independence. The early Polish immigrants settled primarily in five areas of tiny Rhode Island, a state of textile mills. The five areas were the Olneyville neighborhood of Providence, Central Falls, Warren, Woonsocket, and Coventry/West Warwick. Polish Homes and other clubs were established in these areas, and three are still in existence. Casimir Pulaski Memorial State Park is in Chepachet, RI, but aside from this, plus a small representation in the Museum of Work and Culture in Woonsocket, and a few Polish markets, the Polish presence is best represented by its Roman Catholic and Polish National Catholic churches.

Rhode Island has had six Roman Catholic churches established for Polish-speaking Catholics. The oldest parish is St. Adalbert's (Providence). Two are no longer in existence but three churches remain, in order of founding, they are: St. Stanislaus Kostka (Woonsocket), Our Lady of Czenstochowa (Quidnick, Coventry), and St. Joseph (Central Falls).

Our Lady of Czenstochowa Church, Coventry, RI (Joan Tomaszewski)

terior is modern, painted white with a large amber-colored window at the front. An icon of Our Lady of Częstochowa is prominently displayed. Our Lady of Czenstochowa (the current spelling of the Church) and nearby St. Vincent de Paul parishes are served by one priest, while maintaining separate mass times and other activities. The parish holds a Polish festival, *Opłatek, Święconka*, and Polish picnics. **olcsvp.org**

PROVIDENCE
Casimir Pulaski Statue

Roger Williams Park in Providence has twenty-eight distinctive statues throughout the park, including one of Casimir Pulaski on horseback, sculpted by Guido Nincheri. It was donated by the Brigadier General Casimir Pulaski Bi-Centennial Committee of Rhode Island to honor the 200th birthday of Pulaski and was unveiled on "Justice for Poland Day" in 1953 before three thousand people. The 8-foot-high granite base weighs forty tons and was quarried and sent by train from Barre, Vermont. An interactive map of the park gives more information. **www.rwparkguide.org**

Pulaski statue in Roger Williams Park, Providence, RI (Kenneth C. Zirkel CC BY-SA 4.0)

St. Adalbert Church

St. Adalbert Church was founded in 1902 and is the oldest Roman-Catholic parish in Rhode Island and one of the oldest Polish American Roman Catholic parishes in New England. It was built in the Romanesque style and presents a stately picture at 866 Atwells Avenue. It is 130 feet long and 52 feet wide with a bell tower 93 feet high, constructed of red brick mixed with terra cotta in the shape of a cross. A distinctive feature of the church is the painting above the main altar by Adam Styka, one of Poland's renowned religious painters, son of Jan Styka. His work reveals clarity and an insight into areas of human emotion and religious mysticism. Directly above the main altar the Blessed Virgin Mary as Queen of Poland is surrounded by some of Poland's saints and blessed: St. Adalbert, St. Stanislaus Bishop and Martyr, St. Stanislaus Kostka, St. Andrew Bobola, St. Casimir, St. Hyacinth (Jacek), St. Hedwig (Jadwiga), St.

St. Adalbert Church, Providence, RI (Kenneth Zirkel CC-BY-SA-4.0)

John Kanty, Blessed Kunegunda, Blessed Bronisława, Blessed Chester, and Blessed Ladislaus of Gielniów. A Polish Language School is held at the Parish. The annual summer Polish American Festival is well attended. Masses and Polish feast day events are celebrated in Polish.
www.stadalberts.us

WOONSOCKET
St. Stanislaus Kostka Church
St. Stanislaus Kostka Church at 174 Harris Avenue was incorporated on March 1, 1905, and registered in the Rhode Island Historic Preservation Report of 1976. It is uniquely classified as a "Shingle Style" structure, mingling medieval architectural form. Very much like St. Lawrence Church in North Providence, which was erected about 1906, the designs were by Murphy and Hindle of Providence. The wooden "shingle" form of the church is very much like country churches of Poland. In 1923, Jacob Ginalski, a parish sexton, created the altar that now stands in the church. It was painted by A. Brunelli of Dorchester, Massachusetts. St. Stanislaus Kostka is a vibrant church to this day, maintaining many Polish activities and traditions.

St. Stanislaus Kostka Church,
Woonsocket, RI
(Joan Tomaszewski)

SOUTH CAROLINA

AIKEN
Josef Casimir Hofmann marker

Josef Casimir Hofmann (Józef Kazimierz Hofmann) was a Polish pianist born in 1876. He was a child prodigy making his piano debut at six years of age and performing as a soloist with the Berlin Philharmonic Orchestra at age nine. He made his American debut in 1887, playing to a packed house at the Metropolitan Opera in New York when he was just eleven years old. In 1889, he settled in America and eventually founded the Curtis Institute of Music in Philadelphia. He is also credited with the invention of the air brake and held fifty-nine other patents. In 1919 he and his wife opened the Fermata School for Girls in Aiken, SC, now the Fermata Club at 841 Whiskey Road, a private

Josef Casimir Hofmann marker, Aiken, SC (Larry Gleason)

club which has a small historical marker in the dining room. There is also a large outdoor bronze marker honoring its most famous citizen denoting it as the site of the former Hofmann House. Some of his diaries and letters can be viewed at the University of South Carolina Library.

COLUMBIA
Street marker

A marker was placed at the intersection of Gervais Street (US 1) and Main Street stating that the surrounding north-south street pattern was laid out in 1786 with streets mostly named after Revolutionary War heroes, including the Polish-born Count Pulaski.

MYRTLE BEACH
Colonel Francis S. "Gabby" Gabreski marker

The marker to honor this brave and distinguished Polish American can be reached from Gabreski Lane north of Pampas Drive. It is on the right when traveling north, located at the entrance to the Base Recreation Center. Gabreski was born and raised in Oil City, Pennsylvania, joined the Army Air Corps in 1940, and was serving in Hawaii during the attack on Pearl Harbor. In 1942, then-Captain Gabreski (Franciszek Stanisław Gabryszewski) was assigned to the European Theater Operation as a liaison to the British Royal Air Force's Polish 315th Fighter Squadron flying combat missions in their Supermarine Spitfire Mark IXs. He then joined the 56th Fighter Group "Wolfpack" and destroyed twenty-eight enemy aircraft in aerial combat (surpassing Captain Eddie Rickenbacher's record of twenty-six enemy aircraft destroyed during World War I). Gabreski also served in a combat role during the Korean War and was awarded the rank of colonel in 1950.

Ninety Six National Park, Fort Star, SC (Larry Gleason)

NINETY SIX
Ninety Six National Historic Site

This is the site of the first, although inconclusive, American Revolutionary War land battle in South Carolina—the Battle of Savage's Old Fields in 1775. British Loyalists constructed a fortified outpost at this location in 1780, consisting of a wooden stockade around a village, a star-shaped redoubt surrounded by eight-foot-deep ditches and abatis placed thirty feet in front. It was garrisoned by 550 British Loyalists commanded by Lt. Col. John Cruger. On May 22, 1781, commander of the American Southern Department, Maj. Gen. Nathanael Greene, looking to eliminate the last British possession in the interior of South Carolina, at the head of 1,000–1,500 troops, began siege operations against the strategic British outpost. Under chief engineer of the Southern Department, Colonel Thaddeus Kosciuszko, the Patriots began digging approaches and two tunnels to undermine the star redoubt's fortifications. Only thirty yards away and just a few days before the anticipated completion of the tunneling work and setting of the mines, a relief column of 2,000 Irish regulars, led by Lord Rawdon, marched from Charleston, reaching Ninety-Six on June 21st, breaking the Patriot siege. Outnumbered, Gen. Greene was forced to retreat towards North Carolina after coming so close to success. Upon relieving the Ninety-Six garrison, on July 3rd the British evacuated the fortification, deeming it too difficult to support, and marched back to Charleston, never to return. The fort's embankments and about thirty-five feet of Kosciuszko's tunnel have survived since 1781. The fort is original although the trenches have been reconstructed. Two markers detail Kosciuszko's contributions in the siege. **www.nps.gov/nisi/index.htm**

SOUTH DAKOTA

CRAZY HORSE
Crazy Horse Memorial

In the heart of the Black Hills, seventeen miles southwest of Mt. Rushmore, there is a complex of buildings with a welcome center, Indian Museum of North America, an educational and cultural center. This is the site of the Crazy Horse Memorial carved by a Boston-born sculptor of Polish descent, Korczak Ziolkowski whose home and studio are on the grounds and include a sculpture of the Polish eagle among other of his works of art. The Mountain Carving Gallery includes a Carrara marble head of Paderewski which won first prize at the New York World's Fair in 1939,

Crazy Horse Memorial in the Black Hills of South Dakota (Aleksandra Ziółkowska Boehm)

and which got the attention of Chief Henry Standing Bear, who petitioned the sculptor to create a memorial dedicated to the 19th-century war leader who fought against the U.S. government and died in the Black Hills War. Starting in 1947, Korczak dedicated the rest of his life to creating this memorial—the face alone is 87 feet tall. He passed away in 1982 but the work on the sculpture, intended to be 563 feet by 641 feet, is continued by his family to this day. **crazyhorsememorial.org**

GRENVILLE
St. Joseph's Church

Visitors to the glacier lakes area of South Dakota can visit the small predominately Polish town of Grenville, founded in 1914. The first Polish settlers came to this area from Minnesota in 1879 and then from Chicago once the Chicago, Milwaukee and St. Paul Railroad built a line through the area. Almost all the municipality's street names can be tied to a Polish historical or literary figure. Founded in 1885, St. Joseph's Catholic Church serves as the largest landmark in the city and now shares a priest with Sacred Heart Church in Eden. A visit to the church cemetery overlooking Waubay Lake contains many gravestones with Polish language inscriptions. The town's population (currently 54) never surpassed 275 residents, but St. Joseph's Parish lost five men in World War I.

St. Joseph's Church, Grenville, SD (Steven Leahy)

TENNESSEE

BARTLETT / MEMPHIS
Polish Catholic Mission at Church of the Nativity

The Polish Catholic Mission was established at the Church of the Nativity at 5955 St. Elmo Road in Bartlett in 1989 by the Polish immigrants in Memphis and its surrounding area. It provides monthly and special holy day Polish language Masses, a small lending library for children, and sponsors gatherings and events around Polish feast days.

Overall Memphis Polonia activities are coordinated through the "Polish American Society of Memphis," founded in 1978 by a group of descendants of the early-20th-century Polish immigrants. They host a traditional *Wigilia,* cultivate Polish traditions and culture through their activities, and display exhibits at area festivals. They have sponsored the **Nicolaus Copernicus School of Polish Culture & Language** since September 2006.

www.pasofmemphis.com / **polish catholicmission.org** / **nativitybartlett.org**

Jureczki House, Bandera, TX (Larry D. Moore CC BY-SA 3.0)

TEXAS

ANDERSON
St. Stanislaus Kostka Church

The first wave of Polish immigrants came to Anderson County and Grimes County in Texas in 1866 at the request of large landowners, particularly cotton farmers who needed laborers to work the land. Many more from the Wielkopolska region of Poland came in the 1880s. The first piece of property purchased for St. Stanislaus Kostka Parish was filed on December 23, 1880, and the first 40-foot x 60-foot wooden church was built in 1897. Additional acreage was purchased on the north side of the Navasota Anderson Road where the present church at 1511 Highway 90 South was built under the direction of Father N. T. Domanski. It was completed in 1917 and was entirely paid for by the people of the parish. The building features beautiful stained-glass windows, large Stations of the Cross with inscriptions in Polish, and wood carved altars.

saintstans.org

Stained-glass windows in St. Stanislaus Kostka Church, Anderson, TX (James Smock)

BANDERA
Jureczki House

The old Jureczki House is one of the largest and best-preserved Polish pioneer houses in central Texas. The style of the 2-story plastered stone residence—reportedly built in 1876 by Frank Jureczki near the Medina River, exhibits certain Alsatian influences similar to the historic architecture of nearby Castroville. The builder of the house is not recorded, but it seems from the structure's height, plastered limestone, louvered shutters, and proximity to the front boundary line, that he was from Castroville, a stopping point for the Polish immigrants on their way to Bandera. The simple form of this dwelling responds to the climatic conditions of Texas while utilizing local building materials. It reflects the rugged life of Polish emigrants to Texas in the second half of the 19th century.

St. Stanislaus Church

St. Stanislaus Catholic Parish was established in 1855 by landowning Polish immigrants from Upper Silesia. It is the second-oldest parish in Texas after the nearby Immaculate Conception Parish in Panna Maria. After 1875, the Order of the Immaculate Conception, aka, "the Blue Veiled Nuns" came to Bandera.

St. Stanislaus Parish Historical Marker, Bandera, TX (Polish Heritage Center)

Polonia in Austin

The oldest Polish traces in Austin are associated with Helena Modjeska (Modrzejewska), the great Shakespearean actress, who always emphasized her Polish roots. She visited Austin in 1884, 1893 and 1898 and performed at Millett Opera House, at 110 East 9 Street and at the Hancock Opera House (since demolished). When in town, she stayed at the opulent Driskill Hotel which merits a visit. William H. Sandusky, a descendant of Polish immigrants to the English colonies, helped to map the City of Austin in 1839.

The present Polish presence in Austin is extensive. **The Austin Polish Society (APS)** has been active since 2005 cultivating knowledge of Polish culture, history, and language. The society supports a language school and a history club that organizes monthly lectures. APS also organizes concerts by Polish musicians, evenings with Polish poetry, and literary discussions. The flagship event is the Polish Film Festival, which takes place every fall and is a permanent part of the city's cultural landscape. APS also cultivates Polish traditions such as *Wigilia* celebration, Easter Egg painting, a Bigos Cook-off, pierogi parties, and cooking classes. **austinpolishsociety.org**

The Sisters were founded by Fr. Felix Zwiardowski in Panna Maria, the only locally started order of nuns. The original small log cabin church was rebuilt using native limestone in 1876 and that is still the church that is used today located at 311 Seventh Street. Father Antoni Polaniak designed and painted the inside of the church including the ceiling. In 1906 the steeple was completed and it would be redone in 1988 using steel. In 1966, a carillon was donated to St. Stanislaus commemorating the 1,000th anniversary of Poland's adoption of Christianity. Memorabilia from the early Silesian settlers of the parish are on display in St. Joseph's Parish Hall. St. Stanislaus is also a sister parish to St. Michael's in Rozmierz, Poland. **ststanislausbandera.com**

BREMOND
St. Mary Church
In 1878, Fr. Joseph Mosiewicz began to build a brick church in Bremond which was dedicated in 1909. In 1970, the church was torn down and a year later, the current church at 715 North Main Street was dedicated which has a painting of St. Pope John Paul II to the right of the altar. The parish still maintains Polish customs such as sharing of Christmas wafers and Easter food blessing. Each June, the parish hosts a *Polski Dzień* with Polish food and music. **catholicbremond.us**

St. Mary Church, Bremond, TX (James Smock)

CESTOHOWA
Nativity of Blessed Virgin Church and Cemetery

The town was originally named Czestochowa after the patroness of Poland, Our Lady of Częstochowa, but the spelling was later Americanized to the current spelling. A historical marker in front of Nativity of the Blessed Virgin Church at 300 FM 3191 Cestohowa Boulevard reads: "The second Polish colony in Karnes County, the village in this area grew out of a small settlement known as St. Joe and was formally established in 1873. Often, the priest at Panna Maria would conduct services at St. Joseph School in what would become Czestochowa. The 'Mother Colony' church at Panna Maria was destroyed by lightning in 1877 and Czestochowa settlers decided to build their own church which was blessed by Bishop Anthony D. Pellicer on February 10, 1878." Another marker is located near the historic cemetery which contains graves of Poles from the Confederate Army, both World Wars, as well as the Korean and Vietnam Wars. Most grave markers were inscribed in Polish until the 1930s.

Nativity of The Blessed Virgin Church, Cestohowa, TX (James Smock)

ST. HEDWIG
Annunciation of the Blessed Virgin Mary Church and Cemetery

Polish settlers from Upper Silesia and Wielkopolska arrived here in 1855 and built log cabins. Since San Antonio was a half-day wagon ride away, the settlers built their own chapel for their settlement which they initially called "Martinez," but which was called "Polanderville" by their neighbors. After the Civil War, the Martinez community benefitted from the abandonment of the surrounding plantations and the Silesians were able to buy land at very favorable prices. By 1900, the chapel could no longer accommodate the congregation, so it was expanded into the church that stands today at 14011 FM 1346.

Annunciation of the Blessed Virgin Mary Church, St. Hedwig, TX (James Smock)

There are two plaques on the parish grounds: one in front of the church in tribute to the Polish founders and a second at the cemetery which has been designated a state historical site. The sanctuary mural was painted by a Polish Salvatorian priest/artist. The parish constructed the St. Pope John Paul II Community Center which was dedicated and blessed on October 15, 2006. The parish continues Polish Christmas and Easter traditions. **www.sthcc.org**

Polonia in St. Hedwig
The oldest documented log cabin in St. Hedwig was built by, and was the home of, Martin Gorlaszka's family from Poznań, Poland. There is a state marker on the house.

CHAPPELL HILL
St. Stanislaus Church

Chappell Hill, a rural community in Washington County, is in the rolling hills between the cities of Austin and Houston. By 1852, Polish Catholics had immigrated to Chappell Hill, mostly from Wielkopolska. Missionary priests traveled to the area to minister to the faithful in Washington, Austin, Brazos, Colorado, and Nacogdoches counties.

St. Stanislaus Parish in Chappell Hill had some initial bad luck with its churches. The first church was dedicated on November 25, 1894, and destroyed by a hurricane on September 9, 1900. The second church was built in 1901-1902 and destroyed by fire in 1921. The third church was dedicated in 1924 and it is thankfully the present church at 9175 FM Road 1371. The church has statues of Polish saints, and the parish maintains Polish Christmas customs such as *Kolędy* and an annual Harvest Festival (*Dożynki*). **www.ststanislauschappellhill.com**

St. Stanislaus Church, Chappell Hill, TX (James Smock)

International Boundary Marker No. 1, U.S. and Mexico, El Paso, TX (James S. Sullivan)

EL PASO
International Boundary Marker No. 1

As a member of the U.S. Boundary Commission in the years 1851-1855, Karol Radzimiński surveyed 330 miles of the US-Mexico border. He came to the United States seeking asylum after the defeat of the 1830 Insurrection against Russia. He served in the U.S. military with distinction, and finally became a government surveyor. Radzimiński was present at the laying of the foundation for International Boundary Marker No. 1 on the Rio Grande which occurred on January 31, 1855, and signed the official documents buried next to the marker. The marker is in a small park on the exact boundary between Mexico and the United States and designates the beginning of the boundary from the Rio Grande westward to California (about 500 miles). There is a historic description on the monument.

General Casimir Pulaski Polish American Society (GCPPAS), El Paso, Texas

The GCPPAS, at 221 North Kansas Street, Suite 1300, in El Paso is a Polonian fraternal, social, and cultural organization. It covers West Texas and Southern New Mexico as well as Juarez in Mexico. The organization aims to strengthen the bonds of friendship and solidarity between Polish Americans, and cultivate Polish traditions, culture, and language. GCPPAS supports philanthropic and educational programs around Polish history and the contributions of Poles to the development of the United States. It cooperates with local cultural institutions to organize social events linked to traditions such as *Wigilia*, egg coloring (*pisanki*), food blessings, the Polish Film Festival, and El Paso Chopin Piano Festival. The organization prepares events for social meetings with Polish musicians, athletes, filmmakers, and soldiers. Most events are open to the public. **http://poloniaelpaso.org**

HOUSTON

Our Lady of Czestochowa Church

Our Lady of Czestochowa Church at 1731 Blalock Road was established in 1982 to fulfill the spiritual needs of Polish immigrants in the Houston metropolitan area and is the center of Polish religious, cultural, and social life in Houston. The Church is home to several relics of St. Pope John Paul II, St. Faustina (Faustyna) Kowalska, and Blessed Fr. Michał Sopoćko. To the left of the main altar, a large shrine is dedicated to our Lady of Częstochowa. The church also features the Houston Polonia Memorial Plaza, with the bronze statue of St. Pope John Paul II at its heart, dedicated to the memory of those who had visibly enriched the life of the community. The parish is home to the Nicolaus Copernicus Polish Saturday School, as well as three generations of folk-dance groups: "Wawel," "Mini Wawel," and "Babcia Wawel." Our Lady of

Houston Polonia Memorial Plaza, with bronze statue of St. Pope John Paul II at Our Lady of Czestochowa Church, Houston, TX (Rafal Zielinski)

Czestochowa is the host of the semi-annual Polish Festival, the biggest Polish event in the state of Texas, which attract over six thousand guests to sample Polish culture, tradition, and cuisine. **http://polishchurchhouston.com**

LA PORTE
San Jacinto Monument

San Jacinto Monument, La Porte, TX (Gronowski26 CC BY-SA-4.0)

The San Jacinto Monument commemorates the battle for Texan independence from Mexico. It is the tallest stone monument in the world and houses the San Jacinto Museum of History and an extensive library. At this location on April 21, 1836, the army of Texas was commanded by General Sam Houston under the battle cry, "Remember the Alamo! Remember Goliad!" The Texans charged and won the battle. The battlefield's name is derived from the San Jacinto River that flows through this area. The river was named by the Spanish explorers in the late 17th century after the newly canonized Dominican Polish Silesian saint, St. Jacek Odrowąż or San Jacinto in Spanish. There were several Poles from the "November Uprising" of 1830-1831 who fought in the Texas Revolution. Michael Debicki, an engineer, served at Goliad. Others serving with Colonel James Fannin in Goliad were Francis and Adolph Petrussewicz, John Kornicky and Joseph Schrusnecki—all were killed. At the Battle of San Jacinto, Felix Wardzinski, Michael Dembinski, and Frederick Lemsky, plus an additional six Poles served with General Sam Houston on March 21, 1836. In fact, Lt. Col. Felix Wardzinski is accredited with capturing President Santa Anna the day after the battle and presenting him to General Sam Houston. One hundred years later, on June 6, 1936, Wardzinski was listed in the Texas Hall of Fame alongside Sam Houston, the first president of the Republic of Texas, and Stephen F. Austin. **www.sanjacinto-museum.org/Monument**

NEW WAVERLY
St. Joseph Church

St. Joseph Parish was organized in 1869 by the Rev. Felix Orzechowski. Two years earlier, he had come upon forty Polish families that had emigrated as part of the Waverly Emigration Society, a group established to procure foreign agricultural workers. This led to such a great influx of Polish immigrants that one historian described New Waverly as the cradle of Polish immigration in southeast Texas. Mass was celebrated on farms until a church was built in 1877. In 1890, the church was replaced with a larger one and the original building became a school. With continued growth, the third and present church at 101 Elmore Street was built on the same site as the two earlier ones and dedicated in 1906. In December 2019, the celebration of the sesquicentennial of St. Joseph's Parish revitalized interest in its Polish history and saw the reintroduction of Polish celebrations. It is on the state register of historic buildings. **stjosephnewwaverlytx.net**

St. Joseph Church, New Waverly, TX (James Smock)

PANNA MARIA

Immaculate Conception of the Blessed Virgin Mary Church

Immaculate Conception Church is the first Polish church in the United States. The community was established when the settlers arrived and held their first Mass on Christmas Eve, 1854, under a large oak tree which still stands on the church grounds. The first church, made of limestone with a thatched roof, was struck by lightning and burned in 1875.

The present church at 13879 North FM 81 Road was rebuilt in 1878 on the same site with hand-chiseled limestone. The 100-ft. tower and cross were completed in 1882. An addition increased the church to its present size in 1942. The church houses several artifacts and works of art including an 1858 painting of St. Stanislaus, Bishop and Martyr, Patron saint of Poland; a mosaic of the Black Madonna presented to Panna Maria by President Lyndon Johnson in 1966; three chairs used at Pope John Paul II's meeting with Texas Polonia in 1987; and a statue of St. Anne, a gift from Bishop Nossel of Poland. The remains of Panna Maria's founder, Fr. Leopold Moczygemba, rest in the courtyard next to the church.

Immaculate Conception of the Blessed Virgin Mary Church, Panna Maria, TX (John Wojtasczyk)

Texas State Markers

In 1936, over one thousand granite slabs were placed across the state in celebration of the Centennial of Texas Independence from Mexico. Several of them document and honor early Polish settlers. The "White Deer Polish Settlers Marker" mentions that in 1909 Polish families migrated to claim land offered by the White Deer Land Co. In 1913, they built their first church, and the marker is at the local parish, Sacred Heart Catholic Church. Another notable marker is the "Polonia Settlers Marker."

The Polish settlement of Polonia was founded in 1897 and had a store, gin, blacksmith shop, two schools and Sacred Heart Catholic Church. The Polish population retained many traditions from their homeland, but Polonia declined in the late 1930s because of a failing farm economy and the church was razed in 1939. Today the last reminder of the once vibrant village is the still active Polonia Cemetery where the marker is located.

Polonia Cemetery, Polonia, TX
(Jim Mazurkiewicz)

Polish Heritage Center at Panna Maria

Settled in 1854, Panna Maria is recognized as the first and oldest permanent Polish settlement in the United States and the birthplace of American Polonia. More than one hundred families from the region of Upper Silesia joined their countryman, Father Leopold Moczygemba, who had secured land for them in Texas. The original settlers and subsequent waves of their relatives founded several communities, like Cestohowa, Kosciusko, and St. Hedwig, in the surrounding South Texas area as well as settlements as far away as White Deer in the Texas Panhandle.

The Polish Heritage Center at Panna Maria, dedicated in 2021, honors the legacy of these ancestors and celebrates this memorable immigration story. As an education center of national significance, its founder, Bishop John W. Yanta, a descendant of the original settlers, envisioned a destination that would "preserve the sacred memories of generations."

The 16,500-square foot Center at 13909 North FM 81 includes more than three thousand square feet of permanent exhibit space that provides high-tech interactive and immersive experiences from early Polish history to the present. It also includes a theater, library, archives, and collections, as well as genealogy and oral history areas. **polishheritagecentertx.org**

St. Joseph School Museum

John Twohig's 1855 storehouse was used as a church and a school until the St. Joseph parishioners could construct other buildings. The site chosen for St. Joseph's School was the location of the first cemetery before the graves were transferred to the current cemetery site. Construction on the St.

Polish Heritage Center at Panna Maria, TX (Tesi Pugh Photography)

Joseph School building began in 1868 and is recognized as the oldest private Polish school in the United States. In 1934, St. Joseph School became a public school and was called Panna Maria Public School. In 1989, the school was closed but the building on Farm Road 81 remains as a museum with displays of items used by the early Polish settlers, furniture, and photos.

SAN ANTONIO
Shrine of Our Lady of Częstochowa

This Shrine at 130 Beethoven Avenue was built in 1966 by a group of Polish immigrants under the direction of Father Peter Kolton in commemoration of one thousand years of Christianity in Poland. The stations of the cross at the Shrine were made by Walter Marek in the Polish Highlander (*Góral*) style.

The icon of Our Lady of Częstochowa, the "Black Madonna," above the altar was donated by Cardinal Stefan Wyszyński, who had ordained Fr. Kolton in Rome. Kolton decided to come to San Antonio to minister to Polish immigrants following the example of Fr. Leopold Moczygemba and purchased land for the shrine, under the name "Society of Our Lady of Częstochowa." He invited the Seraphic Sisters to San Antonio to maintain the grotto, museum and surrounding grounds. The shrine is open daily and houses a museum of religious articles collected by Fr. Kolton, including valuable relics as well as photographs of famous Poles, and many items belonging to the Polish American actor Pola Negri, whose portrait hangs in the small chapel next to Poland's patron.

Shrine of Our Lady of Częstochowa, San Antonio, TX (Seraphic Sister Emilia Rzeznik)

There are additional Polish American churches throughout Texas that are of historical importance. For more information see:
Polish Heritage Center: **polishheritagecentertx.org**
Polish Texans: **www.polish-texans.com/2011/05/beautiful-polish-churches-in-texas**

STONEHAM
St. Joseph Catholic Mission

This parish at 11323 County Road 304, a mission of St. Mary's in Plantersville, was established in 1909 by Polish immigrants from Grimes Prairie, Stoneham, and Plantersville. The parishioners built a church in the New England style popular at the time with a wood interior reminiscent of Polish Highlander churches. The cemetery was also established at this time and is still open. The church has several original artifacts such as the processional cross, holy water font, bell, and sanctuary lamp. The floor is also from the 1909 church. The main altar was originally a side altar at the Polish church in Buffalo—Church of the Assumption. Each year on the Sunday of Memorial Day Weekend, the parishioners hold a homecoming celebration with Polish food and music. **smsj.org**

St. Joseph Catholic Mission, Stoneham, TX (James Smock)

Texas Polonia Music

A visit to Texas Polonia would be remiss if one did not seek out the traditional Texas Polish village music. Poles came to Texas in the mid-1800s and brought their love of music with them. Due to the segregation of Texas from the rest of the U.S., and the ever-popular country music scene, the fiddle remains king in Texas and in the state's Polish music. Tunes have been passed down orally from generation to generation in the Brazos Valley. The waltz and the oberek are the most popular dances (both of the Mazurka family), along with the polka.

Over time the cross-pollination of tunes produced the well-known "Westphalia Waltz" (*Pytała Się Pani*), "Put Your Little Foot," (*Varsovienne*), and "Maidens Prayer" (*Modlitwa dziewicy*). Since Texas is home to diverse cultures, the musical traditions of many different communities in the state have contributed to its music.

UTAH

BOUNTIFUL
St. Olaf Church

For nearly one-hundred years after the area was first settled by the Mormon pioneers, there were no Catholic churches between Salt Lake City and Ogden. St. Olaf Parish was established May 26, 1943, as a Paulist Mission in a small brick bungalow. As the parish grew, a new church at 276 East 1700 South was dedicated on July 29, 1980. Polish masses and Polish holiday customs are celebrated. **www.stolafut.org**

VERMONT

WEST RUTLAND
St. Stanislaus Kostka Church

St. Stanislaus Kostka Parish, in the foothills of the Green Mountains at 11 Barnes Street, has served Catholics for over 150 years. The first record of Polish settlement in West Rutland was in the year 1890 and work in the marble quarries attracted many fellow countrymen. In the early years, Polish priests would come from Massachusetts and New York to say Masses until the parish was assigned a Polish priest in 1904. The parish still maintains many Polish traditions such as *Opłatek*, blessing of Easter baskets, and Polish dinners. The parish now shares services with St. Bridget Parish in West Rutland and St. Dominic Parish in Proctor.
www.westrutlandcatholic.org

St. Stanislaus Kostka Church, West Rutland, VT (Parish)

VIRGINIA

CHARLOTTESVILLE
Jefferson Library Monticello (University of Virginia)
The Manuscript Division of the University of Virginia Jefferson Library Monticello has a collection of documents and letters between Thomas Jefferson and Thaddeus Kosciuszko and a colored engraving of Jefferson designed by Kosciuszko.

JAMESTOWN
Jamestown Settlement

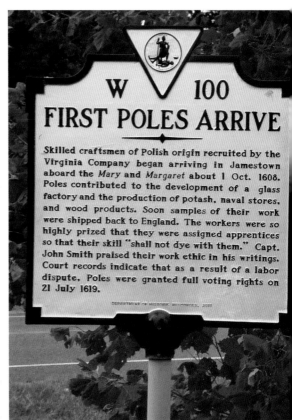

Captain John Smith settled the first English colony on American soil. Polish settlers were invited by Captain Smith, as he knew and valued their industriousness and talents as craftsmen and artisans, having spent several years in Poland. The first Poles arrived in 1608 and made vital contributions as glassblowers, pitch makers, and potash workers. The products they produced were the first exports from America to Europe, other than what the Spanish exported. As more Poles came over, they founded the manufacture of resin, potash, glass products including windowpanes, clapboard, and frankincense. The Poles contributed politically as well. When they were excluded from the council set up by the English they protested, perhaps the first strike in the Americas, and subsequently secured the franchise for the House of Burgesses.

In the middle of the parking lot of the Jamestown Historic Site, among a cluster of flagpoles, you can find a marker listing the names of those who arrived aboard the British ship *Mary and Margaret*. Another roadside historical marker to the Jamestown Poles is located just outside the park. About a mile west beyond the original historic settlement, visitors can view the sheltered ruins of the original glasshouse. **www.poles.org/Jamestown_marker**

Jamestown Colony historical marker, VA (Peter Obst)

Piłka Palantowa / Bat Ball
It is believed that in the year 1609, a handful of Polish craftsmen in Jamestown took a break from their work to engage in a bat and ball game called *piłka palantowa*, or "bat ball." **ourgame.mlblogs.com/polish-workers-play-ball-at-jamestown-virginia-in-1609-a62de06c736**

Polish glass blower in 1608, Jamestown, VA (NPS)

WEST POINT
Our Lady of the Blessed Sacrament Church

The early twentieth century saw the arrival of numerous Polish families to the area in response to newspaper advertisements heralding the availability of jobs and land, thus a large Polish community developed just outside of the town of West Point. Incorporated in 1926, the new town of Port Richmond, annexed by West Point in 1963, became home to the region's largest Catholic population. In 1925, a white frame building, Our Lady of the Blessed Sacrament Church, was built at 3570 King William Avenue and was served by Polish priests. In the late 1970s the church saw an opportunity to offer refuge for Polish citizens suffering religious persecution in Europe. Through the efforts of the Office of Refugee Settlement of the Richmond Diocese, numerous families, formerly residents of camps in Austria, were able to make this their new home. The church oversees two cemeteries, one of which is St. John of Kanti (located on Polish Town Rd.) which was the cemetery of the burned down St. John Kanty Polish Church in nearby New Kent County. It is open for visitors. **https://www.olbs-cathonlic.org**

WILLIAMSBURG
Pulaski Club

The old and somewhat quirky Pulaski Club, created to honor Casimir Pulaski, can be found in historic Williamsburg on Duke of Gloucester Street. The stone marker set in a patch of red bricks and the three benches in front are gifts of John D. Rockefeller, who himself was a member of the Club and helped to fund the restoration of the colonial capital of Virginia. The Pulaski Club, which has not always met in the same place, is one of the oldest and most loosely organized clubs in the country. Since 1779, it holds an annual dinner that always includes a toast to Casimir Pulaski. The number of members is capped at the Polish general's age—one member for each year of his life (he died at thirty-three)—and only male citizens of Williamsburg are admitted.

Pulaski Club, Williamsburg, VA (Edward Pinkowski)

WASHINGTON

ABERDEEN
Polish Hall & Sts. Peter and Paul Church
The historic Polish Hall in this lumber town was opened in 1916. Soon after opening, the hall became too small for the growing Polish community. The structure was extended, and a second story added in the 1930s. The Polish Hall was the focal point of Aberdeen's Polish neighborhood that once hosted several small Polish-owned businesses and a Polish Roman Catholic parish, Sts. Peter and Paul. The parish was closed in 2016 by the Archdiocese of Seattle but the building still stands on the same block as The Polish Hall.

The Polish Hall at 823 West 1st Street is home to the Polish National Alliance Lodge 852 and the Polish Club of Aberdeen. The Polish Club hosts several annual events including a Polish Dinner, *Opłatek*, *Wigilia* dinner, Polish Festival, and an Oyster Feed featuring local oysters from Grays Harbor. **aberdeenpolishclub.com**

ENUMCLAW
Father Michał Fafara gravesite
Father Michał Fafara (1862-1914) arrived in Tacoma, WA, in 1892 through the efforts of Polish National Alliance Lodge 156 to secure a Polish-speaking priest. Father Fafara was the first Polish-speaking priest in the Pacific Northwest. Besides serving the newly formed parish of St. Stanislaus Kostka in Tacoma (now Sts. Peter and Paul Church), Fr. Fafara served as a circuit priest traveling by train, horse, and foot to numerous lumber and mining communities in western Washington where Polish immigrants labored. His regular visits included Enumclaw, Wilkeson, Black Diamond, Aberdeen, and Pe Ell. Fr. Fafara died in 1914 in Enumclaw and is interred in Enumclaw Memorial Park. Inscribed on the impressive grave marker are the words "Pioneer Priest."

LACEY
Cebula Hall, St. Martin's University
Cebula Hall is the home of The Hal and Inge Marcus School of Engineering at St. Martin's University. The building, known for its modern and environmentally sustainable design, is named for Father Richard Cebula, O.S.B., an inspiring professor and priest at St. Martin's Abbey. Father Cebula guided the university's engineering programs and established their reputation for excellence. Cebula Hall is a lasting tribute to an important Polish American scholar and Benedictine priest of Washington state.

Father Michał Fafara grave, Enumclaw, WA (Robert Hicker)

PE ELL
Holy Cross Polish National Catholic Cemetery
Holy Cross PNCC and Holy Cross PNC Cemetery were established in 1916. The Polish community of Pe Ell felt that their requests for a Polish-speaking priest from the Roman Catholic bishop of Seattle were being ignored, so a substantial portion of the Polish-speaking population of the lumber town formed one of the few Polish National Catholic communities west of the Mississippi. The community prospered until the collapse of the local timber industry in the Great Depression and the church was demolished in 2010.

The cemetery was established on land adjacent to the Roman Catholic cemetery. Today it is difficult to see where one begins and one ends. Many of the headstones in both cemeteries bear Polish surnames, so the locals refer to the cemeteries collectively as "The Polish Cemetery." This is to distinguish the site from "The German Cemetery" across town. Holy Cross Polish National Catholic Cemetery is one of two Polish cemeteries in Washington state, the other is located in Roslyn.

ROSLYN
Roslyn Polish Cemetery

Located on a pine-studded hillside above the former mining town of Roslyn in the Cascade Mountains is the picturesque Roslyn Polish Cemetery. It is one of twenty-six separate but adjacent cemeteries representing twenty-four nationalities that worked in the coal mines of this former boom town and gives a good overview of the ethnic make-up of Roslyn at that time. The Polish Cemetery was established by the local lodge of the Polish National Alliance and today the Polish National Alliance Lodge 685 in nearby Cle Elum maintains the Polish Cemetery. The first burial in the cemetery was in 1903. The Polish Cemetery in Roslyn is one of only two Polish cemeteries in the state of Washington, the other is located in Pe Ell.
www.atlasobscura.com/places/the-roslyn-cemetery

Roslyn Polish Cemetery Marker, Roslyn, WA
(Robert Sloma,Kathleen Callum and Jozef Callum Sloma)

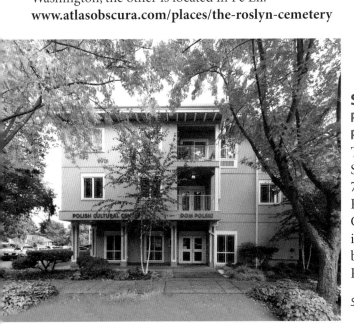

SEATTLE
Polish Hall (*Dom Polski*) /
Polish Cultural Center
The Polish Home Association (PHA) in Seattle was incorporated on November 7, 1918. The building that became the Polish Home (now also called Polish Cultural Center) was purchased in1920 in the Queen Anne neighborhood and became the center of cultural life for the Polish American community, a meeting

Seattle Polish Home, WA (Mike Penney)

St. Peter & Paul Church, formerly St. Stanislaus Kostka, the first Polish church in the Pacific Northwest, Tacoma, WA
(Robert Hicker)

place for Poles and their friends, and a home for many Polish organizations and clubs. The Polish Cultural Center at 1714 18th Avenue offers its members and guests a place to meet and to attend social functions, lectures, film festivals, artistic performances, national holiday celebrations, balls, and more. A Polish restaurant is open on Friday evenings; a library offers books and videos; Polish School provides Polish language classes and scouting; clubs and organizations provide opportunities to volunteer and to contribute to the cultural life of the community. On display are photos of Polish children who were trapped in Siberia in the aftermath of the Bolshevik Revolution and relocated to Poland via Seattle and New York. The PHA sponsors an annual Polish Festival and Pierogi Fest. **www.polishhome.org**

St. Margaret of Scotland Church

The current church building at 3221 14th Avenue West dates to around 1914 but only became a Polish parish in 1992, when the Archdiocese of Seattle combined St. Margaret of Scotland with a neighboring parish and gave the Polish Catholics their own parish home. The Polish Community gathers here for religious holydays and to commemorate Polish historical events. A Katyń Memorial, dedicated in 2008, and a large bronze statue of St. Pope John Paul II are in the church gardens. In the parish hall, there are two rooms run by the John Paul II Foundation with permanent exhibits including the pope's skullcap among other mementoes relating to Pope John Paul II's visit to Seattle in 1984. **www.st-margaret-church.org** *(in Polish)*

Katyń Memorial in the St. Margaret of Scotland Church garden, Seattle, WA (Larry Romans)

TACOMA

Sts. Peter and Paul Church

Originally named St. Stanislaus Kostka, Sts. Peter and Paul is the first Polish parish in the Pacific Northwest. The current church was built in 1924 on the East Side of Tacoma, then home to the largest Polish community in the city. The neighborhood contained several small Polish-owned businesses and The Polish Hall operated by the Polish National Alliance Lodge 156. The church is all that remains today. While originally serving Polish Catholics in the surrounding neighborhoods, today Sts. Peter and Paul Church serves Polish Catholics in the greater South Puget Sound region offering Masses in both Polish and English. **www.parafiatacoma.com**

WILKESON

Our Lady of Lourdes Church & Cemetery

This former mining town, located in the Cascade foothills, was populated by several Slavic-speaking Catholic groups: Poles, Slovaks, and Croatians. Jointly they formed Our Lady of Lourdes Catholic Church in 1894. Although the church at 506 Ash Street closed in 2017 and has been turned into an event venue, the cemetery on Carbonado South Prairie Road dating from 1905, which resembles those in Poland, is still open.

WEST VIRGINIA

WEIRTON
Sacred Heart of Mary Church
This parish was founded by Polish settlers with a strong Marian devotion in 1910, an identity that is reflected in the church's architecture and traditions. The community is still largely Polish and holds an annual Polish festival, a Polish picnic, and continues Polish customs such as Easter basket blessings around the holidays. The church at 200 Preston Avenue has a side chapel dedicated to Our Lady of Częstochowa. Behind the altar is a stained-glass window depicting significant events and historical figures from the history of Poland and Polonia, including Kosciuszko, steel mills, immigrants, and the American Czestochowa shrine at Doylestown, PA.
sacredheartweirton.org

Polish American World War Memorial in Our Lady of Grace Grotto, Wheeling, WV
(Ed Gorczyca)

WHEELING
St. Ladislaus Church and Our Lady of Grace Grotto
Founded in 1902 to serve the local Polonia in the mines and steel mills, this church at 450 Eoff Street was the center of the community. Locally known as St. Lad's, it was the oldest Polish church in West Virginia.

Just a few feet from the building is a Polish American World War Memorial built in 1949 at Our Lady of Grace Grotto that became a memorial to those who served in both world wars. As the city evolved, the church building was sold to a Baptist church, but Masses and Polish holiday gatherings still happen at the grotto.

Polish American Patriot Club
In 1919, the Polish American Political Club—now the Polish American Patriot Club—was started as a civic group with a building to promote the well-being of Polish immigrants and help them assimilate. These days there are few Poles left in the area but the Club still offers scholarships and gatherings. It holds an annual Polish Heritage Day in June at Our Lady of Grace Grotto (*see above*).

WHIPPLE
Whipple Company Store and Museum
The White Oak Valley in the southern part of West Virginia had been heavily populated by Eastern European immigrants, the greatest number of them Poles, coming to work in the mines. There were five mines in the valley around Whipple and Carlisle and the Poles settled in what was called "Hunk Hill," near Sts. Peter & Paul Catholic Church, mainly between 1900 and 1925. The original church was moved to Oak Hill in 1966 where it is still functioning. These were company towns, and the small homes and remnants of the mines still stand as does the Catholic cemetery. Nearby, the Whipple Company Store (built in 1890) had been restored and featured exhibits and artifacts from these mines that have all closed after widespread worker unrest due to working conditions,

Display panel outside Whipple Company Store highlighting the Polish coal miners, Whipple, WV (j.j. prats)

including Polish immigrant workers. At the time of this publication the store was closed but intended to reopen. Outside the store, there is an interpretative display panel highlighting the Polish coal miners. **www.whipplecompanystore.com**

WISCONSIN

CUDAHY

Bust of Casimir Pulaski

Joseph Aszklar, a Polish sculptor who emigrated from Poland in 1908 and settled in the Milwaukee area, had his own art studio. He was commissioned to sculpt a bust of General Casimir Pulaski for Pulaski Park in the Milwaukee suburb of Cudahy to celebrate the 150th anniversary of Pulaski's death in 1929. Money was raised by Milwaukee Poles and sponsored by the Polish Central Association of Cudahy. The bust, which was cast in bronze in Germany, has a time capsule with Polish and American historical documents inside. The unveiling in 1932, a few years after the anniversary of Pulaski's death, drew four thousand attendees. Aszklar also sculpted fourteen life-size outdoor Stations of the Cross, carved from Bedford Stone and set-in grottos, at Holy Hill in Hubertus about 20 miles west of Milwaukee.

EAGLE

Old World Wisconsin

Old World Wisconsin (at W372 S9727 WI-67) is an open-air living history museum that depicts the lifestyles of various pioneer ethnic groups. The Polish area features the home of an elderly immigrant couple, August and Barbara Kruza, who lived in Hofa Park. In 1884, the Kruzas' son-in-law, Frank Stefaniak, built a house for them on the farm where he and his wife Katherine lived. He used a technique known as stovewood construction, in which short logs are stacked up as in a woodpile and mortared together to form walls. The house is divided into two sections separated by a solid wall, each with a separate door. August and Barbara Kruza lived in the larger room and Barbara kept chickens in the other part of the house. In 1989, the Kruza House was dismantled, log by log, and painstakingly reassembled at Old World Wisconsin. It is furnished as a Polish immigrant home would have been in the 1890s. The adjacent garden incorporates Polish heirloom vegetable varieties. Nearby is a replica of a 15-foot-tall wayside cross from Portage County. The Polish custom of erecting wayside crosses and shrines was brought to several rural Polish communities in Wisconsin.

Bust of Casimir Pulaski in Pulaski Park, Cudahy, WI by Joseph Aszklar (Ewa Barczyk)

Kruza House at Old World Wisconsin open-air living history museum, Eagle, WI (Susan Mikos)

Polish Center of Wisconsin, Franklin, WI (Susan Mikos)

FRANKLIN
Polish Center of Wisconsin

The Polish Center of Wisconsin, which stands adjacent to a picturesque lake, lies southwest of Milwaukee in the suburb of Franklin at 6941 South 68th Street. Dedicated in 2000, this impressive structure is in the authentic style of an 18th-century Polish manor house and honors the Poles' tradition of gracious hospitality. The idea for the Polish Center was made possible thanks to the financial success of the first two Polish Fests that were organized in 1982 and 1983 on Milwaukee's Summerfest grounds along Lake Michigan. Polish Fest, now a three-day festival of Polish music, dance, foods, and culture, is held in June each year.

But the Polish Center is more than a beautiful building where cultural and patriotic events, family celebrations, business meetings, and public programs take place. It is a veritable repository of the art of Poland and Polonia, most of it donated by members of Milwaukee's Polish American community, as well as an extensive library run by Polanki, the Polish Women's Cultural Club of Milwaukee. **www.polishcenterofwisconsin.org**

INDEPENDENCE
Sts. Peter and Paul Church

Independence is one of several communities in Trempealeau County that were settled by Poles from two neighboring villages in Upper Silesia—Popielów (Poppeleau) and Siołkowice

Sts. Peter & Paul Catholic Church, Independence, WI (Susan Mikos)

Mecikalski Stovewood Building, Jennings, WI (Susan Mikos)

(Schalkowitz). Polish settlers began arriving in the 1860s and organized Sts. Peter and Paul Parish in 1869. The parishioners worshiped in private homes until 1875, when they built a wooden church. In 1896, they replaced that structure with the monumental brick Gothic Revival church that now stands at 36028 Osseo Road. A 1907 addition made Sts. Peter and Paul the largest church in the diocese of La Crosse. The parish cemetery is located next to the church, and a rectory, built in 1915, is also on the property. Across the street is a former convent building (built in 1901, enlarged in 1932) that may have been the original rectory. The present school was built in 1966, replacing two earlier school buildings. The basement of the church houses a museum that documents the area's history. **www.ssppwi.org**

JENNINGS
The Mecikalski Stovewood Building
The Mecikalski Stovewood Building is situated at the intersection of Highways B and Z in the un-incorporated community of Jennings, originally known as Kościuszko. It was erected about 1899 by Polish immigrant John Mecikalski, who came to Wisconsin from East Prussia with his parents in the 1870s. It is an unusually well-preserved example of stovewood construction (also known as cord wood or stackwall construction), in which the outer walls consist of short logs stacked up

as in a wood pile and embedded in mortar. While this building technique may have originated in Canada, it was used by Polish and German immigrants in the U.S. Upper Midwest. John Mecikalski's building combined living quarters for his family with a general store, saloon, and boarding house for lumberjacks. The Mecikalski Stovewood Building is unique because of its large size and because it is a rare stovewood commercial building. It is listed on the National Register of Historic Places and was restored by the Kohler Foundation in 1987. A friends group maintains it through the Mecikalski Stovewood Foundation and hosts an annual "Stovewood Daze" event in August. On the other side of the road is a Polish cemetery that belonged to St. Mary's Catholic Church. **www.kohlerfoundation.org/preservation/preserved-sites/mecikalski-stovewood-building**

LUBLIN
St. Stanislaus Church
Two churches were established by Polish settlers in this small farming community of barely over one hundred inhabitants—St. Stanislaus Roman Catholic Church and St. Mary's Polish National Church. Early Polish settlers moved up from Chicago and Milwaukee for farming, sawmill, and logging opportunities around 1902. The original church, built in 1908, was called All Saints. The new church at W13381 South Street was built in 1961 and officially became St. Stanislaus Congregation in 1968. There are numerous towns and villages with Polish names in the central farming area of Wisconsin, including Poniatowski, Torun, Krakow, Polonia, and Pulaski, but Lublin remains a robust community and continues to preserve and foster Polish cultural life through an annual summer Lublin Days Festival that brings Polish dance groups and dignitaries from as far away as Chicago as well as surrounding towns.

MILWAUKEE
Bay View Massacre Memorial
Concurrent with the Haymarket riots of 1886 in Chicago, workers in Milwaukee organized strikes demanding an eight-hour workday. On May 3,1886, a general labor strike brought the entire city to a standstill and only one major business was still running, Bay View Rolling Mill, so some one thousand Polish laborers marched to the plant to shut it down. The governor called in the militia and the first arrivals to push back the strikers were the Kosciuszko Guard— their own countrymen and neighbors. The following day an even larger group marched from St. Stanislaus Church to the plant and the confrontation ended with the Sheridan Guard shooting the strikers, resulting in at least half a dozen deaths. Each year a commemoration is held on the first Sunday in May at the site of the State Historical Marker site (Superior Street and Russell Avenue)

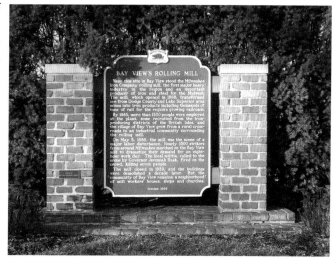

Bay View Massacre Memorial plaque, Milwaukee, WI (2006 Sulfur)

Basilica of St. Josaphat, Milwaukee, WI (Mark Heffron)

Basilica of St. Josaphat

Basilica of St. Josaphat, an architectural gem and center of worship and cultural life, and a remarkable repository of the Polish religious and patriotic experience, is a popular Milwaukee landmark located at 2333 South 6th Street on Milwaukee's near south side.

The edifice was the work of Milwaukee architect Erhard Brielmaier in partnership with the parish's pastor, the Rev. Wilhelm Grutza. By the mid-1890s Grutza realized that the existing St. Josaphat Church was too small to serve its mushrooming congregation, which already numbered twelve thousand. He hired Brielmaier to design a far larger structure, one modeled after St. Peter's Basilica in Rome. After learning that Chicago's Post Office and Customs House was to be demolished, Rev. Grutza purchased all its building materials and had them shipped on five hundred flatcars to Milwaukee for the new church. The project, completed and dedicated in 1901, was turned over to the order of Conventual Franciscans of Buffalo, New York. In 1925, the pastor, Rev. Felix Baran, hired an Italian painter, Gonippo Raggi, to decorate the interior, whose bare walls at the time were painted white. Paintings around the apse include numerous Polish saints with Warsaw in the background, and historical scenes such as *The Miracle of the Vistula*. Large paintings include one with Gen. Kosciuszko leading Polish peasants into battle against Russian invaders and another with Piotr Skarga, a 17th-century Jesuit, preaching before the Polish royal court. In the very top of the dome, there are windows depicting Polish shrines dedicated to the Blessed Virgin. Behind the altar is a painting by Prof. J.S. Zukotynski from 1904 of the *Martyrdom of Josaphat*. Pope Pius XI raised the church to the status of a basilica, the third such edifice in the United States to be so recognized. The Basilica, named in memory of the martyr Saint Josaphat Kuntsevich, is listed on the National Register of Historic Places. Seating up to 1,500, it frequently hosts symphonic concerts and choral events.
www.thebasilica.org

Birds of Knowledge of Good and Evil

A public artwork by Polish sculptor Magdalena Abakanowicz is in a grassy boulevard near downtown Milwaukee, across from the Woman's Club of Wisconsin at 813 East Kilbourn Avenue. The six large aluminum birds in columns were erected in 2001. *(Photo next page)*

Traces of Polonia in Wisconsin

Wisconsinites of Polish birth and ancestry count for ten percent of the state's population so the Polish footprint can be found all over. The Polish presence in Milwaukee and several of its surrounding towns and suburbs remains very visible, as the city (and Wisconsin) was the destination for large numbers of Polish immigrants from the 1860s on. Nearly 90 percent of them hailed from the lands of partitioned Poland that were under imperial German rule before World War I (Poznań, Kashubia, and Silesia). By 1910, Milwaukee, long famed as America's most German (and beer loving) city, was also home to over seventy thousand Poles, 20 percent of its population at the time. Only after 1960 did increasing numbers of their descendants begin the move out of the city into its surrounding suburbs.

The Polish footprint is most visible in Milwaukee's Catholic parishes – eighteen were established before 1940. Each symbolizes the Poles' desire to give of themselves and their resources to make their churches both beautiful temples of faith *and* proud centers of community life.

Magdalena Abakanowicz's "Birds of Knowledge of Good and Evil," Milwaukee, WI (Ewa Barczyk)

Kaszube's Park

A patch of grass near the Milwaukee harbor on South Carferry Drive on Jones Island is the small-est park in the city. This tiny area is the home of Kaszube's Park, dedicated by the City of Milwau-kee in 1981, where the descendants of fishermen from Northern Poland continue to celebrate their heritage at a picnic the first Saturday in August of each year. A historic sign in the park tells the story of the settlers. Until they were removed by the city in the 1940s, the Polish/Kashub fishermen families from the villages on the Hel Peninsula in Poland lived on Jones Island, also a peninsula, for over seventy years. Milwaukee needed the peninsula to build a sewage treatment plant and to create a bigger harbor so the residents were forced to relocate to the mainland.

Historical photographs and artifacts of these early settlers can be found in the **Ruth Kriehn Collection at the Milwaukee Central Library** at 814 West Wisconsin Avenue.

Kosciuszko Monument

This monument, in Milwaukee's Kosciuszko Park at 2201 South 7th Street, dates to 1905 and honors General Thaddeus Kosciuszko. The splendid monument, the work of sculptor Gaetano Trentanove, was funded by the Polish community of the time. On the day of its dedication, over sixty thousand people filled the park. Around 2005, dedicated community activists began the

Kosciuszko Monument, Milwaukee, WI (Susan Mikos)

work of raising the funds needed to restore the monument to its original state. On November 11, 2013, the monument was rededicated in the presence of city, county, church, and community leaders and representatives of the Polish government. That date was fitting since it marked the anniversaries of both Poland's Independence Day and Veterans Day in America.

Pulaski Monument in Pulaski Park

The Monument to General Casimir Pulaski stands in Milwaukee's Pulaski Park, a beautiful 26-acre park on Milwaukee's South Side close to the Kosciuszko Monument. In 1929, the 150th Anniversary of the death of Pulaski, the president of the United States proclaimed October 11th as a Day of National Remembrance in his honor. Soon after, the leaders of Milwaukee's Polish American community initiated a campaign to erect a fitting monument in his memory.

Sts. Cyril and Methodius Church

Sts. Cyril and Methodius Church at 2427 South 15th Street was built in 1893 to serve the spiritual needs of the rapidly growing Polish immigrant community in Milwaukee's South Side. A massive, beautifully appointed edifice, the church for decades was a center of community activity of members of the Polish Roman Catholic Union fraternal organization, headquartered in Chicago. Priests from Poland still celebrate Mass and other liturgical functions in both Polish and English. A Polish Saturday school was created to provide instruction in the Polish language, religion, history, and culture. A large icon of Our Lady of Częstochowa can be found in a side altar, paintings of St. Maximilian Kolbe and St. Pope John Paul II hang by the altar, and the inscriptions throughout the church are in Polish. It has the only Polish language Mass in Milwaukee. **cmmk.org**

St. Hedwig Church

In the years after the establishment of the City of Milwaukee in 1846, devout Polish immigrants and their sons and daughters founded eighteen Catholic parishes in the city, all

Kosciuszko Monuments

Milwaukee's Kosciuszko monument was the third to be erected by the Poles in America. The first was dedicated in Chicago in 1904. Cleveland followed, and Milwaukee came next. Soon after, one was dedicated in Washington, DC (1910), with another at the U.S. Military Academy at West Point, New York (1913). Many more have since been erected.

of them centered around the splendid churches they erected. Saint Hedwig Church (*Jadwiga* in Polish and named in honor of the Polish Queen) was dedicated in 1887 to serve the spiritual needs of the Poles residing on Milwaukee's near northeast side, although the community had been celebrating Mass at another site since 1871. This area was the locus of the city's second largest Polish immigrant settlement. This beautiful edifice, in a Romanesque and Gothic style, on the corner of Humboldt Boulevard and Brady Street, was initially the city's largest Catholic church. The parish itself became the "mother" of two other Polish parishes in the area, one named after St. Casimir (1894) at 2600 North Bremen Street now part of Our Lady of Divine Providence Parish, the second after St. Mary of Czestochowa (1907) at 3055 North Fratney Street. In recent years, the church has been restored to its original luster and is one of three churches that together form the Parish of Three Holy Women. **www.threeholywomenparish.org**

East Brady Street Historic District, Milwaukee
St. Hedwig's Church is part of the East Brady Street Historic District, a historically Polish commercial strip that is listed on the National Register of Historic Places. The adjacent residential area, bounded by Brady Street, Humboldt Avenue, Warren Avenue, and the Milwaukee River, is a historic Polish neighborhood that is also listed on the National Register of Historic Places as the East Village Historic District.

St. Stanislaus Bishop and Martyr Oratory

Driving from Chicago to Milwaukee, visitors will notice the twin church towers of St. Stanislaus as they approach the center of town. This church is named for Poland's first patron, St. Stanislaus Bishop and Martyr. The parish, established in 1866 by Milwaukee's first pioneering Polish immigrants, many of them Kashubian fishermen from nearby Jones Island, is often considered the oldest urban Polish Catholic Church in America. The present church at 524 West Historic Mitchell Street dates to 1873. In the years after, Milwaukee's Polish immigrant community mushroomed in numbers and St. Stanislaus Church became "mother" to a many other parishes founded around the city.

Ship beam from Kashubian settlement, St. Stanislaus Bishop and Martyr Oratory, Milwaukee, WI
(St. Stanislaus Parish)

St. Stanislaus Parish was for generations at the heart of the Polish community, which counted sixty thousand members by 1910. In 1966, St. Stanislaus Church celebrated its centennial. This milestone moment coincided with the millennium of the birth of Christianity and statehood in Poland in 966. To mark these twin events, parishioners funded a giant mosaic of the "Black Madonna of Czestochowa" on the church's outer southside wall and covered its domes in gold leaf, much of which has subsequently eroded. A most unusual element is the beam above the sanctuary which is a historic rood beam from a ship donated by the original Kashubian inhabitants of Jones Island.

In 2008, the Church was dedicated as an oratory of the Institute of Christ the King and Sovereign Priest. With many of its former parishioners having moved away from the neighborhood, the Archdiocese of Milwaukee redefined the Church's mission as a "designated religious community" with members coming to worship from miles away.
institute-christ-king.org/milwaukee-home

Spirit of Polonia or Solidarity Sculpture
This sculpture was erected in 1969 as part of the fifteenth anniversary celebration of Polanki, the Polish Women's Cultural Club of Milwaukee. It is a nine-foot stainless-steel sculpture with three different sized interconnected rings symbolizing unity, harmony, and infinity surrounded by a pool (originally it had a brass sphere which represented earth but that has been lost). It was sculpted by Edmund Lewandowski, a Polish-American Milwaukee-born "Precisionist" artist. He created multiple outdoor sculptures, including a mosaic mural on the west façade of the city's lakefront War Memorial/Art Museum and his art is recognized nationally. The sculpture was renamed "Solidarity" in tribute to the Polish trade union movement when it was moved to its current location on the south side of the Milwaukee County Courthouse at 901 North 9th Street.

Incidentally, the **Milwaukee Public Museum** is located one block to the east at 800 West Wells Street where you can see the Polish House which is part of the Museum's European Village permanent display.

University of Wisconsin–Milwaukee Libraries & Archives: Kwasniewski Photo Collection
The University of Wisconsin-Milwaukee Library is the repository of one of the largest photographic collections documenting Polish Americans. Over 30,000 glassplate negatives taken by Roman Kwasniewski (1886-1980), proprietor of Milwaukee's Park Studio (across from St. Josaphat Basilica and just east of Kosciuszko Park), have been preserved and digitized. They are freely ac-

Polish American Bowling Parlors in Milwaukee
One lively part of the history and heritage of Milwaukee was its durable reputation as "America's Bowling Capital," and Polish Americans made up a large share of the devotees of this classic urban, working-class pastime. While most of the scores of corner watering holes that served up beer and tenpins to the Cream City *Polonia* are long gone, two holdovers from the glory days of Polish-American bowling in Milwaukee survive. In the northerly Riverwest sector, one can still roll at the six-lane **Falcon Bowl** at 801 East Clarke Street, which started as Listwan's Alleys in 1899 and became the home of Polish Falcons Nest 725 in 1945. On the South Side, the **Holler House** at 2042 West Lincoln Avenue remains open for business, as it has been since 1908, when it debuted as Schachta's Alleys. The Holler House is well known for its two antique basement lanes decorated with Polish eagles that still use human pinsetters. As home to the oldest "certified" alleys in the United States, this unassuming tavern draws bowling pilgrims from near and far, including the occasional celebrity. Upstairs, the ground floor barroom abounds in a jumble of bric-a-brac recalling its past as a vintage Polish-American gathering spot.

cessible to everyone. What makes the collection unique is Kwasniewski's success in photograph-ing every aspect of community life in the neighborhoods of Milwaukee's large Polish community, mostly pre-World War II. Not only did he photograph individuals, families, and wedding parties, he took his camera everywhere in covering people at work and play, in business and industry, at cultural, social, and sports events, and at church and fraternal doings.

The UWM Archives also holds the records of most local Polonia organizations. The American Geographical Society Library at UWM holds hundreds of rare historic Polish maps as well as photographs documenting the outbreak of World War II in Poland. **uwm.edu/mkepolonia**

PINE CREEK / DODGE
Most Sacred Heart–St. Wenceslaus Church
Kashubian immigrants came to the Winona/Pine Creek area on the Mississippi River looking for appropriate land for farming. Many of these immigrants moved on to the nearby village of Pine Creek/Dodge, Wisconsin, a few miles away from Winona, Minnesota, but they maintained strong emotional ties to Winona where many found employment in the local sawmills. Bohemi-ans (Czechs) were arriving at the same time and since their language was similar to the Kashu-bians, they all wanted a church that spoke their language. The small wooden church was dedicated in 1864 and almost 85 percent of the parishioners were Kashubians. It is among the oldest reli-gious churches of predominantly Kashubian parishioners in the country. By 1875, they erected a newer brick building on the hill that overlooks the modern-day church at N20555 County Road G. The parish is very much still active and serves families in the community of 500. Pine Creek's population never grew to become a substantial city and many residents moved back to Winona, MN, across the river, where plentiful opportunities existed. The Church is now part of Most Holy Body and Blood of Christ Parish (*see* Winona, MN).   **sacredheartpc.wixsite.com/sacredheartpc**

PULASKI
Assumption of the Blessed Virgin Mary Church
Pulaski is the largest and most successful of five planned Polish "colonies" in the rural area northwest of Green Bay. A Norwegian land agent named J.J. Hof be-gan selling land in the town of Maple Grove to Polish settlers in 1877. The resulting community of Hofa Park was named after Hof, but subsequent settlements were given Polish names: Pulaski (1883), Sobieski (1892), Kosciuszko (1895), and Krakow (1897). In 1887, Hof donated 120 acres to found a Polish Franciscan com-munity in Pulaski. The Franciscans built a friary and a church and established a printery. The present twin-towered Romanesque-style church at 124 East Pulaski Street is the third building of the Assumption of the Blessed Virgin Mary Parish and was completed in 1931. In 1901, the parish erected three brick roadside shrines—one in front of the current church, another on Highway 32 a mile north of the church, and a third a mile south on Shawano County Line Rd.

The Pulaski Area Historical Society
The Pulaski Area Historical Society, at 129 West Pulaski Street, features a small museum dedicated to the history of Pulaski and the surrounding area. The former **Holy Cross Polish National Catholic Church** (1916) is located at 257 North St. Augustine Street. Six miles north of Pulaski on Highway 32 is **St. Casimir Church** (1929) in Krakow. Seven miles to the southwest is St. Stanislaus Church (1935) and cemetery in Hofa Park. **pulaskiwihistory.com**

POLONIA
Sacred Heart Church

The mid-central area of Wisconsin, especially Portage County, has a strong history of Polish immigration. The first settlers came in the mid-1850s including Michael and Frances Koziczkowski and their nine children from an ancient farming Kashubian village of Podjazy. They settled near the town of Polonia as it came to be called, ten miles from Stevens Point, which is the center of Portage County and is often cited as one of the earliest rural Kashubian communities in the country.

Shortly after their arrival, the Kashubian/Polish settlers set out to establish their own religious community. While a few small church communities were established, a permanent church in 1864 was constructed in "Poland Corner" (now called Ellis) but then was moved a mile away to Polonia by the parishioners due to the proximity of several noisy saloons. It was renamed Sacred Heart Church and the parish still exists today, although the present church at 7379 Church Street is from 1934. They have a bi-lingual weekly bulletin. On the right side of the church, tablets honor the first Polish settlers. Visitors to the church cemetery view hundreds of memorials displaying well-known Kashubian names. **www.sacredheartpolonia.com**

Felician Sisters Convent Historical Marker

The order of Felician Sisters was founded by Zofia Wanda Truszkowska in 1855 in Poland; in November 1874, she established a convent in Polonia, WI, which later was converted to a boys' orphanage. The girls were transferred to the new motherhouse in Detroit, MI. The sisters kept expanding and spreading over the entire country and in the 1960s they operated 265 elementary schools, 162 preschool institutions, 32 high schools, and 4 colleges, totaling 85,000 students, as well as 302 catechism centers, 15 orphanages, 9 hospitals, 4 asylums for the elderly, and 29 clinics. A large marker is located on the southeast corner of Church St. and County Highway K on the Polish Heritage Trail in nearby Custer marking the founding of the Felician Sisters in Polonia.

STEVENS POINT
Casimir Pulaski Bust

McGlachlin Park is the site of Stevens Point's memorial to Gen. Casimir Pulaski near the corner of Highway 10 and Soo Marie Avenue. The bronze bust sits on a marble stand and was dedicated on October 11, 1929, the 150th anniversary of Pulaski's death at the Battle of Savannah.

Polonia in Stevens Point

There is a park in town dedicated to Michael Koziczkowski, the first Polish pioneer settler in Portage County. Nearby is Market Square and Main Street, which are on the National Register of Historic Places and several of the buildings still bear the names of the original Polish owners. Various buildings have murals with Polish folk motifs showing how the market square looked when the Polish settlers came to sell their produce in town. Stevens Point is also home to one of the few Polish language newspapers printed in the U.S., *Gwiazda Polarna*. A popular annual city-wide *Dożynki* (Harvest) Festival is held during the third week of August.

It is worth noting that there are several churches founded by Polish settlers in town that can be visited. Although they are no longer actively Polish, they reflect Polish iconography. **St. Stanislaus Church** on Fremont Street, founded in 1913, is now merged with the Neuman Center at the University of Wisconsin-Stevens Point. **St. Peter Parish**, which is now joined with St. Casimir's, was started in 1876 and the present building at 800 4th Avenue dates from 1897. It is considered the oldest Polish church building in Portage County and one that boasts a visit by St. Pope John Paul II whose bronze statute stands outside the church. There is a St. Faustina Room with a stained-glass window of St. Pope John Paul II as well as numerous statues of Polish saints such as St. Hedwig and St. Casimir.

Polish Heritage Trail

Visitors can drive or bike through the Polish Heritage Trail in central Wisconsin around Stevens Point to view sites that represent the rich Polish history of the area, including typical Polish roadside shrines and crucifixes like the ones frequently found in Poland. The brick style used in the photo is strikingly similar to ones in Poland in the Kashubian region in the village of Stężyca not far from Kartuzy, built around 1912. This area is the first Polish rural settlement in the state and the second in the U.S. The trail takes you through rolling farmlands, glacial terrain, and small communities, with impressive churches, creating a pastoral and spiritual landscape not unlike the Kaszuby area in northern Poland from which the earliest Polish settlers came beginning in 1857. Some of the trail goes along Highway 66 which was named the Polish Heritage Highway (from Stevens Point to Rosholt) in 1998.

www.pchswi.org/archives/townships/ heritagetrail.html

Kashubian wayside shrine, Polonia Heritage Trail, WI (Francene Gollon)

Cultural Commons Interactive Garden

Along the Wisconsin River at Pfiffner Pioneer Park next to the Riverfront Arts Center, the Interactive Gardens include a Polish Garden which features a newly added statue, "For Our Freedom & Yours" by Wisconsin Polish sculptor and blacksmith Bolesław Kochanowski, Jr. The work which is 25 feet in height, celebrates the American bald eagle and the Polish white eagle as iconic symbols of each country.

THORP

St. Hedwig/St. Bernard Parish

Completed in 1906, St. Hedwig Church at N14921 Gorman Avenue was the largest rural church east of the Mississippi River. Abandoned since 1970, after many years of political strife between the Polish and German members, the church was slated for destruction. After a studio recorded a concert inside the abandoned church and found the acoustics were excellent, the Hands Foundation leased the church from the diocese of La Crosse, it was deconsecrated, and a major renovation was launched to convert it to a recording studio while still preserving its Polish Catholic history. It is now called the Historic Thorp Quonset Hall, The parishioners of St. Hedwig are now joined with St. Bernard Parish at 109 North Church Street and the combined parish still maintains Polish traditions such as *Opłatek*.

www.handsfoundation.com/st-hedwigs
www.stbernardshedwig.org

"For Our Freedom & Yours" by Bolesław Kochanowski, Jr. in Cultural Commons Interactive Garden, Stevens Point, WI (Irena Fraczek)

St. Hedwig Bell Tower, Thorp, WI (Leon Konieczny)

WYOMING

SHERIDAN
Black Diamond Byway Trail

A good way to learn about Sheridan County's mining heritage is to drive the trail with the 45-minute audio tour that tells the story of those who lived and worked in the historic coal mining towns during the early 20th century. It includes the heavily Polish town of Monarch, one of many mining towns with Polish workers established as "model" towns by the mining companies. To accommodate the influx of workers and their families, the companies provided most miner needs such as houses with running water, electricity, heated sidewalks, and more.

Download the app "TravelStorysGPS" and search for the Black Diamond Byway tour. You can also download it on your computer: **wyoparks.wyo.gov.**

Sheridan County Historical Society & Museum

The starting point for the Black Diamond Trail is the Sheridan County Historical Society Museum at the Bighorns which is located off exit 23 just west of Interstate 90. The Museum houses a diorama of the town and mine once located in Monarch as well as artifacts and a history of Poles. The mine at Monarch closed in 1953, the last of the major underground mines of the County, but the water tower still sits out on the plains.

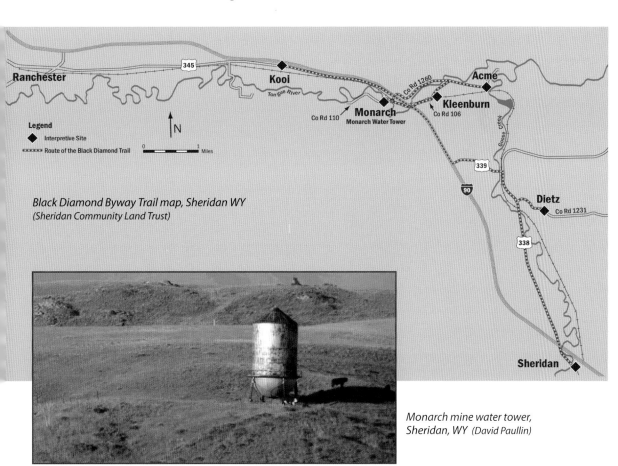

Black Diamond Byway Trail map, Sheridan WY
(Sheridan Community Land Trust)

Monarch mine water tower,
Sheridan, WY (David Paullin)

Poles in Northern Wyoming

Sheridan County is in north central Wyoming, a long way from Poland. However, in the early part of the 20th century Poles began immigrating and migrating to the scenic valley beneath the Bighorn Mountains, a comforting setting like many of their villages in Poland.

It was the coal mines that drew the Poles. Underground mining was very labor intensive and served as a source of employment for people looking for new opportunities. Expansion of the railroads to the West created a demand to power the locomotives and provided the transport for this needed commodity. The railroad was also the primary way Poles traveled from Eastern coal fields and Atlantic ports to Wyoming.

Poles were one of over thirty ethnic groups to work extracting coal in Sheridan County. The mines and camps are gone and there are few physical structures left from that era. However, with the leadership of the Sheridan Community Land Trust, the State of Wyoming created the Black Diamond Trail which honors the people who lived and worked in the underground coal mines. The trail has markers for those interested in the background of the mines and towns in Dietz, Acme, Carneyville, Monarch and Kooi.

Many of the immigrant Poles came from agrarian backgrounds. Some of these folks saved money earned in the mines, homesteaded, and purchased property to establish farms and ranches nearby. Many have stayed in the family for over one hundred years.

State of Wyoming Visitor Center

On the eastern side of exit 23 for Interstate 90 is the Wyoming Information Center. Inside this comfortable stop for travelers, one not only gets a spectacular view of the Big Horn Mountains but you can see the life-sized metal sculpture of a miner. This piece was created by a Polish miner, John Kuchera, who worked and lived in Monarch. It was purchased by the United Mine Workers of America and the Monarch Mine employees dedicated it in 1973 as a "memorial to coal miners, past and present."

Wyoming Room, Sheridan County Public Library

The library has a section devoted to Wyoming history with an extensive collection of the papers and pictures documenting the Polish workers in the mining towns. The Wyoming Room has many pictures and painting of Poles and hanging prominently is a large portrait by the Polish painter Jan Wałach of Paweł and Anna (Juroszek) Karch, painted in 1929 in Poland. Paweł's younger brother was a coal miner and farmer in Sheridan County, but it is not known how the painting in its original frame got to Sheridan. It was donated to

John Kuchera sculpture of a miner, Wyoming Vistor Center, Sheridan, WY (WYDOT and Sheridan Travel and Tourism)

Portrait of Paweł and Anna (Juroszek) Karch by the Polish painter Jan Wałach, Wyoming Room, Sheridan County Public Library, Sheridan, WY (Sheridan County Fulmer Public Library)

the Wyoming Room collection in 2015 by the Kohut family who also had ties to the area. The painter's studio with other paintings is open to the public in Istebna (Beskid Mountains area) in Poland. There also is a very complete genealogy of most of the Polish families that lived in the County. This work was done by Tom Legocki, the grandson of Polish immigrants who lived in the mining camps. Research papers and pictures by Stan Kuzara, son of Polish immigrants, are housed there as well.

CANADA

Polonia in Canada

There are several umbrella Polish organizations in Canada that have branches throughout the provinces, each with their own buildings and memberships. Listed below are several of the main bodies.

The Polish Alliance of Canada is the oldest ethnic organization in Canada. It was created in 1907. It is an amalgamation of various Societies of Mutual Aid for the "Sons of Poland," the Society of St. Stanislaus and the Progressive Polish Union. According to the PAC, the organization aims to carry out "cultural, charitable and social activities, cultivating Polish traditions and promote the rich heritage of Polish culture" via PAC Branches, Polish Women Circles, Youth Groups, PAC-Mutual Aid Societies, and affiliated organizations. The guiding slogan of the Alliance is: Brotherhood-Tolerance-Education. **www.polishalliance.ca**

The Canadian Polish Congress promotes awareness of and respect for Poland's history and heritage and the contributions of Poles to the culture of Canada and the world. It was incorporated in 1933 and changed its name to the present one in 1944. Currently, there are numerous districts represented across Canada including dozens of funds, federations, committees, societies, clubs, combatants' societies, and associations across the country under the CPC organization. **kpk.org**

The Polish Canadian Women's Federation was founded in 1956 by Jadwiga Dobrucka with the goal of preserving cultural values and making a positive contribution to Canadian society. Currently, it has twelve active branches across the Province of Ontario. More specifically, its initiatives, according to Branch #8 in Ottawa is "organize women of Polish origin for the purpose of preserving their cultural values and making a contribution to Canadian society. The organization is charitable in character and based on democratic and Christian principles." The Federation publishes a semi-annual bulletin entitled "Informator," which helps to communicate and exchange ideas and achievements. To achieve their ends, the PCWF organizes many social gatherings, festivals, lectures, poetry recitals and other cultural events. **http://www.federacjapolek.ca/**

ALBERTA

CALGARY

Our Lady Queen of Peace Church

The current church at 211 Uxbridge Drive NW, consecrated in 1968 (an earlier church was built in 1958), was built in the shape of a First Nations tipi. A statue of St. Pope John Paul II stands next to the church, commemorating his pilgrimage to Canada in 1984 and his visit to Calgary in 1969. The church was renovated in 2009-10 when new stained-glass windows, designed by Andrzej Florczak, were installed, including images of St. Maximilian Kolbe, the Black Madonna, a scene from Warsaw with the castle and King Zygmunt's column, Polish Winged Hussars, as well as the Polish flag interwoven through the stained-glass windows in the vestibule. Several of the windows are sponsored by members of the community and cultural groups. The parish hosts a Polish library to assist the school in promoting Polish language and culture. **queenpol.org**

Our Lady Queen of Peace Church, Calgary, Alberta (OLQP Parish)

COLEMAN

Crowsnest Pass Polish Hall

Coleman's Polish Society of Brotherly Aid was formed in 1916 and the Polish Hall was constructed at 1406 82 Street in 1927 to meet the needs of the growing organization. At the time there were an estimated 240 members, and a place was needed to hold language, dance, and drama classes, as well as to host the library and choir practice. Many members contributed to building the hall with recycled bricks used from the Rocky Mountains Sanatorium in Frank. The exterior of the hall was later covered in stucco (c. 1930). In 2009, the building was designated as a Provincial Historic Resource and hosts Polish events.

Crowsnest Pass Polish Hall, Coleman, Alberta (Joshua Blank)

Holy Rosary Church, Edmonton, Alberta
(Holy Rosary Church)

EDMONTON
Holy Rosary Church
Since 1913, the Holy Rosary Parish has been serving the needs of its Polish-speaking community, but with the arrival of the post-World War II Polish immigration a new building was needed, and the enlarged church at 11485 106 Street was finished in 1959. In 1966 a monument was created to honor Canada's centenary and the 1,000th anniversary of Christianity in Poland; in 2008 a bronze statue of St. Pope John Paul II, created by Czesław Dzwigaj of Kraków, was erected outside the church. Daily Masses are in Polish. **hrp.ca**

Our Lady Queen of Poland Church

As the Solidarity immigration in the 1980s increased, the need for another Polish parish in Edmonton was met in 1989 by converting an empty building at 9906 83rd Avenue into a church on the southside of town while Holy Rosary Parish continued to serve the northern part of the city. A large painting of our Lady of Częstochowa hangs on the wall behind the altar. The large bells were poured in Poland. Robert Bober created an artistic Way of the Cross and Bruno Stasiak created a sculpture of Christ on the cross for the church. Polish ecclesiastical traditions and Polish national holidays are celebrated as well as Masses in Polish. Christmas and charity concerts are notable events at the parish. **www.mbkp.com**

Polish Centennial Monument

In 2021, the Canadian Polish Congress, Alberta Society, spearheaded the dedication of a monument on the Alberta Legislative grounds commemorating one hundred years of Polish settlement in Alberta. The monument is in the shape of an open torch with a pictorial history of the waves of immigrants to Alberta carved in the metal. Bronze plaques on granite slabs surround the monument outlining the five phases of immigration from 1895 to 1995, in both Polish and English.

Polish Centennial Monument, Edmonton, Alberta (Canadian Polish Congress)

KRAKOW
Precious Blood Church

In the small locality known as Krakow, located on Range Road 173 north of Township Road 542, a small church remains as a testament to the efforts of local Polish settlers. The original freestanding church was built on the homestead of Fr. Franciszek Olszewski in 1907 to replace a two-story structure that was built in 1902 and housed a boarding school, convent, and chapel, all dedicated to St. Casimir. It was the first Polish parish in Alberta. The current church was built in 1934-35. Mass and grave blessings are held at the site once a year. Open via special permission or appointment.

Precious Blood Church, Krakow, Alberta (Grant S. Wilson)

Our Lady of Lourdes Grotto, Skaro, Alberta (Lech Galezowski)

SKARO

Our Lady of Good Counsel Church

The Polish community of Skaro is approximately 50 miles north of Edmonton. The first settlers arrived in the late 1890s. The first modest chapel was built between 1901-04, but the Polish population soon outgrew it. In 1918, almost a thousand people gathered for the consecration of the second church. Then in 1959 that church was dismantled, and the present-day structure (at 570010 AB-831) was finished in 1960. Elaborate stained-glass windows highlight the family names of the early settlers. The cemetery next door has the graves of the early settlers. The church is now part of Our Lady of the Angels Parish in Saskatchewan. **olafortsask.caedm.ca**

Our Lady of Lourdes Grotto

In 1918 the pastor of Our Lady of Good Counsel Church, Rev. Antoni O.M.I. Sylla, who had started the movement to create a similar grotto in Rama (*see* Rama, Saskatchewan: Our Lady of Lourdes Shrine), began the construction of a replica of the "Grotto of Our Lady of Lourdes" in France on the parish grounds. The idea appealed to parishioners who brought 600 wagon loads of stone to construct the shrine under the chief architect, Fr. Philip Roux. The Grotto consists of a semicircular stone wall with a large cross on top of the monumental crucifix which can be seen from a distance. An original wheelbarrow from the construction still stands at the site. A yearly pilgrimage to the grotto takes place August 14th–15th that attracts thousands of people and Vespers are recited there in Polish.

ST. MICHAEL/WOSTOK

St. Michael the Archangel Church & Memorial

When Polish settlers arrived in the area around 1896, the first Masses were held in residents' homes until a log chapel was constructed at the turn of the century. Between 1914 and 1915, a larger church was built at 561064 Rge Road 184. On the right wall in the sanctuary is a painting of St. John Kanty, in honor of the name of the former chapel. The interior was painted by Peter Lipinski, who hailed from Galicia and painted approximately forty-five churches in the province. The church committee asked the Canadian Pacific Railroad to rename the station. A memorial recognizing the original chapel was built in 1940. In 1976, a monument honoring the original pioneers was blessed by the archbishop. The parish is now served by Our Lady of the Angels in Fort Saskatchewan. **www.olafortsask.caedm.ca**

BRITISH COLUMBIA

VANCOUVER

Dom Polski

The Zgoda Polish Friendship Society was established in 1926 by the first significant wave of Poles arriving in British Columbia who came from Japan where they had served in the Russian Armed Forces during the Russo-Japanese War of 1904 and were taken prisoner by the Japanese. Most were economic immigrants who did not want to return to Poland since it was not a free country. Dom Polski was built in 1956 by the local architect Roman Zurawski. The Society hosts many cultural and social events in the community, such as an annual *Dożynki* festival and Polish music events, and it sponsors Polonez, a Polish dance group that performs internationally.
www.polishsocietyvancouver.ca

Polish Veterans Association in British Columbia Home

The Veterans Association actively organizes commemorations such as Polish Independence Day, remembrance of the Katyń Massacre, as well as Polish dances and food events. The Vancouver organization began with the arrival of Polish soldiers in the latter half of the 1940s and is associated with the Polish Combatants Association. The building at 1134 Kingsway contains a bas-relief "Pegasus' Net" by the Polish Canadian artist Ryszard Wojciechowski which symbolizes the human creative work and was made to commemorate the awarding of the Nobel Prize in Literature in 1996 to Polish poet and essayist Wisława Szymborska.

St. Casimir Church

This parish has been a gathering place for the community since it was established in 1944. In 1948 the new church at 1187 East 27th Avenue was officially consecrated. A memorial plaque built into the wall of the church commemorates, "Those who died in the defense of democracy during the martial law imposed in Poland from 1981 to 1983." The tablet was funded by the Society of the Friends of Solidarity and was unveiled on December 13, 1983. There is a sheetmetal bust of Polish Cardinal Stefan Wyszynski sculpted by internationally awarded Polish Canadian artist Ryszard Wojciechowski in 2000. (Wojciechowski has another sculpture "Rhapsody" in North Vancouver in Centennial Hall.) The Polish School meets in the parish. **www.stcasimirs.bc.ca**

VICTORIA

White Eagle Polish Association Dom Polski

This Hall in James Bay, at 90 Dock Street a block away from Ogden Point and minutes from downtown, has been the focal point of cultural activities in Victoria with frequent concerts, dances, educational lectures, events, films, and a library on the premises. The White Eagle Polish Association sponsors the White Eagle Band, a Polish language school, and a Polish language magazine *Stromy*. The post-World War II emigres created this organization in 1950 and in 1954 they built the hall to bring Polonia together. **victoriapolishhall.com**

MANITOBA

COOK'S CREEK

Cook's Creek Heritage Museum

Situated in the oldest Galician settlement in Western Canada, Cook's Creek Heritage Museum is in the former rectory of St. Michael's Parish at 68148 Highway #212. The rectory was built in 1937 and under the guidance of Fr. Alois Krivanek was converted into a museum in 1968 to preserve the area's heritage. Inside, artifacts, costumes, and furniture from the neighboring Slavic communities are showcased. Additionally, several buildings have been moved to the site, including a blacksmith shop, pioneer house, and Polish-style wayside shrine which is considered the smallest chapel in Canada. The museum also hosts "Polish chat" sessions. **www.cchm.ca**

Cook's Creek Heritage Museum, Manitoba
(Heritage Museum)

St. Michael Church

In 1899, the first Mass was celebrated in the unfinished church located about twenty miles northeast of Winnipeg. It has the distinction of being the second oldest Polish church in Western Canada, after the Church of the Holy Ghost in Winnipeg. In 1922, the church caught fire and was rebuilt. It is thought that the earliest burials in the cemetery date from 1910. Since many markers have disappeared over time, a monument was dedicated to the Polish pioneers in 1980. **www.stmichaelsrc.com**

St. Michael Church, Cook's Creek, Manitoba
(Grazyna and Lech Galezowski)

EAST SELKIRK

St. Stanislaus Kostka Church

In 1899, an immigration clearing hall opened in East Selkirk which brought thousands of immigrants to the area, many of whom were Poles from Galicia, and they settled in nearby localities. The present-day St. Stanislaus Church at 702 Old Henderson Way was built in 1937 although an earlier log chapel was built as early as 1912 to serve the Polish immigrants in the area. The nearby St. Stanislaus Cemetery has a plaque dedicated to the early settlers.

St. Stanislaus Kostka Church, East Selkirk, Manitoba
(Lech and Grazyna Galezowski)

GIMLI
Sts. Cyril and Methodius Church
Built by its Polish parishioners, this church is located west of the town of Gimli on Highway 231. Fire destroyed two earlier churches on the site, but it was continually rebuilt and served the Polish community for many years. Restored in 2000 after being vacant for a long time, the church hosts small celebrations from time to time. It was designated as a municipal heritage site and became known as the "Little White Church on the Corner." Open via special permission or appointment.

LADYWOOD
Sts. Peter and Paul Church stone cairn
A cemetery of the former Sts. Peter and Paul Church is located on Provincial Trunk Highway 12. Polish settlers began arriving in the area in 1893. The construction of a church by the Polish families began in 1901 and the first Mass was celebrated in the structure on June 29 although it did not yet have a roof. A new church was built in 1936 south of the original church and cemetery. The building is no longer a church and became a private home. However, in 1999, a stone cairn with a plaque was erected by the faith community on the original location of the first church (now in the cemetery).

Sts. Cyril and Methodius Church, Gimli, Manitoba (Desiree Rolfe)

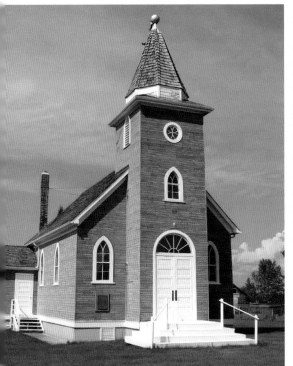

MELEB
St. Michael of Archangels Church
The name of the church is a reminder of the many Michaels among the pioneers, including the builder, Michael Gottfried. In 1918, the first Mass was celebrated and afterwards services in Polish and Latin were conducted until 1960 when the population declined. The building was renovated in 1988, declared a municipal heritage site by the District of Armstrong in 1989, and canonically closed in 1998. A plaque was installed on the side of the building in 1991 to commemorate the history of the Polish parish and highlight the challenging work of the volunteers who renovated and preserved the church after its closure. Open via special permission or appointment.

St. Michael of Archangels Church, Meleb, Manitoba (Gordon Goldborough)

Monument to Polish and Ukrainian Immigrants

A monument was erected in 1957, adjacent to the Ukrainian Catholic Church of the Blessed Assumption on Rd117 N and across the road from the St. Michael of Archangels Polish Roman Catholic Church, to commemorate the Ukrainian and Polish immigrants who settled in the Meleb area between 1900 and 1950. Their work resulted in the establishment of three schools, models of which are displayed in nearby Meleb-Park-Cumming Schools Reunion Park.

SPRINGFIELD

First Poles Monument

In 1817, the De Meuron Swiss Regiment recruited by Lord Selkirk arrived on the Red River. It included at least ten Polish soldiers. When the unit was disbanded, the Poles stayed and settled since Poland was partitioned at that time. After the great flood of 1826 most of them left for other parts of Canada and the United States. A monument, in Birds Hill Provincial Park, commemorates these first Poles. An affixed plaque naming the original settlers was funded by

Monument to Polish and Ukrainian Immigrants, Meleb, Manitoba (Gordon Goldborough)

the Association of Polish Priests in Manitoba. The monument was unveiled on June 24, 1971, and is located near the Pine Ridge Cemetery.

WEST ST. PAUL

Polish Combatants Association Branch #13 Monument

This monument located at the Holy Ghost Cemetery is dedicated to the memory of veteran members of the Polish Combatants Association Branch #13 who fought on the battlefields in Europe. A list of locations and names of the deceased veterans are inscribed on the monument. The unique triangular shape of the monument is an intentional design as it is a common feature in Polish wayside shrines, but also signals for a passerby to pause and offer a prayer to Our Lord. The inscription "Mother of God of *Kozielsk,* Pray for Us" refers to the many Polish officers murdered by the Soviet KGB in 1940 in the Katyń massacres. The three branches of the Polish Armed Forces are listed: Air, Navy, and the Underground Army. The inscription says "For our Freedom and Yours" with the emblem of all Polish Combatants Association branches across Canada. On the other side of the monument are emblems of major Polish units that fought in battles in World War II.

First Poles Monument, Springfield, Manitoba (Lech & Grazyna Galezowski)

WINNIPEG

Andrew Mynarski Statue

This bronze statue by Charles Johnston in Vimy Ridge Park was dedicated in 2015 and commemorates Andrew Mynarski, a World War II Canadian Pilot-Officer of Polish descent who was shot down over France in 1944 while trying to save the plane's tail gunner. He died of burns sustained while trying to save his fellow comrade. For his bravery, he was posthumously awarded the highest British War medal, the Victoria Cross. In addition to this statue a school and the Royal Canadian Legion #34 are named after him. (*See also* Ottawa: Andrew Mynarski Bust.)

Andrew Mynarski statue, Winnipeg, Manitoba (CC BY 3.0)

Holy Ghost Church

In 1899, a wood-frame Gothic church was built to serve the growing number of Poles, Ukrainians, Slovaks, and Germans who resided in the north-end of Manitoba. The parish became the focal point of Polish culture in Manitoba following the construction of the first Polish school in Canada in 1902 and a rectory in 1903. It also served as the base for Oblate missionary activity in Polish communities across Western Canada. The wood-frame church was remodeled several times and then demolished in 1986 to make way for the present church at 342 Pritchard Avenue. The pulpit and altar were custom built for the visit by Pope John Paul II. The original bells from 1902 are housed in towers outside. The roof of the structure is striking and has an arrangement of triangular forms that allows for fenestration. The Manitoba Heritage Council erected a plaque on the site in 2012 honoring the history of the Poles. The parish holds Masses and prayer services in Polish and hosts a Polish festival.
www.holyghost.ca

Manitoba Museum and Planetarium

To commemorate the 500th anniversary of the birth of Nicolaus Copernicus, Polish organizations and churches across Winnipeg funded the installation of a state-of-the-art solar telescope in the Copernicus Room at the Manitoba Museum and Planetarium in 1973. The telescope is located between the Planetarium and Museum Research Tower.

Ogniwo Polish Museum

Originally started in 1992 with the help of the Polish Canadian Women's Federation Branch #7, this museum at 1417 Main Street has a wide selection of artifacts from Polish settlers across Manitoba as well as archival and photographic holdings. Not only does the museum preserve artifacts, but it also fosters a love of Polish art, culture, and traditions. Its library includes over one thousand titles, many of which are rare and out of print. It also holds language classes, hands-on workshops, and lectures on various subjects and activities. **polishmuseum.com**

Ogniwo Polish Museum in Winnepeg (Gordon Goldsborough)

Polish Airplane Crash Monument,
Winnipeg, Manitoba
(Gordon Goldsborough)

Polish Airplane Crash Monument
A stone monument in Albrin Lake Park at 40 Lake Abrin Bay was erected by the Polish community in memory of the president of Poland, Lech Kaczynski, his wife, and the ninety-four Polish citizens who died in a plane crash on April 10, 2010, in Smolensk (near Katyń), Russia.
www.mhs.mb.ca/docs/sites/ // polishairplanecrash.shtml

St. Andrew Bobola Church
After the formation of the Archdiocese of Winnipeg in 1915, Polish residents of St. Boniface still attended Holy Ghost Parish. In 1953 excavations began for this new Polish church at 541 Marion Street. The stained-glass windows include one of St. Pope John Paul II with an emblem of the Polish eagle. A shrine to St. Faustina Kowalska is left of the main altar and one to St. Pope John Paul II is on the right. The patroness of the parish is St. Faustina, and her relics are in the shrine. A permanent **Shrine to Divine Mercy** was dedicated in 2007 and is open to the public. Masses and devotions are in Polish. **www.standrewbobola.ca**

St. Mary's Polish National Catholic Church
The oldest parish of the PNCC in Canada was founded in Winnipeg in 1904. A new church at 365 Barrows Avenue was dedicated in 1968, designed by Stan Pupek. An icon of the Black Madonna hangs over the altar. It is affiliated with the smaller St. Joseph Parish, founded by Polish settlers in 1924 in Libau, and St. Joseph's Mission in Beausejour. Masses are in Polish and a Polish language school for children is sponsored by the parish. The cemetery dates to 1911 with the graves of the original settlers. **www.stmarypncc.ca**

200 Years of Polish Immigration to Manitoba Plaque
On October 22, 2017, an unveiling ceremony took place for a plaque in the Manitoba Legistlative Building at 450 Broadway that honors two hundred years of Polish immigration to Manitoba. The first Poles came to the territory with Lord Selkirk's expedition in 1817. Manitoba was a gateway for Polish immigrants to the west who formed many émigré cultural and social groups, particularly in Winnipeg. Fundraising efforts for the plaque were coordinated by the Canadian Polish Congress Manitoba District.

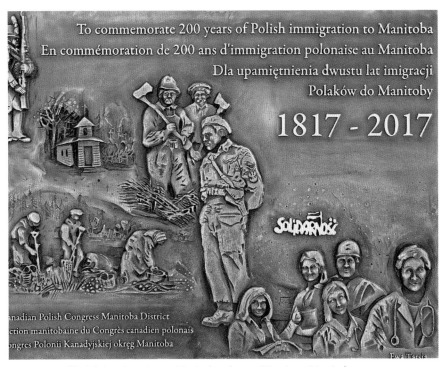

200 Years of Polish Immigration to Manitoba plaque, Winnipeg, Manitoba
(Canadian Polish Congress Manitoba District)

NEWFOUNDLAND AND LABRADOR

FLATROCK
Blessing of the Fishing Fleet Memorial

In 1984 Pope John Paul II made a historic pastoral visit to Flatrock, Newfoundland for the blessing of the fishing fleet and a papal address as part of his first visit to Canada. A rock and brass monument is erected in the place the Pope spoke.

Blessing of the Fishing Fleet Memorial, Flatrock, Newfoundland (Magicpiano CC BY-SA 3.0)

NOVA SCOTIA

GLACE BAY
Plaque to First Polish Settlers
Unveiled in September 2020, a plaque in the Dawe Avenue recreation field, across from Holy Cross Church, commemorates the hardworking Polish immigrants who came to work in the nearby coal pits circa 1900 and set up a community. In addition to a brief history of the Polish community, the plaque includes numerous photos documenting the area. The project was funded by individual donors as well as the St. Michael's Polish Benefit Society and the Glace Bay Polish Heritage Project.

Plaque to first Polish settlers, Glace Bay, Nova Scotia (Joshua Blank)

HALIFAX
Polish Emigration Memorial Monument "Pier 21"
Unveiled in 2018, this monument is made from southern Polish sandstone. A bronze plaque, also from Poland, on the stone reads: "A stone from Poland in honor of emigrants from Polish lands who contributed to the creation and development of Canada, which in return offered them shelter and new prospects." The first recorded Polish immigrant, Dominik Barcz, arrived on Canadian soil in 1752. Visitors can see the monument outside the Canadian Museum of Immigration at Pier 21 in Halifax and view exhibits in the museum which include the history of Polish immigration to Canada.

Polish Emigration Monument, Halifax, Nova Scotia (Polish Consulate N.S.)

St. Faustina Kowalska Polish Mission Church
This Mission was established in 1984 as the sole Polish Mission in Halifax, right after Pope John Paul II's visit to Canada. In the beginning, the location of the mission was St. Joseph Church in Halifax, but now it is located at St. Anthony Church at 26 Courtney Road in the Dartmouth neighborhood. A picture of the Black Madonna adorns the church. A permanent Polish library was established. Polish national holyday ceremonies and other cultural events are celebrated and after Sunday Mass in Polish, parishioners gather in the Church Hall for traditional coffee and cake. Since 1990 a Polish Festival is organized each year.
www.halifaxyarmouth.org/parishes/parish-directory/item/saint-faustina-kowalska-polish-mission

SYDNEY

St. Mary's Polish Church

Since 1901, the Cape Breton region welcomed Polish Canadians to work in the steel mills. The center of the Polish community is St. Mary's Parish, located in the Whitney Pier neighborhood at 21 Wesley Street. It is one of the longest-standing Polish communities in Canada. Established in 1913, with the assistance of St. Michael's Benefit Society which provided insurance to nearby steel workers, the wooden modified Gothic-style church was designed after a Polish church in Quebec. It was rebuilt in 2016 after a fire and continues to host spiritual and cultural activities for the community. The altar for the rebuilt church was donated by parishioners in Wisla, Manitoba. A shrine to St. Faustina contains her relics, a painting of St. Pope John Paul II hangs from the old pulpit, and statues of St. Casimir and St. Stanislaus

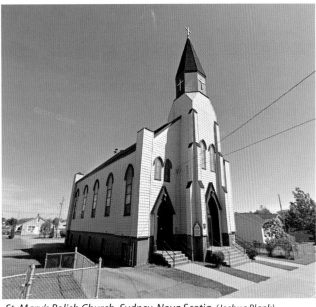
St. Mary's Polish Church, Sydney, Nova Scotia (Joshua Blank)

adorn the Gothic altar. A painting of Our Lady of Częstochowa by John Tynski hangs in the left nave. This is the only Polish church in Atlantic Canada, and it is recognized by the province as a historical site and was placed on the Canadian Register of Historic Places in 1984.
www.stmaryspolishparish.ca

St. Michael's Polish Village Hall / Dom Polski

The current hall at 954 Victoria Road that dates from 1949 replaced an earlier hall that was in operation as early as 1911. Run by the St. Michael's Polish Benefit Society, the hall is a municipally designated landmark. It hosts numerous celebrations and cultural activities for the Polish community and is home to the Pogoria Polish Folk Ensemble. The Polish Canadian Society of Nova Scotia is active in promoting Polish Heritage by sponsoring events in various locations around the city, including an annual Polish Festival.

St. Michael's Polish Village Hall Park, Sydney, NS (Dom Polski)

ONTARIO

Cathedral in the Pines, Barry's Bay, Ontario (Joshua Blank)

BARRY'S BAY
Cathedral in the Pines
A short drive down Old Barry's Bay Road and a turn down Kopernik Road leads you to the Cathedral in the Pines. Started in 1953 by Fr. Ignatius (a decorated chaplain of the Polish Army and Polish Scouts) as a retreat, it is now under the auspices of the Franciscans. Summertime Masses are celebrated in a large outdoor chapel with the image of Our Lady of Częstochowa overlooking Wadsworth Lake. There are roadside shrines throughout the terrain resembling ones found in the Polish countryside. A monument to Fr. Ignatius and another one marking one thousand years of Christianity in Poland are on the site with the inscription "Polonia Semper Fidelis" as a memorial of the millennium of Christianity of the Polish Nation.

Mission Church of the Assumption Memorial Cairn
Constructed in 1896 on property west of the village off Siberia Road, the Mission Church served the growing needs of Polish Kashub and Galician settlers who were too numerous to be accommodated in nearby Wilno. A cairn and plaque, donated by Don Etmanski of Syracuse, NY, was unveiled in 1974 to mark the site where the church was located before it burned down. A memorial dedicated to the parishioners buried in the cemetery was unveiled in 1996.

St. Hedwig Church
Kashubian settlers were the first and most numerous who came to this region. They initially worshipped in

St. Hedwig Church, Barry's Bay, Ontario (Lech and Grazyna Galezowski)

Mission Church of the Assumption Memorial Cairn to settlers, Barry's Bay, Ontario (Zita Glafcheskie)

a small mission church around 1900 but in 1915 the current church was dedicated, built by parish volunteers. An adoration chapel is dedicated to the Black Madonna. The church is located on Karol Wojtyla Square. Polish traditions and holy days are celebrated.
www.sainthedwigchurch.com

St. Pope John Paul II Monument

In 1980, parishioners of St. Hedwig Parish decided to name the street that passed through the church property after Pope John Paul II, using his given name Karol Wojtyła. The monument is 6 by 12 feet, with a curvilinear base, and built of red and white brick in equal proportions. A total of 1,014 bricks were used to represent each year of Poland's participation in Christianity. The plaque on the monument has inscriptions in Polish and English.

St. Pope John Paul II Monument, Barry's Bay, Ontario (Joshua Blank)

Szare Szeregi Monument
This monument in the middle of a field at the inter-section of Old Barry's Bay Road and Vistula Road near the Polish Scout Camp in Kazuby was complet-ed in 1994 and honors the Polish girl and boy scouts and guides, known as *Szare Szeregi* (Grey Ranks), who perished during the Warsaw Uprising in 1944 or were sent to Nazi concentration camps for serving in the paramilitary underground Polish Scouting As-sociation during World War II. Built to resemble the corner of a bombed-out church building, the site fea-tures a compass pointed towards Warsaw and is often adorned with flowers and mementos. Another stone with a plaque was erected in 2014 to commemorate the 70th anniversary of the Warsaw Uprising.

Zurakowski Park
Opened in 2003, this triangular-shaped park at the corner of Opeongo and Kelly Streets commemorates the life of the decorated pilot Janusz Żurakowski (1914–2004). While in the Polish Air Force, he es-caped to England in 1940 and served in World War II. After immigrating to Canada, he was a test pilot for the famed supersonic CF-105 Avro Arrow. A long-time resident of the area, he is commemorated by a statue and a scale model of the Arrow in the park. Numerous Polish Canadians donated to the project and worked on the construction of the park and model.

Szare Szeregi Monument, Barry's Bay, Ontario (Joshua Blank)

BRESLAU
Polski Dom
Several Polish groups in the region came together to purchase a property with an event hall at 2711 Shantz Station Road in 1999. It was adapted into a cultural center with the goal to unite all Polish-Canadians living in this region to cultivate their heritage and pass it on to their children. Numerous events are held, including New Year's Eve parties *(Sylwester)*, the Polish Veterans An-nual Picnic, the yearly Polish Harvest Festival *(Dożynki)*, and St. Andrew's Eve (*Andrzejki)*.
www.polskidom2000.com

BURLINGTON
Polish Cultural Center and Banquet Hall
Built in 1970, this center at 2316 Fairview Street is owned by the Polish National Union of Cana-da, Branch 17 Burlington, and serves as the home for the National Polish Community of Canada (a member of Canada Polish Congress), Mikołaj Kopernik Polish School, Scomora Theater, Pol-ish Ladies Club, Polish Scouts, and others. It supports the Polish community of Burlington and Toronto through many cultural events and celebrations held in this newly renovated building that is open to the public. **zwiazeknarodowypolskiburlington.ca**

ETOBICOKE
St. Teresa Church
St. Teresa Parish was established in 1924 although the current church building at 100 Tenth Street dates from 1967. Since the end of World War II, many Polish families moved into the area and Masses are conducted in Polish and English. The parish is also home to a scouting troop and the Podhale dance troupe. There are several large stained-glass windows, one that depicts St. Pope John Paul II with the monastery of Częstochowa behind him, and another of the Black Madonna. There is also a large carved relief of Our Lady. **stteresaset.archtoronto.org**

GUELPH
Polish Hall
Guelph is home to Branch 11 of the Polish Alliance of Canada which runs the Polish Hall at 5 Empire Street. It is a gathering place for the community and hosts numerous Polish folk and cultural events for different age groups, as well as offering Polish meals.

HAMILTON
Dom Polski & Royal Canadian Legion Polish Veterans Branch #315
Located at Solidarnosc Place at 722 Barton Street E, this Dom Polski is home to many celebrations and events, including gatherings for John Paul II Polish School. The original building from the 1920s has been renovated to double its size according to plans by Zebroski Associates.

Dom Polski, Hamilton, Ontario (Joshua Blank)

St. Stanislaus Kostka Church
Polish-speaking people in this area initially attended Mass at St. Ann Parish until 1912 when St. Stanislaus Kostka Church was built at 8 Saint Ann Street. The Mutual Benefit Society of St. Stanislaus Kostka was established the same year. The Society organized a library and night school for new immigrants. Parishioners have developed schools, sports teams, scouts, and choirs. Cardinal Karol Wojtyła (the future Pope John Paul II) visited the church twice, in 1969 and 1976, and there is a life-size statue of him as well as one of St. Stanislaus. The church has several active groups and Mass is said in Polish. **www.stankostka.ca**

KITCHENER
Royal Canadian Legion – Polish Veterans Branch 412
Founded in 1946 by Polish veterans and members of the community, this branch is named in honor of General Władysław Sikorski, leader of the Polish forces during World War II. Various organizations hold meetings and events in their building at 601 Wellington Street N, including the Kujawiacy dance ensemble. The branch also sponsors soccer teams, t-ball teams, individual athletes, and two hospitals. **https://www.royalcanadianbanquet.com**

Sacred Heart Church
This parish was started as a Polish Mission in 1904 and the church building at 66 Shanley Street was dedicated in 1918. There are a number of parish organizations, including a Polish school. The parish welcomed many Polish families after World War II and again in the 1980s with the Solidar-

ity emigres. An icon of the Black Madonna is located by the altar. *Opłatek*, the blessing of food baskets, and other Polish traditions are maintained, and Masses are offered in Polish. **http://kitchenercr.com**

LONDON
Dom Polski / Polish Hall
The Polish National Association (PNA), founded in 1920, purchased an old church at 554 Hill Street. With the influx of the post-World War II Polish population, a larger venue was needed for cultural events. In 1958 the construction of a new hall at the same site started. In conjunction with the Polish Hall, the PNA purchased, in 1977, 37 acres in Nilestown and built a recreation center and soccer fields. Many Polish cultural and festive celebrations are held here.   **http://www.polishhall.org**

Our Lady of Czestochowa Church
In the 1950s, the steadily growing Polish population in London led to the opening of a Polish church which was constructed in 1954. In the 1980s, many immigrants were sponsored from Poland leading to a newly rebuilt church at 419 Hill Street in 1996. The icon of Our Lady is displayed prominently behind the altar that is surrounded with quotes of St. Pope John Paul II in Polish. Windows depict Polish historical events. Masses are in Polish, and the parish sponsors a Polish dance group.

MISSISSAUGA
Canadian Polish Research Institute
Established in 1956 by Dr. Wiktor Turek, the Institute focuses on research on the history, culture, language, and social changes of the Polish ethnic minority in Canada. The chief goal is to collect and preserve documents concerning the life and work of Polish immigrants. They publish many works relating to Canadian Polish emigration and host seminars and lectures. **www.the cpri.org**

St. Maximilian Kolbe Church /
John Paul II Polish Cultural Centre
By the 1970s the Polish-speaking population in the western areas of greater Toronto—namely Mississauga and Brampton—increased to levels large enough to sustain a new parish. The church building at 4260 Cawthra Road was completed in 1983 and blessed during Pope John Paul II's visit to Canada. Over the years, the parish has sponsored many refugee families and established the John Paul II Polish Cultural Centre, run by the Maximilian Kolbe Foundation, beside the church in 1994. The Centre hosts numerous so-

John Paul II Polish Cultural Centre Patriots' Monument, Mississauga, Ontario (Canadian-Polish Congress)

cial, cultural, business, and recreational gatherings and events in Polish and English as the suburb has become a focus of Polonia activities. The center has a concert hall, stage, library, and club. The Polish Patriots' Square has a monument dedicated to Polish patriots. **www.kolbe.ca**

Spiral of Victory Monument
The ground-breaking took place in July 2021 for the first memorial in Canada dedicated to Polish airmen, ground personnel and Women's Auxiliary Air Force serving in the Polish Air Force

International Railroad Bridge from U.S. side (Jacquie Pason)

alongside RAF during World War II. The metal and concrete monument, by Polish Canadian artists Ania and Wojtek Biczysko, is composed of two main parts: the obelisk, which is a slender pyramid on a triangular base, with inscriptions and symbols on all three sides; and the dynamic, upper composition that includes sculptures of three aircrafts symbolizing "battle in the air." It includes a red and white checkerboard on each side which is the symbol of Polish Aviation. The main sponsors are the Institute of National Remembrance in Poland and Polish Veteran Affairs Canada. The project was organized by the Maximilian Kolbe Foundation and is located outside the John Paul II Cultural Centre (*see entry above*).

NIAGARA FALLS
Casimir Gzowski Provincial Plaque
Located south of Clifton Hill on the Niagara Parkway, a plaque commemorates the achievements of Casimir Gzowski. Born in Russia of Polish parents, Gzowski immigrated to Canada in 1841, and became the first chairperson of the Niagara Parks Commission (1885-1893). He designed the International Railway Bridge (*see entry below*). (*See also* Toronto, Ontario: Sir Casimir Gzowski Park.)

International Railway Bridge
Spanning 1,113 meters in length, the three-section, single-track iron international bridge linking Fort Erie and Buffalo, New York, was designed by Casimir Gzowski and David Lewis Macpherson. It was officially opened on November 3, 1873.

NIAGARA-ON-THE-LAKE
Camp Kosciuszko and Niagara-on-the-Lake Museum

Camp Niagara was used previously to train the Canadian Expeditionary Force, but 22,395 Polish soldiers were stationed here between October 1917 and March 1919 for their basic and special training before going to fight in France under General Józef Haller ("Haller's Blue Army"). While the camps are long gone, the Commons can be toured as well as the Butler's Barracks. It is a National Historic Site of Canada. The Niagara-on-the-Lake Museum contains a Blue Army uniform from a volunteer in Gen. Haller's army, recruitment posters, army artifacts, and pictures and documents of Camp Kosciuszko. There is a good online exhibit of the museum found on their website.

Haller Army Cemetery & Memorial

Visitors can tour the cemetery and view a commemorative plaque in Polish and English. The plaque outside the gate, dedicated in 2000 after the site was restored, gives information about the Canadians and Americans who sacrificed their lives for Polish independence and the Polish organizations that worked to preserve the site. There is a memorial to the twenty-six Polish recruits who died during training due to influenza in the camp. A pilgrimage by the Polish community is made to the site every year in June.

Blue Army recruitment poster at Camp Kosciuszko Museum, Niagara-on-the-Lake, Ontario (LAC E-010754113)

Haller Army Cemetery & Memorial , Niagara-on-the-Lake, Ontario (Terry Polewski)

OTTAWA

Canadian Airmen Memorial Plaque

A plaque commemorating the twenty-six Royal Canadian Air Force airmen shot down by the Germans while carrying out supply operations over Poland during World War II is in Confederation Park across from City Hall (110 Laurier Avenue W). The Canadian airmen flew their missions mostly during the Warsaw Uprising of 1944, trying to support the heroic Poles who fought there, surrounded by over twenty divisions of the German army. The plaque, funded by the Montreal Association of Former Soldiers of the Polish Home Army, was unveiled in 1964, twenty years after the uprising. The Home Army Cross (AK) was added to the monument in 1995.

Canadian Airmen memorial plaque, Ottawa, Ontario (Ottmem)

Canadian Tribute to Human Rights

This monument, created by Melvin Charney in downtown Ottawa at 220 Elgin Street, celebrates the principles of the worldwide human community. Started in 1983, it was inspired by the Polish Solidarity Trade Union movement, which was a non-violent struggle for basic human rights. Hundreds of organizations, individuals, businesses, and governments at all levels helped to build this monument. In November 1989, Lech Walesa took the first steps on the symbolic pathway leading to the ceremonial arch at the center of the tribute. The Canadian-Polish Congress and St. Hyacinth Polish Parish are among the more than forty names listed on a special plaque as major donors. The monument was unveiled in 1990 by the Dalai Lama.

Canadian Tribute to Human Rights, Ottawa, Ontario (Andrevruas CC BY-SA 3.0)

Dom Polski

The Polish Combatants Association Branch #8 acquired the property in 1952 and moved into the current building at 379 Waverly Street in 1970. The venue has been a center for cultural activities for over a half-century and houses a library which contains over three thousand titles. Much of the social and cultural life of the Polish community in Ottawa, such as meetings, seminars, lectures, banquets, and rehearsals, takes place here. Of note recently is the Polanie Dance Group performance which was attended by the Polish president and first lady in 2016.

Andrew Mynarski Bust

The "Valiants Bust" of the Canadian American World War II hero was added at the Cenotaph War Memorial in 2006. (*See also* Winnepeg: Andrew Mynarski Statue.)

Dom Polski, Ottawa, Ontario (Jozef Semrau)

St. Hyacinth Church

After World War II, the Polish immigration to Ottawa increased and a permanent place of worship was needed. The first Mass in the new church was celebrated on August 4, 1957. The Stations of the Cross were sculpted by E. Koniuszy. The picture of Our Lady of Częstochowa was painted by B. Rutkowski and was blessed in Poland at Jasna Góra where the original icon is located. In 1969, Cardinal Wojtyła visited the parish and brought relics of St. Hyacinth, and he again visited as Pope John Paul II in 1984. The parish was redecorated in the early 1990s and new stained-glass windows were installed, including one depicting St. Pope John Paul II. The parish also has a relic of St. Faustina Kowalska. The parish hosts a Polish children's choir, celebrates Polish holy days, and sponsors sales of Polish foods, bazaars, films, and cultural events. **swjacek.ca/en**

SARNIA

Our Lady Queen of Peace Church

The city of Sarnia received a considerable number of Polish immigrants and displaced persons after World War II. Some worked on local farms and then moved into the city for employment in the petroleum industry. In 1952, a mission church, Our Lady of Mercy, was established to accommodate the growing Polish population. In 1969, a new church at 566 Rosedale Avenue, Our Lady Queen of Peace, was dedicated and Polish Masses continue to be said there along with observances of Polish religious and national holidays. There is a bronze bust of St. Pope John Paul II on a marble slab to the right of the altar as well as a replica of the icon of Our Lady of Częstochowa on the arch. The church is now part of a family of seven parishes in the area. **sbrcfp.dol.ca**

Our Lady Queen of Peace Church, Sarnia, Ontario (Rev. Jan Burczyk)

Polish Hall

Constructed in 1951, Polish Hall at 173 Exmouth Street is home to social and cultural events for the community. It holds Friday night dances as well as the Annual Fall Bazaar. The hall is operated by Branch 14 of the Alliance of Poles in Canada, which was founded in 1936. **www.polishhallsarnia.ca**

ST. CATHARINES

Canadian Polish Society (CPS) Niagara Banquet Hall

From Fish Fridays to Polish Food Festivals, the Niagara Banquet Hall at 43 Facer Street hosts events of the Canadian Polish Society, which was founded in 1928 to promote Polish culture. The Society also runs Ontario Polonia Park in nearby Niagara-on-the-Lake where the annual Dożynki Festival is held. **www.cpsfacer.ca**

Our Lady of Perpetual Help Church

This church building at 5 Oblate Street dates to 1886 but only since 1914 has it been a Polish parish. A wave of post-World War I migrants rejuvenated the community. Further industrial growth on the peninsula brought more Poles to the area after World War II. The parish celebrates Polish holy days and traditional national events. The stained-glass windows in the church depict Polish iconography including a window with King Jan Sobieski at the Battle of Vienna. *Gorzkie Żale, Dożynki*, and Easter basket blessings are celebrated in Polish. **www.ourladyofphchurch.ca**

Royal Canadian Legion Polish Veterans Branch 418 Hall

This branch was initially formed in 1956 to give returning veterans and their families assistance. Since then, they have been involved in many community activities and celebrated their 70th anniversary in April 2016. Many Polish celebrations and events are held at the hall at 294 Vine Street, and their outdoor soccer fields host local leagues and teams.

THUNDER BAY

Millennium Mound and the International Friendship Garden

Over a dozen Polish groups worked together to create and unveil the Millennium Mound in the International Friendship Garden in 1967. On the mound are two stone pillars with a giant eagle monument that links them. A plaque on the site informs visitors that the mound and monument commemorate Canada's centenary as well as the 1,000-year anniversary of Christianity in Poland. A statue of Our Lady of Częstochowa was erected in the garden by the Polish Women's Club of Fort William in 1969. The monuments are located near the intersection of Victoria Avenue East and Hyde Park Avenue.

Millennium Mound, Thunder Bay, Ontario (Joshua Blank)

Port Arthur Polish Hall

This building at 102 Court Street S, formerly St. Stephen's Ruthenian Presbyterian Church, was purchased and renovated by the Polish Pilsudski Mutual Benefit Society, which was started in 1928. Over the years, many organizations have used the hall including: the Polish Women's Club, Polish Combatants Branch 1 (Royal Canadian Legion Branch 219), the Canadian Polish Congress Thunder Bay District, and currently the Polish Alliance of Canada Branch 19. The building was designated as a heritage site by the City of Thunder Bay in 2004 because of its cultural significance and the building's design. The wood fronted façade of the building is reminiscent of early-1900s community halls. The city of Thunder Bay was previously known as Fort William and Port Arthur.

Port Arthur Polish Hall, Thunder Bay, Ontario (Polish Alliance)

St. Casimir Church

The original wooden church was opened in 1922 in Fort William and was named Holy Rosary Parish. It is said that an early priest criticized the parishioners too frequently and the parish was almost taken over by the Polish National Catholic Church in the 1930s. In 1936, the name was changed at the behest of the parishioners. The current church at 613 McKenzie Street was constructed in 1952–1953. Many Polish saints are depicted in the stained-glass window. Polish language Masses are said and Polish holy days are celebrated. **www.directorydotb.ca** (*click 'Central'*)

St. Mary Queen of Poland Church

The post-World War II Polish community in Port Arthur began gathering and holding Masses in several locations until the church at 93 Algoma Street was finally dedicated on August 22, 1965.

It was built by Stefan Zysko's construction company. The parish community continues to hold numerous Polish cultural events and religious celebrations. Mass is said in Polish. A painting of Our Lady of Częstochowa hangs on the altar and an outdoor shrine dedicated to her is the site of outdoor Masses. After Pope John Paul II died, the parishioners erected a bronze plaque in his memory. **www.directorydotb.ca** (*click 'Central'*)

TORONTO

Katyń Monument

The large bronze structure with a crack running through the center in Beaty Boulevard Park was erected in 1980. It is dedicated to the 22,000 Polish POWS who disappeared in 1940 from camps in the USSR and those murdered by the Soviet Secret Police and found in mass graves in Katyń. The monument was designed by Tadeusz Janowski. One side is in English, and one side is in Polish.

Katyń Monument, Toronto, Ontario (Alex Laney CC BY 3.0)

Museum and Archives of Polish Combatants Association in Canada (PCA)

Organized in 1983, this museum maintains an extensive collection of items from the Polish Armed Forces that fought on the Allied side in the West during World War II. It has a collection of over twenty uniforms from the 2nd Polish Corps, 1st Polish Armoured Division, Polish Air Force, Polish Navy, and Polish Home Army. In addition to the original uniforms, maps, and photographs other war items are on display. Among the more unique items is a replica of an officer's uniform worn by a major in Gen. Haller's Blue Army as well as the jacket worn by Colonel Michal Gutowski of the 2nd Armoured Division and recipient of the Virtuti Militari war medal for bravery. The

Polish Combatants Association Museum, Toronto, Ontario (Tomek Bakalarz)

museum is located at 206 Beverley Street at Polish Combatants Association Branch #20 which is the national PCA/SPK headquarters.

The PCA/SPK was primarily for the veterans of the Polish 2nd Corps who fought alongside British and Canadian troops during the Italian Campaign of 1943-45, under the operational command of the British Eighth Army. PCA was established in 1946 to help the demobilized Polish soldiers adjust to their new lives as civilians and exiles. The individual branches, thirty across Canada, were organized by the immigrant Polish soldiers in the cities and towns where they were settled by the Canadian government after World War II. **spk20.ca**

Our Lady Queen of Poland Mission Church
Polish Canadians living in Scarborough and other eastern boroughs of Toronto usually travelled a long way through the city to attend Polish Mass. With an influx of Solidarity era migrants in the 1980s, planning for a new parish in Scarborough was initiated in 1986 and the church at 625 Middlefield Road was consecrated in 1997. Most Masses are in Polish as are commemorations of Polish holy days. A painting of the Black Madonna and St. Pope John Paul II are found near the altar.

St. Pope John Paul II Monument
Located outside the St. Stanislaus-St. Casimir's Polish Credit Union building at 220 Roncesvalles Av-

St. Pope John Paul II Monument, Toronto, Ontario (Alaney2K CC BY-SA 3.0)

enue, the monument was privately commissioned by the community, designed by Alexander von Svoboda, and unveiled in 1984. A plaque was erected in July 2002 at the same site by the members of the credit union to commemorate the visit of the Pope for World Youth Day.

St. Casimir Church
Established in 1944 and built between 1948 and 1952 at 156 Roncesvalles Avenue, this was the third Polish parish in the Toronto area. Over the years, the parish has been a center for community and cultural life in the neighborhood. Masses are in Polish, and an icon of the Black Madonna hangs near the altar. There is an active Polish Saturday school and Polish religious holy days are observed. **www.kazimierz.org/en**

Toronto's Roncesvalles Avenue
Known by many as "Polish Street" or "Roncy," this area was considered the cultural and commercial capital of Polonia. Several Polish restaurants, delis, and shops are still open. The street is closed off during the annual Polish Festival as thousands of people pack the neighborhood. A branch of St. Stanislaus-St. Casimir's Polish Credit Union, the office of *Gazeta*, Toronto's Polish language newspaper, the headquarters of the Canadian Polish Congress and St. Casimir Church are all located on Roncesvalles Avenue.

St. John Polish National Catholic Church

This Gothic-revival church at 186 Cowan Avenue was completed in 1887 and was originally known as the Cowan Avenue Methodist Church. The building was acquired by the Polish National Catholics in 1953 and is now the seat of the PNCC diocese in Canada. Hand-carved reredos and the baptismal font were designed by the noted local artist Eugene Chruscicki. The altar area has quotes from the Bible in Polish and Masses are offered in Polish and English. **www.stjohnsparishofthepncc.com**

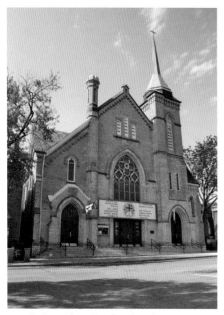

St. Stanislaus Kostka Church, Toronto, Ontario (Lech and Grazyna Galezowski)

Sir Casimir Gzowski monument in Sir Casimir Gzowski Park, Toronto, Ontario (Alex Laney CC BY 3.0)

St. Mary Polish Church

This parish was founded in 1915 and for many years it has served as a center for culture, schooling, and education. A library was set up along with a dance group and drama circle. In the 1930s, there were around three thousand parishioners and the Felician Sisters arrived to do pastoral work. In 1954, a new church at 1996 Davenport Road was blessed and in 1967 the parish was visited by Cardinal Karol Wojtyła (later Pope John Paul II). A stained-glass window above the altar has the Polish Blessed Mother with a prayer to her in Polish. Masses are conducted in Polish, English and Latin. **stmarysdavenport.archtoronto.org**

St. Stanislaus Kostka Church

The yellow-brick church at Denison Avenue was built in the Gothic revival style in 1879-80 as the West Presbyterian Church. This is the oldest Polish ethnic parish in the Toronto area and fourth oldest in Canada. A plaque in the narthex commemorates the generosity of Eugene O'Keefe, a Toronto brewing magnate who bought the property to build the church and donated it to the diocese, which then sold it to the Polish community for a dollar. A larger-than-life statue of St. Stanislaus is seen in the original Gothic altar. In the late 1930s, the Felician Sisters arrived from Buffalo to administer to the community as well. Since then, it has been a hub of culture for the community through its school and Polish language classes, as well as dance and choir groups. **ststanislauskostkato.archtoronto.org**

Sir Casimir Gzowski Park & Monument

Between Lakeshore Boulevard West and Lake Ontario sits Sir Casimir Gzowski Park, dedicated to the eponymous civil engineer and railway developer. A large concrete monument with a bronze bust by Frederick Dunbar was unveiled and dedicated in 1968. Funding for the project was provided by the Institute of Engineers, the Polish community, and the City of Toronto. The monument outlines Gzowski's life and accomplishments and was designed by Richard Dzwonnik.

VAUGHAN
Paderewski Park
Located in Vaughan in the northern area of greater Toronto at 9700 Highway 27, this park is maintained by the Polish Army Veterans Association (PAVA), Post 114, Toronto (*Stowarzyszenie Weteranów Armii Polskiej w Ameryce Placówka 114 Toronto*). Many Polish commemorative events take place in their headquarters in the park as well as wreath laying and Mass at the Memorial to the Battle of Monte Cassino. The split dark marble monument commemorates the Polish soldiers who lost their lives during the series of assaults by the Allies in Italy against the Axis forces during the Italian Campaign of World War II in 1944. The Polish II Corps played a decisive role in the Allied victory and advance toward Rome. PAVA has planted the "Oaks of Remembrance," ,dedicating them with plaques outlining their contributions. Recent tree dedications include Ignacy Jan Paderewski and Witold Pilecki, a Polish World War II resistance leader and co-founder of the Secret Polish Army resistance movement in Auschwitz Extermination Camp.

Battle of Monte Cassino Monument, Paderewski Park, Vaughan, Ontario (PAVA Post 114)

WELLAND
Sts. Peter and Paul Church
The first Polish residents in this region are thought to have come from Buffalo and Detroit c1905 with more settlers coming from Europe the following decade. In 1912-1913, Sts. Peter and Paul Church was built off Beatrice Street where many Polish-speaking people resided. The church was renovated in 1996 but a fire destroyed the church soon after the renovation. The new church at 300 Chaffey Street continues Polish customs such as Easter basket blessings, *Gorzkie Żale*, and Polish Mass. **www.sppchurchwelland.com**

Sts. Peter and Paul Church, Welland, Ontario (Lech and Grazyna Galezowski)

WILNO
Polish Kashub Heritage Museum and Skansen
This museum, located on Highway 60 across from the Wilno Tavern, was opened in 2002. Settled in 1859, Wilno is the oldest Polish settlement in Canada, the first Canadian Kashubian settlement and is also known as the Kashub heartland of Canada. The site, which is run by the Wilno Heritage Society, features several restored pioneer buildings, family stones dedicated to the first families, and a gift shop where books about the settlement can be purchased. Inside

Wilno-Barry's Bay-Kaszuby Trails
This 35-km bike/walking trail along an abandoned railway bed offers an opportunity to explore some of the Polish communities in Renfrew County. The route begins in the village of Wilno, the first Polish settlement in Canada and home to a thriving artisan community, and ends in Barry's Bay which was settled by Poles, mainly Kashubs, beginning in the 1860s. **www.ontariotrails.on.ca**

*One of the buidlings in
Kashub Heritage Museum
and Skansen, Wilno, Ontario
(Joshua Blank)*

*Unveiling of the First Polish Settlement plaque, Wilno,
Ontario (Zita Glofcheskie)*

the buildings, re-created scenes from years past and seasonal displays show the history of the Polish Kashub settlers who immigrated to the region. The park is open year-round, but the museum is only open in the summer months. **www.wilno.org**

Shrine Hill Canada's First Polish Settlement Plaque

Shrine Hill is located on Shrine Hill Drive on Hwy 60 and was chosen for the Archaeological and Historic Sites Board of Ontario plaque commemorating the area as "Canada's First Polish Settlement." It was unveiled in 1972.

St. Mary Our Lady of Częstochowa Church

This church is located at 17325 Highway 60 on Shrine Hill. This is the oldest Kashubian Polish parish in Canada dating to 1875. It was originally founded as St. Stanislaus Kostka Church. In 1936, the current church was built to replace the older one that burned. The parish hall holds gatherings, cultural events, and lectures sponsored by the Wilno Heritage Society. The parish is under the pastoral care of the Oblate Fathers of the Assumption Province (OMI) and is regularly staffed with Pol

*St. Mary Our Lady of Częstochowa Church, Wilno,
Ontario (St. Mary Parish)*

St. Stanislaus Kostka Pioneer Cemetery, Wilno, Ontario
(Joshua Blank)

ish-speaking pastors so bilingual Masses are offered. Two Polish icons are found in the Church: the replica of the statue of *Matka Boska Sianowska* (Queen of the Kashubs) which was dedicated in 2004 (the original statue is in the village of Sianowo in Poland) and Our Lady of Częstochowa. **www.stmaryswilno.com**

St. Stanislaus Kostka Pioneer Cemetery
Near St. Mary Church on Church Street is St. Stanislaus Kostka Pioneer Cemetery with the graves of the original Kashubian Polish settlers. It is open to visitors.

Wilno Tavern
Originally the Exchange Hotel which was opened in 1903 by a recent Polish arrival to Canada, Ignacy Słominski, this property has seen many boarders, diners, and drinkers pass through its doors over the years. Now the Wilno Tavern, it is a favorite stopping place on Highway 60 for Polish food. It is listed as a historic pub and one side is painted with colorful traditional Kashubian folk motifs.

WINDSOR
Astrolabium & Sundial of Mikołaj Kopernik
Located just south of downtown in Jackson Park, the sundial was dedicated in 1954 to the City of Windsor by "the citizens of Polish origin and descent on the celebration of its Centennial Year." The 15-foot-tall granite monument with a sundial on top was designed by Col. Jan Jazwinski and erected under the direction of Chester Sadowski. It was restored in 2017 by Polish organizations.

Holy Trinity Church
Polish immigrants started arriving in Windsor after 1906 and the official blessing of the new church at 1035 Ellis Street E took place in 1919. There is a Polish language school and Masses are said in Polish. The parish celebrates Polish religious and cultural events, such as *Jasełka* and *Dożynki*.

Polish Club Windsor
This facility at 1275 Langlois Avenue, affectionately known as *Dom Polski*, was completed in 1930 by the Polish Peoples' Home Association, which was founded in 1925. Over the years, countless cultural events and celebrations have taken place at the hall and it continues to be the center of activity in the Polish community. In 1941, it became a recruiting center and headquarters for the Polish Army in North America. Both

Astrolabium & Sun Dial, Windsor, Ontario
(City of Windsor)

the Polish Club Windsor & Polish Beach Club are owned and operated by the Polish Peoples' Home Association of Windsor. Polish food is served. For more information on Polish activities in Windsor visit the Polish Centre website: **poloniawindsor.ca // www.polishclubwindsor.ca**

QUEBEC

MONTREAL
Holy Cross Polish National Catholic Church
Although the current church at 3330 Laurier Avenue E was completed in 1969, this Polish National Catholic parish has been in existence since the 1950s. Inside the church, the Stations of the Cross are done by folk sculptor Tomasz Ligas. A copper niche was created in the vestibule that holds four urns with ashes of victims from World War II concentration camps. Over the years, hundreds of parishioners have celebrated Polish artistic and cultural events. The parish also sponsors a Polish school for the community.

Mikołaj Kopernik Statue
This bronze statue of the Polish astronomer is a copy of the 1830 work by the Danish sculptor Bertel Thorvaldsen that stands in Warsaw, Poland. The Canadian replica is a gift from the Canadian Poles to all the people of Canada for the country's centenary and was unveiled on November 12, 1966, on the grounds of Expo '67 in Montreal. In 2011, the statue was moved to its current location outside the Rio Tinto Alcan Planetarium at 4801 Pierre-de Coubertin Avenue.

Kopernik Statue, Montreal, Quebec (Salajro CC BY-SA 4.0)

Grosse Île Memorial
This island was often the first stop for many immigrants coming into Canada. Large quarantine buildings were set up on the island as it processed immigrants between 1832 and 1937. Many of the Polish-Kashub settlers who would later settle near Wilno/Barry's Bay had to pass through here before continuing their journey. Some Polish immigrants succumbed to cholera and typhus epidemics and are buried on the island and the monument is a tribute to them.

Our Lady of Czestochowa, Montreal, Quebec (F. Czarnowski)

Our Lady of Czestochowa Church

Described by a local guide as, "…the marrying of the religious art of the Middle Ages with that of the modern age," Our Lady of Czestochowa is a picturesque stone church from 1947 located in the Sainte Marie neighborhood of Montreal at 2550 Gascon Avenue. The architect was Zygmunt Kowalczuk, and the interior was painted by Father Bernard Kazimierczyk, a Franciscan priest who was vicar of the church for twenty-three years (1930-1955), and Stefan Katski. Scenes depicted include the baptism of Polish Christianity and the beatification of St. Maximilian Kolbe. The woodcarvings were created by Paul Barbaud and the church arches were carved by the Italian sculptor Sebastian Aiello. Stained-glass windows executed by André Rault in Rennes depict saints as well as the Polish emblem and Polish eagle. A large statue of Our Lady is above the entrance doors and her icon is prominent behind the altar. On a side wall, a marble plaque commemorates the Smolensk plane crash in 2010 in which Polish President Kaczynski perished. To the right of the entrance doors, there is a large bronze statue of St. Pope John Paul II. Religious, cultural, and social activities are celebrated. Masses are in Polish.

Sts. Michael and Anthony Church

Perhaps the only Polish church with a minaret-inspired belltower, Sts. Michael and Anthony at 5580 Saint Urbain Street was built in 1914-15 for the then predominantly Anglophone community using a plan by Aristide Beaugrand-Champagne. The architect drew inspiration from the Hagia Sophia and fused Byzantine, Romanesque, and Gothic elements. The interior was decorated by Guido Nincheri (1885-1973) and one of his stained-glass windows depicts Our Lady of Częstochowa. The Stations of the Cross were copied from Martin Feuerstein's (1856-1931) in the Church of St. Anne in Munich, Germany. A plaque commemorates the visit of the then Cardinal Karol Wojtyła in 1969. There is a shrine to St. Maximilian Kolbe. Masses and religious and cultural events are celebrated in Polish. **www.franciszkanie.org/kanada/smsa** *(in Polish)*

Sts. Michael & Anthony Church , Montreal, Quebec (Mourial CC BY 3.0)

SASKATCHEWAN

EMERALD
White Eagle Sacred Heart Church & Cemetery
In 1915, Polish immigrants constructed a church 17.5 kilometers north of the village of Kelliher on Warren Road. After several decades, a new church was needed, and in 1960 parishioners worked together to build one. It is a single story, wood-frame church with a historic cemetery established in 1916. The building was designated a Municipal Heritage Site in 2004. A plaque on the front exterior of the church outlines the history of the early Polish founders. The church building is open only via special permission or appointment, but the cemetery is open.

RAMA
Mission Church of St. Anthony
A large contingent of Poles from Galicia (Austro-Hungarian Empire) settled the area between 1904-1910. In 1921, Poles built St. Anthony Church at 104 1st Street N which has paintings of Our Lady of Częstochowa and St. Pope John Paul II near the altar. The church is a mission church part of St. Patrick Parish in nearby Sturgis. **stpatricksturgis.ca**

Mission Church of St. Anthony, Rama, Saskatchewan (Lech and Grazyna Galezowski)

Our Lady Of Lourdes Shrine
Under the direction of the pastor of the church, Rev. Anthony Sylla O.M.I., the community began constructing a stone replica of the famous French "Our Lady of Lourdes Shrine." Upon completion of the Grotto in 1941, the first public pilgrimage was held in August and attended by thousands. Three years later, a cross was placed on top of the nave. Around 1958-1959, the "Way of the Cross" stations were created from fieldstones and were added around the outside of the hill. A tradi-

Our Lady of Lourdes Shrine, Rama, Saskatchewan (Lech and Grazyna Galezowski)

tional pilgrimage is held every year on August 14th–15th and continues to draw pilgrims of all ages near and far with hundreds in attendance. It is considered one of the most popular and beautiful places to visit in the province of Saskatchewan. (*See also* Skaro, Alberta: Grotto of Our Lady of Lourdes) **www.ramashrine.ca**

REGINA
Nicolaus Copernicus Plaque
In 1973, to mark the 500th anniversary of the birth of Copernicus, the Polish community of Regina unveiled a plaque at Campion College. The text on the plaque is in English and Polish.

St. Anthony Church
Begun in 1931, this church at 2275 Atkinson Street is the home of the Polish community in the capital city of Saskatchewan; many Polish parishioners contributed funds for stained-glass windows to be made in Rennes, France, by Andre Rault which were installed in 1954 and include St. Stanislaus, St. Casimir, and a special window of *Matka Boska Ostrabramska* (Our Lady of the Gate of Dawn) above the entrance. The colors in these windows resemble raw jewels as the artists utilized the *dalle de verro* technique (faceted glass which yields bright colors). A painting of Our Lady of Częstochowa hangs near the altar. A statue of St. Pope John Paul II was constructed to commemorate the Pope's visit to Canada. The Polish library in the parish dates to the 1920s. Polish traditions continue to be celebrated and masses are in Polish.
www.stanthony-regina.org

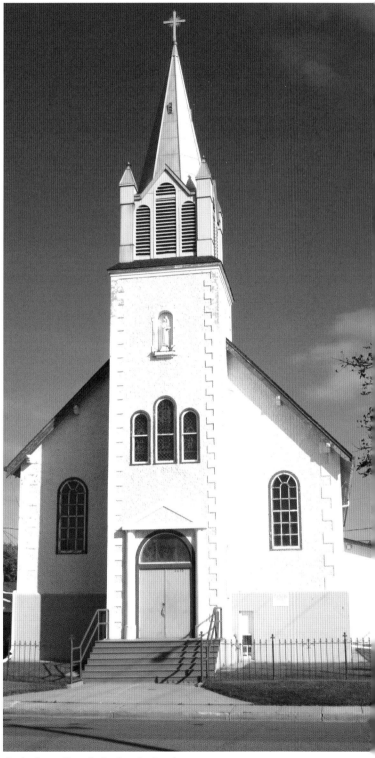

St. Anthony Church, Regina, Saskatchewan (Lech and Grazyna Galezowski)

Stained-glass window at Our Lady of Czestochowa Church, Saskatoon, Saskatchewan (OLC Parish)

SASKATOON
Our Lady of Czestochowa Church
This church at 301 Avenue Y South was consecrated in 1965 after approximately sixty Polish-speaking families helped to raise funds for its construction. A Polish school and a Women's Society were started in the following years. Above the choir loft the large stained-glass window depicts Our Lady of Częstochowa with the monastery of Jasna Góra in Poland in the background. To celebrate the visit of Pope John Paul II in 1984, a bronze statue of the Pope sitting with his arm on the shoulder of a child was unveiled in front of the church. The church continues to hold Polish Masses, and celebrate Polish customs and historical events.

CENTRAL AMERICA & CARIBBEAN

COSTA RICA

SAN JOSÉ
Fryderyk Chopin Bust
The bust of Chopin in front of the National The-ater was donated by the Polish community in Cos-ta Rica and dedicated in April 2006. The style of the bust is reminiscent of the flamboyant pose by Wacław Szymanowski's famous Chopin sculpture in Łazienki Park in Warsaw, Poland, with wind-blown hair, lowered eyelids, and closed mouth.

Statue of Pope John Paul II
A modern Italian Carrara marble statue of St. Pope John Paul, flanked by two figures is found at the Metropolitan Cathedral to honor his visit in March 1983. It was sculpted by local artisit Jorge Jimenez Deredia. The statue stands12 feet high and weights 25 tons. His visit was considered the most impor-tant event in the Cathedral's history. The Cathedral is a beautiful neo-classical building from the 1870s with rich art and history.

Fryderyk Chopin bust, San José, Costa Rica
(Christopher Ziemnowicz)

St. Pope John Paul II Statue in front
of Metropolitan Cathedral, San José
(Michael Miller)

CUBA

HAVANA
Fryderyk Chopin Bench

A life-size bronze figure of Chopin sits on a bench in Havana, in the Plaza de San Francisco, just opposite the former home of the Marquis of San Felipe and Santiago. It is a simple and modern statue sculpted by the award-winning Polish sculptor Adam Myjak.

Fryderyk Chopin Bench, Havana, Cuba
(Emmanuel Huybrechts CC-BY-SA-2.0)

GUATEMALA

GUATEMALA CITY
St. Pope John Paul II Statue and Sculpture

There are two depictions of St. Pope John Paul II who visited the country in 2002. A bronze statue sits atop a fountain on the plaza of Paseo Cayalá, a wealthy area just on the outskirts of the capital. A giant metal open air sculpture is located a few meters from a similar one of St. Hermano Pedro de Betancourt on Plaza de la Paz. The pope canonized this saint during his pilgrimage to Guatemala City in 2002.

HAITI

CAZALE

Monuments to the Victims of Cazale Massacre

In 1969, the regime of François Duvalier sent soldiers to Cazale in a crackdown on Communist students and intellectuals in the area and to enforce his political ideology known as *noirisme* ("Blackism"), through which he claimed to promote the black masses against "mulatto elites." Hence, the Duvalier dictatorship targeted mulatto sectors of society seen as illegitimate members of the nation and the citizens of Cazale were known to be a light-skinned village because of intermarriage with Polish soldiers. In response to harassment from soldiers, residents lowered the black and red flag of the Duvalier regime and raised a traditional red and blue Haitian flag. Soldiers then burned houses and brutally massacred thirty residents with an unknown number listed as "disappeared." The victims are commemorated with a plaque and flagpole in the center of the village. The memorial plaque is in several languages, including Polish.

*Cazale Plaque to the Victims of Cazale Massacre
(Polonia na Haiti)*

Our Lady of Częstochowa

For many Haitians, Our Lady of Częstochowa has special significance. The icon resembles Ezili Dantou, a Voodoo goddess and similarly dark-skinned mother figure who holds an infant child. Some scholars trace the syncretic iconography to the Polish Legions sent to Haiti by Napoleon to suppress the Haitian Revolution. One of the soldiers may have brought a prayer card or lithograph with the image. For the Haitian diaspora in the United States, the connection is vibrant and commemorated each year in a pilgrimage to the Shrine of Our Lady of Częstochowa in Doylestown, PA.

Vierge Noire Grotto and Place Jean Paul II
Outside of St. Michel Church is a small grotto with an icon of Our Lady of Częstochowa, also known in Haiti as the *Vierge Noire*. The surrounding plaza is named after St. Pope John Paul II and commemorates his 1983 visit to Haiti, when the Pope met with a delegation from the village, recognizing its Polish heritage.

Cazale's Descendents of the Polish Legions
In 1796, enslaved Africans in Saint-Domingue led a revolution against the French and prevailed over successive waves of relief forces from Europe, including over five thousand Poles sent by Napoleon. In Saint-Domingue, some Polish soldiers joined with the Haitians, refusing to fight on behalf of a colonial empire while they lacked autonomy in their own homeland. After the formal establishment of a new government in 1804, Jean-Jacques Dessalines, a leader of the revolution and Emperor of Haiti from 1804-06, gave remaining Poles full citizenship, rights, and land. The descendants of these Poles who intermarried with Haitians are centered in Cazale. The etymology of "Cazale" may be derived from "Ca' Zalewski," meaning "house of Zalewski," one of the first Polish settlers. Although the Polish connection with Haiti has been understudied, it has garnered significant attention in recent years. The 2014 Polish Pavilion at the Venice Biennale curated by Joanna Malinowska explored this history through production of Poland's national opera, *Halka*, in the village. In 2017, the "1st edition of the Day of Solidarity of the Polish People with the Polish Community in Haiti" was established with a visit to Cazale of the Polish Consul stationed in Bogota. There was a performance of Polish popular songs and dances by young artists from Cazale. The inhabitants of the village of Cazale (also known as La Pologne), located about seventy kilometres from the country's capital, Port-au-Prince, refer to their Polish origin and consider themselves descendants of the soldiers of the Polish Legions and are immensely proud of their Polish heritage. The local cemetery has survived in the village, where most of the names are Polish. The Christopher & Elizabeth Mission (run by Polish philanthropists Krzysztof and Elżbieta Szybiński) introduces Polish culture to Cazaliens, through the medium of videography and via the Polish children's channel CazaleTVPologne.

HONDURAS

TEGUCIGALPA
St. Pope John Paul II Statue
The large gold statue stands in front of the massive Basilica de Nuestra Señora De Suyapa commemorating the papal visit in 1983.

PANAMA

PANAMA CITY
St. Pope John Paul II Statue
A large statue of St. Pope John Paul II is located at Albrook Mall to commemorate his visit in 1983. The statue is a gathering place for the Polish community for historical celebrations.

Hacienda Santa Rosa, Leon, Guanajuato, Mexico

MEXICO

COAHUILA

SALTILLO
Karol Beneski's Grave

Karol Beneski is a big Polish personality in Mexico's history. Originally from Poland where he was a lieutenant colonel retired from the Prussian army, when he immigrated he first tried to enlist in the United States army but was told no more soldiers were needed. He then went to Mexico where he joined the Mexican army and worked closely with Agustin de Iturbide, the first emperor of Mexico after it gained independence from Spain in the 1820s. Beneski became a politician in Mexico and left a book of memoirs about life working for the Mexican emperor. He is buried in the Catedral de Santiago in Saltillo.

GUANAJUATO

LEÓN
Hacienda Santa Rosa

In 1943, 1,434 Polish refugees, mainly orphans who fled the war in Poland through Siberia, Iran, Karachi, and Australia finally found a home in Mexico. In the previous year, an agreement had been signed between Mexico and the Polish government-in-exile to aid the Polish refugees, some of whom were in Iranian camps. The building of Hacienda Santa Rosa was not large enough so, with aid provided by the US, UK, and Polish government-in-exile, many new buildings were added including a school, hospital, and swimming pool. After the war, only a few of the refugees went back to Poland; the majority moved to the United States. Those who remained in Mexico joined the earlier Polish exiles from the 1920s, becoming intellectuals, artists, and scientists. Today, the Hacienda Santa Rosa functions as an orphanage for Mexican children run by the Salesian Fathers. A large plaque on the grounds commemorates the memory of this fascinating story of Polish emigres. In 1993, the Chicago group "The Poles of Santa Rosa" organized a 50th anniversary reunion; four years later they visited Santa Rosa unveiling a commemorative plaque that honored their Mexican hosts for their hospitality and kindness. Two documentaries have been made about this story: "Santa Rosa: An Odyssey in the Rhythm of Mariachi" and "From Poland to Santa Rosa, after One Thousand Days," produced by Piotr Piwowarczyk and Slawomir Grunberg.

JALISCO

GUADALAJARA
Chopin Monument

The *Monumento a Federico Chopin* is in the Jardín Chopin on Avenue Alcalde (colonia de Barranquidas). It was unveiled in 2001 to honor the composer. The sculpture shows a very foreboding, frowning countenance, with eyes as narrow slits and no smile and his elongated fingers holding the collar of his jacket. It has an "unfinished" texture.

PUERTO VALLARTA
Posters International Art Gallery

This gallery at Leona Vicario 233 houses an extensive collection of mainly post-World War II (Socialist period) Polish artwork collected by Martin Rosenberg since the 1980s. The largest component of the "Rosenberg Collection" are the vintage movie posters that represent the period 1945-70 which were printed in very small quantities, making them very rare. All the recognized Polish artists are rep-

Chopin Monument, Guadalajara, Mexico (meacultura)

resented, particularly those whose works won international awards or had shows in museums and educational institutions. Mr. Rosenberg had his first public exhibition in 1990 at the Polish Museum of America in Chicago and it was the largest showing of vintage Polish posters ever shown outside of Poland. He continues to display his collection globally. The collection also includes many pre-1945 posters covering theater, music, jazz, opera, dance, sports, circus and rare product advertising and represents works of the leading artists from the Polish School of Design.
www.rosenbergcollection.com

CIUDAD de MÉXICO

MEXICO CITY
St. Pope John Paul II Statue

This statue of St. Pope John Paul II near the side entrance to the Metropolitan Cathedral of Mexico City has an image of the Virgin of Guadalupe superimposed on the front and is made entirely of more than seven million keys donated by Mexicans. The plaque states that this was done to show that the Mexican people had given the Pope the "key to their hearts," a dedication highlighting his five papal visits. The statue was done by Artist Francisco Cardenas Martinez.

*Statue of St. Pope John Paul II and the Virgin of Guadalupe made of more than seven million keys
in front of Metropolitan Cathedral of Mexico City (Thelmadatter)*

Statue of Ignacy Jan Paderewski, Mexico City, Mexico (Sarumo74 CC BY-SA 4.0)

Statue of Paderewski

The statue of the Polish musician and diplomat Ignacy Jan Paderewski can be found on Paseo de la Reforma, the main avenue of Mexico City. It is the work of the Spanish sculptor Miguel Baquidano Camps. This three-meter bust depicts Paderewski with a Polish eagle on his chest. The sculpture was initially unveiled in 1945 at the Palace of Fine Arts in Mexico City. However, the Polish Communist People's Republic blocked the project at that time and it took sixty years before the sculpture was finally placed on the Paseo de la Reforma.

YUCATAN

IZAMAL
Convento Franciscano
Izamal is a city in the Yucatan known as "The Yellow City." When Pope John Paul II visited this small city in 1993, he gifted to the people a crowned statue of the Blessed Virgin Mary. There is a small statue of St. Pope John Paul II in front of the Franciscan Convent of Saint Antonio de Padua.

Appendix I: Chicago, City of Neighborhoods Map *(see sidebar page 41)*

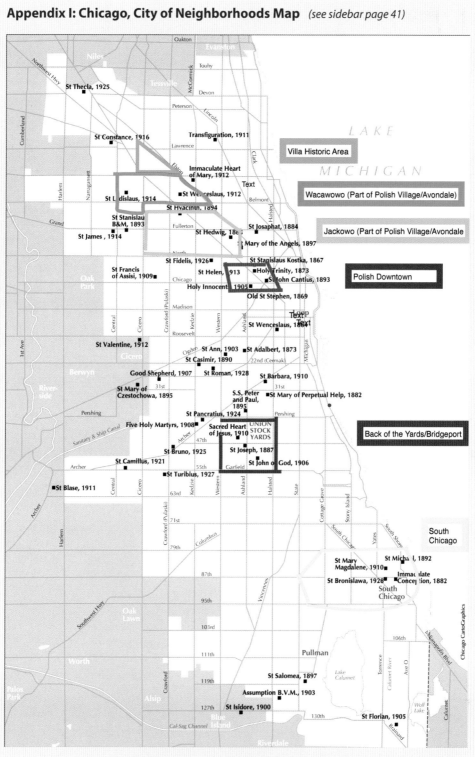

Oakton
Evanston
Niles
Touhy
Tessville
McCormick
Devon
Northwest Hwy
Peterson
Lincoln
St Thecla, 1925
Clark

LAKE

St Constance, 1916
Transfiguration, 1911
Lawrence
MICHIGAN
Cumberland

Villa Historic Area

Immaculate Heart
of Mary, 1912
Elston
Harlem
Narragansett
Text
Wacawowo (Part of Polish Village/Avondale)
St Ladislaus, 1914
St Wenceslaus, 1912
Belmont
St Hyacinth, 1894
Jackowo (Part of Polish Village/Avondale
St Stanislau
B&M, 1893
Fullerton
St Josaphat, 1884
Grand
St James, 1914
St Hedwig, 188
St Mary of the Angels, 1897
North

St Fidelis, 1926
St Stanislaus Kostka, 1867
Oak
Park
St Francis
of Assisi, 1909
St Helen, 1913
Holy Trinity, 1873
Polish Downtown
Chicago
St John Cantius, 1893
Holy Innocents 1905
Old St Stephen, 1869
Crawford (Pulaski)
Madison
Central
Cicero
Kedzie
Western
Ashland
Text
Text
St Wenceslaus, 1864
Roosevelt
Michigan

1st Ave
St Valentine, 1912
Cicero
Ogden
St Ann, 1903
St Adalbert, 1873
Berwyn
St Casimir, 1890
22nd (Cermak)
River-
side
Good Shepherd, 1907
St Roman, 1928
St Barbara, 1910
31st
31st
St Mary of
Czestochowa, 1895
St Mary of Perpetual Help, 1882
Pershing
S.S. Peter
and Paul,
1895
St Pancratius, 1924
Pershing
Sanitary & Ship Canal
Five Holy Martyrs, 1908
Sacred Heart
of Jesus, 1910
UNION
STOCK
YARDS
Archer
47th
Back of the Yards/Bridgeport
St Bruno, 1925
St Joseph, 1887
St Camillus, 1921
55th
St John of God, 1906
Archer
Garfield
St Turibius, 1927
St Blase, 1911
Central
Cicero
Kedzie
Western
Ashland
Halsted
State
63rd

Crawford (Pulaski)
71st
Cottage Grove
Stony Island
Harlem
79th
Columbus
South Chicago
Yates
South Shore
South
Chicago
87th
Vincennes
St Michael, 1892
St Mary
Magdalene, 1910
Immaculate
Conception, 1882
St Bronislawa, 1928
South
Chicago
95th

Oak
Lawn
103rd
106th
Indianapolis Blvd
Chicago CartoGraphics
111th
Pullman
Torrence
Calumet River
Ave O
Worth
Crawford
119th
St Salomea, 1897
Lake
Calumet
Palos
Park
Assumption B.V.M., 1903
Alsip
127th
St Isidore, 1900
Wolf
Lake
Calumet
Southwest Hwy
Blue
Island
130th
St Florian, 1905
Cal-Sag Channel
Brainard
Riverdale

ADVISORY COMMITTEE

I wish to acknowledge and express my thanks to the members of the Advisory Committee who provided invaluable input, lent their expertise, and provided encouragement throughout the project:

John J. Bukowczyk *Wayne State University*
Mary P. Erdmans *Case Western University*
Czeslaw Karkowski *Hunter College*
Anna D. Jaroszyńska-Kirchmann *Eastern Connecticut State University*
Anna Muller *University of Michigan-Dearborn*
James S. Pula *Purdue University Northwest, Emeritus*
Pien Versteegh *Avans University of Applied Sciences in Breda, the Netherlands*
Gavin Moulton *Assistant to the Editor, Ph.D. student Notre Dame*

CONTRIBUTORS

This is a list of individuals and organizations who assisted with this project in identifying sites, submitting entries, and/or submitting photographs. I list the states for which they provided information, not where they might reside.

Matthew Adams, GA
Michael Addicks, TX
Lady Amanda, ND
Tom Antonishak, OH
Jeremy Atherton, IL
Frederick Augustyn, D.C.
Tomek Bakalarz, Manitoba
Flo Baker, TX
Dr. Karen Ballek, WY
Ewa Banasikowski, MN
Janet Barczyk, IL
Dale Bennington, Dublin, OH
Małgosia Bielak, CO
Joshua Blank, Canada
Allen C. Browne, D.C.
James Buhlman, NY
John Bukowczyk, MI
Romuald Byczkiewicz, CT
Kathleen Callum, WA
Mary Castellano, ME
John Cebrowski, TX
Marta Cieslak, AR
Peg Cieslak, NC

Alexander Clegg, MI
Andrew Cordner, Canada
Bill Coughlin, MA
F. Czarnowski, Montreal
Sebastian Czerwinski, NJ
Andrew Deskur, NY
Mark Dillon, MN
John Dunn, GA
Janusz Duzinkiewicz, IN
Joanne Dzengielewski, MA
Ellen Engseth, MN
Mary Erdman, OH
William Fischer, Jr, IN, PA
Alvin M. Fountain II, NC, SC
Patrick Fulks, AR
Lech and Grazyna Galezowski, Canada
Krzysztof Gajda, TX
Kathy Garmon, MI
Larry Gleason, GA
Zita Glofcheskie, Manitoba
Gordon Goldborough, Manitoba
Francene Gollon, WI
Laurie Gomulka Palazzolo, MI

William Hal Gorby, WV
Ryszard Gbiorczyk, IL
Andrzej Gołębiowski, NY
Victoria Granacki, IL
Edyta Grzelakowska, NY
Anne Gurnack, Minnesota, WI
Michael A. Guzik, S.J.
JD Hancock, D.C.
Ann Hanlon, WI
Mark Heffron, WI
Theresa Batto Helbert, TX
Michael Herrick, NY
Robert Hicker, WA
Virginia Hill, TX
Thomas L. Hollowak, MD
Andrew Jameson, MI
Czeslaw Karkowski, NY
Keith Kaszubik, VA
Matthew Keagle, NY
Mary Ann Kedron, NY
Alexsander Kirchmann, PA
Donald Kohler, St. Petersburg, FL
Anna D. Jaroszyńska-Kirchmann, CT
Tim Kirchmann, CT, PA
Alina Klim, MI
Leonard Kniffel, MI
Mark Kohan, NY
Don Kohler, FL
Leon Konieczny, WI
Iwona Korga, NY
Regina and Allen Kosub, TX
Betty Kowalik, TX
Edward Krolikowski, GA
Kathy Krysiak, MA
Joanna Kukla-Pownuk, TX
Mike Kurtin, TX
Marian Krzyzowski, MI
Chris Kuklinski, WI
Jack Kulpa, MN
Alex Laney, Toronto
Fr. Joe Laramie S.J, MO
Stephen M. Leahy, IA, NE, SD
Mark Levandoski, MI
Joe Mabel, Portland, OR
Logan Mabey, GA
Barbara Macejewski Lee, TX
Karen Majewski, MI

Clara Malak, TX
Brian Marshall, TX
Wojtek Maslanka, NY
Alexander Matusiak, CO
Dr. Jim Mazurkiewicz, TX
Margaret Meub, Austin, TX
Susan Mikos, WI
Richard E. Miller, NY
Susan Moczygemba, TX
Anthony Monczewski, MD
Gavin Moulton
Maureen Mroczek Morris, CA
Tom Napierkowski, CO
Peter Obst, PA
Dominic Pacyga, IL
Mariusz Palka, MI
Mitchell Panek, FL
Panna Maria Parishioners, TX
Cindy Pasiuk, MN
Jacquelyn Pason, NY
Andrzej Pazdziora, CA
Kryssy Pease, MN
Neal Pease, KS, MO, OK, NE, ND
Mike Penney, WA
Mark Peszko, NY
Donald Pienkos, WI
Mark Pienkos, FL
Piotr Piwowarczyk, Mexico
Fr. Len Plazewski, FL
Terry Polewski, Manitoba
Fr. Stanisław Poszwa, MO
Sr. Genowefa Potachała, MI
Ted Pugh Photography, TX
Cheryl Pula, NY
James Pula, IN, NY, MD, PA
Michael Retka, MN
Desiree Rolfe, Manitoba
Larry Romans, D.C., WA
Joanna Ruszczyk, TX
Barbara Rylko-Bauer, MI
Seraphic Sister Emilia Rzeznik, TX
Nancy Schlesiger, NE
Brian Scott, NY
Józef Semrau, Ontario
Camille Shaw, LA
Colter J. Sikora, IL
Donna Singleton, AR

Christopher Siuzdak, ME
John Skibiski, MA
Małgorzata Skrodzki, NY
Jozef Callum Sloma, WA
Robert Sloma, WA
Keith S. Smith, DE
James Smock, TX
Joanna Sokołowska-Gwizdka, TX
Matthew Stefanski, NJ
Tracy H. Sugg, MS
James S. Sullivan, TX
Robert Synakowski, NY
Frank Szelag, MA
Taida Tarabula, Cuba
Marcin Tatjewski, NJ
Leigh Thelmadatter, Mexico
Rosalie Titzman, TX
Joan Tomaszewski, RI
Ronald Trigg, IN

Anna Harley Trochimczyk, CA
Maja Trochimczyk, CA
John Trombetta, NH
Kasia Trznadel, IL
Krystyna Untersteiner, WA
Kathleen Urbanic, NY
Pien Versteegh, MA
Leon Washut, WY
Teresa Wiacek, MI
Grant S. Wilson, Alberta
John Wojtasczyk, TX
Małgorzata Wozny, MI
Dr. Rafal Zielinski, TX
Christopher Ziemnowicz, Costa Rica
Frederick Zimnoch, MA
Aleksandra Ziółkowska-Boehm, SD
Kenneth C. Zirkel, MA, RI

Special thanks to the following institutions who gave permission to use photographs from their collections:

American Legion Archive, Chicago, IL
Arizona Polish Club, AZ
Basilica of St. Josaphat, Milwaukee, WI
Canadian Polish Congress, Manitoba District
Canadian-Polish Congress, Mississaugua
Chicago Park District
Consulate General of the Republic of Poland in Chicago, Consulate Archives
Cooks Creek Museum, Manitoba
East Bay PolAm Organization, Martinez, CA
Fort Pulaski National Monument (Joel Cadoff), Cockspur Island, GA
Immaculate Heart of Mary Parish, Marche, AR
Kosciuszko Foundation, Washington, D.C.
Kuryer Polski, Milwaukee, WI
Meacultura, Guadalajara, Mexico
Miami Polish American Club of Miami (PACOM)
Orchard Lake Schools Polish Mission, MI
Our Lady of Czestochowa Parish, Bay City, MI
Our Lady of Poland Parish, Southampton, NY
Our Lady Queen of Peace (Fr. Jan Burczyk), Sarnia, Ontario
Our Lady Queen of Poland, Calgary
Our Lady of Czestochowa Parish, Bay City, MI
Our Lady of Częstochowa Parish, Phoenix, AZ
Poles in America Fdn. (PIA), Philadelphia, PA
Polish Alliance of Thunder Bay Canada

Polish American Association of Sarasota
Polish American Congress, Western New York Division
Polish American Council of Texas
Polish American Fire Company #4, Pennsylvania
Polish Army Veterans Association, Post 114, Toronto
Polish Arts Club of Buffalo (PAC)
Polish Arts Club of Trenton, NJ
Polish Club Windsor Canada
Polish Heritage Center, Panna Maria, TX
Polish Library Building Association (PLBA), Portland, OR
Polish Museum of America (PMA), Chicago, IL
Polish Nobility Association Foundation (PNAF), Anneslie, MD
Polonia Music
Shrine of Our Lady of Czestochowa Doylestown PA
St. Casimir Polish National Catholic Church, Rochester, NY
St. Charles Borromeo Parish, Du Bois, IL
St. Hedwig Parish, Manchester, NH
St, Mary's Church, Otis, IN
St. Mary's Parish, Parisville, MI
St. Mary's Church, Wilno, Ontario
St. Mary of the Angels Church, Chicago, IL
St. John Paul II Parish, Perth-Amboy, NJ
Saskatchewan Archives
Trenton Polish Arts Club, NJ
Polish Room, University at Buffalo, NY
Villa Maria College, NY
Walsh County Historical Society, NE
Wibaux Museum (Lida Schneider), MT
Wyoming Sheridan Community Land Trust (Brad Bauer)
Wyoming Information Center Sheridan (Nancy Herdt)

FOR FURTHER READING: SELECTED BIBLIOGRAPHY

Here is a short selection of general histories of Poles in America with a few representing the major Polish communities. Many churches and organizations have published their own histories and issued commemorative books and you can find copies in libraries by searching the online database **worldcat.org.** For a more detailed and pictorial overview of specific Polish communities, Arcadia Publishing has over a dozen different books available for purchase: **arcadiapublishing.com.** A good starting place might be **The Polish American Encyclopedia.** There are several journals that have wide-ranging articles on Polish American topics: **The Polish Review** (quarterly journal published by the Polish Institute of Arts & Sciences of America) and **Polish American Studies; A Journal of Polish American History and Culture** (biannual journal published by the Polish American Historical Association).

Brożek, Andrzej and Wojciech Worsztynowicz. *Polish Americans: 1854-1939.* Warsaw: Interpress, 1985.

Bukowczyk, John J. *And My Children Did Not Know Me: A History of the Polish-Americans.* Bloomington [etc.]: Indiana University Press, 1988.

Bukowczyk, John J., ed. *Polish Americans and Their History. Community, Culture, and Politics.* Pittsburgh: University of Pittsburgh Press, 1996.

Dolan, Sean, Stanisław Andrzej Blejwas and Daniel Patrick Moynihan. *The Polish Americans.* New York; Philadelphia: Chelsea House Publishers, 1992.

Erdmans, Mary Patrice. *Opposite Poles: Immigrants and Ethnics in Polish Chicago, 1976-1990.* University Park, Pa: Pennsylvania State University Press, 1998.

Galazka, Jacek, and Albert Juszczak. *Polish Heritage Travel Guide to U.S.A. & Canada.* Cornwall Bridge, CT: Polish Heritage Publications, 1992.

Galezowski, Lech and Grazyna Galezowski. *In the Footsteps of Polish Pioneers on the Canadian Prairies: Exploring Churches and Chapels 1899-1914.* Toronto: Canadian Polish Research Institute, 2018.

Galush, William J. *For More Than Bread: Community and Identity in American Polonia, 1880–1940. East European Monographs.* New York: Columbia University Press, 2006.

Greene, Victor R. *The Polish American Worker to 1930 : The "Hanky" Image in Transition.* New York: The Polish Information Center in America, 1976.

Heydenkorn, Benedykt, and Frank Renkiewicz. *The Polish Presence in Canada and America.* Toronto: Multicultural History Society of Ontario, 1982.

Jaroszyńska-Kirchmann, Anna. *The Exile Mission: The Polish Political Diaspora and Polish Americans, 1939-1956.* Athens: Ohio University Press, 2004.

Kozak, Jacek. *How the Polish Created Canada.* Canada: Dragon Hill Publishing Ltd., 2011.

Kruszka, Waclaw. *A History of the Poles in America to 1908. Part I: A General History of the Polish Immigration in America; Part II: The Poles in Illinois; Part III: Poles in the Eastern and Southern States; Part IV: Poles in the Central and Western States.* Washington D. C.: The Catholic University of America Press, 1993 - 2001.

Kubiak, Hieronim. *The Polish National Catholic Church in the United States of America from 1897 to 1980 : its Social Conditioning and Social Functions.* Warszawa: Państwowe Wydaw. Naukowe; Kraków: nakł. UJ, 1982.

Majewski, Karen. *Traitors and True Poles : Narrating a Polish-American Identity, 1880-1939.* Athens: Ohio University Press, 2003.

Morawska, Ewa. *Bread with Butter: The Life-Worlds of East Central Europeans in Johnstown Pennsylvania 1890-1940.* Cambridge: Cambridge University Press, 1985.

Morawska, Ewa T., Benedykt Heydenkorn and Rudolf K Kogler. *Poles in Toronto : (in their own perception).* Toronto, Ont., Canada: Canadian-Polish Congress, Canadian-Polish Research Institute, 1982.

Pacyga, Dominic A. *American Warsaw: The Rise, Fall, and Rebirth of Polish Chicago.* Chicago: University of Chicago Press, 2019.

Pienkos, Donald. *PNA: A Centennial History of the Polish National Alliance of the United States of North American.* Boulder: East European Monographs, 1984.

Pula, James S. *Polish Americans: An Ethnic Community.* New York: Twayne Publishers,

Pula, James S., ed. *The Polish American Encyclopedia.* Jefferson, N.C: McFarland, 2011.

Radziłowski, John and Ann Hetzel Gunkel. *Poles in Illinois.* Carbondale: Southern Illinois University Press, 2020.

Thomas, William I. and Florian Znaniecki. *The Polish Peasant in Europe and America.* New York: Octagon Books, 1974.

Walaszek, Adam. *Peasants, Poles, Ethnics : Polish Immigrant Workers in the United States of America, 1880-1925.* New Britain, Conn.: Polish Studies Program, Central Connecticut State University, 1998.

Znaniecka Lopata, Helena. *Polish Americans: Status Competition in an Ethnic Community.* Englewood Cliffs, N.J.: Prentice-Hall, 1976.

ONLINE RESOURCES:

The Am-Pol Eagle. A weekly English language newspaper with both current and historical articles focused on Western New York State. **ampoleagle.com**

Gwiazda Polarna (North Star). A bi-weekly general interest Polish-language newspaper published in Stevens Point, WI, since 1908. **gwiazdapolarna.net**

Historical Markers Database. This database is arranged by location but you can narrow to topics and ethnicity. **www.hmdb.org**

Kuryer Polski. The original newspaper was the first Polish language newspaper in the US begun in 1888 in Milwaukee and published until 1962. It was then reactivated in 2020 as an online portal of information of Polish and Polish American news and is published in both Polish and English versions. **kuryerpolski.us/en**

Parafie i Kościoły Polskie w Stanach Zjednoczonych (Polish Parishes and Churches in the USA). An ongoing project of The Research Center of Polish Migration and Immigrant Pastoral Care of the John Paul II Catholic University of Lublin (KUL) documenting Polish churches in major Midwest and Eastern Polonia centers, with illustrations. **www.kosciolypolskiewusa.com**

Polish American Journal. This monthly English-language publication since 1911 includes many pieces on Polish history, culture, and sites. **www.polamjournal.com**

Polish American Liturgical Center. Located in Orchard Lake, Michigan this is an extensive digitized collection of histories of Polish American Churches. **liturgicalcenter.org**

Polonia Music. In addition to Polish heritage music, this website includes overviews and links to traditional Polish cities, events, customs, stores, and restaurants, in both the US and Canada. **www.poloniamusic.com**

Radzilowski, Thaddeus and Dominik Stecula. ***Polish Americans Today: a Survey of Modern Polonia Leadership.*** Hamtramck: PIAST Institute, 2010. Provides demographic information. **www.piastinstitute.org/uploads/6/9/8/8/69881853/polish_americans_today_ebook.pdf**

INDEX